SCHOOL LAW
FOR THE
1990s

Also in
The Greenwood Educators' Reference Collection

Planning In School Administration: A Handbook
Ward Sybouts

SCHOOL LAW FOR THE 1990s

A HANDBOOK

Robert C. O'Reilly
and
Edward T. Green

The Greenwood Educators' Reference Collection

GREENWOOD PRESS
New York • Westport, Connecticut • London

Library of Congress Cataloging-in-Publication Data

O'Reilly, Robert C., 1928–
    School law for the 1990s : a handbook / Robert C. O'Reilly and
Edward T. Green.
        p.   cm.—(The Greenwood educators' reference collection,
ISSN 1056–2192)
    Includes index.
    ISBN 0–313–27817–2 (alk. paper)
    1. Educational law and legislation—United States. I. Green,
Edward T., 1921–   II. Title. III. Series.
KF4119.07   1992
344.73'07—dc20   91–27237
[347.3047]

British Library Cataloguing in Publication Data is available.

Library of Congress Catalog Card Number: 91–27237
ISBN: 0–313–27817–2
ISSN: 1056–2192

First published in 1992

Greenwood Press, 88 Post Road West, Westport, CT 06881
An imprint of Greenwood Publishing Group, Inc.

Printed in the United States of America

The paper used in this book complies with the
Permanent Paper Standard issued by the National
Information Standards Organization (Z39.48–1984).

10 9 8 7 6 5 4 3 2 1

Contents

Preface

The notion that people should all be governed by and be responsive to a common set of laws is accepted by twentieth-century Americans—to a degree. Rules that are admired are most easily accepted, and most easily enforced; however, since ours is a pluralistic and multicultural society with many viewpoints and backgrounds represented in the general population and the public schools, not every rule is admired by all, and many Americans view some rules as downright oppressive.

Considered as an occupational group, the teachers and administrators of American elementary and secondary schools compose what is perhaps the largest single group of rule enforcers in society. Operating under legislative statutes, court cases, board policies, program regulations, and so on, there is no end to the part of the educator's professional task that calls for those persons to be on-the-spot rule enforcers in an adult-to-child relationship.

Viewed historically, it might be said that the first American schools that originated in response to mandates from Massachusetts legislators were simple, straightforward, no-frills institutions. Yet, it is conceivable too that many of the affected citizens who had to develop and maintain in those schools a basic curriculum grumbled some about that mandating legislative body. A retrospective view from the twentieth century may not have been the reality view of the times. There is in the American nature an aversion to governance, to imposed rules of behavior. There is a gravitation toward the concept of independence, of freedom for decision making. Still, groups of people, that is, society, necessitate some rules and some common agreements on both acceptable and unacceptable behaviors.

In a sense, schools are miniature societies. Schools are also part of a larger society. Institutionalized education has a monetary cost; that money must be raised from the citizens. Calls for curriculum extension and development have costs. Mandated programs coming from the federal or state government, or locally requested grass-roots curriculums, can be carried out only in some kind of recognized and accepted set of rules. If not mutually acceptable, the rules must be, at least, tolerated by all who are affected by them. Rules and costs combine, sometimes.

The rate of social change in America has been increasingly rapid. Although the conventional public school district that evolved in the nineteenth century continues to be the basic governance unit through which the obligations of public education are carried out, some of those general social changes are reflected in school districts themselves. Some districts have grown so large that just by virtue of size, any realistic expectation of local governance must be reformulated. For example, in a school district enrolling hundreds of thousands of pupils, it can hardly be seriously contended that such a political subdivision has the operational characteristics generally associated with localism. Should those districts be sub-divided? Should they be dismantled? Should localism be forsaken? What stip-ulations should the laws impose? Should states create new educational policy that governs public school district size?

Although there are, on the opposite end, many exceedingly small school districts, the total number in the nation is decreasing steadily, and there are now about 15,000 of those political subdivisions created to offer public education. California has about 1,000 districts for 27 million people; Nebraska has nearly 1,000 districts for 1.7 million people. Can both states be correct, or are both in need of new statutes, restructuring the school districts in each state? If new structures for their education delivery systems are developed, what should they look like? From where should the new laws originate, state or federal level? Some changes in district organization and governance are occurring. Evolutionary change will be by law—case law, statutes, referendums, or by some other way. Change is one sign of the times, and change indicated the need for retitling this text. So, this second edition is *School Law for the 1990s: A Handbook*.

The laws affecting schools exist within a much broader legal framework. Nonetheless, for teachers and administrators, the discrete part of the law that pertains to schools, especially, is an area of law that can be separated out, studied, and understood and, through study and understanding, make for greater ease and efficiency in school operation. Some laws are categorically specific to schools. This handbook takes both the broader and the narrower aspects of the law and combines them to provide an extended understanding of the realities in which professionals must perform as employees in elementary and secondary schools. Legal applications to higher education settings are minimal.

The content of the text reflects the experiences that the authors have had in a long-term engagement with public schools. Among others, the experiences in-clude teacher, building principal, superintendent, and board of education mem-ber. Each professes school law for preparing school administrators in their respective institutions, and each does substantial consulting with school districts.

Such contacts with practicing school administrators have provided a setting from which the authors address problems that relate to school law. Administrative experiences have been matched with knowledge of school law to lead readers toward an understanding of basic legal principles. Those legal principles are topically treated by chapters that are devoted to aspects of schooling. Not all of the law pertinent to schools has been included. The authors' experiences and professional contacts were the deciding force on which topics to include and which to exclude. Fine legal distinctions such as might be essential to a law student are not emphasized. Legal principles for professionals in elementary and secondary schools are emphasized. The result is a professional guide that is usable for teachers with an interest in school law, for graduate students preparing for school administration, and for school administrators in need of a precise but succinct treatment of the law and schools.

From those professional and academic experiences and with those goals, organization of the text evolved, and pertinent material was selected. The flow of authority in the American polity is depicted, from the constitutional power grant of the Tenth Amendment to the development of policy by a local school board. Statutes and cases have been selected to provide some sense of the national picture yet to make clear that each state may be the critical force in decision making about its schools. The hierarchy of law is described so that students can recognize that in the event of conflicts between a constitutionally protected right and particular state statutes, and if that conflict is litigated, the federal judiciary will set aside the state statutes. The hierarchy does prevail.

The cases not only should be a source of information but also should have practical value when professionals are confronted with similar situations in job settings. They should stimulate reflective thought and discussion, leading readers to consider what courts might decide if similar issues of one kind or another from their own school were to be litigated. For students who are serious about knowing school law comprehensively, selected major cases should be identified and prepared in brief form for a long-term reference. A brief, answering to the criteria of scholarliness and practicality, can handily be set into a structure of seven parts.

1. Identification should include the names of the litigants, the primary source of the report, the court that pronounced the decision, and the date.
2. Action should be a statement of what the plaintiff desires.
3. Facts should be a recitation of the pertinent, predominant evidence as that was developed for and recounted by the last court to hear the case.
4. Question(s) should be the specific, limited inquiry that was allowed in the last court hearing the case.
5. Answers should be the response of the court, "yes" or "no" or whatever else might be an accurate and suitable answer to the question.

    (Note: Actually, inasmuch as lower and higher courts may address the same case by way of different questions, it might enhance accuracy and understanding to identify every question by every court involved in the hearings of a case, up to and including the United States Supreme Court, if the case is appealed that far.)

6. Reasons that are revealed by the court for the answers given, and that substantiate the court's decision, should be listed. Frequently, five or six reasons might be given.

7. Application should reveal the general—or specific—applications of the findings to the current organization and operation of schools.

A well-written, precise, seven-part case brief can be done for most major cases in 400 to 500 words. Techniques for finding cases in the law-reporting systems are given in chapter 1.

The authors acknowledge the stimulating conversations with many colleagues in the National Council of Professors of Educational Administration (NCPEA) and the National Organization for Law in Public Education (NOLPE). Graduate students in classes of school law at both institutions have presented many challenges as the actions of legislatures and courts have been questioned in the best scholarly fashion. Many of those same students have provided research assistance. Finally, a special thanks is due Miss Inga Ronke, University of Nebraska at Omaha, a patient typist for much of this manuscript.

SCHOOL LAW
FOR THE
1990s

1

The Legal System and Location of Cases

THE LEGAL SYSTEM

Recognizing the need for nonviolent resolution of conflict, people acknowledged the advantages of a system of laws. Laws are external guides to acceptable behavior in society. Earlier in human history, conflicts were resolved by brutality or force. Laws provide an alternative—the use of words to work out disputes. Laws can be operational in a wide variety of political systems, ranging from open participation democracies to closed absolute dictatorships. Some of this early teaching of law as part of societal enlightenment emerged coupled with religion. Every social system has its own unique group of law-enforcing government officials, using its own set of laws.

In the United States of America, law has been conceptualized as the minimum restraint that must be imposed on individuals to achieve an acceptable level of social orderliness. Whether it is the revolutionary spirit, the frontier spirit, or something else, it is clear that since American citizens came into their own in 1776, there has been a steady resistance to power increases by central government authorities. Americans want to make most of their decisions for themselves with minimum guidance from governing officials. Not incidentally, that prevailing spirit of those early Americans provides the basis for much of the litigation centering on schools—people want to make decisions for themselves and for their children.

At the same time, those Americans of the late eighteenth century candidly recognized that some laws were necessary if property rights were to exist. Likewise, the same concept called for laws to protect certain rights of citizens in regard to individual freedoms. To incorporate such concerns and give them political reality, a constitution was adopted that called into being a three-part government, one in which checks and balances were provided. The Constitution called for a United States Congress (Article I); an executive, the president of the nation (Article II); and a judiciary consisting of one supreme court and necessary inferior courts (Article III). By the mid–1780s it was apparent to many that the Articles of Confederation should be set aside in favor of a more powerful central government.

Over the decades, certain constitutional parts selected from the whole document have proved to be most pertinent to education and to schools. Chiefly, these are restraints imposed in all settings and certainly including schools where children are compelled by law to attend.

1. Article I, Section 8
   The Congress shall have Power to lay and collect Taxes, Duties, Imposts and Excises, to pay the Debts and provide for the common Defence and general Welfare of the United States; but all Duties, Imposts and Excises shall be uniform throughout the United States. . . .

2. Amendment I
   Congress shall make no law respecting an establishment of religion or prohibiting the free exercise thereof; or abridging the freedom of speech, or of the press; or the right of the people peaceably to assemble, and to petition the Government for a redress of grievances.

3. Amendment IV
   The right of the people to be secure in their persons, houses, papers, and effects, against unreasonable searches and seizures, shall not be violated, and no warrants shall issue, but upon probable cause, supported by oath or affirmation, and particularly describing the place to be searched, and the persons or things to be seized.

4. Amendment IX
   The enumeration in the Constitution, of certain rights, shall not be construed to deny or disparage others retained by the people.

5. Amendment X
   The powers not delegated to the United States by the Constitution, nor prohibited by it to the States, are reserved to the States respectively, or to the people.

6. Amendment XIV, Section 1
   All persons born or naturalized in the United States, and subject to the jurisdiction thereof, are citizens of the United States and of the State wherein they reside. No state shall make or enforce any law which shall abridge the privileges or immunities of citizens of the United States; nor shall any State deprive any person of life, liberty, or property, without due process of law; nor deny to any person within its jurisdiction the equal protection of the laws.

Much of the essence of what can and must be done, or not done, in the nation's elementary and secondary schools is determined by consulting the pertinent portions of the Constitution, the baseline for all the statutes that have followed. Considered totally, all law of origin that is focused on elementary and secondary education is within the rubric of school law. The United States Constitution provides a reference point from which to continually revise laws that bear on schooling, an indicator of what states should, or should not, do.

With the Constitution as the benchmark or primary reference point, a substantial experience has developed concerning the relationship of the federal government and education. The executive branch is little involved; the legislative is involved more than that but still less than the judiciary. The judiciary is deeply involved in many decisions that are mandatory or influential on local school districts, and that level of influence has increased markedly since World War II. The judiciary has been central in the enforcement of civil rights legislation, pointing out directions for statutes and administrative guidelines that are aimed at the operation of schools.

Any survey of such a government structure as the legal system is definitionally brief, and fine points must be omitted. This text is a survey in only one area. Nonetheless, a general picture, resting on specifics and basic principles, is a necessary base from which a student of school law can make some important connections. For example, out of a case concerning agricultural subsidies, *United States v. Butler*, 297 U.S. 1 (1936), the right of the United States Congress to act broadly within Article I, Section 8, was recognized. Presumably, that congressional power can transfer to other areas of general welfare, for example, education. The Supreme Court interpretation that legitimized earlier but unquestioned action by Congress concerning education paved the way for such later statutes as the National Defense Education Act of 1958 and the Elementary and Secondary Education Act of 1965.

Education is not a government function mentioned in the United States Constitution. The Tenth Amendment is a plenary power grant, stating that all functions not given to the federal government are to become state functions, or functions of the people. Federal powers are restrictive and proscriptive. State powers are much broader; theoretically, states have all power not reserved to the people or the federal government.

In the American political system, a representative democracy, two streams of governmental action exist. Not only does the federal government consist of three parts—the legislative, executive, and judicial—but the same is true for every state. Each has its own constitution, one harmonious with the United States Constitution. That is, before territories were admitted to the United States, conflicts between territorial constitutions and the United States Constitution were removed. State constitutions may be ''stricter'' than the United States Constitution, and on some issues, such as separation of church and state, many are more strict. So, there are federal and state streams of government speaking about education, but the vast bulk of school law comes from the states.

Every state legislature is active—passing, amending, and repealing laws. Educational policy is a changing political process. Those laws can be different from laws on a similar subject in another state but cannot contradict federal statutes or the Constitution. Legislation is often tested by citizens who believe that there are contradictions, who feel adverse effects from it. The test is by way of the

American procedure of judicial review. In its political system, Britain accepts the principle of parliamentary supremacy. There, laws enacted by the federal government—Parliament—become the laws, without question. Although a common political heritage is shared by the English-speaking peoples, in the American political system another principle prevails. It is called judicial review. In the American system, the laws passed by any legislature—state or federal—may, with cause, be called into question to determine whether they conflict with either the state constitution or the United States Constitution. Courts resolve that conflict, if it exists, and those decisions become part of case law, that is, law derived from court decisions in cases brought before them.

Suppose, for example, that a state legislature mandated some additional part of the secondary curriculum for all the schools and that a teacher found it ethically offensive to be so directed to teach that new part. That teacher might seek relief in a state court, challenging the power of the legislature to be so prescriptive. The state court would examine the state constitution and decide, yes or no, on the amount of power conveyed to the legislature by the state constitution. Or, perhaps that teacher might seek relief in the federal judiciary, asserting that the mandate to teach the new curriculum was contradictory to personal religious beliefs, beliefs protected in the First Amendment of the Constitution. Admittedly, the example is grossly oversimplified at several points. Yet, it portrays accurately three aspects of the legal system: (1) the role of state legislatures; (2) the separate question of roles of state and federal courts; (3) the rights of citizens to question government actions. In the example, the judiciary served as a kind of political safety valve, reassuring individual citizens who, when they wish to do so and are willing to face some costs, may challenge the actions of legislatures. Such challenge may not be done on a citizen's whimsy; there must be some probable cause. It is clear, however, that the action of one citizen may be enough to overcome the action of a legislature—if the court so decides.

For schools and questions that have some base in education, the disputes frequently seek court orders or damages. Damages are generally for a money amount—restitution for some wrong, an injurious thing done by the school or its employees. Court orders are negative or positive. Injunctions are orders to cease and desist; a mandamus is an order to start and do something. In abbreviated form, the judicial system is depicted in figure 1.1, showing the parts that are commonly involved in school law.

To assist in understanding the system and the linkages, a concise explanation of two real school arguments should be helpful. In *Wisconsin v. Yoder*, 406 U.S. 205 (Wis., 1972), Wisconsin's compulsory education law forced Amish children, and all others of specified age, to attend secondary schools. The legislature had passed that compulsory education law. The secondary curriculum, also under the general control of the legislature, had parts that violated the religious beliefs of the Amish, forcing children to inquire into some deeper meanings of life that the Amish considered closed areas. Amish parents objected and brought suit. Argued before the Wisconsin Supreme Court, that decision decreed that compulsory education laws of the state violated the free (religious) exercise clause of the First Amendment, which had been made applicable to all of the states by the Fourteenth Amendment. The state of Wisconsin, through its attorney general, appealed to the United States Supreme Court, and Chief Justice Warren Burger delivered the Court's opinion, affirming the Wisconsin decision. So, the compulsory education laws of all the states, as they applied to Amish children who had completed the eighth grade, were set aside by the Supreme Court's decision. Other actions have occasionally been brought against compulsory education as out of step with a democratic society, but the *Yoder* case was specific to the group and the reason for exception.

In *Epperson v. Arkansas*, 393 U.S. 97 (Ark., 1968), a secondary teacher was constrained by state law from teaching Darwin's theory of the origin of species in a biology class and was mandated to teach the story of origin as found in the Book of Genesis. In a final appeal to the United States Supreme Court, her suit was upheld; the Court found the mandating Arkansas statute in conflict with the First Amendment. In addition, the Court commented, "Public education in our nation is committed to the control of state and local authorities." Still, a constraint on state authority was found in the establishment of religion portion of the First Amendment.

There is certainly no intention in this book to diminish the role of legislators in making laws that affect schools. Every state constitution has conveyed to its legislature some kind of responsibility to provide for public education. Some of those constitutional clauses are general and some are quite specific. Some even specify the role to be played by a state department of education. So, the legislatures created, in any rational way they desired, the public school districts that are charged as the local agencies for the educational effort of the state. It is the whole effort of the legislative branch, combined with the judiciary branch, that has chiefly impinged on education, forming it into what it is and reforming it as new ideas and contentions are expressed within the nation's political system.

LOCATING COURT CASES

Cases are carried before courts and argued there. The decisions of the lower, or inferior, courts go unrecorded, in the main. From figure 1.1, four types of courts may be seen to be courts of record:

1. United States district courts
2. United States courts of appeal
3. State supreme courts
4. United States Supreme Court

There are more than 150 courts of record, any of which may handle some kinds of questions related to schools and all of which report their findings in the reporter

Figure 1.1
The Judiciary

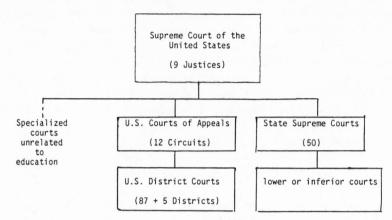

systems. The reports are not transcripts but are summary recapitulations, with conclusions. Authoring judges are usually identified.

Legal citations, as the device for locating any given case, are different from other scholarly citing systems but are simple, short, and accurate. Cases have names. Generally, those are the names of the plaintiff and defendant—*Smith v. Jones*. Although those positional labels, plaintiff and defendant, in that hypothetical case may change on appeal, and although new labels may be used—appellant and appellee—the basic statement still is the critical truth. Cases have names.

Civil cases predominate in school litigation. Very little of it involves criminal law. In civil cases, damages or court orders are what is sought. So, in *Smith v. Jones*, Smith may have wanted a court to order Jones to do, or not to do, something; or, Smith may have sought some kind of damage award from Jones for an alleged injury.

Real citations have not only names but numbers as well. The numbers reveal the volume and page number of a book in which the case can be found, as reported by the deciding court. For example, in a real case in which the defendant was the state because a state law was being challenged, the citation was *Meyer v. State of Nebraska*, 262 U.S. 390, 43 S.Ct. 625, 67 L. Ed. 1042. This case originated from a complaint filed in 1920 and decided by the Supreme Court in 1923. It can be found in volume 262 of the *U.S. Reports* (the reports of the United States Supreme Court decisions), commencing on page 390. It also occurs in other primary reporting systems, the *Supreme Court Reporter* and the *United States Supreme Court Reports, Lawyer's Edition*. Also recounted in the *American Law Review* (ALR), it is enough for school law students to know about and be able to find cases in the primary reporting source. In the example of Meyer, with three citations, the first one listed is the primary source. In this text, the general rule is to give the citation to the primary source. The identification of each case is the same as was suggested in the Preface for the writing of a case brief. If Meyer had not been appealed to the United States Supreme Court, the decision of the Nebraska Supreme Court would have been final, and that court's decision was reversed—overruled—by the United States Supreme Court. The state court's decision can be found in the *Nebraska Reports* and also in the *Northwest Reports*. There is a reporter system for each state supreme court. In addition, every such decision is carried in the regional reporter system, for example the *Northwest Reports*.

After it is located, a case should be read in order to clearly understand the primary aspects of the case. What was the argument? What was the judgment? Who won, the plaintiff or the defendant? Remembering that higher courts report their actions on the appeals of decisions from lower courts, the reader must come to know what happened in the lower court, separating that part of the report from the final reporting court's action. It is the last decision that really counts. The seven parts of a case brief, as set forward in the Preface, provide a suitable descriptive format for students of school law:

1. Identification of the case
2. Action sought
3. Facts of the case
4. Questions raised by the court
5. Answers given by the court
6. Reasons that support the answers
7. General applicability to school settings

It is a rather mechanical approach to reading the report of a case, but it is also an assurance that, if the reader can grasp how those seven parts fit, the case will be understood.

In addition to locating and reading the cases, a reader needs a few additional technical concepts for an accurate understanding. The Bill of Rights preserved to the people certain individual liberties. Each amendment in the Bill of Rights places prohibitions and limits on the powers of governments. Originally, those power restrictions were applicable to the federal government only; however, interpretations by the Supreme Court of the Fourteenth Amendment made them applicable to state governments as well.

Interpretations of the Fourteenth Amendment have led the Supreme Court to consider such questions as the meaning of "privileges," "liberty," and "due process of law," as those terms occur in the Fourteenth Amendment, Section 1: "No state shall make or enforce any law which shall abridge the privileges or immunities of citizens of the United States; nor shall any state deprive any person of life, liberty, or property, without due process of law; nor deny to any person within its jurisdiction the equal protection of the laws." Considerations over the past century have revealed several philosophical-legal positions that can

stand more or less scrutiny as logical systems in which applications and relationships between the Bill of Rights and the Fourteenth Amendment can be used
to settle civil disputes. The currently prevailing view of the Supreme Court is
one of the least rigorous in terms of its ability to meet the tests of a system of
logic and one of the most flexible in terms of its ability to allow the justices a
great deal of discretion in interpretation of what the Court should say. Readers
of cases should anticipate that operational viewpoint of the Court as a necessary
aspect of understanding why Court opinions sometimes are finally rendered as
they are. It provides a vantage point of general understanding and an ability to
anticipate or predict decisions. It also serves to explain why many decisions are
made by split panels of judges. With nine justices on the U.S. Supreme Court
and each confident of his/her ability in scholarship in the law, split decisions—
for example, of 6 to 3—are common. The justices and the lower judges exercise
their substantial discretion when they address a conflict, interpret the law, and
make a decision.

Emanating from all of this legal activity in the three major branches of government is administrative law. This includes the policies, rules, guidelines, and
so on at local levels, and from state agencies. Speaking practically, it is administrative law that composes the bulk of school law, but professional educators
need to understand its place of origin. It can be developed only on authorization,
such as from statute, and is subject to judicial review to test for its compliance
with either federal or state constitutions. It may be tested against statutory or
case law too. It is the specific refinement of the more general body of law,
specific to particular instances and local settings.

2

School Districts and
Boards of Education

BOARDS OF EDUCATION

Boards of education are unique American institutions. These boards are charged
with the management of school districts and are created as state entities having
authority to manage local education agencies (LEAs). The powers and organizational patterns of boards of education vary from state to state and, within many
states, according to the sizes and types of public school districts.

Major board functions include hiring a superintendent of schools, establishing
policy for the district, overseeing state laws, reviewing local programs, and
setting the budget. Public school boards are legally distinct from other governing
boards such as city councils and county commissioners. Well over 75 percent
of American public school board members are elected from within their district;
the rest are appointed, and patterns for appointment vary. Boards have no inherent
powers; their powers can be expanded or curtailed by state legislatures. Court
decisions may also alter the power base for an LEA board. Board members must
fulfill a dual function: (1) service as a representative of some constituency; (2)
service as a trustee of the school district's mission and resources. To manage
more than 15,000 LEAs, there are nearly 100,000 school board members in the
nation.

Although most members of LEA boards are elected officials, some states
provide for their appointment. In *Irby v. Virginia State Bd. of Elections*, 889
F.2d 1352 (1989), the appointment method was challenged on the premise that
blacks failed of appropriate representation. Virginia's statute providing for appointed school board members was supported by the court because the plaintiffs
failed to show that it had a direct discriminatory effect on school boards across
the state. Similar suits have been brought by other minorities, and sometimes
with different claims for underrepresentation. Court rulings have varied because

such cases have local peculiarities in population and operate under varying state statutes. For example, in *McNeil v. Springfield Park District*, 666 F.Supp. 1208 (Ill., 1987), the plaintiffs demonstrated that it was possible to create a subdistrict in which over 50 percent of that population would be minorities. With a seven-member board of education elected at large, the plaintiffs contended for the necessity of dividing the territory into subdistricts, stipulating that the present condition was in violation of the Voting Rights Act of 1965. Analyzing the plaintiffs' data, the LEA board demonstrated that only 43 percent of the voting-age minority citizens lived in the described area of the subdistrict, and the court found no violation of the 1965 act.

Local boards of education derive their powers from the state constitutions, state statutes, federal laws and court decisions. Such powers may be expressed—those that are statutory (mandatory) requirements; or they may be implied—those that evolve from delegated powers. The courts have provided fairly broad interpretations of the implied powers and have thus encouraged freedom and experimentation somewhat beyond that which the legal structure might suggest. Unless a practice not expressly permitted by statute is challenged judicially, it may continue to grow and spread until it becomes generally accepted practice. If it is challenged and sustained, it acquires a status as if permission for the practice had been given through statute. One of the early examples of this process can be found in the Michigan decision of 1874, *Stuart v. School District #1 of Kalamazoo*, 30 Mich. 69 (1874). In that instance, the Kalamazoo school board extended the common school system to include a high school, hired a superintendent of schools, and levied a tax to pay for the extensions, thereby establishing a process that spread across the nation and was not judicially challenged to the extent that it was impermissible.

Boards of education have been charged with managing the affairs of an LEA and with administering the state laws that apply to the public schools that compose that public school district. The board is the governing unit for those political subdivisions charged with the responsibility for education in that state.

Local boards of education are composed of members who have been selected by a process defined in the statutes or the state constitution. The members serve in their official capacity only when sitting in a duly constituted board of education meeting during which they are to transact the business of the district in accord with the authority granted to them by constitution, statutes, or court decisions.

In some states (Michigan and New York), boards are considered to be bodies corporate; in others (Georgia), the school district is considered to be the body corporate. Not all problems of local operation can be foreseen and planned for in statutes. In such situations, many boards opt for the autonomy of the corporate concept and set their own direction. For example, when parents change residence, moving to another public school district, must the affected children be disenrolled on the moving day, or tuition payments demanded? Advocacy for the welfare of children argues for continuity of instruction if the new residence is nearby. In metropolitan areas that have several school districts, this is a common occurrence. If boards allow such children to continue in attendance, and without charge, are the interests of the LEA taxpayers being ignored? Lacking a statutory mandate, boards may establish their own direction via policy, choosing whatever direction that particular board in that specific LEA might decide on. That is, boards have many powers that are similar to those of private corporations. With a choice made either way, board action would be an example of a board acting within implied powers. Some citizen might give the decision a court test to determine if it was right, or wrong.

THE BOARD OF EDUCATION AND THE STATE

The Tenth Amendment of the United States Constitution states, "The powers not delegated to the United States by the Constitution, nor prohibited by it to the States, are reserved to the States respectively, or to the people." The state constitutions make provisions for education within the particular state. As examples, the state of Georgia places the responsibility for public schools on the state, which, in turn, delegates this responsibility to the State Board of Education; Section 1, Article XI, of the New York State Constitution instructs the legislature to provide for a system of free common schools wherein all the children of the state may be educated.

The determination of those policies and statutes that govern the operation of the schools stems from the legislature, which, in turn, has delegated those matters of day-to-day management of the schools to local school districts. These same legislatures have made provisions for local governing boards. Since local school districts are creatures of the legislature and have been created, altered, or dissolved by legislative acts, local boards of education depend for their existence on state constitutional or legislative processes. Thus, local boards of education have no power or authority except that which is provided through constitutional or legislative enactments for them.

In each state, a governing body at the state level is responsible for carrying out the constitutional and legislative mandate for providing public schools. One state, Hawaii, has one school system; thus, the state board of education is, at the same time, the board of education for the school system. The other 49 states have governing bodies at the state level which are responsible for carrying out the constitutional and legislative mandate for providing public education. These vary in name and structure and provide for a state department of education to carry out the administrative and organizational functions of the state board of education. In Georgia, Michigan, and several other states, the governing bodies are state boards of education, whereas the New York Board of Regents has the responsibility for the governance of the public schools.

Technically, then, it must be recognized that even though local boards of education provide for the day-to-day operation of the schools, local board of education members, regardless of the manner in which they are appointed or elected, are state, not local, officers. This applies even if local board of education members are appointed by the mayor; they are state, not municipal, officers. In whatever manner they gain office, it can only have been as statutorily specified for that kind of school district in that state. This question arose early, and in *Ham v. Mayor of New York City*, 79 NY 459 (1877), the ruling was that even when appointed by the mayor, the school board members should not be considered as municipal officials because the legislature could change that method at any time.

The Georgia State Department of Education is the administrative unit and organization through which the policies, directives, and powers of the state board of education and the duties of the state superintendent of schools are administered. Section 3, Article VIII, of the Michigan State Constitution provides:

Leadership and general supervision over all public education, including adult education and instructional programs in state institutions, except as to institutions of higher education granting baccalaureate degrees, is vested in a state board of education. It shall serve as the general planning and coordinating body for all public education, including higher education, and shall advise the legislature as to the financial requirements in connection therewith.

The New York State Education Department is the administrative arm of the board of regents. These three state systems—Georgia, Michigan, and New York—are representative of the remaining systems in the United States.

The prevailing pattern by which states make known their presence in the educational enterprise is through a state board of education. The actual name may change from state to state, but such functions as overseer and program leader are commonly shared. Some states have seen fit to abolish that department of state services, and in the late 1980s, other states were considering such action.

THE BOARD OF EDUCATION AND INTERMEDIATE SCHOOL DISTRICTS

The nature and responsibility of the intermediate school districts vary from state to state. In general, they are formed by a group of local school districts to provide services to the component districts which otherwise could not be economically or efficiently provided for. This "shared service" concept is found, for example, in the formation of Regional Education Service Areas in Georgia, Area Education Agencies in Iowa (AEA), and Boards of Cooperative Educational Services (BOCES) in New York. Most states have some such intermediate education units.

In New York, the Boards of Cooperative Educational Services are voluntary, cooperative associations of school districts in a geographic area, which have joined forces to provide educational or auxiliary services more economically than each could provide by itself. Such services may include, but not be limited to, education for handicapped students, vocational education, drug and health education and services, continuing (adult) education, staff development, data processing, consultative services, psychological and psychiatric services, co-operative purchasing, and repair and maintenance of equipment. The services supplied are those that each component school district may request, subject to approval, in some instances (e.g., New York State) by the appropriate division in the state education department. State statutes may direct the narrowness or breadth of service that the intermediate unit can develop.

Governance of the intermediate school district is through a board of control. Members of these boards are selected, usually, by electors designated by the local school district board of education or by the local board of education itself, sometimes by district and sometimes at large. Michigan and Nebraska are examples of states that provide an alternate method of selection—election at popular elections in the intermediate district.

The financing of intermediate districts varies and may be through the payment of service and administrative costs by the component districts, as in New York; through direct allocations from the state board of education and service fees from component districts, as in Georgia; by allocations derived from legislative appropriations, as in Iowa; or by combinations thereof. Wide variances in financial support systems exist from state to state, each provided for in statute.

The intermediate school district is a service unit that serves more than one local school system and is, thus, an intermediary between the state and the local school. The state may give it extended autonomy or high control. These units are governed by specific statutory enactments, such as the Quality Basic Education Law in Georgia, State Code, sections 32–628a through 32–636a, and New York's Educational Law, Section 1950, Boards of Cooperative Educational Services. It should be noted that these intermediate districts are shared service units in contrast to the type of intermediate districts that are found in major metropolitan areas, for example, the New York City Public School District. These latter districts were created for the purpose of decentralizing inordinately large school systems, with subdistricts in a large district, each having substantial autonomy.

THE BOARD OF EDUCATION AND THE LOCAL SCHOOL DISTRICT

Legally, the local board of education is considered to be the governing body of the public school district, the LEA. Where the duties and powers of the school district have been delineated, these, then, are considered to be the duties and powers of the board of education. The very existence of the board of education is dependent on the existence of the school district.

Legislative enactments that provide for the organization and establishment of school districts provide, also, for the selection of boards of education. Such enactments include the qualifications, method of nomination and selection, terms of office, duties and responsibilities, procedures for removal from office, composition of the board of education, remuneration of board members, reimbursement for expenditures in the line of duty, and such other specifications as may be pertinent to that particular state and the operation of the local boards.

Since boards of education depend on statutory authority for their acts, duties, and responsibilities, a search of each state's education code can provide the specific information that is applicable to that particular state. As an example, these states cited in this chapter have the following citations pertaining to school districts and boards of education, giving a comprehensive description of board powers and obligations:

Georgia — Chapter 2, Article 3, Sec. 20–2–50. County Boards of Education
Chapter 2, Article 8, Part 4, Sec. 20–2–490. Local Tax for Public Schools

New York — Education Law, Section 1709. Powers and Duties of a Board of Education of Union Free School Districts (applicable, also, to Central School Districts)
Education Law, Section 2503. Powers and Duties of City Boards of Education of Cities under 125,000 Population.

Only the board of education can act for the LEA and exercise the powers that have been granted by the statutes and the state constitution. Further, a board of education has authority over a single school district. It is the governing body for one local education agency (LEA).

In a time when declining student registrations are common in public school districts, numerous LEA boards have made moves to close attendance centers. Frequently, such moves, viewed as necessary by boards, are received with hostility by patrons. In *Parents' Council v. Boston Schools*, 542 N.E.2d 1043 (Mass., 1989), the board moved aggressively and rapidly to close a building. Accused of violating its own policy for conducting a hearing on school closings, the board paused in its activity, held the hearing, and then voted to close the school. Board actions were supported by the court when it observed that board members could approach a wide variety of problems with an inclination toward a specific decision. In *Haynes v. Kanawha County Board*, 383 S.E.2d 67 (W. Va., 1989), the lower court ordered the board to hold a second public hearing on a school closing. With one hearing already accomplished and a decision made, the board appealed, contending that it was obligated for one hearing only. Agreeing, the West Virginia Supreme Court held that the LEA board was responsible for facilities, including the closing of some schools when that was necessary.

In some states, the qualified electors of a school district meet in an annual meeting of the district. Those voters who attend these meetings have been granted specific statutory authority by the legislature. They are empowered to act on a variety of items, including adoption of the district's annual budget, election of board of education members, and the transaction of such other business as may be properly brought before the meeting. Questions sometimes arise as to which body holds the ultimate authority over controversies occurring in the conduct of the school district's business. In *State v. Anderson*, 22 N.W.2d 516 (Wis., 1946), it was held that a school board is not inherently superior to the annual school district meeting that elects the board. Only when the statutes specifically place a matter within the control of the board of education may the board overrule an action of the school district annual meeting. Statutes on this matter vary from state to state. Court decisions may influence a legislature to act with statutory clarifications as its intent.

Another area in which questions arise is that dealing with the transfer of power when district reorganization takes place. Generally, the powers possessed by the previous board of education are transferred to the successor board. One major concern in district reorganization is the effect of such reorganization on contracts. In *McClure v. Princeton Reorganized School District R-5*, 307 S.W.2d 726 (Mo., 1957), it was held that contracts entered into by a previous board of education must be honored by the successor boards. Unless there is a statutory prohibition, generally the successor board has the same powers as its predecessors. So, when an LEA "disappears," its obligations and opportunities still remain for its successor.

THE BOARD OF EDUCATION AND MUNICIPAL BODIES

It should be remembered that the local board of education derives its duties and powers from legislative enactments. These statutes prescribe the authority granted to the board of education to manage and control the operations of the school district that it governs. It follows, then, that the municipal authorities may not contravene the legislative intent by limiting or controlling the authority granted to the local board of education. Given the facts that some school districts have coterminus boundaries with a municipality of the same name, the separateness is not always clear. Still, budget realities are always separated.

Fiscally independent boards of education are free to adopt budgets—subject in certain jurisdictions to a referendum by the qualified voters of the district; they can levy—or cause to be levied—taxes within the constitutional or statutory limits prescribed by the state and can expend the funds received in accordance with the prescribed fiscal procedures. Fiscally dependent boards of education, although having the authority to determine the budget, must depend on another body—for example, the board of estimate, the city council, or the county board of commissioners—to provide the funds to underwrite the budgetary needs of the school district. In this latter instance, that other local governmental body becomes the fiscal agent and, thereby, assumes some indirect control over the school district's educational program. If the funds requested by the board of education are not granted, the two bodies—the board of education and its fiscal agency—shall confer in an attempt to reach a satisfactory agreement on funds. Some of governance is negotiations and compromises. When an agreement has been reached, the budget must be amended accordingly. It is in this manner that the "outside" fiscal agency can exercise some control over the school district's affairs.

SOURCES OF BOARD POWERS

In *Board of Education of Oklahoma City v. Cloudman*, 92 P.2d 837 (Okla., 1939), the court defined, judicially, the powers of a board of education as follows: "The school board has and can exercise those powers that are granted in express words, those fairly implied in or necessarily incidental to the powers expressly granted, and those essential to the declared objects and purposes of the corporation."

Powers and authority residing in a board of education come from three sources: the state constitution, legislative enactments, and judicial decisions. Those powers granted by the state constitution can be changed only through amendment of that document; powers granted by legislative enactment can be modified as the legislature may see fit; and powers decreed by judicial decision may be changed only as the decision is reversed by a higher court or superseded by a new opinion.

Unless the statutory authority granted to a board of education proves to be unconstitutional, the courts will not interfere with it. Where express legislative approval has not been given, the courts must determine whether the statutes clearly imply authority to pursue the activity or whether the activity is necessary to accomplish the school district's purpose. Challenges to a board of education's authority are often found when that board has embarked on educational innovations. Typically, such challenges maintain that these innovations are beyond the powers of the board of education. However, courts have given a broad interpretation to the notion of implied powers of LEA boards. That judicial attitude has been apparent from the *Kalamazoo* case and it is a condition which has encouraged boards to think freely about their powers.

The decision as to how the statutes are to be construed rests with the court. Courts in certain jurisdictions have held that the statutes that confer power or impose duties on the boards of education must be given strict construction. They hold that the statutes must be viewed not only as grants of powers but also as limitations of that power. Courts in other jurisdictions see the matter differently and give the statutes a more liberal construction. As a general rule, wherever doubt exists as to whether a board possesses a given power, the courts will deny the power's existence.

The rule *ejusdem generis* states that a general grant of power following an enumeration of specific powers is to be interpreted as applying to the same general kind of powers as those that are specifically mentioned. Thus, if specific powers regarding the provisions of educational programs have been conferred on the board of education, a general provision granting powers to the board of education to do those things that are necessary for maintaining the educational program does not expand the specific powers.

Boards of education, as state bodies, have been created to perform a state function. They have been granted the necessary authority to act when the occasion demands action. Thus, the board of education possesses powers that have been conferred on it by statute. Not only may the board of education exercise these powers, but the board must act when the situation requires the board to exercise its granted powers.

BOARD POWERS AND DUTIES

No state constitution or statutes are inclusive enough to provide for every act that may be performed by a local board of education. It can be noted that many of the practices being followed in American schools were first implemented by one or more local boards of education before those practices were specifically authorized by the statutes. Included in this list might be educational data processing, programmed instruction, nongraded groupings, and the use of paraprofessionals.

Examination of developments in educational programs reveals other areas that were introduced by boards of education before authorization by the legislature and are now provided for by legislative enactment. Among these are pupil health services, school food services, guidance and counseling services, and machine accounting practices and procedures.

Boards of education assumed that those powers were implied to permit them to carry out the expressed duties with the expressed powers defined in the statutes. The powers of local boards of education may be changed at any time by the same authority that granted the powers—the legislature. The courts have agreed that because it is not possible to foresee and legislate particularly for every problem that may arise in the administration of the schools, boards of education may exercise implied powers so that they might carry out the express powers granted by the statute. The doctrine of necessity is the assumption of the implied powers necessary to carry out the express powers granted by the statute and the educational functions of the school district. However, in the eyes of the law, boards of education have implied powers related to education only. For example, a board might note that a street by a school lacks speed control or traffic lights. The board has no control over city streets and cannot act beyond a request to city officials for a remedy of an unsafe condition; the board cannot install traffic lights. Boards of education are not vested with inherent powers. Even though the courts, when in doubt, under common law are inclined to find against an implied power, most courts tend to construe implied powers broadly when dealing with educational matters.

One of the fears under this tendency is that boards of education will be permitted to expend funds for any purpose that they deem to be for the educational cause of children. "Not so," said the Georgia Supreme Court in ruling on the question of whether the school lunch program may be tax supported as an "educational expense." The court ruled that "educational purposes" could not be construed to include the feeding of children. *Wright v. Absalom*, 159 S.E.2d 413 (Ga., 1968). This might be a cue to the legislature to extend the definition of the term "educational expenses" to include specified health and nutrition programs.

Unless the courts find decisions to be arbitrary, capricious, or unreasonable, they have utilized a rule of expediency as a basis for sustaining board actions that to the court appear to utilize implied powers to provide educationally sound programs and practices. The court's determination will be based on the particulars presented and the outcome of such a proceeding cannot be predicted perfectly. If the court wishes to apply a strict construction, limitations may be placed on the board of education's powers. A remedy for this would be to seek a change in the empowering statute to provide express powers to cover the board of education's action. Should the court interpretation of the board of education's implied powers be extended, this could result in "judge-made law," wherein judicial approval is given to educational programs which were not considered when the legislature enacted the statutes that conferred express powers on boards of education.

One area of board of education powers that should be examined is that of delegated powers. A common law principle is that a delegated power may not be further delegated by the body or the person to whom it was originally delegated by statute. Boards of education, to whom the legislature has delegated specific powers, must exercise the powers that have been delegated. Before exercising these powers, the board may seek counsel and advice from parties who may be affected by their decision, but the final decision must be made by the board of education.

With the development of collective bargaining in the public sector, contracts have been written, sometimes including nondelegable powers. Such contract provisions are null and void. A Georgia case in which the board of education granted a teacher's association the right to allocate at least $339,600 as increased economic benefits among the board's professional employees was denied by the court in *Chatham v. Board of Public Education*, 204 S.E.2d 138 (Ga., 1974). This case was further complicated by the fact that the state of Georgia had not enacted a public employee bargaining law.

In summary, then, boards of education have no powers or duties other than those expressed by or implied from delegating statutes. Although courts may be fairly liberal in construing implied powers broadly, each case is determined on its merit under the particular circumstances presented to the court. When acting in undefined areas, administrators need to use conservative common sense in advice to LEA boards.

CONTINUING NATURE OF THE BOARD

Where a school district exists, by the nature of the statute provided for its existence, there too is the provision that a governing body shall be formed to manage the day-to-day operations of the school district. The answer to a question as to whether one board of education can bind a future board to take a specific action on a proposition that may come before the successor board in the future turns on the statutory authority given to the board of education. If statutory authority is granted to a board of education to undertake an action that will cover a period of time extending into the future, and the board does so in good faith without intent to defraud another, succeeding boards will be bound by the action.

There has been much litigation over this question of binding future boards of education. Even though the courts are not in complete agreement on the question, the weight of the evidence leads to the conclusion that a board of education may enter into a contract extending beyond the terms of office of its individual members (i.e., three, four, five, or whatever years the term of office may occupy) even without the benefit of legislative enactment. Georgia is one state that has provided for continuity of a board of education and settled this issue. Where the board of education has been declared a continuing body through the statutes, it can be argued that it would be contrary to public policy to limit the board's contractual powers to the official life of its individual members. Such a restriction would not answer for tests of common sense and administrability.

An area where the matter of a continuing board of education is of much concern involves incurred debt. States make provisions to protect against an abuse of the power and authority to incur debt by providing for public bond referendums before the issuance of such debt instruments. In addition, many states have constitutional limitations on debt as well as the ability to tax, limitations that serve as protections against the misuse of the debt-incurring powers of boards of education. Because there are such wide variations in state statutes with regard to entering into contracts that extend beyond the term of office of individual board of education members and because there are conflicting court decisions, LEA boards should seek legal advice regarding their state statutes relative to their power to enter into obligations extending beyond their term of office and, thereby, binding successor boards.

BASES FOR BOARD POWERS: STATUS, ROLES, AND FUNCTIONS

The board of education's primary functions are goal setting and policy-making. In addition, major responsibilities assigned to boards of education include the selection and appointment of the superintendent of schools and the approval of the annual budget. The board should develop and adhere to strong, workable policies so that the district might be operated in an efficient manner. Boards of education do not have plenary powers in many situations. Their authority to make policies is proscribed by the Constitution of the United States (through the Fourteenth Amendment), the state constitution, state and federal statutes, federal and state court rulings, attorney general opinions, and state board of education policies. Written board policies establish a legal base for the board of each LEA, carry the force of law, and provide direction when questions arise.

In *Mullin v. Board of Education of East Ramapo School District*, 421 N.Y.2d 523 (1979), the court held for the defendant when it weighed the balance between the teacher's interest "as a citizen in commenting upon matters of public concern and the intent of the State as an employer, in promoting the efficiency of the public services it performs through its employees." In part, the court relied on *Pickering v. Board of Education*, No. 205, 319 U.S. 568 (Ill., 1968) in arriving at its decision.

In *Mullin*, the teachers' union had developed a "success card" and was mailing this to the parents of the pupils in the school system. The board of education sought and obtained an injunction against this practice. The union appealed. The court, in its decision, supported the board of education's contention that the teacher's union had violated board policy concerning communication with parents through the use of the "success card." The board of education's contention was that establishment of educational policy was within the sole province of the board and the school administration and that this included, for example, the function of systematic communication from the school to parents. The court agreed.

Policies must be consistent with and may not contravene the statutes. Thus, under the provisions of its policies, a board of education must act only in the manner prescribed or authorized by statute. Where boards of education choose to ignore the duties imposed by the statutes, their failure to comply with the statutes may—and frequently does—result in legal action that contests the board of education's act. Even if the board of education should successfully defend the action, there are those who consider the board to be suspect.

The general rule is that a board of education can act only as a body at a meeting that has been legally called and held. No individual member of the board of education has power to legally act for or bind the board of education. If a board of education's actions are to be considered valid, the board must act at the time, in the place, and in the manner prescribed by law.

There are two types of actions that govern or describe the board of education's behavior. The first type is discretionary acts, which require the full consideration, counsel, and deliberation of the entire board of education. The board cannot delegate to an individual or to a committee any act that requires the exercise of discretion. The second type is ministerial acts (e.g., in several states a board may direct its presiding officer to execute a contract in the name of the board), which are somewhat mechanical in nature and do not require the board's discretion. Moreover, ministerial acts are typically those acts mandated by the state; the local board merely acts for the state.

Many boards of education have adopted a committee system to assist in the conduct of the board's business. Committees have no power to act; they may investigate a situation, report their findings, and make their recommendations to the entire board of education for consideration and action. Committees are designed to discover information, make recommendation, and influence action by the board.

THE BOARD'S AUTHORITY AS RULE MAKER

Boards of education have the implied power to make and enforce reasonable rules and regulations for the efficient conduct of the schools. The key word here is *reasonable*. Because the scope of rules and regulations is so wide, the courts have been asked to consider a vast range of cases. The general presumption by courts is that boards of education have acted reasonably in reaching their determination. Except where a fundamental constitutional right of the plaintiff is involved, the burden of proof is placed on the plaintiff. In the matter of rules and regulations, we are dealing with discretionary powers of the board of education. Where such powers have been exercised, it remains for the court to examine such actions to determine if they were arbitrary, capricious, unreasonable, or unlawful. It has been established that a court will not substitute its judgment for that of the board of education where the board's judgment has been reasonable. The finding in *Parrish v. Moss*, 106 N.Y.S.2d 577 (1951), supports this thesis.

However, an LEA board's power to make and enforce rules and regulations is not unlimited. If such rules and regulations conflict with existing statutes and/or constitutional provisions, they are invalid when challenged. Should a subsequent statutory enactment conflict with a board of education's rule or regulation, such enactment automatically repeals the board's rule or regulation.

It is virtually impossible to foresee every emergency situation that might arise. Thus, it is also impossible to promulgate rules and regulations to meeting every contingency. Consequently, the court held in *Tanton v. McKenney*, 197 N.W. 510 (Mich., 1924), that a reasonable rule that may be adopted by a teacher or a school administrator and that is not inconsistent with rules or statutes adopted by a higher authority shall be binding on pupils.

With the adoption of rules and regulations by a board of education comes the obligation to provide due process to those to whom the rules and regulations will apply. Such due process requires notice. Notice may be provided by the publication of the rules and regulations and the placement of them in the hands of the people who are to be subject to these rules and regulations. As an example, in the realm of secondary students, the publication of the rules and regulations in a student handbook and the provision of the handbook to each and every student will suffice.

An area where boards of education have been called on to use discretionary powers is in determining a "cut off" date for entrance to school. If the statute or the state constitution provides a "free" public education for all children, beginning with age six, does that mean that entry could/should/must occur on the sixth birthday?

One such case was brought before the supreme court of Montana. In *State ex. rel. Ronish v. School District, Fergus County*, 348 P.2d 797 (Mont., 1960), the board of education had adopted a rule that a child must be five years of age on or before October 31 to be enrolled in kindergarten during that school year. The board provided, further, that parents could request a test to determine if a child whose birthday fell between November 1 and November 15 could be enrolled in the kindergarten at the commencement of the fall term. The parents of a child whose birthdate was November 18 sought to enroll their child, claiming that the statute provided for schools to be open to all people between the ages of six and twenty-one and that the cut-off date was arbitrary. Their request was denied, and they sought judicial relief. The question before the court was, "Does a school board have power under our Constitution and statutes to set an arbitrary date, after the beginning of a school term, after which a child who reaches his sixth birthday may not be admitted for that particular term?" The court answered the question in the affirmative and held, further, that the board of education had made a reasonable rule that was not in conflict with the intent and purpose of the state statute.

Once adopted by a board of education, rules must be administered equitably and in like manner to all persons similarly situated. An example of this requirement is found in *Wood v. School District No. 65*, 309 N.E.2d 408 (Ill., 1974), wherein an Illinois appellate court held that if the board of education used a mailing list to communicate with parents about a referendum, that list must be made available to others within to express their opinions in the same matter; that is, matters of public concern deserve equal treatment.

If the test to determine the validity of a rule or regulation is its reasonableness, then it follows that there should be a "paper trail" that provides a record of facts on which the rule or regulation is based. Such evidence should show the procedures (e.g., study of facts, consultations with experts in the matter, review of similar situations in other districts, public hearings on the matter, and a determination that the rule or regulation is educationally sound) that the board of education has followed.

LEA AUTHORITY IN CURRICULUM AND ACTIVITIES

Each state legislature has enacted statutes related to the curriculum of the public schools. It has been well established that the legislatures have plenary power over the curriculum, except where there are constitutional restraints. Further, compulsory attendance laws have been held to be valid. The issue of whether all children who are governed by these compulsory attendance laws must attend public schools was decided in *Pierce v. Society of Sisters*, 268 U.S. 510 (Or., 1925), where the Supreme Court of the United States held, "The state [Oregon] may reasonably regulate all schools and may require that all children attend some school, but the state may not deny children the right to attend *adequate* private schools and force them to attend only public schools."

With the requirement of compulsory attendance, it might be expected that there would be challenges to the curricular determinations of legislatures, state boards of education, and local boards of education. That expectation is the reality of much of the legislation involving schools.

One such challenge is found in *Epperson v. Arkansas*, 393 U.S. 97 (Ark., 1968). The challenge in this instance was to individual freedom. In 1928, the state of Arkansas enacted a statute that prohibited teachers in any state-supported school from teaching the Darwinian theory of the evolution of man. The Supreme Court of the United States found that the statute was unconstitutional on the ground that the establishment of religion clause of the Constitution was breached. Because the statute proscribed a discussion of the subject, which was considered by a religious group to be in conflict with the Bible, the statute was held to be in violation of the First Amendment's prohibition of state establishment of religion as incorporated through the Fourteenth Amendment.

The state of Nebraska enacted a statute that prohibited the in-school teaching of any subject in a foreign language or of any modern foreign language to children who had not yet completed the eighth grade. A private school teacher who had been convicted for teaching German to a child who had not yet completed the eighth grade appealed the conviction. In *Meyer v. State of Nebraska*, 262 U.S. 390 (Neb., 1923), the court held that a state law that prohibits the teaching of modern foreign language to children in kindergarten through eighth grade is unconstitutional. The state legislature, in enacting the statute, had reasoned that children who knew English through grade eight would be better citizens. The court held that this reason was unconstitutionally arbitrary and therefore was insufficient to support the limitation to teach. The court affirmed that the power of the state over curriculum in general in the tax-supported public schools was not in question. The main thrust of this decision was the constitutional right of an individual to pursue an occupation that was not contrary to the public interest, the right of parental choice, and the educational rights of children.

Religious exercises in the schools, for example, the recitation of the Lord's Prayer and Bible reading, were barred in *School District of Abington Township Pennsylvania*, 374 U.S. 203 (Pa., 1963). This put to rest marked disagreement within the various states as to the constitutionality of Bible reading as a religious exercise. It did not deny the study of the Bible or the study of religion from a literary or historical position.

Implied delegated powers of boards of education have given rise to the inclusion of courses of study and organizational patterns that are not mandated by the state but that have been offered locally over a period of time. Local boards of education can exercise the same powers when proposing to delete from the curriculum courses of study that have involved substantial expenditures of funds. This especially is true when the challenge attacks physical education programs, including the construction of stadiums and gymnasiums. In *McNair v. School District #1*, 288 P. 188 (Mont., 1930), such action by the board of education was sustained.

Textbooks have been involved in much controversy. The legal right of the state to prescribe textbooks was upheld in *Leeper v. State of Tennessee*, 53 S.W.

962 (Tenn., 1899), and in subsequent cases. The entire area of supplementary textbook selection and instructional material selection has been held to be within the implied powers of boards of education. Barring state mandates or constitutional restrictions to the contrary, boards of education cannot be compelled by the courts to offer particular instruction, to use a specific book in a particular way, or to remove a book from use in the curriculum.

In recent times, boards of education have been faced with challenges rooted in civil rights. In *Lau v. Nichols*, 414 U.S. 563 (Cal., 1974), the Supreme Court of the United States held that non-English-speaking Chinese students in the San Francisco School District were entitled to relief as a class from the district's policy of providing special English instruction for only a portion of those eligible for such instruction. The court based its decision on Title VI of the Civil Rights Act of 1964, which bars discrimination under federally assisted programs on a ground of "race, color, or national origin." The regulations for the implementation of *Lau* became increasingly uncertain as proponents and opponents polarized in the early 1980s. The United States Court of Appeals for the Tenth Circuit held similarly to *Lau* for Spanish-surnamed students in *Serna v. Portales Municipal Schools*, 499 F.2d 1147 (N.M., 1974). However, not all litigation involving the necessity for a bilingual curriculum has had identical findings, as pronounced in *Guadalupe*.

Guadalupe Organization v. Tempe Elementary School District, 507 F.2d (USCA 9th, 1978)

Generalization

Local school boards must take affirmative steps to assure that school children are not denied access to educational opportunities because they lack skill in English; however, this does not mean that boards must provide a curriculum to maintain or extend the non-English language skills of those students.

Description

This was an action to compel the board of the LEA to provide non-English-speaking children with a bilingual-bicultural education. The Guadalupe Organization was a nonprofit group formed to represent the interests of elementary school children of Mexican-American and Yaqui Indian origin. It was alleged that of the 12,280 children in the Tempe Elementary School District #3, approximately 18 percent were Spanish-speaking Mexican-Americans or Yaqui Indians and that in one school, Guadalupe Elementary, 554 of 605 students were Mexican-American.

Four discriminatory acts, violating constitutional rights or civil rights, were charged: (1) failure to provide bilingual instruction taking into account the special educational needs of Mexican-American or Yaqui Indian students; (2) failure to hire enough teachers of Mexican-American or Yaqui Indian ancestry; (3) failure to structure a curriculum that minimally takes into account the particular educational needs of the two ethnic groups; (4) failure to structure a curriculum reflecting some of the historical contributions of the ethnic groups to the state of Arizona and to the United States. At the same time, it was agreed by all that the school district did provide educational programs designed to cure existing language deficiencies of non-English-speaking students.

The court acknowledged cases from the United States Supreme Court, including *Keyes* from Denver and *Lau* from San Francisco. It then declared that the LEA had fulfilled its equal-protection duty to children of Mexican-American and Yaqui Indian origin when it adopted a curriculum designed to cure existing language deficiencies of the non-English-speaking students. There was nothing in the equal-protection clause to impose on the district a duty to provide for a bilingual-bicultural education. Neither did the Civil Rights Act of 1964, Title VI, require the school district to provide non-English-speaking students with a bilingual-bicultural curriculum staffed with bilingual instructors. To provide adequate remedial instruction in English put the LEA in compliance with *Lau* and gave those ethnic groups a meaningful educational opportunity.

Linguistic cultural diversity within the nation-state, whatever may be its advantages from time to time, can restrict the scope of the fundamental compact. Diversity limits unity. Effective action by the nation-state rises to its peak of strength only when it is in response to aspirations unreservedly shared by each constituent culture and language group. As affection which a culture or group bears toward a particular aspiration abates, and as the scope of sharing diminishes, the strength of the nation-state wanes.

The decision of this local school district to provide an educational plan that was predominantly monocultural and monolingual was a rational action, in harmony with a legitimate state interest. The court added that the Constitution neither required nor prohibited bilingual-bilcultural education, that such a decision was a local matter, and that it should be left to local boards of education. In Alaska and Massachusetts, bilingual education is mandated in the state code; like many other states, New Mexico authorizes bilingual education as part of the curriculum.

The responsibility of the state to require students to pursue courses of instruction, and to participate in activities that the state has considered to be essential to the educational development of the student, is rational and reasonable. Balanced against that is the right of parents to guide the rearing of their children and to make a reasonable selection of courses for their children to pursue. It has been well established that the board of education has no legal power to force a student to take a particular subject or course or to participate in any activity that would violate the constitutional right of the pupil or his/her parents. An area involving considerable controversy is the requirement that a student take a particular course or engage in an activity that collides with the religious belief of the child and his/her family. Unless the state or the local board of education can prove that participation is essential to citizenship, the courts are reluctant to abridge the student's constitutional rights and generally have held that the school must excuse the student from those courses or activities.

THE CORPORATE NATURE OF THE BOARD

Boards of education are regarded as public or quasi-public organizations. This has been a consistent holding, and a good example of that judiciary attitude can be found in *Wilson v. Abilene Independent School District*, 190 S.W.2d 406 (Tex., 1945). Public school district boards of education have been referred to as municipal (see *Board of Education v. Stoddard*, 60 N.E.2d 757 [N.Y., 1945]) or as quasi-municipal corporations (see *Rose v. Board of Education of Abilene*, 337 P.2d 652 [Kan., 1959]). Classifications of corporations are distinct and, thus, important. The statutes frequently confer specific powers and place certain limitations on municipal corporations. It is important to know the specific classification of a board of education in order to determine if it comes under the provisions of the statute.

Given a strict constriction, the term *municipal corporation* is applied to a governmental unit that has previously been incorporated for purposes of self-government; its status is, essentially, that of a local agency. This status enables citizens to govern their local affairs, and in order to do so, the corporation has been granted fairly extensive legislative and regulatory powers. On the other hand, the quasi-municipal's primary function is to execute state policy, differing from the reasons for existence of city or county government.

Given these two definitions, and given the source of the board of education's powers and authority, there can be little doubt that the board of education is a quasi-municipal corporation. As such, its powers are limited to those conferred on it by the statutes, either directly or by implication.

However, the issue is not as clear-cut as it may seem. The courts have rather consistently held that school districts and school boards are quasi-municipal corporations. *Daniels v. Board of Education*, 158 N.W. 23 (Mich., 1916), is a very clear statement on this matter. When interpreting certain constitutional provisions and statutory enactments, courts have decided that boards of education and school districts are, for these purposes, municipal corporations. It falls on the court to determine if the intent of the framers of the statute in question meant to include quasi-municipal as well as municipal corporations within the body of the statute. As an example, in the case of *State v. Wilson*, 69 P. 172 (Kan., 1902), the Kansas Supreme Court, in interpreting a statute providing that eight hours would constitute a workday for all laborers employed by the state of Kansas, or by or on behalf of any county, city, township, or other municipality, held that, strictly speaking, cities were the only municipal corporations in the state but that the framers of the statute by the use of the word *municipality* intended to include school districts. Such ambiguousness of key terminology is apparent in the reading of a substantial number of case reports.

In the language of the states included as examples in this chapter, the Code of Georgia Annotated, Section 32–902, holds that the county board of education is not a body corporate with authority to sue and be sued. The state of Georgia operates on the basis of a county school system, and the county board of education is merely the agency through which the county acts in school matters: 54 App 81, 187 S.E. 601.

Section 1701 of the New York Education Law defines the board of education of each union free school district as a body corporate. The section further stipulates that any liability created by a school is a liability of the corporation and not that of the members of the board as individuals. A school board is a continuous corporate entity, and the legality of its contracts is not conditioned by the official life of its members. Such statutory limitation of personal liability becomes exceedingly important in times of litigation for damages in large money amounts.

It is clear from these illustrations that each state has provided statutory definitions of corporate status and powers of boards of education and that they vary, according to the state. A reading of the statutes of the state in which the reader is located will provide specific details on the corporate status of the local board of education.

MEETINGS OF LEA BOARDS

A local board of education is considered to be a legal entity only as a whole. Thus, the board members must act as a board of education, through action taken at a meeting that is duly assembled, having been given proper notice in the manner prescribed by law, and by a present quorum of the membership, as prescribed by the statute, for the conduct of business. A board is not a loose assemblage of individuals. The statutes have established that the board of education's official acts and obligations are those of the district. Board decisions rest with the total board and not with individual members thereof, as characterized in *State v. Consolidated School District #3*, 281 S.W.2d 511 (Mo., 1955).

As a general rule, the legality of a meeting is determined by the manner in which it is called and the manner in which notice of the meeting is given to those who are entitled to receive it. It is required that board of education members be given the opportunity to deliberate on the matters before the board and, thus, that each member receive due notice of the meeting before the meeting is scheduled. Such notice is the responsibility of the board president and the district's superintendents; no board member may be omitted from notice of meeting. In some states, the time for notice is established by statute; in other states, the board of education sets the time, day, and place of the meeting in accordance with its duly adopted procedures.

Many states, through their open meeting laws, require publication of notice of approaching board of education meetings in order to inform the public. Several states require the publication of the agenda that is to be followed at the meeting. It is generally conceded that no state's open meeting law is more demanding of rigid procedure than is Florida's.

One issue involved in notices is the waiver of notice. Courts are in general agreement that the rule regarding notification may be waived if all members of the board of education are present and all agree to act as in *Anti-Administration Association v. North Fayette County*, 206 N.W.2d 723 (Iowa, 1973). It would be well for the clerk of the board of education to have waiver forms to be signed so that this record would be available in the event of a challenge to the legality of the meeting. In states allowing such waivers, two requirements must be met if the formal notice of meetings is to be waived: (1) all members must be present, and (2) all members must agree to act. If a member is present yet refuses to act, even though the remaining members are present and ready to act, the meeting may not be constituted and no action may be taken.

Several situations related to meetings should be addressed. First, it is pertinent to discuss the "Sunshine Laws"—or the open meeting laws. State statutes relating to open meetings require that public business be conducted in full view of the public. The public board of education meeting is a meeting of the board of education members and not a meeting of the public (or a public hearing). Under these conditions, most boards of education have, in their rules of procedure, provided for members of the public who wish to make a presentation to the board of education to be heard. Commonly, a place is made for such speakers on the agenda. Unless provided for and recognized by the presiding officer of the meeting, members of the public have no standing to participate in the meeting because regular meetings are not open forums but are meetings, as necessary, of the governing board to conduct the business of the school district.

Second, questions about quorum frequently arise. State statutes define quorums and the requirements for voting. In the education section of the Code of Georgia Annotated, Section 20–2–57 defines *quorum* as follows: "A majority of the board shall constitute a quorum for the transaction of business." The General School Laws of the State of Michigan provide that "a majority of the board shall constitute a quorum." In the State of New York, the General Construction Law, Section 41, controls and provides that a quorum is a simple majority (more than half) of the total number of board members. However, for final action to be taken on any proposition, an affirmative vote of a majority of the total members of the board is required. (If a board has nine members and a majority of five is present at a meeting, legal resolutions would require all five votes—and a 3-to-2 or a 4-to-1 vote would not be legal.) The number of members authorized by the statutes is the determinant of a quorum. A vacancy on the board of education does not reduce the number of members required for a quorum, one impetus to a board to fill vacancies promptly.

Third, executive sessions merit attention. Specific statutory provisions pertain to executive sessions. In general, three matters may be considered in executive sessions: purchase of real property, personnel matters, and discussions with the attorney who represents the board of education. Most statutory provisions stipulate that executive sessions are for discussion only, with formal action to be taken in an open meeting. That is, voting may not be a part of executive sessions because voting must be disclosed publicly. Moving to an executive session shall be by a majority vote of the board of education. The purpose of the executive session must be stated in the motion. As an example, in the state of Georgia, when actions are taken in an executive session, the vote of each member shall be recorded in official minutes of the session and shall be open to public inspection. More commonly, votes are not taken until the board has returned to open session and is operating in a regular manner.

Pointing out two situations dealing with executive sessions demonstrates some of the problems that arise in the interpretation of the statutory provisions for such sessions. In *Karol v. Board of Education Trustees, Florence USD #1*, 593 P.2d 649 (Ariz., 1979) *rehearing denied*, April 24, 1979, a teacher challenged a board's action as it developed from an executive session in Arizona. The board discussed personnel matters—termination and renewal of contracts of teachers— in the executive session. After meeting in this executive session, the board reconvened in open session, where it adopted a resolution approving contracts for certain teachers whose names appeared on a list; other names that were identified by asterisks were terminated, but those names were not read aloud. The entire list was attached to the official minutes of the open meeting and was subsequently made public. The court ruled in the board's favor, having found that the board's vote was within the law.

In *Hudson v. The School District of Kansas City, Missouri*, 578 S.W.2d 301 (Mo., 1979), the American Federation of Teachers alleged that the board of education of Kansas City, Missouri, had violated the open meeting law. The union sought injunctive relief from (1) future executive sessions of the board and (2) implementation of board action taken in the meeting. The issue turned on Missouri Law 610.010, which allows closed meetings, closed records, or closed votes in "meetings relating to the hiring, firing, or promotion of personnel of a public governmental body." The board of education, facing a $7 million budget deficit, met in executive session to deal with personnel problems and the possibility of program reductions. The question that the court was to consider was whether a discussion of programs and finances was within the meaning of the open meeting law exception. The court, in striking a balance of state and private interests, said that the discussion of programs and finances should have been done in open session and the discussion of reduction of personnel in closed session. However, the court denied the injunctive relief sought and held that since reorganization had been accomplished, it was not in the state's interest to have everything undone. It held, further, that the board had violated the open meeting law but had handled teacher reductions and administrative demotions according to the law; therefore, on balance, the court found no error and found for the board of education.

Questions dealing with executive sessions tend to be somewhat complicated. Frequently, courts must weigh, as did the court in the previous matter, the balance between state and private interests.

Boards of education may convene in any of three types of meetings. The first is the regular meeting. This term is usually applied to a board of education meeting that is convened at a stated time and place in accordance with either the statutes, practice, or specific action of the board itself. With exceptions, which we will discuss later, the business of the school district is transacted at such meetings. These meetings are held under the open meeting law provisions and are the official meetings of the board of education. Either by statute or board resolution, the day, time, and place of meeting are established at the beginning of the official year. Deviations from these must be announced publicly and are restricted, very often, by statutory requirements.

Special meetings are those called for a special purpose. It has been argued that only the business that was included in the call for the meeting may be transacted. That is, special meetings are generally one-item agenda meetings; however, unless specifically limited to this proposition by statute or board policy, other matters may, with the consent of those present, be discussed. Under some statutes, decisions may be reached at special meetings. Special meetings too are subject to the open meeting law.

The third type of meeting is the emergency meeting. Most states have statutes that permit boards of education to call emergency meetings subject to limiting the discussion to the emergency for which the meeting is called. The key is that a bonafide emergency shall exist. Waiver of notice of such a meeting is permissible if a true emergency does exist. An example of such an emergency would be the loss of a building by fire and the need to take immediate action to house the pupils and staff who were displaced.

Because the actions of a board of education are the legal bases under which the school district operates, meetings at which such actions take place are extremely important. For the board of education's actions to stand judicial scrutiny, the statutory requirements and the board's prescribed procedures for the conduct of meetings must be followed scrupulously.

BOARD PROCEDURES, MINUTES, AND RECORDS

It is difficult to overemphasize the importance of maintaining an accurate and clear record of board of education proceedings. It has been held, consistently, that the board of education speaks through its minutes and records, which constitute prima facie evidence of the board's actions. *Lewis v. Board of Education of Johnson County* 348 S.W.2d 921 (Ky., 1961), is a good example of the value of accurate minutes.

Keeping proper minutes and records is important for (1) taxpayer reference, (2) reference of successor boards of education, (3) updating of the policy manuals of the board of education, and probably the most important of all (4) providing a legal record should actions of the board of education be called into the open for court review in connection with an action or complaint. Statutes requiring that records of board of education meetings be kept usually have been held to be directory in nature, and failure to keep such records under these statutes will not invalidate actions taken by the board of education, as was found in *School District of Soldier Township v. Moeller*, 73 N.W.2d 43 (Iowa, 1955).

Board of education minutes should show what actions were taken by the board and should show that the board acted within the law. The actual vote on each proposal approved should be shown by recording the "ayes" and "nays." Literally, this means that a statement that the vote was unanimous does not meet the requirements of a statute that requires the record to record the "ayes" and "nays," as stated in *Potts v. School District of Penn Township*, 34 A. 290 (Pa., 1937). Recording the "yes" or "no" vote of each board member satisfies the law; if a unanimous vote occurred, it will show.

The board of education speaks through its records. They must be written and approved, and parol (word-of-mouth) evidence will not be permitted to alter the written record. However, courts have generally admitted parol evidence to supply omissions in the record, to provide information needed to reconstruct records that have been lost or destroyed, or to explain sections that appear to be ambiguous. If an action was not recorded in the minutes, officially it never happened; thus, the admission of parol evidence may remedy the omission, under certain circumstances, but it cannot stand in substitution of an unrecorded action.

Sufficient time should be provided to prepare the official record (minutes) of a board of education's actions. The courts have held, however, that these records should be available in a reasonable time. Thus, unreasonable delay resulted in the finding in *Conover v. Board of Education*, 1 Utah 2d 375 (1974): "It seems clear that final approval of the minutes at a board meeting is not a condition to the right of the public to inspect them, provided the board has had ample opportunity to take action on the minutes and has not done so."

Minutes can be amended, usually, to speak the truth of what happened at the meeting in question but may not be amended to reflect a change in mind, for such action might prejudice third parties who may have acted in reliance on the minutes and might open board members as targets for politicking and lobbying to change a vote.

Judicial interpretation, more often than statutory specification, is called on to determine what constitutes an official or public record. A case in point here is *Crabtree v. Board of Education, Wellston City School District*, 270 N.E.2d 668 (Ohio, 1970), in which the court held that although board minutes were not prepared by the person specified in state law, the minutes and proceedings were valid.

The "Right to Know" laws of many states permit copying and reproduction of board minutes (as public records) as well as inspection of the records at reasonable times and places. If there is a change, the cost of reproduction must be reasonable and shall be borne by the citizen requesting the copy.

BOARD HEARINGS

Boards of education are considered to perform duties of a quasi-judicial nature when holding hearings. Statutes frequently require boards of education to hold hearings on such matters as budgets, proposed bond issues, school district re-organization, termination of tenured personnel, pupil expulsions, and other mat-ters where due process is involved—the right to a hearing before an impartial tribunal being one of the steps in due process. In such hearings, the board must adopt a judiciary stance and convene as an impartial tribunal, not as a governing board.

Generally, the statutes specify that hearings must be held, but they may not prescribe the procedure to be followed. In *Board of Education v. Kennedy*, 55 S.2d 511 (Ala., 1951), the Alabama Supreme Court made the following state-ment, which sets forth the generally accepted procedural requirements for a hearing—lacking specific statutory requirements: "No particular form of pro-cedure is prescribed for hearings under the statutes here in question but of course due process must be observed."

Hearings before boards of education are not constrained by the usual formalities observed in court proceedings. Rules of evidence do not apply. However, the courts do agree that the right of a hearing includes the right to be represented by counsel. The question of swearing in witnesses has not been given a definitive answer, but in some states it is a statutory demand. It is very important that the board of education maintain an accurate record of the hearing. This is particularly true if the record is to be reviewed by a court in the event of an appeal. An appeal should be anticipated and planned for.

Where the statutes provide that board of education decisions may be appealed to a higher jurisdiction, generally it is held that all administrative remedies must be exhausted before seeking judicial review. In cases that involve a question of law, the doctrine of exhaustion of administrative remedy is not applicable to the board of education's decision.

Unless the courts can find that the board of education's decision was arbitrary, capricious, or unreasonable, the courts have been very reluctant to substitute their judgment for that of the board in educational matters. Thus, it is incumbent on the board of education to hold as its objectives good faith and fair dealing, basic components of the common law.

Finally, a precautionary note is necessary. Board hearings that conform to procedural obligations must also take note of substantive protections provided in statute and in the United States Constitution. To do less is to open the board, individually, to suit for damages. Liability for individual board members, arising out of their own arbitrary actions, has produced a whole new volume of liability insurance premium costs in public school districts.

Wood v. Strickland, 420 U.S. 308 (Ark., 1975)

Generalization

Misbehavior among students occurs in several levels of severity. Severe pun-ishments for minor infractions are out of phase with concepts of fairness, and expulsion is a severe punishment. Board members who act unreasonably and injure students may be guilty of tortious acts.

Description

The Mena, Arkansas, school board had a regulation prohibiting the use or possession of intoxicating beverages at school. Three high-school girls engaged in a prank, to spike the punch at a high-school party. After their prank was discovered, the board held a hearing and expelled the girls for a period of three months. Seeking relief in the courts, the three eventually took their case to the United States Supreme Court, and Justice White delivered the opinion.

Respondents Peggy Strickland and Virginia Crain brought this lawsuit against petitioners, who were members of the school board at the time in question, two school administrators, and the Special School District of Mena, Ark., purporting to assert a cause of action under 42 U.S.C.A. § 1983, and claiming that their federal constitutional rights to due process were infringed under color of state law by their expulsion from the Mena Public High School on the grounds of their violation of a school regulation prohibiting the use or possession of intoxicating beverages at school or school activities. The complaint as amended prayed for compensatory and punitive damages against all petitioners, injunctive relief allowing respondents to resume attendance, preventing petitioners from imposing any sanctions as a result of the expulsion, and restraining enforcement of the challenged regulation, declaratory relief as to the constitutional invalidity of the regulation, and expunction of any record of their expulsion. . . .

The violation of the school regulation prohibiting the use or possession of intoxicating beverages at school or school activities with which respondents were charged concerned their "spiking" of the punch served at a meeting of an extracurricular school organization attended by parents and students. At the time in question, respondents were sixteen years old and were in the tenth grade. The relevant facts begin with their discovery that the punch had not been prepared for the meeting as previously planned. The girls then agreed to "spike" it. Since the county in which the school is located is "dry," respondents and a third girl drove across the state border into Oklahoma and purchased two twelve-ounce bottles of "Right Time," a malt liquor. They then bought six ten-ounce bottles of a soft drink, and after having mixed the contents of the eight bottles in an empty milk carton, returned to school. Prior to the meeting, the girls experienced second thoughts about the wisdom of their prank, but by then they were caught up from disposing of the illicit punch. The punch was served at the meeting, without apparent effect . . . the board voted to expel the girls from school for the remainder of the semester, a period of approximately three months. . . .

Petitioners as members of the school board assert here, as they did below, an absolute immunity from liability under § 1983 and at the very least seek to reinstate the judgment of the District Court. If they are correct and the District Court's dismissal should be sustained, we need to go no further in this case. Moreover, the immunity question involves the construction of a federal statute, and our practice is to deal with possibly dispositive statutory issues before reaching questions turning on the construction of the Constitution. . . . We essentially sustain the position of the Court of Appeals with respect to the immunity issue. . . .

Liability for damages for every action which is found subsequently to have been violative of a student's constitutional rights and to have caused compensable injury would unfairly impose upon the school decisionmaker the burden of mistakes made in good faith in the course of exercising his discretion within the scope of his official duties. School board members, among other duties, must judge whether there have been violations of school regulations and, if so, the appropriate sanctions for the violations. Denying any measure of immunity in these circumstances "would contribute not to principled and fearless decision-making but to intimidation" . . . the imposition of monetary costs for mistakes which were not unreasonable in the light of all the circumstances would undoubtedly deter even the most conscientious school decisionmaker from exercising his judgment independently, forcefully, and in a manner best serving the long-term interest of the school and the students. The most capable candidates for school board positions might be deterred from seeking office if heavy burdens upon their private resources from monetary liability were a likely prospect during their tenure.

These considerations have undoubtedly played a prime role in the development by state courts of a qualified immunity protecting school officials from liability for damages in lawsuits claiming improper suspensions or expulsions. But at the same time, the judgment implicit in this common-law development is that absolute immunity would not be justified since it would not sufficiently increase the ability of school officials to exercise their discretion in a forthright manner to warrant the absence of a remedy for students subjected to intentional or otherwise inexcusable deprivations.

. . . We think there must be a degree of immunity if the schools are to go forward; and, however worded, the immunity must be such that public school officials understand that action taken in the good-faith fulfillment of their responsibilities and within the bounds of reason under all the circumstances will not be punished and that they need not exercise their discretion with undue timidity.

Nonetheless, after discussing suitable standards of conduct necessary for fair treatment of Americans under the law, and after discussing the need for various kinds of immunity if LEAs are to function, Justice White added:

In the specific context of school discipline, we hold that a school board member is not immune from liability for damages under § 1983 if he knew or reasonably should have known that the action he took within his sphere of official responsibility would violate the constitutional rights of the student affected, or if he took the action with the malicious intention to cause a deprivation of constitutional rights or other injury to the student. That is not to say that school board members are "charged with predicting the future course of constitutional law." . . . A compensatory award will be appropriate only if the school board member has acted with such an impermissible motivation or with such disregard of the student's clearly established constitutional rights that his action cannot reasonably be characterized as being in good faith.

SUMMARY

Local boards of education derive their powers from the state constitutions, state statutes, and court decisions. The Tenth Amendment to the United States Constitution reserves powers not delegated to the United States by the Constitution, and not prohibited by it to the states, to the states respectively; thus, education is provided by the constitutions of each of the fifty states.

Local school districts are creatures of the legislatures and have no power or authority except what is provided through constitutional or legislative enactments for them. In each state, a governing body at the state level is responsible for carrying out the constitutional and legislative mandate for providing public schools.

Intermediate school districts exist in many states. In general, they provide services that the component districts cannot efficiently or effectively provide for themselves. Generally, intermediate districts are service units.

Legislative enactments provide for the selection of local board of education members. The statutes of the fifty states establish the authority for acts, duties, and responsibilities of board members. Only the board of education can act for the school district and exercise the powers that have been granted by the statutes and the state constitution. Board members act in their official capacities only when meeting in a duly constituted meeting of the board of education.

Boards of education have three types of powers: expressed, which are conferred by the constitution, statute, or court decision; implied, which are derived from the specifically stated powers; and necessary, which are required to carry out the operation of the school district.

Boards of education must comply with the common-law principle that governs delegated powers, namely, a delegated power may not be further delegated by the body or the person to whom it was originally delegated. Based on the continuing nature of a board of education, if statutory authority is granted to a board of education to undertake an action that will cover a period of time extending into the future, for example, a capital construction program, and if the board does so in good faith without intent to defraud another, succeeding boards will be bound by the action. It would be wise for any board of education that is considering entering into long-term commitments to seek legal advice on such contracts.

Aside from hiring a superintendent, should that be necessary, a board of education's primary functions are setting goals and making policy. Written policies establish a legal base and carry the force of law. Policies must be consistent with and may not contravene the statutes.

Two types of actions govern a board of education's behavior. They are discretionary, which require the full consideration, counsel, and deliberation of the entire board of education, and ministerial, which are somewhat mechanical in nature and do not require the board's discretion. Where boards of education operate on a committee system, it should be noted that these committees have no power to act; they may investigate a situation, report their findings, and make their recommendations to the entire board of education for consideration and action.

Boards of education have implied power to make and enforce reasonable rules and regulations for the efficient conduct of the schools. Such powers are not unlimited. If the rules and regulations conflict with existing statutes and/or constitutional provisions, they are invalid. Boards of education are obligated to provide due process to those to whom the rules and regulations will apply.

Boards of education are regarded as public or quasi-public corporations. They have been referred to as municipal or quasi-municipal corporations. Since the statutes frequently confer specific powers and place certain limitations on municipal corporations, it is important to know the specific classification of a board of education in a particular state.

The local public school district is considered to be a legal entity only as a whole. Board members must act as a board of education, through action taken at a meeting that is duly assembled, having been given proper notice in the manner prescribed by law, and by a present quorum of membership, as prescribed by statute, for the conduct of business. Due notice of the meeting must be given to each member of the board of education. It is permissible to have a waiver of the notice of a meeting if the following two requirements are met: (1) all members are present and (2) all members agree to act.

"Sunshine," or open meeting, laws require that public business be conducted in full view of the public. The public board of education meeting is a meeting of the board of education and not a meeting of the public. Unless provided for and recognized by the presiding officer of the meeting, members of the public have no standing to participate in the meeting. Quorum is determined by the statutes of the particular state in which the board of education is located.

Specific statutory provisions pertain to executive sessions. In general, these following matters may be considered in such sessions: purchase of real property, personnel matters, and discussions with the board's attorney. State statutes prescribe procedures for executive sessions. These procedures vary from state to state.

Three types of open meetings exist: (1) the regular meeting, which is the official meeting of the board of education; (2) the special meeting, which is a called meeting to deal with a special purpose or situation; and (3) the emergency meeting, which must be limited to the emergency for which the meeting has been called.

The board of education speaks through its minutes and records. Keeping proper minutes and records is important for (1) taxpayer reference, (2) future reference of successor boards of education, (3) updating the policy manuals of the board of education, and (4) providing a legal record. Such records shall be open to public view and shall be made available in a reasonable time after the meeting at which the action was taken.

Boards of education are considered to perform duties of a quasi-judicial nature when holding hearings. Statutes frequently require boards of education to hold hearings on such matters as budgets, proposed bond issues, school district reorganization, termination of tenured personnel, pupil punishment, and other matters where due process is involved.

Where the statutes provide that board of education decisions may be appealed to a higher jurisdiction, generally it is held that all administrative remedies must be exhausted before seeking judicial review. Unless the courts can find that the board of education's decision was arbitrary, capricious, or unreasonable, the courts have been very reluctant to substitute their judgment for that of the board in educational matters.

3

Parent Rights
and Responsibilities

The nuclear family has prevailed in Western cultures for centuries. Prerogatives of deciding what is to happen to offspring have been held by parents. The latter part of the twentieth century is bringing a decrease in the decision-making span of parents, primarily because of new protections being conferred on children by way of statutes intended to curtail child abuse. Nonetheless, it is still true that parental responsibility for the development and upbringing of children is a predominant aspect of American culture; it is true even in a time of decreasing family stability and strength.

Responsibility for the formal education of American children is shared by parents and agencies that function with state purposes, and especially by public educational institutions. In response to the compulsory-education laws that prevail in all but two states, parents must respond and see to it that their children who are in the compulsory-education age range do attend school, or the parents must provide for adequate alternatives in home schooling. To do less is to contribute to truancy, a situation punishable by a fine and/or jail sentence in most states. Parents, then, are responsible for the regular and punctual attendance of their eligible children in school.

Taken as a whole, parents have agreed to release their children into the care and custody of the schools, expecting that the pupils will be kept safe and will learn from what is being taught. It is a trade-off; the schools accept a parental responsibility, and parents expect the schools to provide systematic development for the child. This can promote tension between the home and the school, for the parents' expectations may be high—sometimes even unrealistically high.

While the parent accepts this responsibility to relinquish some child-rearing prerogatives and while the child is in school, progress reports are regularly and periodically sent from the teacher to the parent. They are evaluative reports.

When those reports contain good news, it is easy to convey the message, and it can be accepted with ease. When the reports contain news that the child is failing, the news is often received with an ear that is connected to a sensitized ego. Parents hear the information as, in part, an evaluation of themselves; that is, they had the child who failed.

Parents also have the responsibility to support the school. Aside from membership and work in service agencies of the school and community, this support is a part of the obligations of tax payment. Through property taxes, sales and income taxes, and other kinds of tax, parents function as school supporters—a responsibility that must be accomplished if schools are to be open to all and to operate for school years of reasonable length. These and other responsibilities represent the whole gamut of things that might be gathered together and labeled as school-patron responsibilities. Although parents may choose to enroll their child in a nonpublic school, they may not choose to avoid the obligations of taxes that are collected and spent for public education. In the educational concept, that is another condition of tension between some parents and schools, for many parents with children in nonpublic school have sought relief from the tax obligations, on the premise that they are paying for their own educational costs. That feeling has provided much of the political support for the various voucher and tax-refund plans that have become politically popular.

Once that small number of broad and general responsibilities has been enumerated, parents enter the realm of combined educational responsibilities and rights. For example, Congress passed the Family and Educational Rights to Privacy Act (FERPA) in 1974. The act, also known as the Buckley Amendment, was a consequence of consideration of the legal and ethical aspects of record keeping in schools. The collection and use of information about pupils by schools—and access to that information by parents and qualified others—formed the basis for the political support of that act.

FERPA opened school records to parents. Because many public schools, until the time of this act, had refused to provide open access to pupil records for parents, a modest amount of distrust developed between parents and those schools. That is, were the schools hiding something from the parents? It is true that secrecy can lead to misuse. It can certainly lead to distrust. FERPA provided that school records should be open to parents as an assurance to them. FERPA contained three key features:

1. Parents have the right to be informed about the whole school record of their child and to have some control over it.

2. In like condition, outsiders to the family do not have the right of access to a child's school record, except upon authorization.

3. Parents have the right to challenge information that, upon their reading it, appears to be misleading or incorrect.

It can be seen, then, that this act is a melding of rights into new responsibilities. Although it has carried its own cost for installation and operation through procedures that vary little from state to state, LEAs have had no option but to shoulder those costs, providing a new service to parents. Dropping the veil of record secrecy and providing formal procedures for examining records has surely had its own positive impact. It is a legal requirement that can also be seen as an opportunity to build improved school-home relationships.

Parents have been concerned about other aspects of the school, challenging the right of schools to develop curriculum, establish some courses as required of all students, maintain a curriculum of less than what might be offered under a broad construction of state statutes, and so on. Some of these challenges have found their way into court cases as advocacy for parent and student rights in education has become an organized effort, involving issues such as suspension from school and educational opportunities for handicapped children. Parent advocacy groups prominent during the 1970s included Children's Defense Fund (in Washington, D.C.), Parent Union for Public Schools (in Philadelphia), and Chicano Education Project (in Denver). It is a characteristic of such groups to be aggressive and to move with speed and power against those school practices seen as unproductive or harmful to children. These groups become involved on their own initiative, not waiting for invitations from school officials. They protest, testify, lobby, and sue—and their methods are likely to be abrasive, for their goal is to accomplish change toward their own views, quickly. Schools are not without problems and shortcomings, and parents have a large stake in school quality. Those two factors create a climate that is conducive to the forming of independent parent groups to protect their own interests, as they view them.

THE CURRICULUM

When a school district offers a curriculum to be studied by the elementary and secondary students, that curriculum must meet the minimums established by state statute. However, this does not mean that the maximum program possible under state law must be offered. The governing board of an LEA may decide to offer less because of cost or other sufficient reasons. The case of *State ex. rel. Shineman v. Board, District #33*, 42 N.W.2d 168 (Neb., 1950), illustrated the power of a local board very well. Under the state constitution, the permissive attendance age for children was from age five; by statute, the mandatory minimum age for attendance was seven, a not unusual age among many states. Parents of several children age five contended that their children were ready for school and that the board should establish and admit them to a kindergarten. There was no kindergarten, and the board declined to establish one. On appeal to the state's supreme court, the decision of the LEA was upheld because the Nebraska ''legislatures did not undertake to say . . . that all schools should provide a kindergarten or a beginner grade'' before first grade. General powers were statutorily placed with the LEA. There were no violations of Department of Education regulations. So the parents could not prevail, whatever could be said about the qualitative aspects of their arguments.

The research literature on child growth and development differs on the question of the most appropriate age to start formal schooling. Some findings point to the desirability of an early start; some findings have identified values of a less organized time as most helpful. Some individuals advocate for universal education for all three- and four-year-olds, and such early organized education has come to be the prevailing view, with strong political support.

Beyond the questions of the most appropriate time to start formalized education, parents have been interested in questions of curriculum. That is, they have requested additions, deletions, and exceptions, and local schools that decide to proceed, insisting on their own plan, must be prepared to accept challenges in courts from disappointed parents.

State ex rel. Kelley v. Ferguson, 144 N.W. 1039 (Neb. SC, 1914)

Generalization

The subjects that compose the curriculum are divided between those that are required by state statute and those that are required from electives by the local board of education. Parents must agree to the registration of their children in the former but are entitled to consider excepting their children from the latter group.

Description

Eunice Kelley had been advised by her father that she need not attend the homemaking classes that were required by the local school district and that were held in a building more than one mile from the building where she regularly attended classes. Instead, he stipulated that his twelve-year-old daughter should use that time to study music and that he would pay the fees for private instruction. His request for her absence from the public school class to attend the private instruction was denied. He did not object to her study of any of the other courses required for sixth-grade students: reading, spelling, arithmetic, geography, drawing, writing, and general lessons. The question included not only the rights of parents to control the education of their children but also the rights of an LEA to add to the list of courses required by the state.

The right of the parent to make a reasonable selection from the prescribed course of studies which shall be "carried" by a child in the free public schools of the state is not limited to any particular school of that class or to any particular grade in any of such public schools. . . . It exists at all times and in every grade. In *State v. Bailey*, the sole question involved was the constitutionality of a compulsory education act; one of the grounds upon which the act was assailed being that it was an unauthorized invasion of the natural rights of the parent. The court sustained the law and in support of its holding gave a very good discussion upon the duty and obligation of a parent to educate his child, and illustrated the fact that this duty the parent owes not only to the child but to the commonwealth. If he neglects to perform it, or willfully refuses to do so, he may be coerced by law to execute such civil obligation. The welfare of the child and the best interests of society require that the state shall exert its sovereign authority to secure to the child the opportunity to acquire an education. Statutes making it compulsory upon the parent, guardian, or other person having the custody and children to send them to public or private schools for longer or shorter periods, during certain years of the life of such children, have not only been upheld as strictly within the constitutional power of the Legislature but have generally been regarded as necessary to carry out the express purposes of the Constitution itself.

The matter of education is deemed a legitimate function of the state and with us is imposed upon the Legislature as a duty by imperative provisions of the Constitution. The subject has always been regarded as within the purview of legislative authority. How far this interference should extend is a question, not of constitutional power for the courts, but of expedience and propriety, which it is the sole province of the Legislature to determine. The judiciary has no authority to interfere with this exercise of legislative judgment; and to do so would be to invade the province which by the Constitution is assigned exclusively to the law-making power.

Parents do not have the right to deprive their children of the advantages so provided and to defeat the purpose of necessary appropriations. Wherever education is most general, civilization seems to be of the highest order. The public school is one of the main bulwarks of our nation, and it should not be intentionally undermined; however, it is not an "all in all." Rights of parents must be one voice in the bringing up and education of children.

The state is more and more taking hold of the private affairs of the individuals and requiring that they conduct their business affairs honestly and with due regard for the public good. All this is commendable and must receive the sanction of every good citizen. But in this age of agitation, such as the world has never known before, we want to be careful lest we carry the doctrine of governmental paternalism too far, for, after all is said and done, [the] prime factor in our scheme of government is the American home.

Our public schools should receive the earnest and conscientious support of every citizen. To that end, the school authorities should be upheld in their control and regulation of our school system; but their power and authority should not be unlimited. They should exercise their authority over and their desire to further the best interests of their scholars, with a due regard for the desires and inborn solicitude of the parents of such children. They should not too jealously assert or attempt to define their supposed prerogatives. If a reasonable request is made by a parent, it should be heeded. This court has expressly decided that the parent has a right to make such selection.

We think the action of the respondents was arbitrary and constituted an invasion of the relator's rights under the law. The judgment of the district court is therefore affirmed.

Although not a recent case, and although one containing an out-of-phase demographic concept of the American family, *Kelley* still stands as a good indicator of what a present school administrator might do when faced by a parental request for release from a class. This was not a request that the child be released to get a headstart on an "every weekend at the family cabin" situation. It was a trade-off for one kind of instruction—selected and paid for by the parent—over one course within the whole curriculum, a course that was not on the state's required list. There is a limit to a board's discretion, which must be balanced against what a parent sees as desirable in the matter of educational development of the child.

During the twentieth century, several factors have converged to diminish the understanding of what should be widely accepted in completing the curriculum. That is, what is the meaning of a high-school diploma? Some of those impinging factors include social promotions, increased high-school pupil-retention rates, and the mainstreaming of handicapped children. All three factors increase the span of meaning in a high-school diploma. Many parents firmly believe that in some earlier time, graduation from an American high school stood for competency in academic accomplishment at some higher level than is presently true, and they decry the "lowered standards" for the accomplishment of these contemporary diplomas. In the best of the brief but politically potent tradition of consumerism, their critical interest is based on the question, "Are we getting value from the public schools?" The question is at the heart of school accountability.

For some of those people, the answer to their problem has been to withdraw from public schools and to fashion their own, unique educational program. But such solutions carry many problems of their own. In *State ex. rel. Shoreline Schools v. Superior Court*, 346 P.2d 999 (Wash., 1959), the Washington Supreme Court addressed this very problem. That court established a three-part test as the necessary elements for a school: a qualified teacher, pupil(s) present, and a designated place to hold instruction. For that court, absence of any of the three was failure of the test. Contemporary courts are likely to be less stringent.

The notion of quid pro quo—something received for something given—permeates American society. The concept of contract embodies that expectation. People who support schools, who send their children to schools, have an expectation that the schools will use their time and resources for the optimum development of the child. At graduation time, some parents believe that schools have done very well by their child; others believe the contrary, and a few malpractice suits have been attempted.

Doe v. San Francisco USD, 131 Cal. 854 (1976)

Generalization

Although a child may spend the full complement of years in a school system as a student, the school is not liable for learning achievement at a level less than the parent thinks represents the true learning potential of that student.

Description

Peter W. graduated from the San Francisco public schools, receiving a diploma in 1972. He could not pass the test for enlistment into the armed forces. His reading ability was low, although his I.Q. was average. His parents sought damages of $500,000 from the LEA for the negligent work of the teachers who were employed in the school system. That is, their case rested on the development of a cause-and-effect relationship in which they attempted to establish that the cause of his low ability in reading rested with an ineffective curriculum and a deceptive grade-reporting system. The case was dismissed and appealed.

The novel—and troublesome—question on this appeal is whether a person who claims to have been inadequately educated, while a student in a public school system, may state a cause of action in a tort against the public authorities who operate and administer the system. We hold that he may not.

The appeal reaches upon plaintiff's first amended complaint (hereinafter the "complaint"), which purports to state seven causes of action. Respondent (San Francisco Unified School District, its superintendent of schools, its governing board, and the individual board members) appeared to it by filing general demurrers to all seven counts; we hereinafter refer to them as "defendants."

There were several causes of action set forward in behalf of Peter W., and the court examined each one. Attention to only a few can provide an understanding of the whole suit.

XI. Defendant school district, its agents and employees, negligently and carelessly failed to provide plaintiff with adequate instructions, guidance, counseling, and/or supervision in basic academic skills such as reading and writing, although said school district had the authority, responsibility, and ability [to do so]. . . .

In the closing paragraphs of the first count, plaintiff alleges general damages based upon his "permanent disability and inability to gain meaningful employment;" special damages incurred as the cost of compensatory tutoring allegedly required by reason of the "negligence, acts and omissions of defendants." . . .

On occasions when the Supreme Court has opened or sanctioned new acres of tort liability, it has noted that the wrongs and injuries involved were both comprehensible and assessable with the existing judicial framework. This is simply not true of wrongful conduct and injuries allegedly involved in educational malfeasance. Unlike the activity of the highway or the marketplace, classroom methodology affords no readily acceptable standards of care, or cause, or injury. The science of pedagogy itself is fraught with different and conflicting theories of how or what a child should be taught, and any layman might—and commonly does—have his own emphatic views on the subject. The "injury" claimed here is plaintiff's inability to read and write. Substantial professional authority attests that the achievement of literacy in the schools, or its failure, are influenced by a host of factors which affect the pupil subjectively, from outside the formal teaching process, and beyond the control of its ministers.

We find in this situation no conceivable "workability of a rule of care" against which defendants' alleged conduct may be measured, no reasonable "degree of certainty that . . . plaintiff suffered injury" within the meaning of the law of negligence, and no such perceptible "connection between the defendant's conduct and the injury suffered," as alleged, which would establish a causal link between them within the same meaning.

These recognized policy considerations alone negate an actionable "duty of care" in persons and agencies who administer the academic phases of the public educational process. Others, which are even more important in practical terms, command the same result. Few of our institutions, if any, have aroused the controversies, or incurred the public dissatisfaction, which have attended the operation of the public schools during the last few decades. Rightly or wrongly, but widely, they are charged with outright failure in the achievement of their educational objectives; according to some critics, they bear responsibility for many of the social and moral problems of our society at large. Their public plight in these respects is attested in the daily media, in bitter governing board elections, in wholesale rejections of school bond proposals, and in survey upon survey. To hold them to an actionable "duty of care," in the discharge of their academic functions, would expose them to the tort claims—real or imagined—of disaffected students and parents in countless numbers. They are already beset by social and financial problems which have gone to major litigation, but for which no permanent solution has yet appeared. The ultimate consequences, in terms of public time and money, would burden them— and society—beyond calculation.

The California court made it clear that the parents had not given over custody of the child to the school. Parents still had the responsibility, shared with the school, for the development of the child. Some observers might reasonably assert that low achievements such as Peter W.'s were as much, or more, the responsibility of the parents and the home environment provided by them than of the schools. At the same time, school administrators should take note of this case as a signal calling for the improved evaluation of students, with student achievement levels accurately determined and conveyed to parents with precision.

In a slight variation of the theme of negligence and liability, the New York court decided in *Donahue v. Copiague Schools*, 497 N.Y.S.2d 874 (1978), that it was the duty of the schools to provide education but also that there was no clear basis on which to claim an injury traceable to the schools. Successful suits for educational malpractice have been very rare.

On many other matters, courts have been inclined to embrace parental views. In *Jordan v. Erie School District*, 583 F.2d 91 (Pa. 1978), and other cases associated with it, the court set aside a negotiated contract, between the district and the teachers, that had stipulated how children with handicaps could be transferred from regular classrooms to alternative attendance centers. Agreeing with the mothers who had brought suit on behalf of their children, the court noted that the contract set forward a transfer routine that violated the due process requirements from pertinent Supreme Court decisions.

The stresses that parents face from their experience with schools are several, then. To the extent that parents have felt shunted aside by an educational bureaucracy, an angry alienation is likely to be the result. When, additionally, they then see their children coming through a thirteen-year education with only modest academic achievements, or when they see their child placed for instruction in an assignment to which they object but for which they can discover no real recourse, frustration often drives them to ask, "What can I do to change the system?'' Clearly, legal recourse comes forward as a possible solution, and many parents pursue it.

Extending this consideration of parent-school problems into the area of extracurricular activities, we find a key case in Iowa, a case of disputed eligibility for participation. In *Bunger v. Iowa H.S. Athletic Association*, 197 N.W.2d 555 (Iowa, 1972), a father sought to have set aside the state athletic association's rule on alcoholic beverages. The son was riding in a car during the summer months, and some occupants were drinking beer. When stopped by the highway patrol and brought into court, three youths pleaded guilty; Bunger pleaded not guilty and in court was found to be innocent. Yet, when school officials applied the association's rule, Bunger was declared ineligible for football for six weeks in the fall semester. The Iowa Supreme Court set the rule aside, labeling it too sweeping, invalid, and unreasonable.

That is not to say that schools lack power to regulate the drinking of alcoholic beverages by students. Courts have recognized that schools have a valid interest in deterring the consumption of alcohol among students. In *Braesch v. De-Pasqueale*, 265 N.W.2d 842 (Neb., 1978), parents were initially successful in their suit on behalf of their children who had, admittedly, been drinking alcoholic beverages. Eventually, the school district policy and the administration of that policy prevailed when the Nebraska Supreme Court set aside the injunction that had been issued against the school. Initially, the school had prevented the students from continuing in interscholastic sports, and the injunction had been issued at the instigation of parents. The state's high court held "that the rule prohibiting the use of alcohol and drugs by participants in the high school's interscholastic basketball program served legitimate, rational interests, and a penalty of expulsion for the season was not arbitrary or unreasonable" as one means to curtail the use of alcoholic beverages by high-school students.

Parents of those children who have unusual athletic ability have a natural desire to secure opportunities for their children. Public performance is a strong motivator. Schools provide some of those opportunities through interscholastic sports, and denial of participation for rule breaking is a very serious consequence for a student. When participation is conditioned on the student's meeting rules of good personal health and hygiene, when those rules are reasonable and circulated to all participants, and when due process is afforded to any suspected offenders, parents must accept the consequences of offending behavior—even if it means that their children will be denied participation. On the other hand, the schools must accept such obligations as fairness, reasonableness, and advance notice of rules addressing eligibility to participate.

Specialized aspects of curriculum have created problems for parents when, viewing the curriculum provided their children in light of civil rights legislation, they have concluded that the schools not only were shortchanging their children but were in violation of federal statutes such as the Bilingual Education Act of 1965 and the Civil Rights Act of 1964. Such a case originated in New Mexico.

Serna v. Portales Municipal Schools, **499 F.2d 1147** (N.M., 1975)

Generalization

Denial of special instruction in English to pupils who by national origin or ethnicity lack sufficient linguistic skills is a deficiency in the educational program and is violative of civil rights generally and of widely held educational goals.

Description

Statistical evidence indicated that many of the students knew very little English. They spoke Spanish at home and had grown up in a Spanish-influenced culture. One consequence apparently was a lower achievement level than that demonstrated by their Anglo-American classmates and a higher percentage of school dropouts. Of the four elementary schools in the Portales schools, Lindsey School consisted of nearly 86 percent Spanish-surnamed children, and the ethnic composition of the students in the other elementary schools was 78–88 percent Anglo-American.

During an evaluation of the Portales Municipal Schools by the New Mexico Department of Education in 1969, the evaluation team concluded that the language arts program at Lindsey School "was below average and not meeting the needs of those children." Notwithstanding this knowledge of the plight of Spanish surnamed students in Portales, appellants neither applied for funds under the Federal Bilingual Education Act, 20 U.S.C. 880b, nor accepted funds for a similar purpose when they were offered by the State of New Mexico. Undisputed evidence shows that Spanish surnamed students do not reach the achievement levels attained by their Anglo counterparts. . . . The Portales school curriculum, which has the effect of discrimination even though probably no purposeful design is present, therefore violates the requisites of Title VI and the requirement imposed by or pursuant to HEW regulations.

Appellants argue that even if the school district were unintentionally discriminating against Spanish surnamed students prior to institution of this lawsuit, the program they presented to the trial court in compliance with the court's memorandum opinion sufficiently meets the needs of appellees. The New Mexico State Board of Education (SBE), in its Amicus Curiae brief, agrees with appellants' position and argues that the trial court's decision and the relief granted constitute unwarranted and improper judicial interference in the internal affairs of the Portales school district. After reviewing the entire record, we are in agreement with the trial court's decision. The record reflects a long standing educational policy by the Portales schools that failed to take into consideration the specific needs of Spanish surnamed children. After appellants submitted a proposed bilingual-bicultural program to the trial court, a hearing was held on the adequacies of this plan. At this hearing expert witnesses pointed out the fallacies of appellants' plan and in turn offered a more expansive bilingual-bicultural plan. The trial court thereafter fashioned a program which it felt would meet the needs of Spanish surnamed students in the Portales school system. We do not believe that under the unique circumstances of this case the trial court's plan is unwarranted. The evidence shows unequivocally that appellants had failed to provide appellees with a meaningful education. There was adequate evidence that appellants' proposed program was only a token plan that would not benefit appellees. Under these circumstances the trial court had a duty to fashion a program which would provide adequate relief for Spanish surnamed children.

Serna, with only two languages in the school community controversy, was a comparatively simple case. That simplicity tends to obscure the fact that the American cultural and economic mainstream demands English proficiency, but it is indicative of the demographic fact that, increasingly, the United States is a multicultural nation. Educational efforts that fail to incorporate diversified needs are surely focused on an extremely narrow interpretation of the role of the school.

Not all such cases have resulted in court orders to install new programs of language instruction (see *Guadalupe v. Tempe Schools*, 587 F.2d 1022 [1978]). Yet it is still true that parents who see substantial deficiencies in a curriculum, deficiencies that do not promise to raise the language skills and academic achievement of their children to socially productive levels, may call for the legal rights of the children.

Parental residency location has been a major determiner of where children can attend school for free public education. By 1990, 20 states had enacted laws that provided for choice or open enrollment, patterns allowing students to cross over public school district boundaries. In *Rogowski v. New Hartford School District*, 730 F.Supp. 1202 (N.Y., 1990), the attending child lived with an aunt in one school district during the week but returned home to another district on weekends. On discovering this, the school district denied the student further attendance, and the court supported the position of the school district; that is, she was not denied attendance rights because she was free to attend in the district where her parents resided. This was a restriction on parental rights; however, if parental choice and open enrollments become increasingly popular among the state legislatures, the restrictions of residency as a qualification for school attendance will fade.

CURRICULUM AND RELIGIOUS CONFLICTS

Many of the conflicts originating from within schools and focused on religion have involved the rights of teachers—and what they may teach. Some have had characteristics that addressed the rights of many people, parents and teachers included. For example, *Meyer v. State of Nebraska*, 262 U.S. 390 (Neb., 1923), not only touched on the rights of teachers and pupils but also included the rights of parents in the selection of a school for their child—in this case, the selection of a school where instruction in a foreign language was part of the schoolwork and was desired by the parents.

Ironically, it was *Westside Community Schools v. Mergens*, 110 S.Ct. 2356 (Neb., 1990)—another Nebraska case—that has set the tone for interpreting the Equal Access Act of 1984. Mergens, a student at Westside High School, sought use of a room in the building in which a group of religious believers would convene for worship. She was denied. Eventually, before the Supreme Court, the ruling went against the school as the Court examined—and defined—the terms *closed forum*, *limited open forum*, *open forum*, and *noncurriculum groups*. In essence, Justice Sandra Day O'Connor wrote for the majority and noted that with a closed or open forum, no question would arise. However, if a school had a limited open forum, and if any recognized groups used school space for meetings not directly related to the school's curriculum, requests for group recognition and use could not be denied (see *Mergens*, chapter 6).

Mergens is in harmony with a perceptible parental sentiment that has seemingly swept across the nation and that might be described as a broad rejection of the public school curriculum. Parents who are avidly religious and who subscribe to beliefs that have been styled as Fundamentalist Christian, have withdrawn their children from public schools for registration in private schools sponsored by their own church. Or some have been withdrawn for instruction in a home tutorial setting or merely for separation from the public schools, which the parents see as morally bankrupt and utterly lacking in ability to influence positively the educational development of their children. Some children have even been placed in foreign residential schools (see *Matta v. Board of Education*, 731 F.Supp. 253 [Ohio, 1990]).

An appeal was made in *Faith Baptist Church v. Douglas*, 207 Neb. 802 (1981), to the United States Supreme Court, but the appeal was denied. The Nebraska court ruled that the private school that featured a curriculum integrally tied to the fundamentalist religious beliefs of the parents was, like public schools, subject to the compulsory-education laws of the state; that is, pupil-attendance records had to be reported to the state department of education (SDE). Moreover, the court supported teacher certification and curriculum minimums from the SDE, both of which had also been rejected by the school at Faith Baptist. The state's court declared that the SDE rules were reasonable and related to the state interest in quality education and did not contravene the constitutional rights of church-related schools. Similarly ruling in *State v. Moorehead*, 308 N.W.2d 60 (Iowa, 1981), the Iowa court put the burden of proof on the parents. It charged them to show that their children, registered in nonpublic unapproved schools, received an education that was the qualitative equivalent of public education. Not all states have held that public schools establish the standard to be met, and at least in Kentucky the powers of the SDE have been restricted, but most states have followed the lead first enunciated in *Pierce v. Society of Sisters*, 268 U.S. 510 (Or. 1925).

In *People v. DeYonge District*, 449 N.W.2d 889 (Mich., 1989), the parents engaged in home schooling were convicted of violating the state's compulsory education laws, and they appealed. Considering the state's requirement for certificated teachers, the court found the requirement not in violation of parental rights in either the First or Fourteenth amendments. Home schooling need not have religious beliefs as central to judicial findings. In *In re Welfare of B.K.J.*, 451 N.W.2d 241 (Minn., 1990), the question centered on the habitual truancy of a teenager. He had been directed by a parent not to attend school but to be educated in the home. Because his absence from public school was not voluntary, but was a result of parental discretion, the decision was that he could not be classified as truant.

Cude v. Arkansas, 377 S.W.2d 816 (Ark., 1964), is an example of an extremely difficult dispute between parent and school. The Cudes subscribed to a religious belief in which the body itself was a holy temple not to be violated. Vaccination was perceived as an intrusion, a violation, an insult to the body. School regulations forbade attendance of all who had not been vaccinated against smallpox, and that excluded three of the Cudes' children. The exclusion placed Archie Cude in a position of contributing to truancy, and he had repeatedly been arrested and fined for it. Finally, the question faced by the Arkansas Supreme Court was whether the children should be taken from the parents by court order, placed in the custody of a social agency for a short while, and vaccinated. The ruling went against the parents. The court stated that parents lacked a legal right to prevent vaccination, that the risks to the child and the community in regard to a communicable disease exceeded the parental rights in the matter of the free practice of religious beliefs.

Since there was doubt whether the Cudes' children would be welcomed back into the household after the vaccination because the purity of the body had been violated, this was a major question; that is, this involved the permanent separation of children from their natural parents as the consequence of a court order. In a sociolegal conflict having no good resolution, the court opted for the legal side. Other states have commonly addressed the problem beforehand, providing in their vaccination statutes a waiver option to be selected by those parents who find themselves in religious opposition to the requirement. The Nebraska legislature, after mandating immunization, provided an option for "parents or guardians [who] shall object thereto in writing on the grounds that such . . . immunization is contrary to the religious tenets of an established church of which he or she is a member or adherent." Even more broadly, North Carolina provided exemption to "members of a religious organization whose teachings are contrary to [the obligation of immunization]." It is possible, then, to provide for religious freedom along with obligations for personal and community hygiene. Those states that provide exemption on parental demand also stipulate new controls over school attendance; for example, in times of wide occurrence of a disease, uninnoculated children may be denied attendance.

Parents have been involved in many of the mandates issued to school districts about new and extended services, bringing suits in courts and lobbying in legislatures. Some observers have noted that the educational enterprise has extended far beyond the basic mission of schooling for children and now embraces health care, medical care, nutrition, social welfare, and so on. During the 1970s and 1980s there was a plethora of court decisions and statutes that altered the character of the public schools. The general direction was to put new obligations on schools and remove some responsibilities from the home—from parents. The percentage of school budgets supporting the primary mission of basic schooling decreased as special-interest mandates materialized, using the school as society's organization to carry out their particular mission—all within the school's budget and its calendar. Although the role and the function of public schools were expanded, the passage of those decades made it very apparent that all of the malaise of society could not be solved by even such a hardy organization. In the broader sense, these new obligations that were put on schools must be candidly seen as privileged legislation, which is what they are. Public schools have become increasingly politicized agencies that respond to mandates for new kinds of services. The proportionate decrease of the public school effort in basic schooling not only has decreased some of its educational effectiveness but also has brought a new set of problems for educators, including disappointment with the academic accomplishments of children. Some parents have sought restrictions on the extent of the curriculum, and some of those questions had arisen before.

Board of Education v. Barnette, 319 U.S. 624 (W.Va., 1942)

Generalization

Even a curriculum that is broadly conceived by a state board of education must also recognize individual rights that are specified in the Bill of Rights, including freedom of religion.

Description

A religious denomination, the Jehovah's Witnesses, had developed through its church doctrine a patriotic position statement toward the United States of America. That position included statements of allegiance and obedience and also included a statement of respect for the flag, acknowledging it as a symbol of "freedom and justice for all." The doctrinal statements had been developed to set forward clearly its patriotic position, for its beliefs forbade participation in the flag salute ceremony itself.

Under statute, the West Virginia State Board of Education was charged to teach, foster, and perpetuate "the ideals, principles and spirit of Americanism" and to increase knowledge about both state and national government. In this context, the state board stipulated that the "flag is an allowable portion of the schools thus publicly supported." Continuing, then, the board resolved that the salute to the flag of the United States should become a regular part of the programs in public schools and that all teachers and pupils should join in the salute, "honoring the Nation represented by the Flag." Refusal to join in the salute was defined as insubordination leading to expulsion, delinquency, fines, and jail terms. In effect and intent, it was a civics curriculum add-on.

In this setting of conflict, the parents of children who had to reject some stipulation brought suit, seeking relief under the First Amendment and its application to the states through the Fourteenth.

Appellees, citizens of the United States and West Virginia, brought suit to the United States District Court for themselves and others similarly situated asking its injunction to restrain enforcement of these laws and regulations against Jehovah's Witnesses. The Witnesses are an unincorporated body teaching that the obligation imposed by law of God is superior to that of laws enacted by temporal government. Their religious beliefs include a literal version of Exodus, Chapter 20, verses 4 and 5, which says: "Thou shalt not make unto thee any graven image, or any likeness of anything that is in heaven above, or that is in the earth beneath, or that is in the water under the earth; thou shalt not bow down thyself to them nor serve them." They consider that the flag is an "image" within this command. For this reason they refuse to salute it.

Children of this faith have been expelled from school and are threatened with exclusion for no other cause. Officials threaten to send them to reformatories maintained for criminally inclined juveniles. Parents of such children have been prosecuted and are threatened with prosecutions for causing delinquency.

The Board of Education moved to dismiss the complaint setting forth these facts and alleging that the law and regulations are an unconstitutional denial of religious freedom, and of freedom of speech, and are invalid under the "due process" and "equal protection" clauses of the Fourteenth Amendment to the Federal Constitution. The cause was submitted on the pleadings of a District Court of three judges. It restrained enforcement as to the plaintiffs and those of that class. The Board of Education brought the case here by direct appeal.

The freedom asserted by these appellees does not bring them into collision with rights asserted by any other individual. It is such conflicts which most frequently require intervention of the State to determine where the rights of one end and those of another begin. But the refusal of these persons to participate in the ceremony does not interfere with or deny rights of others to do so. Nor is there any question in this case that their behavior is peaceable and orderly. The sole conflict is between authority and rights of the individual. The State asserts power to condition access to public education on making a prescribed sign and profession and at the same time to coerce attendance by punishing both parent and child. The latter stand on a right of self-determination in matters that touch individual opinion and personal attitude.

This case caused the Court to reconsider a 1940 decision in *Minersville Schools v. Gobitis*, 306 U.S. 604, another case from West Virginia with the same religious group and same point of contention. In *Barnette*, the Court stated that the authorities in West Virginia had exceeded constitutional limits on their power by compelling the flag salute. *Gobitis* and all other similar rulings were reversed, and the West Virginia regulations were enjoined. An excellent example of the balance of power between the parent and the schools was created. Incidentally, this is the most immediate reversal by the Supreme Court of a school law case that it had adjudicated, pronounced in 1940 and reversed in 1943.

PARENTS' RIGHTS IN SPECIAL EDUCATION

The enactment of P.L. 94–142 (the Education for All Handicapped Children Act of 1975, renamed in 1990 as the Individuals with Disabilities Education

Act—IDEA) brought parents into a more responsible role with clearly defined rights. Congress, in the preamble to the law, set forth the purpose: to assure that *all* handicapped children have available to them "a free appropriate public education and related services designed to meet their unique needs." In the 1989–90 school year, over 4 million schoolchildren received special education (SPED) services (see chapter 7).

When schools began programs that were auxiliary to the formal education endeavor, questions about those programs followed. Who should pay the costs of transporting children to the place where formal education occurred? Who should pay the costs of feeding the children after they got to the place where formal education occurred? Such questions are more than philosophical—for example, what is equitable?—and are fraught with operational complexities—what costs are politically acceptable?

In *Warren v. Papillion Schools*, 259 N.W.2d 281 (Neb., 1979), a question arose over transportation paid for by the school district. When school consolidation had occurred, it had been understood by the parents who lived in the newly added school territory that bus transportation, paid for by the district, was a part of the attraction to consolidate. By Nebraska statute, children living more than four miles from their attendance center had to be transported at public expense. The reason for the statute was to encourage regular attendance. However, the consolidated area was within the four-mile limit, and after initially providing transportation under its discretionary powers, the local board halted that service in 1976 and suggested that parents pay for bus service by neighborhood contract, should the parents want it. The parents sued, but the Nebraska Supreme Court ruled against them, saying that even if some oral agreements had been made about pupil transportation, they were unenforceable because the official public records of merged public school districts were not open to the collateral attacks.

When LEAs make decisions on operations, they are often compromises between requests for programs and the operational funds that are available. In *Welling v. Livonia Board*, 171 N.W.2d 545 (Mich., 1971), the plaintiffs sought a court order requiring the local board to provide a full day of instruction for all students. Due to a lack of funds, school was on half-day sessions, and certain subjects were being taught on a compressed schedule. The state constitution conferred power to the state board of education to administer the public school system, but the state department of education (SDE) had no rule or regulation that prohibited the practices of the Livonia board, which was faced with a lack of funds.

No clear legal duty was shown on the part of Michigan LEAs. The SDE had not promulgated any regulations specifying the number of hours in a school day. The LEA was doing no more than exercising its reasonable discretion about the need to constrict or reduce a program, and with no state statute or regulation as mandate, LEAs were not required to provide a full day of instruction to certain students. Out of such cases and out of the plethora of reports issued in the 1980s about the shortcomings of education, most states now stipulate a school year described in both days and hours. Half days are inadequate.

As alluded to earlier, and as evident in *Welling*, above, public school districts frequently have less than enough money to operate programs that are desirable and desired. This had led local boards to search for other revenue sources. A number of cases have indicated that public school districts are sharply restricted in fees that can be assessed against students, but the procedure goes on, and public schools engage in selling items, charging admissions, and organizing many programs so that students themselves raise funds for operational costs. All of those activities are endeavors to provide extended programs through funding that does not show in operational budgets or in tax levies. It is an operational mode in which there must be serious legal reservation, even though off-budget programs have a political attraction.

Some states mandate that textbooks will be purchased by each LEA to rent, or offer free of charge, to students. Some states make that an option to each LEA. No state provides an option to its LEAs to engage in rental or sale of such basic items of the educational experience with the intention of making money from students. Short of that extreme, many LEAs have developed fee-charging systems.

In *Bond and Fusfeld v. Ann Arbor Schools*, 171 N.W.2d 557 (Mich., 1969), parents sought relief from the imposition of fees levied that included the purchase of some books and supplies used in classwork. They sought refund of all such fees already collected as well. The court's decision was split, according to the items purchased. It was decided that school districts were not required to furnish books and supplies at no cost at all to students in elementary and secondary schools, for the Michigan constitution could not be so broadly construed, even though the constitution included a section using the term *free education*. On the other question, the school was ordered to cease the assessment and collection of general fees and to discard the material ticket system, used for many of the laboratory classes. No order for refund by the district was issued, but that was only a recognition of an administrative inconvenience, and it was a clear signal to other LEAs that if in the future they engaged in similar fee-collection practices aimed at children compelled by statute to attend and did not adhere to the ruling in *Bond*, refunds might be ordered.

SUMMARY

The interest of parents and schools in the education realm is unified but is characterized by some ambiguities too. Parents may want more than schools can offer. They may think that more should be accomplished than is, in reality, possible when the constraints of "regular" public schools are superimposed against the developmental patterns of children and the consequences of socio-economic classes. Sometimes, parental disappointments have created opposition to public schools and/or have caused parents to search for educational programs that are more harmonious with their own concept of education—generally, non-public schools.

People who operate the schools—the teachers and administrators—have found that parents, as they come to view the school that their child is assigned to attend, can either be allies or not. Consideration of the array of parental interests and the generally understood mission of the schools can be distinguished in the variety of cases brought by parents. The central thread of those cases is that parents want something seen to be advantageous to their child, something that is not being provided. Direction for every LEA can be seen in a thoughtful examination of those interests, and although not every interest can be satisfied, consideration of the interests is vital and necessary, for public schools cannot endure long without strong parental support. There are other publics, some large in number, that are strongly opposed to publicly supported, ''free'' education.

Parents are responsible for sending children to school punctually and regularly. They also have certain rights in the whole educational endeavor. The National Committee of Citizens in Education compiled a list of rights to which parents are entitled by either federal or state laws, and a selection of five specific items from that list is fairly representative of parental rights:

1. To take legal action against school officials in incidents of unreasonable physical force used as discipline
2. To appeal administrative decisions placing children in classes for students designated as troublesome or disruptive
3. To visit the child's classroom during the school day after notifying the school office
4. To request the absence of the child from studying subjects or joining activities objected to on religious, moral, or other reasonable grounds
5. To examine records and, upon cause, to challenge any record seen as unfair or untrue

4

Certification, Contracts, and Retirement

CERTIFICATION

The schools employ several different categories of professionally specialized personnel. The standards of preparation for each type have evolved, and now, approaching the end of the century, those standards are conceptually similar from one state to another, with only a few exceptions. At the same time, it is necessary to point out that state mandates in statutes or regulations are changing the specifics for certification (or licensure) in a majority of the states. Too, the intensity of attempts at control over certification is increasing for teachers and administrators alike.

In the historical development of public school districts, a relatively simple system of identification of candidates and selection of applicants prevailed. The school districts of the late nineteenth and early twentieth centuries were, typically, small. The geographical area was limited by district boundaries, and even though some of those districts were extensive, the population was small. The exceptions to that rule were the large city school districts, but there were not many of them.

Overwhelmingly, school districts were small and provincial, and personal acquaintance was common. School board members knew, personally, many of the candidates for positions as teachers. As time passed, conditions changed, and a lack of personal familiarity enforced the proposition that all beginning professionals should have a credential attesting to minimum competence to teach children and to likelihood of success as a starting teacher. Insofar as possible, uniformity within each state was also accepted as one goal for teacher certification. The state certificate became that credential of uniform minimum competence. It has evolved in the direction of greater uniformity with the goal of enhanced competence. Certification has had the continuous support of the National Education Association (NEA) and the American Federation of Teachers (AFT).

There are several ways to develop a credential that will assure some minimum competence. With states in charge of certificate issuance, each has designed its own pattern. For some occupations, such as barbers, morticians, and engineers, states have generally opted for an examination following the completion of some academic program. Success in the examination is accepted as proof of competence, and a license is issued. The license allows the citizen to then seek work in the specific occupational area. For those candidates who fail the examination, no license is issued. The effect is denial of the right to seek jobs in that occupational area. Success in the examination, more specifically than in the academic program, is the indicator of whether a license should be issued. A license may not be quite synonymous with a certificate, but the two are parallel in that each is a necessary prelude to entry into certain occupational settings. Conceptually, the words are synonymous.

Every professional working in a school must have a certificate. Aides do not need certificates; neither do secretaries, custodians, lunchroom workers, and so on. Such workers are integral to the operation of a school and may regularly be in contact with students, but they are not in charge of students in an instructional setting. For every employee who has responsibility for some aspect of the instruction of a child, an appropriate certificate is a must.

Boards may not be held liable for payment for services to employees who have failed to obtain a proper certificate or who have obtained one through fraud. In contemporary American school districts, boards of education cannot personally know the applicants for teaching positions, except in very small school districts. The unwavering demand that all applicants have, or be eligible for, proper certification provides a necessary protection for school boards and for the children who will receive instruction from the candidates finally selected. Local boards may add to the rigor of state certification requirements, enhancing the teacher qualifications for their district, but they may not reduce them or set them aside.

All teachers must have certificates appropriate to the grade levels in which they will teach and/or to the subject area for which they will have responsibility. Specialized certificates must be possessed by other school employees, such as counselors, principals, supervisors, librarians, and teachers of handicapped children. The certificate is a necessary part of the job seeker's credentials, for it is an acknowledgment from the state's department of education that a minimum level of competence is present. It is not an assurance of success in the job for which it specifies competence, but it does assure likelihood of success, providing a pool of eligible applicants from which successful candidates can be selected and assigned.

The certificates that might be sought as a prelude to job search within a school system differ from licenses only in that their issuance is not generally dependent on a score on an examination. This characteristic of difference is fading as states join the political expedience for accountability. The result has been a sharp increase in test taking for both prospective teachers and administrators, as well as new titles for credentials. Many states now issue a beginning teacher's license with an acceptable test score.

People who desire to be teachers know that it is a lawful occupation and that they may, in American freedom of choice, choose to be a teacher. The route to certification is through a bachelor's degree including certain specifics, according to the kind of certificate desired. Colleges and universities engaged in the preparation of teachers have designed programs containing courses and information appropriate to certain tasks in schools. Students who are in those institutions make choices and commit to one program. The institutions, through liaisons with their own state department of education (SDE), have gathered the necessary coursework and information into programs of study for students. Once those programs are approved by the SDE, students may study in the programs, knowing that after completion they will be eligible for a bachelor's degree from the institution and an appropriate certificate from the SDE. Issuance of the certificate after program completion is not a question. It will be issued on application and evidence of completing an approved program. This procedure is used in some form in every state and is called the approved program procedure for certification. It is not the only approach. Current professional literature reveals some strong preferences in a growing number of states for certification on examination during, and after, completing an approved program, as well as the expansion of what constitutes an approved program of studies.

If there are mitigating factors, then certificate issuance may not be automatic. For example, a student might have attended an institution lacking a teacher preparation program approved in advance by the SDE; or, the candidate might have a criminal record or lack some other statutory requirement. Such applications do not form a large group, however. Typically, certification is an entitlement upon evidence of academic accomplishment and adequate test scores, and a chief state school officer may not deny a qualified applicant the appropriate certificate.

The entire teacher occupational episode is represented by the time line of certificate, contract, job performance, retirement. Certificates are necessary for teachers, and even though, in a way, they represent a property interest for the teacher, certificates are issued by the state for its own convenience and may be subject to forfeiture. In *Hodge v. Stegall*, 206 Okla. 161 (1952), the Oklahoma Supreme Court upheld the state's commissioner of education in revoking a teacher's certificate for cause and with due process. That is, the certificate is not a contract between the teacher and the state, and when a teacher accepted a certificate, the issuance may be conditioned by the state and must be accepted by the teacher—or face loss of the certificate. Still, teachers are not without due process as a defense. In *Williams v. Turlington*, 498 So.2d 468 (Fla. 1986), the teacher had been charged with incompetence, insubordination, immorality, and misconduct, and a complaint asked for temporary revocation. The professional practices commission imposed a heavier penalty: permanent revocation without opportunity for reinstatement. Since the complaint specified a temporary revocation, the holding was in favor of the teacher on the basis that the proceedings were unfair.

Cases detail individual situations. Yet, the same general principles that emerge in individual cases apply to negotiated contracts for groups of teachers. Under the California Educational Employment Relations Act, the part-time teachers of the Santa Monica Community College organized and bargained for a contract. In *Santa Monica Community College District v. Public Employment Relations Board*, 169 Cal. 460 (1980), the California Court of Appeals upheld a Public Employees Relations Board (PERB) ruling that the part-time teachers had been victims of an unfair labor practice when the employing board granted pay raises to full-time faculty but withheld pay raises for part-time faculty after the latter group declined to waive its right to collective bargaining under California law.

For that great bulk of teachers who perform satisfactorily through an occupational lifetime, retirement in accord with the statutes of each state tells what their rights and obligations will be. In *Payne v. Board of Trustees of the Teachers' Insurance & Retirement Fund*, 35 N.W. 553 (N.D., 1948), the North Dakota Supreme Court stated that the relation between teachers and the retirement fund was contractual in nature and that the state had created a trust fund from which to pay annuity claims under the controlling statute—and that qualified teachers could not be denied.

At one end of the employment continuum are certificates, which are not contractual in nature. At the other end is retirement—a pension or an annuity—which is contractual and cannot be denied nor withheld from those who are qualified to file against the fund.

STATUTES AND TEACHING

Statutes from the many states are substantially uniform on how people may come to be legally designated as teachers, counselors, principals, and so on. Excerpts from the three states of Oregon, Nebraska, and Connecticut span the nation and reveal the similarities.

A teaching certificate provided for in this section shall qualify its holder to accept any instructional assignment from preliminary through grade 12 for which he has completed the professional requirements established by the rules of the Teacher Standards and Practices Commission.

A basic teaching certificate shall be issued on application to an otherwise qualified person who has competed an approved teacher education program and meets such other requirements as the Teacher Standards and Practices Commission may consider necessary to maintain and improve quality of instruction in the public schools of the state. (Oregon Revised Statutes 342.145 [1] and [2])

No person shall be employed to teach in any public, private, denominational, or parochial school in this state who does not hold a valid Nebraska certificate or permit issued by the State Board of Education legalizing him to teach the grade or subjects to which elected, except that no Nebraska certificate or permit shall be required of persons teaching exclusively in junior colleges organized as part of the public school system.

The State Board of Education may, for just cause, revoke any teacher's certificate or administrator's certificate or suspend such certificate for such period of time as the board, in its discretion, shall determine. Just cause may consist of any or more of the following: (1) incompetence, (2) immorality, (3) intemperance, (4) cruelty, (5) crime against the law of the state, (6) neglect of duty, (7) general neglect of the business of the school, (8) unprofessional conduct, (9) physical or mental incapacity, or (10) breach of contract for teaching or administrative services. The revocation or suspension of the certificate shall terminate the employment of such teacher or administrator, but such teacher or administrator shall be paid up to the time of receiving notice of revocation or suspension. The board shall immediately notify the secretary of the school district or board of education where such teacher or administrator is employed. It shall also notify the teacher or administrator of such revocation or suspension and shall enter its action in such case in the books or records of its office; Provided, no certificate shall be revoked or suspended without due notice from the board and an opportunity given the teacher or administrator to explain or defend his conduct. (Revised Statutes of Nebraska 79–1233 [1] and 79–1234)

Any board of education may authorize the superintendent or supervising agent to employ teachers. Any superintendent or supervising agent not authorized to employ teachers shall submit to the board of education nominations for teachers for each of the schools in his jurisdiction and, from the persons so nominated, teachers may be employed. Such board shall accept or reject such nominations within thirty-five days from their submission. Any such board of education may request the superintendent or supervising agent to submit multiple nominations of qualified candidates, if more than one candidate is available for nomination, for any supervisory or administrative position, in which case the superintendent or supervising agent recommends such candidates. If such board rejects such nominations, the superintendent or supervising agent shall submit to such board other nominations and such board may employ teachers from the persons so nominated and shall accept or reject such nominations within one month from their submission. The contract for employment of a teacher shall be in writing and may be terminated at any time for any of the reasons enumerated in subdivisions (1) to (6), inclusive, of subsection (b) of this section, otherwise the contract shall be renewed in writing prior to March first in one school year that such contract will not be renewed for the following year, provided, upon the teacher's written request, such notice shall be supplemented within five days after receipt of such request by a statement of the reason or reasons for such failure to renew. Such teacher may, upon written request filed with the board of education within ten days after the receipt of such notice, be entitled to a hearing before the board, or, if indicated in such request and if designated by the board, before an impartial hearing panel established and conducted in accordance with the provisions of subsection (b) of this section, but without the right to appeal provided in subsection (f) of this section, such hearing to be held within fifteen days of such request. The teacher shall have the right to appear with counsel of his choice at such hearing.

(b) ... Employment ... may be terminated at any time for one or more of the following reasons:

(1) inefficiency or incompetence;

(2) insubordination against reasonable rules of the board of education;

(3) moral misconduct;

(4) disability, as shown by competent medical evidence;

(5) elimination of the position . . . ;

(6) other due and sufficient cause. . . .

(c) For the purpose of this section, the term "teacher" shall include each employee of a board of education, below the rank of superintendent, who holds a regular certificate issued by the state board of education.

(d) After having had a contract of employment as a teacher renewed for a fourth year in any one municipality or school district, any teacher who leaves his employment as a teacher in such municipality or school district, and is subsequently re-employed in such municipality or school district or who is subsequently employed in any other municipality or school districts shall become subject to the provisions of subsection (b) of this section after eighteen months of continuous employment unless, prior to completion of the eighteenth month following commencement of the employment in such town, such teacher has been notified in writing prior to March first in accordance with the provisions of subsection (a) of this section that such contract will not be renewed for the following year irrespective of the duration of employment under the then existing contract beyond the date of said notification or unless, for a period of five or more years immediately prior to such subsequent employment such teacher has not been employed in any public school within the state. (Connecticut General Statutes Annotated Title 10, sec 10–151, a, b, c, and e)

Some states, in considering what should be done about teacher certification, merely acknowledge that teachers must be certificated and then name an agency to develop and administer standards. Typically, that agency is the state board of education, a subunit, or a commission on teaching competence. Other states have become statutorily specific about the criteria for certification, the methods for hiring, and the means for maintaining a position as a teacher. State legislatures are in command of the question "How can a teacher's certificate be obtained?" and may handle certification procedure any way they see fit.

In 1977, the Oregon Legislature added a stipulation that every applicant for a teacher's certificate must "hold a recognized first aid card." Another add-on from that same era was the Oregon legislators' mandate that every teacher certificate applicant must "demonstrate knowledge of Title VI of the Civil Rights Act of 1964" and of other similar federal and state statutes aimed at the pro-hibitions of discrimination against protected classes of citizens. The legislature passed such substantive requirements along with the procedural aspects of the state's Teacher Standards and Practices Commission, specifying names and types of certificates. The tendency to modify requirements and make them more com-plicated or more rigorous, revealed in the Oregon example, is common among the states.

In this brief survey of certification statutes that apply to professionals in education, it is important to note that in an era that has seen *accountability* flourish as a catchword, the essence of that catchword has come to teacher certification.

National Education Association v. South Carolina, 434 U.S. 1026 (S.C., 1978) Reported at 445 F.Supp. 1094 as United States v. State of South Carolina

Generalization

States set the requirements for teacher certification. They may have to prove the direct relationship between their requirements and the job, if disproportionate numbers of applicants, separated by race, are disqualified at the point of meeting the requirements.

Description

The National Teacher Examination (NTE) results disqualified a substantially higher proportion of blacks than whites among applicants for teacher's certificates in South Carolina. Among those who passed the NTE, a larger percentage of black than white teachers were placed in lower-paying classifications as one consequence of their test scores. The record of the lower court was accepted and affirmed by the Supreme Court. The lower court noted:

The evidence in the record supports a finding that South Carolina officials were concerned with improving the quality of public school teaching, certifying only those applicants possessed of the minimum knowledge necessary to teach effectively, utilizing an objective measure and providing appropriate financial incentives for teachers to improve their academic qualifications and thereby their ability to teach. We conclude that these are entirely legitimate and clearly important governmental objectives.

Plaintiffs have asserted four acts by the State indicating discriminatory intent: (1) The decision in 1945 to institute an NTE requirement; (2) The decision in 1956, effective in 1957, to institute an absolute rather than relative score requirement; (3) The decision in 1969 to revise the absolute score requirement to include the Area Examinations as well as the Common Examinations and raising the previous required scores; and (4) The decision in 1976 to change the single composite score requirement to separate composite score requirement for each teaching field, and in all but one case raising the required scores again. We conclude for the following reasons that such actions by the State were not motivated by an intent to discriminate because of race.

We are unable to find any discriminatory intent from these facts. Although the historical background of segregated schools might provide some basis for the inference urged by plaintiffs, any such inference has been rebutted. The committee based its recommendation concerning the NTE in part on its conclusion that the tests ''can be scored objectively and impartially and their use would not be subject to the accusation that they are used for purposes of discrimination.'' The Board's extensive study is viewed as an earnest effort in its time, and provided reasonable support for its decision to institute an NTE requirement. The Board's knowledge of differential impact, without more, does not support a finding of discriminatory intent.

In considering whether defendant's use of the NTE bears a fair and substantial relationship to these governmental objectives, we conclude that it does.

The record supports the conclusion that the NTE are professionally and carefully prepared to measure the critical mass of knowledge in academic subject matter. The NTE do not measure teaching skills, but do measure the content of the academic preparation of prospective teachers.

In any decision-making process that relies on a standardized test, there is some risk of error. The risk of excluding truly qualified candidates whose low test score does not reflect his or her real ability can be decreased by lowering the minimum score requirement. That also increases the risk of including an unqualified candidate whose low test score does reflect his or her real ability. The State must weigh many facets of the public interest in making such a decision. If there is a teacher shortage, a relatively high minimum score requirement may mean that some classrooms will be without teachers, and it may be better to provide a less than fully competent teacher than no teacher at all. But to the extent that children are exposed to incompetent teachers, education suffers. It may be that education suffers less than would be the case if classrooms were overcrowded due to lack of teachers. We think it is within the prerogative of the State to accept some unqualified teachers under circumstances where that is judged by the State to be on balance in the public interest, and that such an action by the State is not a violation of Title VII.

We also conclude that defendants' use of the NTE for salary purposes bears the necessary relationship to South Carolina's objectives with respect to its public school teaching force. Although the NTE were not designed to evaluate experienced teachers, the State could reasonably conclude that the NTE provided a reliable and economical means for measuring one element of effective teaching—the degree of knowledge possessed by the teacher. Having so concluded, defendants could properly design a classification system relying on NTE scores for compensating teachers and providing incentives for teachers to improve their knowledge in the areas that they teach.

We believe that a distinction for pay purposes between those who are qualified as well as between those who are not qualified survives the business necessity tests. There appears to be no alternative available to the State, within reasonable limits to risk and cost, for providing the incentive necessary to motivate thousands of persons to acquire, generally on their own time and at their own expense, the necessary additional academic training so that they will be minimally competent teachers. Having made the investment of four years in an undergraduate education, it seems reasonable to try to upgrade the talent of unqualified teachers where possible, rather than rejecting them altogether.

Two justices took no part in this decision; two others, Byron White and William Brennan, dissented. With the acceptance of the district court's findings by a majority of the Supreme Court, South Carolina has continued to use testing as a way to differentiate between the most and least competent teachers and to indicate this, first, by the certificate itself and, second, by a rank system for the determination of pay.

Generally, the statutes not only set forward the procedures and qualifications for acquiring a certificate but also identify the agency responsible for carrying out the legislature's bidding. That agency has wide latitude in how it provides for certification and how it creates eligibility for jobs in schools. The specific conditions of contracts, including contract initiation, ratification, fulfillment, and termination, are addressed by the legislatures so that teachers and boards may know the specifics of their labor relations. Some districts may impose their own "special" requirements on top of state minimums. In *Thomas v. Board of Examiners of Chicago Schools*, 651 F.Supp. 664 (Ill., 1988), the applicant for a principalship claimed that the oral interview was unfair and that she was disconcerted by interrupting tactics. The court upheld the board of examiners' tactics as a good test to determine ability to handle conflict and stress, a common situation for principals. Contracts are not assured, then, merely on possession of a certificate.

Every state also has candidly recognized the possibility of failure or of trust misplaced, for certification is an indicator of trust conveyed from the state to a citizen. Certification can be suspended or revoked as a protection for children. It is the most drastic action that can be taken against a professional. For that reason, the professional needs the protection of both substantive and procedural due process. That is, the reasons for the consideration of revocation must be of importance, and those reasons must be examined by an impartial board or panel to determine that they truly exist, if requested by that teacher. The conflicts of contract termination, continuation, and certificate revocation can be seen in the following case.

Erb v. State Board of Public Instruction, 216 N.W.2d 339 (Iowa, 1974)

Generalization

The duties of a teacher are limited in comprehensiveness. Challenges to a teacher's effectiveness on grounds of immorality must show an unfitness to teach, a reflection on instructional ineffectiveness.

Description

This was an appeal of a certificate revocation. Erb and another teacher in the same school formed an adulterous liaison. The other teacher's husband became aware of it, documented it thoroughly, and presented his findings to the local board of education with a demand for Erb's dismissal as morally unfit to teach. Erb offered to resign; however, because his teaching had been so effective, the local board declined to accept the resignation, an action in harmony with the superintendent's recommendation. At that time, the matter was brought to the attention of the Iowa Board of Public Instruction, which convened, considered the situation, and voted 5 to 4 for certificate revocation.

Erb had never intended that an offer to resign should rise to certificate revocation, so he took his cause to court, finally reaching the Iowa Supreme Court. That court declared that a teacher's adultery was not sufficient grounds for certificate revocation, basing its decisions on reasons that were both substantive and procedural: (1) substantial evidence that Erb was morally unfit to teach was lacking; (2) the conduct of a teacher away from the school has limited relevance in determining fitness to teach; (3) there was a lack of evidence that retention of the teacher, as desired by the local board, would have an adverse effect on the school; (4) when sitting as a board of examiners, the state board's power is specific to the protection from harm of a local school district and cannot be lawfully exercised for another purpose; (5) the board of examiners failed to make findings of fact as a base for their decision; and (6) disapproval of the private conduct of a teacher by individual board members is not a sufficient base from which to call for certificate revocation, an extreme professional penalty.

We emphasize the board's power to revoke teaching certificates is neither punitive nor intended to permit exercise of personal moral judgment by members of the board. Punishment is left to the criminal law, and the personal moral views of board members cannot be relevant.

The board voted five to four to revoke Erb's teaching certificate and without making any findings of fact or conclusions by law, ordered it revoked. Revocation was stayed by trial court and then by this court pending outcome of the certiorari action and appeal. Trial court held Erb's admitted adulterous conduct was sufficient basis for revocation of his certificate and annulled the writ.

There was no evidence other than that Erb's misconduct was an isolated occurrence in an otherwise unblemished past and is not likely to recur. The conduct itself was not an open or public affront to community mores; it became public only because it was discovered with considerable effort and made public to others. Erb made no effort to justify it; instead he sought to show he regretted it, it did not reflect his true character, and it would not be repeated.

The board acted illegally in revoking his certificate. Trial court erred in annulling the writ of certiorari.

Although the court noted that an immoral act might be a basis for certificate revocation, in this instance the local school district board had decided that Erb's teaching was not impaired and had voted unanimously not to accept his tendered resignation. Immoral acts that lead to allegations of unfitness to teach must be examined by way of due process where certificate revocation is concerned.

CONTRACTS

With a certificate in hand, a citizen is legally a teacher and may enter the job market. Eligibility for employment presupposes a certificate. That means that the person may become an applicant for a contract. Typically, contracts are written in a form prescribed by the SDE and include all of the elements of contract found in common law. Teachers are sellers, and boards are buyers. There are five basic elements that describe contract as a condition:

1. Agreement is mutual
2. Parties are competent

3. Considerations are specified
4. Subject matter is legal
5. Agreement is as required by the law

The first element pertains to the job description and compensation level that is agreed to by both parties. The second element specifies that the board is legally competent and that the teacher has—or will possess at an appropriate time to start work—the necessary certificate. The third element includes the job description and time of performance along with the total compensation for those professional services. The fourth element is a mutual assurance that the job and its performance will not be a violation of law. The fifth element is an assurance that the contract is in agreement with the statutory specifics of how a teacher's contract must be made, in that state. The precise format for contracts may vary a little from state to state, but substantially the contracts are the same, and in all states, contracts must be written.

The contract is the document of proof that an agreement was reached between a teacher and a board of education. The teacher promises to deliver services within the certificated scope of competence for some term, that is, for some specified period of time; the board promises to pay for those services at some rate.

Boards of education engage in such varied business that contracts become a common part of operating the school district. Here, the focus of attention has been on personnel and on personnel contracts. The basic elements of contract, above, pertain not only to personnel contracts but to contract law generally and to all other aspects of contract in which boards normally engage. Several of those other aspects of school operation, in which contracting plays a key role, are treated elsewhere in this text.

The centrality of the certificate applies in any setting, public or private. In *DeVico v. Catholic Diocese of Rockville* 508 N.Y.S.2d 886 (1986), a teacher claimed breach of contract on the premise that he had accomplished tenure and could not be dismissed. He cited the teacher's handbook to show that he had accomplished tenure by acquiescence; however, that same handbook included the entire set of rules for tenure by acquiescence. Two stipulations were pertinent: a minimum academic credential of a bachelor's degree and a state teacher's certificate. Having neither, DeVico lost his case.

Initial employment for every teacher new to a particular job setting is the time when the characteristics of hiring and contract are distinctly present. Subsequently, contracts for reemployment or contracts developed through collective bargaining may obscure some of the basic elements. When a teacher candidate is among the finalists for a job, and when an interview with a school district's personnel officer is progressing happily, the job seeker is in final negotiations for the job. If agreement is reached, the job may be offered and a contract tendered. If the candidate signs the contract, he or she may leave the interviewing thinking that the job is secure, but strictly speaking, that is not so in most states. Connecticut is an exception and is one of the states where, when a superintendent is acting as a personnel officer, with the power to hire having been conveyed by the local board, that superintendent can conclude the contract.

Legislatures have vested the hiring power in boards of education, and ordinarily, they cannot delegate that power to any of their officers or employees. Contract forms, signed by teacher applicants, go into a file for board action. In the natural order of events, and at the board's next regular meeting in a *pro forma* action, the board votes on the job candidates and ratifies the contracts. Legally, boards have the option to review and refuse applicants nominated or recommended for hiring; ethically, refusal would be another matter. After ratification, the contract becomes a firm and binding agreement for the services from the teacher and compensation from the board.

Contracts place a teacher in a job setting with an obligation to perform as an instructional leader. Teachers generally want flexibility of assignment minimized; school administrators and boards generally want great flexibility in teacher assignments. This conflict, concerning place of assigned work and duties prescribed, gives rise to many problems because each of the parties interprets the contract to serve its own cause. Extracurricular assignments have been frequent sources of misunderstanding between boards and teachers. Generally, contract forms are written to provide some flexibility and include such clauses as "and such other assignments as may be appropriate and in keeping with the policies of the board." Such a generic clause means that teachers may be assigned to supervise students in locations other than a classroom and that teachers may be assigned to those extracurricular activities that harmonize with their teaching assignment. It does not mean that teachers are to be indiscriminately assigned to teaching duties for which they lack certification and in which their probability for success is low. The question cannot be finally and conclusively settled for every teacher for every year; some uncertainty must be accepted as a fact of the mix in school. Accommodations must be developed that will withstand the reasonable and prudent man test.

BROKEN CONTRACTS

Contracts can be broken. That is not to say that all parties to the contract will be pleased that it is broken. Displeasure may prevail. A broken contract may occur by mutual agreement to dissolve it or by a unilateral decision. When a contract is broken without mutual consent, it is breached. A teacher may breach a contract by declining to perform a specified service; a board may breach a contract by not paying for services rendered.

Historically, boards have seldom been in breach of contract. That is, design of curriculum, staffing for it, budget development, and tax-receipt systems are so closely aligned that boards typically (1) hire the minimum staff necessary; (2) have jobs for every person hired; and (3) have money in the treasury for every position filled. When boards do breach a contract, it is for lack of money. More often than not, many teachers, rather than only one, are involved. Boards might find that they are unable to pay all teachers at a regular payroll time and decide to pay none or decide to pay all but one particular teacher group. In the 1930s, when large proportions of levied taxes were delinquent and uncollected, school board treasuries suffered. Many teachers were paid with promissory notes called no-fund warrants. Occasional incidents of shortage of funds, especially in a few large city school systems, have recurred in the 1970s and 1980s. However, incidents of breach by a board are rare, considering that in 1990 there were about 15,000 operating school districts.

Most contract breaches are committed by teachers. It is a part of American capitalism that every worker hunts for the best job to be found; for teachers, that generally means the job offering the most money. Just because most teachers work in the public sector does not mean that they are less interested in job improvement than are any other American job seekers. Teachers differ from other job seekers, though, in the fact that they become parties to contracts for some term. Ordinarily, that term is for one year. What is a teacher to do when, after signing a contract with one district, another job—higher paying and more desirable—materializes in another school district? Or when a job materializes in an entirely different work arena? That question cannot be treated here in its ethical dimension; here, the considerations are legality and practicality.

If the teacher writes a letter of resignation, requesting release from the contract, how can it be viewed by the board to which it is addressed? Is it a request or a *fait accompli*? Is it an item for *pro forma* acceptance by the board or an item for real discussion and action on its merits? Legally speaking, a letter of resignation may be refused. If the teaching manpower pool is complete and balanced, if the area of performance is in short supply, if there is not enough time to find a replacement, or if other sufficient reasons exist, the board may hold the teacher to the contract and demand performance. Practically, there are problems in such board action because even though teachers subscribe to and practice demanding professional ethics, many teachers' performances would slump if forced to stay where they did not wish to be. Practically, boards of education accept letters of resignation on demand—in a real sense, a contract breach—because the alternative of an unhappy, dissatisfied teacher is not a good prospect for an outstanding instructional leader. The board, through practical action, relieves the teacher of a choice that might lead to an actual, legal breach and identification as the defaulting party.

In *Strayer v. Remsen-Union Community School*, 688 F.Supp. 1275 (Iowa, 1987), an LEA board refused a letter of resignation. Other teachers had been released from their contracts in this district, and Strayer sought release to accept a job in another district. Iowa statutes forbid consummating a teacher contract in one district while a valid contract with another district is in force. Strayer had sought a midsummer release, past the time when an LEA might find the best replacement. The state court ruled that the LEA did not act arbitrarily, that Strayer was denied no rights, and that he was subject to the demands of the contract, in part because the plaintiff failed to demonstrate that a replacement of equal quality could be hired.

On the question of remedies for a contract breached by a board, affected teachers can pursue for money damages. Amounts of actual loss can be calculated and established. Recovery of money is the appropriate remedy, with the amount being equivalent to the amount lost by the board's breach. Not every denial of payment from a board is a breach. Other circumstances may have an overriding effect. Several specifics of contracts and breaches are well illustrated in the following cases.

Oates-Ulrich v. Okemos Board, 415 N.W.2d 213 (Mich., 1987)

Generalization

Tenure statutes will be strictly interpreted. For designation as tenured, a teacher must meet all provisions of probation in Michigan.

Description

Two professional employees—a school social worker and a school psychologist—sought tenure and were denied because, although each possessed a teacher's certificate, neither had been involved as a teacher. Each had worked in nonteaching positions for two years.

Petitioner Oates-Ulrich worked for the Okemos Public School District in the capacity of social worker. With the exception of one approved educational leave of absence, she had been so employed since 1975.

Petitioner Meese worked for the school district as a school psychologist since 1979.

In March, 1982, petitioners were informed by the Okemos Board of Education that they were deemed not to have obtained tenure as classroom teachers. As a result, petitioners filed a petition with the State Tenure Commission for a declaration of their rights under the teacher tenure act, claiming to have achieved tenure status by operation of law. Although not required for their positions, both petitioners at that point in time held Michigan provisional teaching certificates, which subsequently expired without renewal.

The only issue now properly before this Court is whether petitioners had, in fact, obtained tenure. They argue that because they were certificated under Article III by holding Michigan provisional teaching certificates, they were automatically entitled to tenure at the conclusion of two years of satisfactory performance in their assigned positions. We disagree.

Accordingly, we conclude that there was competent, material and substantial evidence on the whole record to support the State Tenure Commission's findings. The circuit court correctly affirmed the commission's ruling.

Affirmed.

Rules that govern contracts generally apply to contracts in public schools. Contracts must be mutual, definite in the terms of provisions, and free from fraud. Boards may not be deprived of choice and discretion in hiring by incomplete or erroneous information, and action taken under those conditions may be rescinded.

Meier v. Foster School District #2, 146 N.W.2d 882 (N.D., 1966)

Generalization

Inadequate planning for curriculum and staff by boards of education cannot be an adequate basis for teacher dismissal during the term of a contract. Lack of need for the services of a contracted teacher is not a sufficient basis for discharge.

Description

In a suit for damages, Dorothy A. Meier charged the board with breach of contract. Having been hired to teach home economics for a specified salary, Mrs. Meier made visits to the homes of several prospective students before the actual school year began. She was paid a part of her contracted salary amount for that work and was notified when teachers were to report for work at their assigned buildings.

Later, she was summoned to a special meeting of the board of education two days before her initial workday. She was informed that, due to a low registration in home economics, all classes were being cancelled. The board asked for her resignation. She declined and declared herself ready, available, and qualified to teach as stipulated in her contract. The board then sent her a special-delivery letter notifying her that there would be no home economics classes, that her contract was null and void, and that no money beyond that already paid would be paid.

We believe that it is immaterial whether a sufficient number of pupils were enrolled in the home economics courses in September 1958 to secure federal assistance for the home economics program for the 1958–1959 school year, because it is our view that the school district became obligated to pay Mrs. Meier the salary specified for the term specified when the contract was executed in February 1958. To hold otherwise would permit school districts to arbitrarily avoid commitments which teachers may have been induced to rely on to their detriment.

Generally, in the absence of any statutory or contractual provision to the contrary, the mere fact that a teacher's services are no longer necessary will not justify the dismissal of the teacher without further compensation prior to the expiration of his period of employment under a valid contract fixing a definite period of employment.

In action for breach by contract by a public school teacher, the measure of damages is the wages which would have been paid under the contract alleged to have been breached, less any sum actually earned or which might have been earned by the teacher by the exercise of reasonable diligence in seeking and obtaining other similar employment.

. . . We therefore conclude that Mrs. Meier is entitled to recover from the school district the amount of her salary less $267 paid to her, or a total of $4,183. The judgment of the trial court is reversed, and the case is remanded with instructions to the trial court to enter judgment in the sum of $4,183 plus interest thereon at the rate of four per cent per annum.

Ruling for Meier, the court agreed that the board had breached the contract and had denied compensation. A contingency about numbers of registered students could have been a part of the offered contract, but it was not. Neither was any board policy on minimum class size made a part of the contract. The board action was arbitrary, lacking any legislative or contractual base. Damages for the denial of employment can be determined. Having secured no alternative employment, Meier was entitled to the whole amount for the school year.

CONTRACT NONRENEWAL

Nonrenewal of teacher contracts is the area in which most disputes over contracts arise. Teaching has historically been a transient occupation in that many people who entered it did so with the full anticipation that they were passing through a time in their life that would lead them into another occupation. Well into the twentieth century, large numbers of females taught until they married, then left to become full-time homemakers. Many males taught while on the way to some other, more lucrative occupation. Such people had but limited interest in the protection of employment continuity.

The public nature of schoolteaching has provided a fertile ground for the development of pressures leading toward the dismissal of specific teachers. Teaching is not an occupation that has the protections characterizing civil service. Actually, many reasons can be identified as having contributed to relatively short terms for teacher employment, but from the viewpoint of teachers, the remedy was to get more thoughtful control over the contract portions specifying the term, that is, the length of time of employment. One way to such control has been through legislated mandates on contracts and their structure.

American school years have never been calendar years. School years are shorter, with state legislatures specifying some minimum number of days. Typical school years are about 175 to 180 teaching days, and in interoccupational comparisons, it is a short work year. Even for that very small group of school districts that demand a 200-day work year, it is still, comparatively, a short year. That is a problem in equitable compensation, but it is only the first step to recognition of the larger problem: For how many years should a teacher be hired, and how much continuity of employment should be provided by the local public school district?

Boards of education desire stability in the local teaching corps. One indicator of that desire can be seen in the historical terms of the contract: one contract for one year. Education is an enterprise with a large call on manpower. It is labor-intensive. Traditionally, boards have made one grand effort each year to fill all of the teaching positions and have then hoped that every position would be ably filled, with a high-quality performance for the school year. In its generic sense, the phrase *contract term* means any period of time, mutually acceptable and stipulated in the contract. For teaching services, it has come to mean something specific. A teaching contract is for the term, for the school year. From the board's viewpoint, that length provides instructional continuity and still allows for personnel change when instructional effectiveness is questioned.

If boards have found a term contract to be a desirable length of time, teachers have, increasingly, found it to be too short. Much professional effort has been devoted to extending the time of the contract beyond one year. In state after state, legislatures have responded to the political action of teacher associations, providing for two developments in teacher contracts: (1) continuing employment contracts, and (2) tenure contracts. Teachers, wanting more job stability, have pursued it through statutory contract refinement.

Continuing contracts provides that all personnel may assume continuation unless specifically notified to the contrary. Statues specify a time when notification must occur, and if during that time there is no notification from the board to the teacher, then continuation as an employee is automatic. There is also a time for information flow of an opposite nature, that is, resignation; and if no resignation is tendered during that time, a board may assume continuation is automatic for every employee who has not resigned during that period. Both characteristics of continuing contract contribute to faculty stability.

Another word that has come to have a specialized meaning in teacher contracts is *tenure*. It means continued or permanent employment after a time of trial or probation. It means continued employment until death, retirement, dismissal for just and specified cause, or elimination of the position due to financial exigency. Probation periods are usually from two to five years, with designation as a tenured teacher coming after successfully completing the probationary period. Statutes in some states do not actually use the word *tenure* but describe a condition of permanent employment after a probationary period. With or without the name, statutory tenure has become quite common as state legislatures have described permanence and due process as integral characteristics of employment in local school districts. For teachers, tenure represents maximum security in harmony with academic freedom. For boards, it represents a reduction in personnel management flexibility and increased burdens on administrations to prove instructional ineffectiveness if a teacher is to be dismissed via a hearing. From the vast amount of litigation in the general area of contract management, including tenure, four cases in the area of nonrenewal have been selected as illustrations of important legal principles.

Boyce and Others v. Board of Education of the City of Royal Oak, 257 N.W.2d 153 (Mich., 1977)

Generalization

Faced with financial exigency and within the statutes of the state, local boards may lay off probationary personnel on short notice when whole programs are eliminated.

Description

This board action originally included the dismissal of some tenured teachers; eventually, only probationary teachers lost jobs. Five weeks before the layoff, the affected teachers received notifications that they would be dismissed and that programs and positions were being eliminated in the middle of the school year due to economic considerations. The contract for the year included the following phrase: "The School District will not terminate . . . unless there is in the judgment of the Board of Education . . . insufficient revenue during the school year to continue the payment of the salary called for in this contract."

Ruling in favor of the board, the court noted that when economic conditions require it, a board can lay off tenured teachers as well as those on probation. The board was in compliance with the master contract provisions and with individual contracts and had acted in good faith. Although the contract called for fewer days of notice than the state statute demanded for tenured teachers, that did not apply to probationary teachers.

Confusion about employment status sometimes comes with employees assigned to noninstructional tasks. Schools employ many supportive personnel, but it is the category of employment that creates eligibility for statutory protection. Employees who, coincidentally, also have a valid state teacher's certificate are not entitled to the benefits and provisions of the tenure statute by virtue of that certificate. For example, a person with a teacher's certificate might be employed as an aide. When the contract specifies that position, the certificate is irrelevant.

Ryan v. Aurora City Board of Education, 540 F.2d 222 (USCA 6th, Ohio, 1976)

Generalization

Practices and policies of local boards of education cannot exceed statutory grants of power, but boards can change their own policies. Teacher entitlement to continued employment is based in state statutes.

Description

Ryan and three other teachers had been employed by the Aurora, Ohio, schools for varying lengths of time, from two years to eight years. In common, all were labeled as nontenured teachers working under limited contracts, all of which expired in the spring of 1973. The local board, acting under the appropriate state statute, voted not to renew the contracts, after timely written notification to each teacher. No reasons for nonrenewal were given, and no requests for hearings were granted.

The teachers did not claim violation of statute but based their claim to employment continuation on a portion of the board's 1965 policy manual:

1. Any teacher recommended for dismissal must have been clearly informed of his status by the superintendent and completely aware that such a recommendation is being made with definite reasons for the action.
2. Teachers who are not to be reappointed shall be given the reasons and notified in writing by the clerk-treasurer of the school district as confirmed by the board on or before April 30th.

The teachers contended that tenure, in the sense that it is continuous employment, was implied by board policy. Since the board acted in accord with the statutes, but not in accord with its own policies, the teachers contended that the board had violated their civil rights and denied them the due process granted them under the Fourteenth Amendment.

Acknowledging that the local board acted within state statutes, the court tacitly agreed that board policy could unilaterally be changed by the board. The court also stated that nontenured teachers cannot lay claim to entitlement to continued employment, for to do so would, in effect, amend the Ohio tenure statute. Implied promises of contract continuation do not create a property interest for probationary teachers. Boards are not bound to give reasons why they decide not to renew contracts. Nonetheless, boards are not free to handle personnel any way they like, including changed assignments.

Romano v. Harrington, 664 F.Supp. 675 (N.Y., 1987)

Generalization

Administrators are not free to change the extracurricular assignments of teachers during a contract year, except as provided for in contract.

Description

Romano was a tenured English teacher in the New York City Schools and had been the faculty advisor to the Port Richmond High School newspaper, the *Crow's Nest*, for six years. That was an extra-pay assignment. A controversial article, condemning the establishment of the Martin Luther King holiday, appeared in a February 1984 issue.

Plaintiff did not agree with the views expressed in the article, but he worked with the author on successive re-writes to make sure it complied with the paper's journalistic standards. The article was not censored by plaintiff or reviewed by the school administration prior to its publication.

On February 8, 1984, just after the distribution of the article, defendant Margaret Harrington, Principal of Port Richmond High School, met with plaintiff and terminated his position as faculty advisor. Defendant Harrington, in a letter to plaintiff dated February 15, 1984, memorialized the substance of their meeting. In essence, she felt that he had not taken appropriate steps to ensure balanced reporting, especially given the history of racial conflict at the school and the sensitivity of the King holiday issue; she claimed he had not been accessible to different groups of students within the student body; she found his professional judgment lacking; and she rated his performance, as faculty advisor to "The Crow's Nest," as unsatisfactory for the fall term of 1983. Although plaintiff has remained at the school as a tenured English teacher, plaintiff's position as faculty advisor was terminated effective immediately.

However, plaintiff was not seeking to further his personal beliefs through his relationship with the school newspaper and its staff. His advisory function is not akin to those who join together for the purpose of literary expression, political change or religious worship. See Olson, 687 P.2d at 439 (citing Tribe, 702–03). Although plaintiff worked with the students in editing and preparing the articles for publication, advising and supervising a student organization is not an activity which falls squarely within the ambit of the freedom of association cases.

Whether the retention rights provided for in the collective bargaining agreement and any implicit understandings surrounding this provision give plaintiff a constitutionally protected property interest in his job as faculty advisor is not readily ascertainable on the basis of the existing record. The wording of the provision in the agreement certainly implies that a faculty advisor who has performed satisfactorily for two years may continue to serve in their per session job absent an unsatisfactory rating from the school. On its face, the provision appears to guarantee continued employment absent sufficient cause for discharge, and thus may create a protected liberty interest.

The court refused to accept the school district's request for a summary dismissal and created the opportunity for Romano to bring another suit, based on examination of factual evidence as measured against constitutional claims and due process causes for action.

Teachers can be dismissed for actions that occur away from schools. In *In re Shelton*, 408 N.W.2d 594 (Minn., 1987), a Minnesota teacher had formed a corporation with two other teachers at Blooming Prairie High School. They were in the computer business, and Shelton engaged in theft and forgery, taking more than $40,000 from the corporation over a two-year period. Discovered, Shelton made payments in restitution and continued to teach, but he had trouble keeping order in his classes. At the end of that school year he pleaded guilty to swindle and theft. The LEA board voted to discharge him on grounds of immorality. Shelton completed restitution, served thirty days in jail, and was placed on probation. He sought reinstatement, but after examining the conditions in the school and the state statutes, the Minnesota court ruled in favor of the board.

When considered as a group, the preceding cases reveal that boards of education cannot exceed their grants of power from their respective legislatures, that teachers cannot create for themselves employment rights exceeding what has been provided by statute, and that both parties to the contract, board and teacher, must accept the contractual limits of their state and for their type of school district. To some extent, labor relations in the elementary and secondary school sector have developed from the political tension generated by teacher associations (unions) speaking their demands to legislators on the one hand and, on the other hand, associated school boards speaking different messages to the same legislators. Gradually, employment conditions are changing. Due process, just cause, and long-term employment are becoming much more prevalent as conditions of contracts for teachers and administrators.

RETIREMENT

Sixty-five years of age has been the magic time when teachers and other workers are expected to have achieved enough financial independence to cut away from work and its attendant regular paycheck. American workers, through a wide spectrum of careers, accepted age 65 as the time to retire. For nongovernmental employees, federal legislation—including all of the social security statutes and amendments—harmonized on that age. With social security the expanded worker coverage that has come with each decade since its passage, and its articulation with existing pension and retirement plans, 65 remained the accepted age for retirement through the middle of the twentieth century.

Increasingly, the appropriate time for retirement is becoming a more flexible concept—a more individualized choice—and at least three major factors have influenced the change. First, for those people who wanted to retire before age 65, social security was altered, opening the choice to initiate claims and retire at age 62. Significant numbers of American workers, including teachers, have saved and invested so that even with the reduced claims that can be made against social security and retirement plans at age 62, a sufficient financial independence exists to consider quitting work. Second, the time spent in retirement has become much more attractive than it was in the first half of the century. Retirees can do many things. Many opportunities have been developed expressly for the mature, retired adult. Things that take time demand that people be unhampered by work schedules. The prospect of an extended number of leisure years, including an acceptable level of financial support and excellent health services, has proved attractive to many Americans, and a tendency toward earlier retirement has occurred. Specifically for teachers, many school districts have attempted to grapple with the problems of declining enrollment by offering bonuses to teachers who would voluntarily retire at earlier ages, reducing the teacher corps by that technique. In *Cedar v. Commissioner of Education*, 269 N.Y.S.2d 661 (1967), it was decided that a school district could offer a lump-sum payment as an incentive to early retirement, and when accepted, the payment was a purchase of tenure rights from the teacher by the board.

From a strictly legal viewpoint, money paid to teachers at the time of a voluntarily elected early retirement cannot be in the form of a bonus, or labeled a bonus. The method of payment must be harmonized with the statutes declaring how boards of education can spend money for professional personnel services. A variety of formulas have been developed by which amounts of such early retirement money can be calculated and legally paid to professionals.

Third, an anomaly in retirement patterns has further contributed to the newly developing flexibility of retirement age. Callously, but picturesquely, it is realistic to think of every worker as a cog in the nation's industrial machine. Cogs do wear out, and observations led to the conclusion that the productive capability of sixty-five-year-old cogs was on the downside. That is, the human physique and intellect passes a point of maximum capability and thereafter declines. Although this is a safe generalization, it is certainly not true for all individuals. If the generalization indicated the suitability of an arbitrary retirement age, 65 years, the exceptions indicated a need to consider an alternative for some American workers because, in the twentieth century, life expectancy has been continually extending.

Americans have been arriving at age 65 with increasingly hardy physiques. Now, the anomaly is that whereas some have opted to retire—even retire early—and enjoy time without the obligations of work, other workers have fought to preserve the right to work, on the premise of adequate physical and mental vitality. Others have opted for an extended work life, coupling that increased physical vitality with their desire to continue to build a retirement fund through those few additional years of work.

Some indication of what rulings are reasonable in regard to retirement can be found in public employment outside of education. In *Weisbrod v. Lynn*, 383 F.Supp. 933 (D.C., 1974), a federal employee was subjected to the Federal Employees Mandatory Retirement Act. Reaching the age of 70, the maximum allowed in the law, Weisbrod was retired against his wishes. He sought reinstatement, alleging a constitutional infringement, and pursued his case through three court hearings. He was denied. In *Massachusetts Board of Retirement v. Murgia*, 427 U.S. 307 (Mass., 1976), the issue was retirement at age 50, stipulated in Massachusetts law for state police officers. Speaking on lowered efficiency and prime physical condition, the Court found for the state in a per curiam decision with one dissent.

From the field of education, Zimmerman claimed protectable property interests past age 70. The Connecticut Teacher Retirement Act allowed for employment past 70. In *Zimmerman v. Branford Board of Education*, 597 F.Supp. 72 (Conn., 1984), the plaintiff was hired in two successive one-year contracts, after reaching the age of 70. Seeking a third, he was refused and brought this suit. Ruling that this claim was without merit, the court found for the board.

In 1978, Congress passed the Age Discrimination in Employment Act Amendments. That statute was in the heritage of the civil rights legislation of the 1960s and 1970s and extended the categories in which employment discrimination was unlawful to eight, although the categories are not equal in the intensity of judicial scrutiny to which they may be subjected:

1. Race
2. Color
3. Religion
4. Sex
5. National origin
6. Physically handicapped
7. Pregnancy
8. Age

Together with earlier statutes dealing with age and employment, the 1978 legislation contained a three-part intent on the part of Congress. It was the intent of Congress, first, to assist older workers to keep or regain employment; second, to deter the establishment and continuation of upper age limits as disqualifications for work; and third, to promote employment of older workers based on what is known of their ability, rather than on an arbitrary age-based decision. Now, employers may not discriminate against employees on the basis of age in such areas as hiring, promoting, transferring, or continuing. Although some employment categories are exempted—for example, state patrol officers—teachers and school districts are within the scope of the legislation. Protected citizens are those who are at least 40 but less than 70 years of age. This statute complicated the intentions, procedures, and economics of retirement in public school districts.

Before 1978, school districts faced occasional suits from teachers who wanted to continue their professional life beyond age 65, even in districts with policies mandating retirement at 65. With that legislation as a watershed, what was appropriate on one side is not necessarily equally appropriate on the other.

Monnier v. Todd County Independent School District, 245 N.W.2d 503 (S.D., 1976)

Generalization

When school policies concerning mandatory retirement are within the state and federal statutes, teachers cannot demand that the policies be waived.

Description

Goldie Monnier was 67 years old and had taught for 12 years in the Todd County Schools. Local board policy stated, "Mandatory retirement of teachers at age 65 will become effective July 1, 1968 unless there is a specific request from the Principal or Director of Elementary Education that the retirement age be waived with an annual review of each teacher receiving such a waiver."

Monnier had received two one-year renewals. When she was approaching the end of the second renewal, it was recommended to the superintendent that she not be rehired and that she be retired in accord with policy. She was informed by the superintendent that she would not be recommended for continued employment. The protection of the state's continuing contract law ceased at age 65. She requested a hearing and was denied.

Faced with a policy that was complementary to the state's statutes, Monnier was left without an argument. The teacher was not entitled to a hearing or to due process, generally. Contractual rights are not contractually abridged when a mandatory retirement coexists with state statutes.

Monnier occurred and was heard before the action of Congress in 1978, in which the 40–70 age group became a protected age group. Obviously, local school board policy cannot contravene federal statutes. Yet, there is not any necessary contradiction, either, between statutes or policies that end tenure at some such age as 65 and the federal statute. If that condition prevails, subsequent contracts can be offered for terms of one year, renewable on satisfactory performance. Age cannot be a reason for nonrenewal.

Retirement plans deserve the surveillance of the people who expect to benefit from them. This is especially true if the plan does not vest in each individual for whom, eventually, there is an anticipation that the money will be paid. In *Dodge v. Chicago Board of Education*, 302 U.S. 74 (Ill., 1937), the question of legislatively diminished retirement eligibility arose. In its original form, the teacher's retirement pension was $1,500 per year. About two decades later, the legislature reduced the annual retirement amount to $500. The case traveled a usual appeal route, and the Supreme Court sustained lower courts, finding that the teachers, not having contributed to the fund, really had no annuity, no vested rights, and no contract rights; rather, they had a pension, the annual amount of which had been set by the legislature. Therefore, it was appropriate for the legislature to periodically examine the pension payments and adjust them as deemed appropriate.

Americans are enjoying an extended vitality in their lives, and many are finding real physical vigor in those later years. Many are choosing to remain active in their careers, into their late 60s. It is their statutory right to defer retirement. To assure that children continue to receive high-quality instruction puts a new obligation on the shoulders of school administrators who conduct personnel evaluation. Complete personnel evaluation systems must be in place and operational to assure necessary and fair scrutiny of those older teachers as they perform their roles of classroom instructional leader. Classroom effectiveness, instructional strategies, and job versatility provide indices of competence that should be evaluated before recommendations for renewal of one-year contracts. Assuming teaching competence, the earliest mandatory retirement age has become 70 years.

SUMMARY

Professional careers in elementary and secondary schools now attract over 2.25 million persons. Teachers, principals, librarians, counselors, and others must possess certificates attesting to minimum competencies for their jobs. The 50 state departments of education issue certificates in correspondence to the academic programs completed by the applicants, and to a large extent, those certificates are transferable among the states. An increasing number of states demand each applicant pass some kind of examination, in addition to completing an approved academic program in teacher preparation.

With eligibility for a certificate, citizens can join the manpower pool pursuing jobs in education. Certificates must come before contracts.

5

Administering Staff Personnel

INTRODUCTION

State government is the repository of power under which public schools function. That power source is direct, mainly through the Tenth Amendment, the plenary power grant from the federal to the state governments, and through Article I, Section 8, of the Constitution, which calls for action to provide for the general welfare. In turn, as territories became states, state governments commonly made constitutional provisions of their own. Two states provide adequate illustrations. Article IX, Section 5, of the California Constitution stipulates, "The legislature shall provide for a system of common schools by which a free school shall be kept up and supported in each district." The Nebraska Constitution, Article VII, Sections 1 and 2, declares, "The Legislature shall provide for the free instruction in common schools of this state of all persons between the ages of five and twenty-one years." And, "The State Department of Education shall have general supervision and administration of the school system of the state." To consolidate those positions, the Nebraska Supreme Court enunciated a viewpoint shared widely with other states in *Kosmicki v. Kowalski*, 171 N.W.2d 172 (Neb., 1969), stating in no uncertain terms, "The state is supreme in the creation and control of school districts, and may, if it thinks proper, modify or withdraw any of their powers, or destroy such school districts." This was a reiteration of the pronouncement in *State v. Haworth*, 23 N.E. 946 (Ind., 1890) when the Indiana court stated: "As power over schools is a legislative one, it is not exhausted by exercise. The legislature, having tried one plan, is not precluded from trying another."

School districts are political subdivisions of the state, sometimes called local education agencies (LEA). Governed by local boards of trustees, they provide instruction for the local boys and girls. To discharge that function, school districts hire teachers and assign them posts. Teachers are the instructional leaders, carrying the school board's charge directly into the classroom.

Historically, while the nation was developing, the number of such districts was large, the geographical territory in each district small, and the pupil registration, also, small. Through the late nineteenth and twentieth centuries, changes have been at work in the opposite direction: the number of districts has decreased, geographical territories have enlarged, and pupil registrations, by district, have increased. (This is not a discussion of the consequences of reductions in the American birthrate; it is a general observation on the condition of public school districts.)

When districts were very small and the intellectual demands on teachers were much less than at present, boards could know, personally, many of the candidates for teaching positions. When, commonly, school boards had three, four, or five persons in the entire membership, and when that board operated a school district under the laws of its state with one or two teachers as the whole faculty, familiarity prevailed. Other reasons beyond size materialized to further contribute toward the likelihood that any board hiring a prospective teacher would have some personal familiarity with the applicant. Presently, with public school district faculties numbering into the hundreds, and some numbering into the many, many thousands, local district boards need help and some protection when applicants come forward, seeking to fill teaching vacancies. One such protection is teacher certification. In effect, it is a guarantee of some minimum performance level to be expected of that teacher by the board. Many people, aspiring to become teachers, do not because they never qualify for the certificate. In a way, the certificate is a sorting device, a legal document attesting to certain professional skills.

To teach is to be a leader, to lead children by professional skills toward some higher development. The teacher combines several uniquely cultured and developed abilities, along with an intellectual capital in some academic area. For example, the English teacher not only must be knowledgeable in literature and in the skills of composition—the intellectual capital—but also must know the sociology and psychology that impinges on learning, the technology and materials by which students can be better directed in their learning, and the organization of the curriculum in a fashion to optimize learning. The teacher must know the basics and refinements of pedagogy. In a sense, the operation of the local schools has not changed over the many decades, for the local boards still search for the highest competence that might be attracted to their particular school. Yet, in another sense, a change has occurred that substantially affects how the teacher functions after having been hired. Typically, boards want to see evidence of continued professional growth.

Within the professional ranks of school administrators, it is widely conceded that personnel management is one of the tasks that is least well done. There are several contributing reasons. First, it is difficult for an administrator to observe a teacher in action and to conclude that performance is so poor as to indicate incompetence; there is a wide range of quality, from clearly understanding to barely acceptable, that is acknowledged as suitably competent, enough to meet minimum standards in most school districts. Second, and connected to the first, there are not many evaluative systems or instruments that are, themselves, acceptable to both teachers and principals. This lack of basic evaluation tools and techniques leaves the evaluator in a vulnerable position when an assessment is questioned. Third, there is no longer any appreciable academic distance to speak of between the evaluator—the principal or supervisor—and the person being evaluated—the teacher. For those decades in which principals were by statute or regulation demanded to have higher academic degrees than teachers, there was an academic leverage that supported the judgments of principals. Nowadays, the evaluation setting will quite typically involve people at academic parity, each of whom can claim a professional expertise, couched in advanced university degree work, as an adequate basis for performance, whether the teacher carrying out instruction or the principal carrying out evaluation. It is a kind of academic stalemate, centered on the implied question "Who are you to tell me that my teaching is faulty and should be changed?" Other observations could be made to show that personnel management in education is difficult. Suffice it to generalize, however, that teachers, who are trained to make hundreds of independent professional decisions every working day, do redirect pressure on administrators who, observing teachers at work, proceed to make recommendations or directions for change.

That work environment and relationship is a far cry from the labor-management setting that typifies the private employment sector and much of the public sector other than schools. It is unique. It causes difficulties for personnel administration. The differences of opinion about the suitability and accuracy of professional assessment have stimulated a fairly large number of questions, which in turn have become cases to be settled at court. When this unique aspect is added to such procedural techniques within the organization as teaching assignments, reduction in force, and so on, the administration of the personnel who constitute the professional faculty emerges as a large problem in school operation. Many of those same problems exist in the administration of classified personnel.

ADMINISTERING THROUGH REWARDS AND PENALTIES

To entice teachers toward higher levels of proficiency, boards may reward certain kinds of things or may penalize for not doing certain kinds of things. In other circumstances, teachers may earn certain rewards, as seen in the following cases.

Harrah Independent School District et al. v. Martin, 440 U.S. 194 (Okla., 1979)

Generalization

Local boards of education may demand that teachers engage in some sort of structured professional growth plan, including university coursework.

Description

As one aspect of personnel development, the board of this LEA had demanded that teachers should, periodically, return to school to earn appropriate additional college credits—five semester hours every three years. Martin refused to return to college for additional work but had attained designation as a tenured teacher under Oklahoma law.

Respondent, hired in 1969, persistently refused to comply with the continuing education requirement and consequently forfeited the increases in salary to which she would otherwise have been entitled during the 1972–74 school years. After her contract had been renewed for the 1973–74 school term, however, the Oklahoma Legislature enacted a law mandating certain salary raises for teachers regardless of the compliance with the continuing educational policy. The school board, thus deprived of the sanction which it had previously employed to enforce the provision, notified respondent that her contract would not be renewed for the 1974–75 school year unless she completed five semester hours by April 10, 1974. Respondent nonetheless declined even to enroll in the necessary courses and appearing before the Board in January, 1974, indicated that she had no intention of complying with the requirement in her contract. Finding her persistent noncompliance with the continuing education requirement "willful neglect of duty," the Board voted at its April 1974 meeting not to renew her contract for the following year.

The school district's concern with the educational qualification of its teachers cannot under any reasoned analysis be described as impermissible, and respondent does not contend that the Board's continuing education requirement bears no rational relationship to that legitimate governmental concern. . . . There is no suggestion here that the Board enforced the continuing education requirement selectively; the Board refuses to renew contracts of those teachers and only those teachers who refuse to comply with the continuing education requirement. . . . That the Board was forced by the state legislature in 1974 to penalize noncompliance differently than it had in the past in no way alters the equal protection analysis of respondent's claim.

With the legislature's action in 1974, the Harrah board was forced to shift its ground in order to keep in place its demand for academic renewal of all teachers and to penalize those who failed to comply. The sanction changed in severity, but the board was not precluded from action that was rationally related to the Board's desire for teachers to accept an obligation for continuing education and development. Martin's petition for reinstatement was denied, and the circuit court of appeals was reversed as the United States Supreme Court let the board policy and action stand.

Burnett et al. v. Durant Community School District, 249 N.W.2d 626 (Iowa, 1977)

Generalization

In the endeavor to continually upgrade the performance of teachers, it is reasonable and rational for boards of education to provide rewards or remuneration for costs incurred by teachers as they pursue approved graduate study.

Description

The board of the Durant schools contractually provided that teachers could get university tuition-cost reimbursements up to $320 if (1) the teacher returned to Durant as an employee in the next school year, and (2) the courses taken were approved in advance by the superintendent. Twenty-five teachers got such approval, took their courses, and applied for reimbursement of costs in the following school year. They were denied payment by the local board on the advice of the county attorney, who stated that the board had exceeded its authority and that part of the contract was void. To some extent, this dispute hinged on the question of timing, for the contract was made in 1971–72, and clarifying statutes were not enacted until 1976. The Iowa Supreme Court held for the teachers and stated:

The 1972 Attorney General's opinion relied on by the county attorney in advising defendant and by the trial court in its ruling had asserted school districts in Iowa could not expend funds to pay teachers on sabbatical leave or reimburse them for tuition for approved graduate studies. The trial court's decision upholding the board's position was made in 1974, and the amendment was enacted in June, 1976 during the pendency of this appeal. It appears the amendment was enacted in response to the attorney general's opinion and resulting controversy.

Considering these circumstances and the language of the affected statutes, we think the amendment was enacted to clarify rather than change existing law.

We hold that defendant had authority to agree to reimburse plaintiffs for tuition expense incurred by them in undertaking approved graduate studies in consideration of plaintiffs' teaching services in the current and ensuing contract years. The trial court erred in holding otherwise.

REVERSED.

U.S.D. #480 v. Lila Epperson and Oleta A. Peters, 551 F.2d 254 (Kan., 1977)

Generalization

Satisfactory performance extending over several years (here, 17 and 11 years) by a teacher in a school district can make that job a property right. This is true whether or not the state has a tenure law that demands procedural due process as a part of any dismissal proceedings.

Description

Peters and Epperson had taught in Unified School District #480, Seward County, Kansas, for 11 and 17 years, respectively. In 1971–72 they were president and president-elect of the local unit of the National Education Association. Under Kansas law for continuing contract, they were timely notified that their teaching contracts would not be renewed for 1972–73. The reason for dismissal given by the board was budgetary cuts caused by decreased enrollments.

Peters and Epperson were of the firm view that the refusal of the school board to renew their teaching contracts was not really caused by budgetary problems, but on the contrary was in retaliation for the exercise by them of their First Amendment right to free speech in connection with their NEA activities. In any event, Peters and Epperson retained counsel, and asked the board for a hearing. The board, on advice of its counsel, refused this request for a hearing, believing that a teacher was not entitled to a hearing upon the refusal to renew a one-year teaching contract because of budgetary problems.

In a series of lawsuits and countersuits extended through several years, three substantive questions finally emerged for court action, and those questions were addressed by this court.

1. Did the school district board deny Peters and Epperson procedural due process?
2. Did that local school board qualify for the governmental immunity promised under the Eleventh Amendment?
3. Were the teachers due any money damages?

After citing such references as *Perry v. Sinderman*, (1972) and *Wood v. Strickland*, (1975), the circuit court examined Kansas statutes.

We conclude that "on balance," School District No. 480 in Seward County, Kansas, and its school board members acting in their official capacity, are not the alter ego of the state, but are more like a municipality, for example, and hence do not enjoy Eleventh Amendment immunity.

And under Article 6, section 2(b) of the Kansas Constitution the State Board of Regents has "control", in addition to "supervision," over all institutions of higher learning. We know that a typical state board of regents really runs the state university, whereas the State Board of Education in Kansas merely "supervises" the local school districts with the latter having a high degree of autonomy.

In *Harris* we held that a local school district in Utah was an alter ego of the State of Utah. However, an influencing factor in that case was the possibility that a money judgment rendered in federal court against the school district might be paid, at least partially, out of state funds. In the instant case, as referred to above, it is agreed, and was so found by the trial court that any money judgment which might be entered in favor of Peters or Epperson against District No. 480 would be raised by special levy within the district, and would not come from the state.

The judgment is reversed and the case remanded to the trial court with direction that it determine the damages fairly attributable to the failure of the school board to afford Peters and Epperson their Fourteenth Amendment right to a pre-termination hearing. We recognize the damage question, and the extent of any such recovery, may itself be a troublesome one.

A local school district that dismisses teachers whose employment has been extensive enough to create a property right places itself in jeopardy by dismissing without a hearing. Although individual board members may not be liable, the district treasury must be the source of money to satisfy damages suffered from loss of the job.

In education, there is an observable tendency toward the all-or-none rule in personnel administration. That is, after teacher evaluation occurs, and administrative judgment is that the performance is incompetent or on the verge of incompetence, the tendency is for a recommendation of dismissal. Fines, suspensions without pay, extensions of probation, and similar management devices are used at minimum levels in school personnel relations. Incompetence, or instructional ineffectiveness, can be determined by low results in tests of pupil progress, as in *Scheelhaase v. Woodbury Schools*, 488 F.2d 237 (Iowa, 1974). Another court also agreed with a board designation of incompetence in *Board of Education of Sioux City v. Morz*, 295 N.W.2d 447 (Iowa, 1980). There were 14 specified deficiencies in four different performance categories. The board followed due process into a termination hearing, and its decision to dismiss was upheld by the Iowa Supreme Court. Indicators of low pupil achievement and mediocre teaching performance were accepted by courts as sufficient evidence to support teacher dismissal on charges of incompetence. In *Dohanic v. Department of Education*, 533 A.2d 812 (Pa., 1987), the Pennsylvania Court affirmed a hearing tribunal decision that an LEA board had acted appropriately in a dismissal for immorality. In *Clark v. Omaha Board of Education*, 338 N.W.2d 272 (Neb., 1983), another dismissal for immorality was upheld on the evidence that, among other statements, the plaintiff, while conducting a racially integrated class, had referred to some disruptive black students as ''dumb niggers.''

Boards are not always successful in attempts to dismiss teachers. In *Bruton v. Ames Community Schools*, 291 N.W.2d 351 (Iowa, 1980), the plaintiff had taught from 1974 to 1977. Then she was employed for one year part-time on a contract that incorporated a one-year-only clause. Near the end of that year she was notified of nonrenewal because of that clause, and she brought suit. In the Iowa Supreme Court she was successful when the court pointed out that nonprobationary teachers are guaranteed the right of renewal by statute, except for just cause. Boards and administrators need to know the law and adhere to it, restricting their actions in rewards and penalties to what is reasonable and allowed.

CONSTITUTIONAL FREEDOMS

Americans have certain rights and liberties that are protected in the Constitution. The Bill of Rights stipulates what those are. Yet, these rights are not entirely clear when applied to specific situations that may include contradictory aspects. From situational disputes, cases are carried to courts for resolution. For teachers, the most important part of the Constitution is the First Amendment and its application to the states through the Fourteenth Amendment.

The First Amendment states:

Congress shall make no law respecting an establishment of religion, or prohibiting the free exercise thereof; or abridging the freedom of speech, or of the press; or of the right of the people peaceably to assemble, and to petition the government for a redress of grievances.

Although many controversies have developed from the portion dealing with religion, since public schools must address religion, that portion has not often been invoked for individual teachers. Individually, teachers are most interested in the freedoms of speech, of peaceful association and assembly, and of the right to petition the government. In considering how teachers may act within these grants of liberty and freedom, many operational questions arise.

Can a board of education curtail the things teachers say in classrooms—or out in public? Can teachers join one or another organization with impunity? If teachers see flaws in the operation of some government unit, can they become actively—even publicly—critical of it? Because it seems that American citizens want to maximize those liberties, to stretch them and make them personally comfortable, questions of propriety, ethics, practicality, and legality frequently come together in such cases.

As an occupational group, teachers have been held to a more rigorous code of conduct in their personal lives than has been demanded of other professional workers in American society. Now, in the late twentieth century, there is a discernible trend toward extending more freedom to teachers and demanding less of them as models. Still, teachers and administrators must be practical about their work setting and must be ready to exercise some judicious restraint in their public behavior. In *Nicasio Board v. Brennan*, 95 Cal. 712 (1971), a teacher provided an affidavit for a friend who had been arrested. In the affidavit, the teacher stated that she personally had used marijuana for several years and had enjoyed its benefits. The affidavit became well publicized, even though that had never been the intent of the teacher-author. She was dismissed, and the court upheld the board's action. Commonsense judgment enters into decisions that teachers make about what they will say in public.

In *Muskego-Norway Schools v. Wisconsin Employment Relations Board*, 151 N.W.2d 617 (Wis., 1967), a superintendent engaged in thinly disguised intimidation of a teacher, Carston Koeller. Koeller was a primary author, from the local education association, of a proposal for faculty welfare. Although unqualifiedly recommended for rehiring, he was fired, and the superintendent offered to recommend him for a life teaching certificate only if he did not appeal his dismissal. He appealed. Finding for the teacher, the Wisconsin Supreme Court stated that his dismissal was based on his activities in the local education association, a constitutionally protected citizen's choice.

In *Beilan v. Philadelphia Schools*, 357 U.S. 399 (Pa., 1958), the Court found that Herman Beilan was not fired for being a member of certain political groups in the 1940s, but rather for his own incompetence evidenced when he refused to enter into conversation of this topic when it was raised by his superior, the superintendent of schools. That is, fitness to teach may be determined through inquiring conversations by an administrator, and refusal to speak and respond is, in its own way, an indicator of incompetence.

So, legally speaking, teachers may select their own associations, for that is a protected citizen's right. Practically, some associations may be so unwise, so troublesome, that to admit to membership may indicate incompetency of some sort by that teacher. At the same time, a teacher may not dodge legitimate inquiries about associations by an officer representing the local board of education, when the answers to such questions will play a part in determining fitness to teach.

Pickering v. Board of Education, District #205, 391 U.S. 563 (Ill., 1968)

Generalization

Teachers are as free as any other citizens to participate in all aspects of democratic governments—including public criticism of governing boards—so long as that participation does not detract from their performances as instructional leaders in classrooms.

Description

Marvin Pickering was a teacher in the Township High School of Will County, Illinois, and was fired because he wrote to the local newspaper a letter that criticized the way in which the local board of education and the superintendent had spent money for the improvement of the school district's physical plant. A bond issue of over $5 million had been passed by the voters in 1961, and Pickering questioned several of the expenditures from that fund. The board held a full hearing and decided that his letter was "detrimental to the efficient operation and administration of the schools of the district." Pickering contended that his writing of the letter was a constitutionally protected activity under the First and Fourteenth amendments. The Supreme Court examined the Illinois statutes that applied and the manner of their application and held that Pickering's "rights to freedom of speech were violated," reversing the Illinois Supreme Court.

The Board dismissed Pickering for writing and publishing the letter. Pursuant to Illinois law, the Board was then required to hold a hearing on the dismissal. At the hearing the Board charged that numerous statements in the letter were false and that the publication of the statements unjustifiably impugned the "motives, honesty, integrity, truthfulness, responsibility and competence" of both the Board and the school administration. The Board also charged that the false statements damaged the professional reputations of its members and of the school administrators, would be disruptive of faculty discipline, and would tend to foment "controversy, conflict, and dissension" among teachers, administrators, the Board of Education, and the residents of the district. Testimony was introduced from a variety of witnesses on the truth or falsity of the particular statements in the letter with which the Board took issues. The Board found the statements to be false as charged. No evidence was introduced at any point in the proceedings as to the effect of the publication of the letter on the community as a whole or on the administration of the school system in particular, and no specific findings along these lines were made.

An examination of the statements in appellant's letter objected to by the Board that they, like the letter as a whole, consist essentially of criticism of the Board's allocation of school funds between educational and athletic programs, and of both the Board's and the superintendent's methods of informing or preventing the informing of, the district's taxpayers of the real reasons why additional tax revenues were being sought for the schools. The statements are in no way directed towards any person with whom the appellant would normally be in contact in the course of his daily work as a teacher. Thus no question of maintaining either discipline by immediate superiors or harmony among coworkers is presented here. Appellant's employment relationships with the Board, and, to a somewhat lesser extent, with the superintendent, are not the kind of close working relationships for which it can persuasively be claimed that personal loyalty and confidence are necessary. . . .

The public interest in having free and unhindered debate on matters of public importance—the core value of the Free Speech Clause of the First Amendment—is so great that it has been held that a State cannot authorize the recovery of damages by a public official for defamatory statements directed at him.

In sum, we hold that, in a case such as this, absent proof of false statements knowingly or recklessly made by him, a teacher's exercise of his right to speak on issues of public importance may not furnish the basis for his dismissal from public employment.

With Pickering as a "trail blazer," it is now apparent that teachers may have substantial leeway in critical comments, when those comments center on a public policy question and when the organizational distance—for example, from superintendent to teacher—is enough that the controversy will not impinge on job performance by the teacher.

Perry v. Sinderman, 408 U.S. 593 (Tex., 1972)

Generalization

When people are successively employed on annual contracts that involve work evaluation and recommendations, competence must be deduced from those successive contracts. At some point, public-employment-sector workers develop a property interest in a job as a consequence of time spent in the job and cannot be summarily fired. Rather, they are entitled to the procedural protection of the Fourteenth Amendment.

Description

Robert Sinderman taught in the Texas state colleges from 1959 to 1969. In 1965, he was appointed to the faculty at Odessa Junior College and received three successive renewals of his one-year contract. Although there was no systematic provision for tenure on that campus, the faculty handbook declared that each faculty member should feel that "he has permanent tenure as long as his teaching services are satisfactory.'' In May 1969, the regents voted to renew Sinderman's contract.

During that year, as president of the Texas Junior College Teachers Association, Sinderman had made public statements and given legislative testimony contrary to some stated positions of the regents. He was labeled insubordinate at the time of the regents' vote not to offer another contract and was not allowed any hearing to question the basis on which his employment was terminated.

The Supreme Court decision, written by Justice Potter Stewart, included the following comments:

For at least a quarter century, this Court has made clear that even though a person has no "right" to a valuable governmental benefit and even though the government may deny him the benefit for any number of reasons, there are some reasons upon which the government may not act. It may not deny a benefit to a person on a basis that infringes his constitutionally protected interests—especially his interests in freedom of speech.

. . . the respondent's allegations—which we must construe most favorably to the respondent at this stage of the litigation—do raise a genuine issue as to his interest in continued employment at Odessa Junior College. He alleged that this interest, though not secured by a formal contractual tenure provision, was secured by a no less binding understanding fostered by the college administration.

. . . the respondent offered to prove that a teacher, with his long period of service, at this particular State College had no less a "property" interest in continued employment than a formally tenured teacher at other colleges, and had no less a procedural due process right to a statement of reasons and a hearing before college officials upon their decision not to retain him.

A written contract with an explicit tenure provision clearly is evidence of a formal understanding that supports a teacher's claim of entitlement to continued employment unless sufficient "cause" is shown. Yet absence of such an explicit contractual provision may not always foreclose the possibility that a teacher has a "property" interest in re-employment.

Holding a much stronger view of the interests of the teacher, Justice Thurgood Marshall dissented, stating, "Every citizen who applied for a government job is entitled to it unless the government can establish some reason for denying the employment.'' To some extent, Marshall's view permeated the practical application of the decision, for *Sinderman* has made it necessary for any public board, acting to dismiss a tenured or long-term employee, be ready to explain why that employment should not be continued. School administrators must know where the burden of proof lies. That burden is not on the affected employee.

A case that will surely have far-reaching effects in establishing the rights of teachers who suffer from severe disease was decided in 1987, and many observers have noted that it is more of a civil rights issue than a public health issue.

School Board of Nassau County v. Arline, 107 S.Ct. 1123 (Fla. 1987)

Generalization

With the development of a legal definition of *handicapped*, people who suffer from severe diseases may qualify as handicapped persons, that is, physically or mentally impaired, and may be entitled to protection from discrimination under the Rehabilitation Act of 1973, Section 504.

Description

Gene Arline suffered from tuberculosis, which periodically recurred in an active form. On the third recurrence within eighteen months in 1979, she was fired by the Nassau County School Board after a thirteen-year career as a primary teacher. She had not listed in her original application that she suffered from tuberculosis, for at that time the disease was in remission. Teaching third-graders, children who by age and development are more susceptible to the disease than are older students, Arline was fired for cause—specifically, risk to others on the basis of having tested contagious. The case went through numerous hearings during eight years of litigation before it came to the Supreme Court. With the specter of AIDS looming large on the educational horizon, the Arline case will surely have wide effects on who must be continued in educational employment. With Chief Justice William Rehnquist and Justice Scalia dissenting, Justice Brennan delivered the opinion of the court.

A trial was held in the District Court, at which the principal medical evidence was provided by Marianne McEuen, M.D., an assistant director of the Community Tuberculosis Control Service of the Florida Department of Health and Rehabilitative Services. According to the medical records reviewed by Dr. McEuen, Arline was hospitalized for tuberculosis in 1957. For the next twenty years, Arline's disease was in remission. Then, in 1977, a culture revealed that tuberculosis was again active in her system; cultures taken in March 1978 and in November 1978 were also positive.

The superintendent of schools for Nassau County, Craig Marsh, then testified as to the School Board's response to Arline's medical reports. After both her second relapse, in the Spring of 1978, and her third relapse in November 1978, the School Board suspended Arline with pay for the remainder of the school year. At the end of the 1978–79 school year, the School Board held a hearing, after which it discharged Arline, "not because she had done anything wrong," but because of the "continued reoccurrence [sic] of tuberculosis."

In her trial memorandum, Arline argued that it was "not disputed that the [School Board dismissed her] solely on the basis of her illness. Since the illness in this case qualifies the Plaintiff as a 'handicapped person' it is clear that she was dismissed solely as a result of her handicap in violation of Section 504." The District Court held, however, that although there was "[n]o question that she suffers a handicap," Arline was nevertheless not "a handicapped person under the terms of that statute." The court found it "difficult . . . to conceive that Congress intended contagious diseases to be included within the definition of a handicapped person." The court then went on to state that, "even assuming" that a person with a contagious disease could be deemed a handicapped person. Arline was not "qualified" to teach elementary school.

The Court of Appeals reversed, holding that "persons with contagious diseases are within the coverage of section 504," and that Arline's condition "falls . . . neatly within the statutory and regulatory framework" of the Act. The court remanded the case "for further findings as to whether the risks of infection precluded Mrs. Arline from being 'otherwise qualified' for her job and, if so, whether it was possible to make some reasonable accommodation for her in that teaching position" or in some other position. We granted certiorari, and now affirm.

The Court engaged in a discussion of the term *handicapped*, searching for the meaning that had been foremost when Congress had enacted the statute.

Within this statutory and regulatory framework, then, we must consider whether Arline can be considered a handicapped individual. According to the testimony of Dr. McEuen, Arline suffered tuberculosis "in an acute form in such a degree that it affected her respiratory system," and was hospitalized for this condition. Arline thus had a physical impairment as that term is defined by the regulations, since she had a "physiological disorder or condition . . . affecting [her] . . . respiratory [system]." This impairment was serious enough to require hospitalization, a fact more than sufficient to establish that one or more of her major life activities were substantially limited by her impairment. Thus, Arline's hospitalization for tuberculosis in 1957 suffices to establish that she has a "record of . . . impairment" within the meaning of 29 U.S.C. §706(7)(b)(ii), and is therefore a handicapped individual.

Petitioners concede that a contagious disease may constitute a handicapping condition to the extent that it leaves a person with "diminished physical or mental capabilities," Brief for Petitioners 15, and concede that Arline's hospitalization for tuberculosis in 1957 demonstrates that she has a record of physical impairment. Petitioners maintain, however, Arline's record of impairment is irrelevant in this case, since the School Board dismissed Arline not because of her diminished physical capabilities, but because of the threat that her relapses of tuberculosis posed to the health of others.

We do not agree with petitioners that, in defining a handicapped individual under §504, the contagious effects of a disease can be meaningfully distinguished from the disease's physical effects on a claimant in a case such as this. Arline's contagiousness and her physical impairment each resulted from the same underlying condition, tuberculosis. It would be unfair to allow an employer to seize upon the distinction between the effects of a disease on others and the effects of a disease on a patient and use that distinction to justify discriminatory treatment.

Finding no congressional intention for such a separation, the Court addressed the general question of ability to perform the assigned work, having settled the issue that a handicapped person could not be denied a job because of the ignorance or prejudice of others. In earlier hearings, it had not been determined whether Arline was "otherwise qualified" to perform her duties as teacher. The Court remanded to a district court to determine whether she was, in fact, otherwise qualified.

PERSONNEL EVALUATION

When administrators function as evaluators of teachers and detect a performance that is unsatisfactory, they are obligated not only to point out what is below standard but also to specify what must be done to upgrade the performance. In *Sanders v. South Sioux Board*, 263 N.W.2d 461 (Neb., 1978), the Nebraska Supreme Court found that the local board had acted in an "arbitrary and unreasonable manner," dismissing Sanders when her current evaluation ratings were good, with a recommendation for renewal, and when there was no record of substantive stipulations for improvement having been given her by the administration.

There can be no doubt that performance accountability has risen to new levels of visibility. Yet, that accountability is shared by teachers evaluated on their teaching performance and by administrators engaged in the process of evaluation and development. When administrators find teachers performing below the standard for that school, those administrators must be prepared to enumerate—or demonstrate—precisely what the teacher must do to improve. And, the entire supervisory-evaluative episode must be documented.

Good documentation provides a baseline for tracing the degree of improvement. That is a practical and ethical minimum for both parties to the evaluation. It is also a legal necessity as the evidentiary base, should some subsequent action be questioned in court. Lack of a systematic evaluation procedure and its documentation led the court to support Sanders, above, because the burden of proof rested on the local board that had dismissed the teacher.

The words that describe the maximum punishment in personnel control vary but include such terms as *fired, dismissed*, and *nonrenewed*. In effect, they mean the same thing: termination of employment. Technically, they are slightly different and are descriptive of precise uses of state statutes. In part, the Nebraska statute states that the teacher's contract "shall be deemed renewed and in force and effect until a majority of the board votes, sixty days before the close of the contract period, to amend or terminate the contract for just cause," (Revised Statutes of Nebraska 79–1254.02). Continuing, the statute directs that the board secretary must give notice of unsatisfactory performance that may be the just cause to terminate, at least ninety days before the close of the contract period. Further, any teacher has the right to request a hearing for the just cause of the dismissal, and the LEA board must convene for that hearing and make its final decision on the evidence presented at the hearing. In practice, teachers designated as probationary have the same rights as do permanent teachers to a due process hearing convened to determine the just cause for dismissal.

The practice in this text is to use the word *teacher* generically as well as specifically. That is, when conditions in schools apply to all certificated employees, the word *teacher* has been used with a generic connotation. In those cases, the world would include teachers, librarians, counselors, and administrators—all of the job positions for which a state-issued certificate is a preliminary to securing and holding the job. When the word *teacher* is used to describe the relationships in an employment hierarchy, it becomes narrower in meaning, for that relationship itself tends to separate teachers and counselors from principals, and principals from superintendents.

Coe v. Paul M. Bogart, 519 F.2d 10 (USCA 6th, Tenn. 1975)

Generalization

Local boards of education have latitude in involuntarily transferring their personnel to other assignments when demotions are not part of the transfer and when increased school effectiveness is an anticipated outcome.

Description

William S. Coe was transferred, against his will, from his position as principal of Sevier County High School, Tennessee. The transfer was made without Coe's receiving any statement of charges against him or opportunity for a hearing before the Sevier County School Board. Coe brought a civil rights action against that board, alleging that he was not given due process when he was transferred. The board contended that it had the right to transfer individuals within the system in order to increase efficiency.

Coe raised two questions: (1) Does a local board and superintendent have the right to transfer a tenured teacher or principal from one location to another or from one job to another without due process? (2) Was Coe, a tenured employee under Tennessee statutes, deprived of a property right within the meaning of the Fourteenth Amendment or of civil rights legislation?

The circuit court ruled in favor of the board of education, commenting:

This is an appeal in an action brought under 42 U.S.C., 1983 and 28 U.S.C., 1343 in which appellant William S. Coe alleged that he was deprived of procedural due process under the Fourteenth Amendment when he was transferred from his position as principal of Sevier County High School without being furnished any statement of charges against him or opportunity for a hearing before the County School Board. Coe had been employed in the county school system for 36 years, the last twelve of them as principal of its largest high school.

Following a trial on the merits, District Judge Robert L. Taylor . . . found that plaintiff was a tenured teacher with the Sevier County system within the meaning of Tennessee's Teacher Tenure Act T.C.A. 49–1401 et seq. He further found that the action of the defendant school board "constituted a routine transfer of personnel within a school system in the interest of administrative efficiency and did not amount to punitive demotion or a deprivation of property."

Our review of the trial record satisfied us that the findings of fact as reported by the trial judge are not clearly erroneous.

Tennessee tenure laws, like those commonly found in other states, did not entitle a teacher or principal to a specific job. The transfer of staff without notice or hearing constituted routine personnel administration. The transfer was motivated by a sincere belief that the effectiveness of that high school could be enhanced under different leadership. The transfer did not diminish the professional integrity of Coe nor force him out of the system; neither did the transfer compel him to accept a demotion or lowered compensation. The transfer was a reasonable consequence of performance evaluation by the superintendent of schools.

In another Tennessee case, the same court spoke to two aspects of termination, also involving the Fourteenth Amendment. The court held that a probationary or nontenured teacher could be discharged at the end of the contract term without any reason being given for such termination of services. However, in *Kendall v. Memphis Board of Education*, 623 F.2d 1155 (Tenn., 1980), the teacher evaluation revealed a performance that was so deficient that a decision was made to fire the teacher at once, abruptly and in midcontract. The court noted that the teacher suffered two injuries, for she received no contract settlement and did not have an opportunity for a due process hearing. The board was found liable for damages, the amount to be settled by the trial court.

In *Imbrunone v. Inkster Public Schools*, 410 N.W.2d 300 (Mich., 1987), three public school districts had joined to provide a magnet school program and had hired one teacher. Under Michigan statutes, the teacher was awarded tenure from the state, a circumstance that one of the districts found objectionable. Through multiple hearings, the finding was for the teacher and against the objecting district.

In a California case, the transfer and reassignment of personnel came to the attention of a grand jury in *Calaveras School District v. Leach, Evans, et al.*, 65 Cal. 588 (Cal. Court of Appeals, 3rd, 1968). The reassignment of a principal as vice principal and a vice principal as teacher resulted in a court order for examination of personnel records by the grand jury. The superintendent appeared before the grand jury but refused to produce the records, and state statute supported his position, there being no criminal conduct involved.

The key point in personnel administration is that adequate records need to be kept. Although it is true that nontenured employees are not entitled to pretermination hearings, and that this question was settled in *Bishop v. Wood*, 426 U.S. 341 (N.C., 1976), when a probationary police officer was dismissed, good personnel records are still ethical and legal minima. Boards cannot act with malice toward any employees, and records must be available to make it clear that fairness has prevailed. Constitutional, contractual, and statutory protection must be met in any manipulation of the school district's manpower pool, and those changes must have their base in an improvement of the educational setting.

PROMOTION AND TENURE

Terms and conditions of employment, as well as the relative permanence of the job, have been concerns of workers since the world of work began to divide into two groups, employees and employers. Workers want to know if they are temporary or permanent. They want to know what must be done to change classifications from temporary to permanent because Americans, fond of making long-range plans, cannot do so when they lack some basic economic understandings. For teachers, the words describing this critical aspect of work life are *probation* and *tenure*.

The underlying concept is that when employees are newly hired, too little is known about the professional performance characteristics to grant employment far into the future. Initial contracts are, typically, for one year. After some time has passed, evaluations have been made, development has occurred, and evidence has been made available that the teacher is a dependable, effective professional, tenure may be granted. The time for that event, the statutory specifics governing it, and the true consequences of conferring a status of permanent employment vary from state to state. The definitions, rights, and obligations are covered by statutes, as seen in the Oregon code.

"Permanent teacher" means any teacher who has been regularly employed by a fair dismissal district for a period of not less than three successive school years, whether or not the district was such a district during all of such period, and who has been reelected by such district after the completion of such three-year period for the next succeeding school year.

"Probationary teacher" means any teacher employed by a fair dismissal district who is not a permanent teacher. (Oregon Revised Statutes 342.805 [4], [5])

Elsewhere in the statutes, a more complete description of the probationary teacher occurs.

Probationary teacher. The district board of any fair dismissal district may discharge or remove any probationary teacher in the employ of the district at any time during a probationary period for any case deemed in good faith sufficient by the board. The probationary teacher shall be given a written copy of the reasons for this dismissal, and upon request shall be provided a hearing thereon by the board, at which time the probationary teacher shall have the opportunity to be heard either in person or by a representative of the teacher's choice.

The district board may, for any cause it may deem in good faith sufficient, refuse to renew the contract of any probationary teacher. However, the teacher shall be entitled to notice of the intended action by April 1, and upon request shall be provided a hearing before the district board. Upon request from the probationary teacher the board shall provide the probationary teacher a written copy of the reasons for the nonrenewal which shall provide the basis for the hearing.

If an appeal is taken from any hearing, the appeal shall be limited to:

(a) The procedures at the hearing;
(b) Whether the written copy of the reasons for dismissal required by this section was supplied; and
(c) In the case of nonrenewal whether notice of nonrenewal was timely given. (Oregon Revised Statutes 842.835 [1], [2], [3])

From the same statutory source, a good, representative definition can be found.

Permanent teacher; permanent part-time teacher. (1) A permanent teacher shall not be subjected to the requirement of annual appointment nor shall he be dismissed or employed on a part-time basis without his consent except as provided in ORS 342.805 to 342.955. (Oregon Revised Statutes 342.845)

Teachers move from one status to another by way of periodic evaluations done during the time they are classified as probationary teachers.

Teacher evaluation; form; personnel file content. The district superintendent of every school district, including superintendents of education service districts, shall cause to have made at least annually but with multiple observations an evaluation of performance for each probationary teacher employed by the district and at least biennially for any other teacher. The purpose of the evaluation is to allow the teacher and the district to determine the teacher's development and growth in the teaching profession and to evaluate the performance of the teaching responsibilities. A form for teacher evaluation shall be prescribed by the State Board of Education and completed pursuant to rules adopted by the district school board. (Oregon Revised Statutes 352.850)

Although the Oregon code differs from many other states in particulars, conceptually it is a good example of how all states have acted to address the question of permanence in public school district employment.

The Nebraska statutes enumerate the specifics under which dismissal can occur. Specifics are strikingly similar to those found in other states. The conditions of unsatisfactory performance are legislatively stipulated.

Just cause shall mean; (a) Incompetency, which shall include, but not be limited to, demonstrated deficiencies or shortcomings in knowledge of subject matter or teaching or administrative skills; (b) neglect of duty; (c) unprofessional conduct; (d) insubordination; (e) immorality; (f) physical or mental incapacity; (g) failure to give evidence of professional growth as required in section 79–12,113; or (h) other conduct which interferes substantially with the continued performance of duties. (Nebraska Revised Statutes 79–12, 107 [4])

The passage from probationary to permanent—tenured—teacher is a critical time in a professional's life. It is a major decision for the employing board, for it signals the start of a long-term commitment, mutually shared. Teachers are eager for accomplishment and designation as tenured. Boards are prone to painstakingly careful and thorough reexaminations of all personnel coming to that point of long-term commitment. In *Holton Schools v. William Farmer*, 259 N.W.2d 219 (Mich. Court of Appeals, 1977), Farmer was told that he would not be rehired at the end of his last year as a probationary teacher because of a program phase-out. He was not told that his work was unsatisfactory. Qualified by certification for four open positions in the school district, he applied but was not hired, being labeled as not the best qualified. Although he had not achieved tenure, he had achieved some seniority, and the court supported his contention that he could not be denied employment until the local board of education comprehensively defined its term *qualified* and he could be identified as clearly outside the group of qualified candidates.

Specific conditions complicate situations. In *California Teachers Association v. Garvey School District*, 240 Cal. Rptr. 549 (1987), at issue was the reinstatement of Grelling, a teacher employed under the status of probationary teacher for the spring semester of 1982. Teaching the next year, he was offered in March 1983 a contract specifying that he would be classified as a temporary employee. Objecting to the classification, he refused to sign the contract; and when he reported for work in September 1983, the building principal told him he had no job. Seeking relief in the courts, Grelling was finally justified when the court decided that he was a probationary teacher and ordered his reinstatement.

Robinson v. Jefferson County School Board, 458 F.2d 1318 (USCA, Ala., 1973)

Generalization

Even among those probationary teachers who are obviously intelligent and accomplished individuals, there is a necessity to accept and work within the policies and regulations of the employing school district.

Description

Carolyn Robinson was a first-year, probationary teacher in the Jefferson County, Alabama, schools. As a probationary teacher, she lacked a constitutionally protected property interest in continued employment, and the Alabama statutes empowered local boards to refuse reemployment to probationary teachers without a hearing. On allegations from the administration, she was dismissed by the school board for her use of profanity in the classroom, for her incompetency and inefficiency in the discharge of her daily duties, and for her inability to relate to ninth-grade students. Robinson, who defended herself, contended that she was not dismissed because of those reasons; rather, she contended that she was dismissed because the principal did not like her, or the way she graded, or the way she arranged her class. The circuit court stated:

The trial court found that the plaintiff was in fact dismissed because of her general ineffectiveness as a teacher. Upon a review of the record, we are unable to say that finding was clearly erroneous.

In light of our holding, we deem it appropriate to make a few observations about the relatively unusual character of this case. The plaintiff appears in this court *pro se*, and she prosecuted her entire case below, through a substantial trial, in her own behalf. The appellant's briefs reveal an understanding of the law and an ability to make legal arguments rare in a layman. Apparently her performance in the trial court was equally impressive; the trial judge stated that he had "never had a case in which anybody has represented himself before in which the party doing so has operated as effectively as has the plaintiff in this case." Her performance led him to suggest that she might prefer the practice of law to returning to teaching. Ms. Robinson's performance as her own counsel leaves no doubt that she is an extraordinarily capable woman. In view of this, the record of this case is a troubling one. It describes the difficulties of an intelligent woman in her first year of teaching, whose ideas differed from those of her superiors in the school organization. We should have hoped that the principal of the school and school board officials and Ms. Robinson, a highly capable woman, could have found some amicable way to communicate and to work out their differences. But whatever may be said of this unhappy breakdown in communications and its cause, the County Board of Education did not violate the plaintiff's constitutional rights. That is all this Court holds.

Affirmed.

Robinson was an instance of regrettable but unreconciled conflict in which a district hired an aggressive, highly intelligent candidate as a teacher and then found that she was unable or unwilling to work within the confines of the organization. Intelligence must be prized among teachers, but organizational teamwork must also be prized—and local boards can demand that.

Blurton v. Bloomfield Hills Schools, 231 N.W. 535 (Mich. Court of Appeals, 1975)

Generalization

Boards are not at liberty to write into contracts clauses that violate state statutes, and teachers who accept and sign such contracts may not be bound by those invalid clauses.

Description

Blurton was employed by the Bloomfield schools on September 7, 1971, and began teaching without a contract as a permanent substitute. She taught fifth grade at one elementary school the entire fall semester of 1971, and near the end of that semester, replaced a teacher who took a maternity leave. In the main body of the form contract it was provided that the term of employment was for one year, starting on or about September 1. Typewritten at the bottom of her contract was the statement: "Prorate from January 7, 1972. Contract to terminate at end of the school year, June, 1972." Near the end of that school year, Blurton received notice that she would not be rehired for the next school year. She sought reinstatement as a teacher, stating that with the exception of three days in January, and permissible leave days, she had taught every day of the 1971–72 school year and that on that performance, the Michigan teacher tenure act stopped the district from discharging her.

Noting that, by statute, no teacher could "waive any rights and privileges under this act in any contract or agreement with a controlling board," the court made its own pronouncement.

By adopting a literal interpretation of the phrase "a full school year," the Legislature's purpose behind the teacher's tenure act would be frustrated. We hold that plaintiff's pleading stated a cause of action. If plaintiff at trial is able to prove the facts alleged in her pleading, we hold she would be entitled to the guarantees (provided in Michigan law).

The statute mandates that a probationary teacher or one employed on a noncontinuing contract must be informed that her work is or is not satisfactory and that she will not be rehired for the following school year at least 60 days before the close of the school year. Defendant contends that it was not required to inform plaintiff that her work was unsatisfactory. It contends it was wholly irrelevant under these facts. We do not agree.

It is our conclusion that a sufficient factual question exists for a trial on the merits of the cause. Reversed and remanded for trial. No costs, a public question being involved.

Although designation as a permanent teacher is a kind of employment security, it does not relieve teachers of the obligation to perform their professional tasks at high-quality standards. When performance falls, for any of the just causes enumerated in statutes, teachers may be dismissed—if their malperformance merits such an extreme penalty. Dismissal must follow correct procedure and rest on evidence strong enough to convince a board of education, sitting as an impartial tribunal at a hearing devoted to that single question, that the board can, by majority vote, decide for dismissal.

Davis v. Callaway School District, **203** Neb. **1 (1979)**

Generalization

When an administration brings to the board's attention a recommendation for teacher dismissal, testimony and documentation must be strong, or the board cannot act in harmony with the administration. The teacher is entitled to present as persuasive a case as possible, having equal rights with the charging administrators.

Description

Anita Davis was a tenured teacher in the Callaway schools. That board terminated her employment in 1976 for "just cause" under Nebraska statutes. Evidence presented to the board of education consisted of testimony from the superintendent, the principal, and three other witnesses, along with a number of exhibits. The superintendent stated that in his opinion, she should be terminated for just cause. The principal concurred with the superintendent's recommendation. Exhibits produced some conflicts. Other witnesses were favorable for retention. The Callaway board voted to terminate the contract of Anita Davis.

Appellant contends that the evidence was insufficient to support the action of the board of education in terminating her employment. The evidence presented to the board of education consisted of testimony from George Wright, the superintendent; David Weber, the principal; Anita Davis; Frank Swathel; Carolyn Kollmeier; and a number of exhibits. The superintendent testified he has observed the appellant and her class personally; student behavior was poor; appellant was too permissive; appellant lacked organizational control; and planning; and appellant did not motivate students. He stated in his opinion she should be terminated for just cause. The principal testified that he had taught for 10 years in the system; he personally observed appellant in her class; discipline was a problem; and appellant needed to improve organization and control. He concurred with the superintendent's recommendation for termination. The testimony of the other witnesses could be summarized as favorable for retention. The exhibits likewise produced conflicts either directly or in inferences to be drawn therefrom.

Appellant argues the decision herein should be controlled by the *Sanders* case. That case is not applicable here. In *Sanders* the expert witnesses charged with the duty of evaluating the performance of the teacher was that her performance did not meet the appropriate standards. They recommended that her employment be terminated and the evidence, including the expert testimony, as a matter of law, was sufficient to support the action of the board in terminating her employment. The language in *Sanders* with reference to a standard of performance should not be interpreted to mean that in every hearing on termination before a board of education there must first be expert testimony establishing the appropriate and acceptable standard of performance before a board may consider whether particular conduct falls below that standard.

In an error, proceeding conflicting evidence will not be weighted and the order of an administrative tribunal must be affirmed if the tribunal has acted within its jurisdiction and there is sufficient competent evidence, as a matter of law, to sustain its findings and order.

The Nebraska Supreme Court held in favor of the local board, ruling that in Davis's dismissal, the procedural and substantive obligations had been met.

Teachers who are tenured sometimes run afoul of board policies or regulations in ways that bring unexpected disputes to the fore. In *Rumph v. Wayne School District*, 188 N.W.2d 71 (Mich. Court of Appeals, 1971), both teacher and board became involved in substantive errors. Having taught for nine years in Wayne, Rumph took a one-year traveling sabbatical leave at half pay, agreeing that he should file an interim and final report. Not receiving any interim report, the board suspended his salary and, on his return, informed him that his breach of contract constituted grounds for dismissal. Bringing suit, Rumph won because the board's dismissal procedure was out of harmony with the state's teacher tenure act; that is, it was procedurally defective. Discharge of a tenured teacher, then, may be made only for reasonable and just cause and only after such charges, notice, hearing, and determination by a board sitting as an impartial tribunal agree that there is sufficient and persuasive evidence to call for dismissal. Administrators who bring charges against a tenured teacher must be confident of the grounds on which they are acting and of the procedures followed in pressing those charges.

JUST CAUSE AND DUE PROCESS

In a sense, the entire structure of events and situations that must be met by a prospective teacher is protection for children. A teacher must be a college graduate, hold a valid teacher's certificate, apply for a job, and survive screening and consideration before the contract is offered and accepted. The structure is an attempt to ensure high-quality instruction in every classroom. After a teacher accepts the job, actual performance as the appointed instructional leader for the students must be periodically evaluated and a judgment made.

Initially, teachers are hired on short-term contracts—normally, of one year's duration. State statutes may differ in particulars, but most states have a specified time when probationary teachers must be told what their future for employment may be. That is, by board decisions that very normally follow administrative evaluations and recommendations, teachers are offered successive contracts or are advised that another contract will not be offered. Unless the duty is mandated in statutes, boards are not legally bound to explain why a successor term contract is not to be offered, for the teacher-as-citizen has no constitutional entitlement to such information. On the other hand, boards are not forbidden to state, privately, the reasoning used in deciding not to offer a successor term contract. Substantively, the choice is up to the board; procedurally, the board must accommodate the statutes of the state.

A teacher's performance evaluation may lead an administrator to seek improvement by replacement. Most improvement is by development of the individual, responding to supervisory questions, recommendation, and directives. Teachers tend to stay on, working over several years, being regularly evaluated, and demonstrating acceptable performance standards. When such work performance records clearly show that acceptable standards have been met, teachers pass from the probationary class into the tenured class of employees. Tenured teachers are protected in their jobs from arbitrary actions of a local board of education and can be dismissed only for just cause and only by due process, if they choose to make use of the latter job-protection item.

Just cause means that there exists a reasonable, proper, and legal motive or reason as a base for some action against the teacher. When the action is so extreme that it may result in termination of a permanent or tenured teacher, that action must be based in the statutes of the state, for tenure is a condition of employment achieved under other, and equally potent, state statutes. Oregon's legislative treatment is typical.

Grounds for dismissal of permanent teacher. (1) No permanent teacher shall be dismissed except for:

a. inefficiency;
b. immorality;
c. insubordination;
d. neglect of duty;
e. physical or mental incapacity;
f. conviction of a felony or of a crime involving moral turpitude;
g. inadequate performance;

    h. failure to comply with such reasonable requirements as the board may prescribe to show normal improvement and evidence of professional training and growth;

    i. any cause which constitutes grounds for the revocation of such permanent teacher's certificate. (Oregon Revised Statutes 342.865)

Like other states, Nebraska defines *just cause* as consisting of most of those items in the Oregon code, as well as "other conduct which interferes substantially with the continued performance of duties." When teachers achieve permanent status in their local school districts, and can be dismissed only for just cause, there is very little chance that any dismissals will occur except for the welfare of the students. Some observers feel that the burden of proof—to discover and document just cause—has shifted too heavily upon administrators and boards and that tenure has protected too many mediocre teachers. No such intention can be discerned by reading the statutes, so if low-quality teaching performance is accepted in some specific situations or settings, it may indicate a lack of systematic, discriminating evaluation and appraisal by the administrators charged with that responsibility.

Due process derives from the Fourteenth Amendment and is a procedural protection that demands a slow, conscientious, and considerate examination of the charges that may be brought against a teacher. For example, a teacher who has been neglectful of a duty assignment, who has had that omission brought up for attention by a supervisor, and who has not remedied the deficient performance may be charged before the board in whatever way the statutes have provided for. Due process demands that an impartial hearing on the charges be allowed, if the teacher so chooses. Suppose it is the teacher's view that the supervisor was prejudiced, withheld information, arbitrarily practiced the authority conferred on the position as supervisor, and lacked substantial supporting evidence of the charge. Only through the exercise of due process could the truth be discovered. Many instances of teacher evaluation are controversial and can be decided only by local boards of education, sitting as impartial tribunals, hearing charges and countercharges, and, finally, making a decision based on the evidence presented. In some states, such disputes may be referred to the commission established to examine questions of professional teaching practices. Some disputes are carried onward through appeals and become court cases.

Cadell v. Ecorse Board, 170 N.W.2d 277 (Mich. Court of Appeals, 1969)

Generalization

Boards of education may proceed against inadequate teaching performance when just cause is charged, and the whole employee relations condition is carried forward within the structure of due process.

Description

Cadell was advised by the superintendent of schools that he was acting in violation of board rules and regulations, especially in regard to job absences, tardies, and falsified sign-in times. He was suspended, pending a due process hearing in which the superintendent would recommend for dismissal. The board, sitting as an impartial tribunal, found Cadell neglectful of his duty on the facts presented by the superintendent. Cadell was dismissed, and he brought suit seeking payment of salary for the balance of the term contract or, lacking that, for the period of the time from suspension to dismissal.

In the present case the grounds for plaintiff's dismissal from employment were absences from duty without properly reporting these absences; tardiness; and falsifying sign-in times. The circuit court concluded that the board's action was authorized by law. Plaintiff did not allege in his pleadings that this action was arbitrary, unreasonable, or beyond the scope of the board's authority. He did allege that his suspension was "without adequate cause or reason." However, the board's decision was a final dismissal from duty, not a suspension.

The circuit court correctly decided that the dismissal of the plaintiff was within the defendant board's statutory authority.

Although the Michigan court upheld the board's action, it did provide one remedy for Cadell. Since he had been dismissed while valid contract was in effect, he was entitled to all salary that had accrued from the time of his suspension until he was dismissed from employment.

diLeo v. Richard Greenfield, 541 F.2d 949 (USCA 2d, Conn., 1976)

Generalization

Tenured teachers may be dismissed for due cause, just cause, or sufficient cause—according to the statutes of an individual state—when dismissal procedures are also harmonious with obligations of due process.

Description

A junior-high teacher had acquired tenure by teaching in the Bloomfield, Connecticut, school system for longer than three years. He was notified by the board that he would be terminated for exhibiting "improper conduct toward students," which was sufficient to constitute "due and sufficient cause" under the Connecticut statute that governed termination of teachers. That notification followed several meetings between school administrators and the teacher, meetings that had failed to relieve or improve diLeo's situation. A hearing occurred at which school administrators, parents, and students presented evidence regarding the teacher's misconduct as charged. Examples included failure to assist students with classwork, making statements with sexual connotations to students, failure to complete lesson plans as directed, and refusals to explain ambiguous textbook material to students. After the hearing, the board of education officially terminated the tenured teacher's employment. diLeo carried the dispute into the courts, contending that Connecticut's teacher-termination statute was unconstitutionally vague and allowing for violation of the rights of due process.

The Second Circuit Court of Appeals found for the local board and did not fault the Connecticut statute, noting that the challenged subsection of the statute, "other due and sufficient cause," was followed by five specific grounds for dismissal. All were clearly stated, each could be understood by a person of reasonable intelligence, and all related to the capacity of teachers to perform professional duties. The conduct of diLeo fell within the core of the statute's delineation of grounds for dismissal. He should have known that the conduct for which he was terminated constituted "due and sufficient cause" for dismissal under state law. Moreover, the board had given him generous notice of the conduct violations it viewed as "other due and sufficient cause in the meetings and notices prior to termination."

Contracts protect teachers but do not relieve them of the obligations to perform at a high standard and in compliance with the reasonable rules of their employing board. In *Skeim v. School District #115*, 234 N.W.2d 206 (Minn., 1975), tenured Minnesota teachers were unsuccessful in their bid to recover salary withheld by the board. Board regulations had stipulated Columbus Day as a normal school day, but the teachers took it as a holiday. Along with some other punishments, the board was upheld in withholding one day's pay. Gradations of punishment for bad performance, less than dismissal, may be meted to tenured teachers for just cause.

In *Zoll v. Allamakee Schools*, 588 F.2d 246 (USCA 8th, Iowa, 1979) a 29-year Iowa teacher was laid off because of declining enrollments. Rose Zoll had written two letters critical of the schools, and they were published in the local paper. The court rejected the school's layoff procedure as subjective and biased. Zoll was awarded reinstatement, back pay, legal fees, and expenses; the court cited a "retaliatory motive" for her nonrenewal. Somewhat similarly, in *Givhan v. Western Line Schools*, 439 U.S. 410 (Miss., 1979), the Supreme Court reversed the U.S. Circuit Court of Appeals, 5th Circuit, and ruled for the teacher, Bessie Givhan. An eight-year teacher, Givhan was terminated after making candid, direct, and private criticisms of school policies to her principal. The high court ruled that having allowed her into the office for discussion of school policies, the principal could not pose as a "captive audience" or "unwilling recipient of her views." The Court construed freedom of speech to include forceful, private expression of personal-professional views.

SUMMARY

In the administration of personnel, the culturally based, widely accepted American concept of fairness must be present. Teachers may not treat children unfairly;

neither can teachers be treated unfairly by administrators or employing boards of education. Reasonable people may view a single situation from different viewpoints, and it is from such divergence that many disputes arise. The disputes call for resolution within a system that is not vague. All parties are entitled to clarity in the statutes, rules, and regulations that will be used as a basis for judging standards of performance. Even with such a carefully laid base, presumed to be constitutionally harmonious, it is still possible, even, inevitable—that all aspects of the operation of a school system will not be seen from identical viewpoints.

Disputes and disagreements create an environment in which due process becomes important. Administrators cannot allow a teacher to continue to teach when students suffer from bad professional performance; neither can teachers become the objects of unreasonable or arbitrary judgments. The insistence on constitutionally provided due process as the procedural arena in which performance problems can be examined after preliminary judgments have been made provides a margin of safety for all parties and creates an atmosphere of reduced hostility where questionable performance can be reviewed more objectively. Tenure laws were never intended to protect incompetence or to protect against any other just cause for dismissal. When just cause exists, it deserves to be exhibited before an impartial tribunal and, on the tribunal's awareness of it and agreement that it exists, to become the base on which even the most severe decisions affecting professional life are made.

6

Administering Student Personnel

Schools exist to educate the children within the community. Compulsory attendance is embodied in statutes that require boys and girls between certain ages to attend instruction. Several states have enacted specific legislation that grants the rights of children of specified ages to attend the public schools. The compulsory-attendance statutes are based on the premise that the state is served by the development of an enlightened citizenry; that is, a public good is created. Thus parents or guardians are compelled to see that their children are educated and are subject to penalties for noncompliance with the statutes.

Students' rights have been the subject of increasing numbers of cases being heard by the courts at all levels. As a result, some substantial changes in the roles of the school administrator have occurred. This school official is being called on to serve as a pupil advocate. There are occasions when this role places the administrator in an adversarial relationship with the board of education. It thus becomes very important that the student of school law be conversant with those rights that have been adjudged to be constitutionally protected. Gone are the days when pupils were expected to leave their constitutional rights outside the schoolhouse.

Tinker v. Des Moines Community School District, 393 U.S. 502 (Iowa, 1969)

Generalization

Students are "persons" under the Constitution. Action by school officials to limit student freedom is permissible only when that action can be defended as educationally necessary and when it is the least restrictive technique that can be used in the control of student behavior.

Description

Several children announced that they planned to wear black armbands to school on certain days. The armband was to express their opposition to the U.S. participation in the Vietnam War. It was their intention to make this passive protest by way of symbolic (but silent) speech. There was no demonstration or any disruption. The school administration feared demonstration, disruption, and confrontation and implemented a policy against such apparel, sending the offending children home.

The school officials banned and sought to punish petitioners for a silent, passive expression of opinion, unaccompanied by any disorder or disturbance on the part of the petitioners. There is here no evidence whatever of petitioners' interference, actual or nascent, with the school's work or of collision with the rights of other students to be secure and to be let alone. Accordingly, this case does not concern speech or action that intrudes upon the work of the schools or the rights of other students.

Only a few of the 18,000 students in the school system wore the black armbands. Only five students were suspended for wearing them. There is no indication that the work of the schools or any class was disrupted. Outside the classrooms, a few students made hostile remarks to the children wearing armbands, but there were no threats or acts of violence on school premises.

The District Court concluded that the action of the school authorities was reasonable because it was based upon their fear of a disturbance from the wearing of armbands. But, in our system, undifferentiated fear or apprehension of disturbance is not enough to overcome the right to freedom of expression. Any departure from absolute regimentation may cause trouble. Any variation from the majority's opinion may inspire fear. Any word spoken, in class, in the lunchroom, or on the campus, that deviates from the views of another person may start an argument or cause a disturbance. But our Constitution says we must take this risk, *Terminiello v. Chicago*, 337 U.S. I (1949); and our history says that it is this sort of hazardous freedom—this kind of openness—that is the basis of our national strength and of the independence and vigor of Americans who grow up and live in this relatively permissive, often disputatious society.

In order for the State in the person of school officials to justify prohibition of a particular expression of opinion, it must be able to show that its action was caused by something more that a mere desire to avoid the discomfort and unpleasantness that always accompany an unpopular viewpoint. Certainly where there is no finding and no showing that engaging in the forbidden conduct would "materially and substantially interfere with the requirements of appropriate discipline in the operation of the school," the prohibition cannot be sustained.

In the present case, the District Court made no such finding, and our independent examination of the record fails to yield evidence that the school authorities had reason to anticipate that the wearing of the armbands would substantially interfere with the work of the school or impinge upon the rights of other students. Even an official memorandum prepared after the suspension that listed the reasons for the ban on wearing the armbands made no reference to the anticipation of such disruption.

Justice Black's dissent represented viewpoints that were prevalent in American society but are fading. He suggested that children came to school to learn and not to attempt to instruct their fellow students—especially in such esoteric areas as international relations. However, Justice Fortas wrote the strong opinion for the court, elevating symbolic speech to a level of "pure speech," and the Des Moines schools lost the case.

The concept of legal rights of children has undergone substantial change during the past two decades. Many questions have arisen concerning these rights. How much freedom should be provided to children in school? Do schoolchildren have the right of self-determination in deciding what their behavior shall be? Are the rights of schoolchildren and adults identical? Are the rights of all children—regardless of age—identical? Undoubtedly, these and other questions of a legal nature will be the basis for court cases and appeals in the future. We are finding that boards of education must review their policies and that school officials must review their procedures in an attempt to avoid costly and time-consuming litigation on the subject of student rights.

The days ahead will require changes in the operation of our schools; many of these changes will call for new, constrained approaches to pupils. The purpose of this chapter is to consider topics such as admission and attendance of students, classification and instruction of students, and control of student conduct, activities, and rights.

ADMISSION AND ATTENDANCE OF STUDENTS

Although some reactionary historians have suggested that compulsory attendance for education is a denial of basic freedoms to children, no court has so held. A nation, if it is to prosper, must rely on an enlightened citizenry. Education is to provide this enlightenment, and thus statutes have required compulsory attendance for instruction. Courts have held that several states have properly exercised their police powers in enacting compulsory attendance laws and thus have denied the charges that these laws infringe on individual liberties guaranteed by the Constitution, as noted in *Concerned Citizens v. Board of Education of Chattanooga*, 379 F.Supp. 1233 (Tenn., 1974).

In its decision in *Pierce v. Society of Sisters*, 268 U.S. 510 (Or., 1925), the Supreme Court struck down an Oregon requirement that, to comply with the compulsory-education statute, all children must attend the public school. Thus parents were assured of the right to direct the upbringing of their children and could send them to private schools, but the state could establish certain minimum standards of education for the schools, public and private. A majority of the states do not exercise such regulatory powers.

Compulsory-attendance ages are established by state statute. For example, Michigan and New York require that parents or guardians having control and charge of a child from the sixth to the sixteenth birthday shall send that child to the public schools during the entire school year. For children who attend nonpublic schools, the requirement is that instruction given to the minor shall be at least substantially equivalent to that given in a public school. (The state of Georgia requires pupils between the ages of seven and sixteen to be enrolled in a public or private school.) As a rule, the local public school superintendent is required to account for all resident children of compulsory-attendance age, whether they are enrolled in public or private school, exempted from school attendance, or taught in the home.

There is one exception to the compulsory-attendance requirement. This was determined in 1972 when the Supreme Court held, in *Wisconsin v. Yoder*, 406 U.S. 205 (1972), that the free exercise of religion clause of the First Amendment prevented a state from requiring Amish children to submit to compulsory formal educational requirements beyond the eighth grade. In the opinion of the Court, the Amish had been convincing in their argument that for almost 300 years, their sustained faith had pervaded and regulated their whole mode of life, and this would be seriously endangered, if not destroyed, by enforcement of the requirement of compulsory formal education beyond the eighth grade. Historically, compulsory age limits were related to child-labor laws. These laws permitted earlier school-leaving ages for those entering agricultural employment. This, in effect, was what the Amish children were doing after the eighth grade.

An issue that surrounds the compulsory-attendance requirement is equivalent instruction. Generally, statutes require that if one elects not to attend public school, one must obtain equivalent instruction elsewhere. Parents and guardians have attempted to meet this requirement through private schools and home instruction. In *State ex. rel. Shoreline School District #412 v. Superior Court*, 346 P.2d 999 (Wash., 1959), the Washington Supreme Court held that home instruction did not satisfy the law covering attendance at a private school. The court stated that there are three essential elements of a school: the teacher, the pupil (or pupils), and the institution (place).

Another issue that becomes entangled with the compulsory-attendance statutes is that of eligibility to attend school. It is held, generally, that eligibility to attend the public schools of a district tuition-free is extended by statute to those school-age youth who are residents of the district. We should distinguish between two terms that are applicable to this issue. *Domicile* is a place where one intends to remain indefinitely, and each person may have only one domicile. A minor child's legal domicile is that of his/her father except in special circumstances such as death of the father or separation or divorce of the parents, where custody of the child has been awarded to the mother or legal charge of the child has been placed in the hands of other persons. *Residence* is a factual place of abode, the place where one is, actually, physically living. It is held, generally, that a child has the right to attend the public school of a district in which he or she is living—unless the child is living in that district solely for the purpose of attending school there. This holding will be found in the *Fangman v. Moyers*, 8 P.2d 762 (Colo., 1932), and *Turner v. Board of Education*, 294 N.E. 2d 264 (Ill., 1973). Statutes providing for interdistrict choice are changing this.

Children living in charitable homes, child-care centers, orphanages, or with court-appointed guardians are, in the absence of contrary statutory provisions, generally considered to be children residing within the school district for school purposes, and the public school system must accept the child tuition-free.

The right of a child to attend school in a district other than that in which he or she resides is dependent on the statutes of the state in which the school district is located. Unless specifically barred by statute, school districts may accept pupils from other districts on payment of tuition. Determination of the tuition is, generally, within the statutory authority of the board of education that is to provide the instruction. As a general rule, boards of education do not accept tuition pupils if the schools are already overcrowded and if these pupils would constitute an excessive burden for the receiving schools. When school districts do accept tuition pupils, if a parent prefers to enroll a child in the schools of a district in which a child does not reside, the parent must pay the tuition. This is true even if the parent owns property and pays taxes in the receiving district, although some states, for example, New York, stipulate that the amount of the tax shall be deducted from the tuition due.

INSTRUCTION OF PUPILS

Various issues are found in this section. The courts have been called on to rule on the issues that have evolved from rules and regulations of boards of education at all levels, as well as from legislative acts and constitutional provisions.

The states have established minimum lengths of school terms. Legislatures have exercised their authority in this matter. The state of Georgia requires a minimum of 175 days of attendance for instruction, whereas the state of New York requires 180 days of instruction. When the legislature has been silent, however, local boards of education may determine the length of the school term. Within the limits established by statutes or the constitution, local boards of education may exercise their discretionary powers in establishing the opening and closing dates of the school year.

Courses of study have been prescribed by state legislatures. Such authority has been assumed as being in the interest of the welfare and safety of the nation and its citizens. The courts have sustained such legislative acts, absent actions that are arbitrary, capricious, unreasonable, or in violation of state or federal constitutions. Once the state has mandated—through legislative enactment or state board of education—that required courses of study be taught, the local board of education must comply with the mandate. Such mandates do not restrict the local board of education from instituting activities that exceed those required.

In enacting statutory provisions for the curriculum, the state may not circumscribe the rights questioned by the state or federal constitution. Typical of this provision have been the attempts by states to prohibit the teaching of certain subjects. An illustration is found in *Mo Hock KeLok Po v. Stainback*, 336 U.S. 368, (Hawaii, 1949), wherein the legislature attempted to prohibit the teaching of any language other than English to children who had not passed the fourth grade. This act was declared to be unconstitutional. In *Steve v. Board of Education of the City of St. Louis*, 233 S.W.2d 697 (Mo., 1950), the court held that when, in the absence of mandatory statutes, a board of education has complete discretion in determining what courses shall be offered, continued, or discontinued, its discretion will not be interfered with by the court.

Challenges have been made to the inclusion of certain topics in the curriculum. One of them that has been hotly debated in recent years is sex education. In *Hobolth v. Greenway*, 218 N.W.2d 98 (Mich., 1974), it was held that the offering of a course authorized by state statutes was not unconstitutional when attendance in a sex-education course was not compulsory, and it was held, furthermore, that the statutory authorization for offering this instruction was not an illegal delegation of authority. With the rapid spread of AIDS, it seems likely that sex education will come to be viewed as more of a personal/community health need. Generally, the courts will not interfere with courses of study that a board of education, acting within the scope of its authority, prescribes.

There are specific instances, nonetheless, where the courts have required programs. They are found, primarily, where the courts have required remedial opportunities. In a recent decision in the matter of *Debra P. v. Turlington*, 474 F.Supp. 257 (Fla., 1979), the court stayed the use of a minimum-competency test, serving as a graduation requirement, for a four-year waiting period until the traces of a dual school system were gone and the students had been provided with remediation for their deficiencies.

A broad construction of the term *curriculum* includes more than the usual academic subjects. In *Mathias v. School District of Trafford Borough*, 35 West [Westmoreland County] 143 (Pa., 1953), the court held that organized sports could properly be included in the school program under the management of the board of education. Furthermore, the court in *Woodson v. School District #26*, 274 P. 728 (Kan., 1929), held that athletics were a part of the regular school program. This is a strained definition.

Questions have been raised about the authority of boards of education to require pupils to wear uniforms for physical education classes. In deciding this issue in *Mitchell v. McCall*, 143 So.2d 629 (Ala., 1962), the court held that required participation in physical education classes did not violate the student's constitutional rights so long as the student was not required to perform any exercise that would be immodest when performed in ordinary wearing apparel. The issue in this instance dealt with the requirement that pupils wear prescribed uniforms that were deemed to be immodest by them or their parents. Contests with parents over minor issues should be avoided.

In many states, the state high school athletic or activities association prescribes rules that govern member schools. Among these rules are those that regulate the eligibility of the team members. One must remember that since many of these cases are decided in particular states, the governing statutes are those of that state and are not applicable, universally, to all 50 states. In *Art Gaines Baseball Camp, Inc. v. Houston*, 500 S.W.2d 735 (Mo., 1973), the court held that the state activities association could lawfully impose a regulation that governed eligibility of secondary school students. In this instance, the provision was that a student who attended a summer camp specializing in one sport for more than two weeks would be declared ineligible to participate in that sport for the following year. One should note that regulations of state athletic or activities associations have not always been upheld. Prevailing opinion in this area is that a board of education cannot delegate its powers to make policy or rules to a state athletic association. An illustration of this application is found in *Bunger v. Iowa H.S. Athletic Association*, 197 N.W.2d 555 (Iowa, 1972), where the court found against the state athletic association rule that made ineligible for athletic competition a boy who used or transported alcoholic beverages or drugs— or who had knowledge that they were being transported in the car he was riding in.

The Education Amendments of 1972, Title IX, Section 901, provided, "No person in the United States shall, on the basis of sex, be excluded from participation in, be denied the benefits of, or be subjected to discrimination under any education program or activity receiving Federal financial assistance." This provision, when applied by means of the regulations that were promulgated to put it into effect, led to considerable litigation. Furthermore, litigation on the extent to which girls may participate on boys' athletic teams was pursued under the civil rights laws. In the first instance, in *Brenden v. Independent School District*, 477 F.2d 1292 (Mich., 1973), the court held that girls were entitled to participate in a boys' interscholastic athletic program if it was shown that they could compete with equal ability and results on those teams and if there were no alternative competitive teams for girls. In the second instance, in *National Organization for Women Essex County Chapter v. Little League Baseball, Inc.*, 318 A.2d 33 (N.J., 1974), the court held that Little League Baseball, Inc., in refusing to permit girls to play on boys' baseball teams, discriminated against the girls and violated the nation's civil rights laws. (See also *Habitz by Habitz v. Louisiana High School Athletic Association*, 915 F.2d 164 [La., 1990]).

ORGANIZATION OF INSTRUCTION

Local boards of education have the authority to determine the grade levels to be maintained in the school district. The large majority of the schools in the United States are organized on a graded system. In *Ashton v. Jones*, 47 Lack. [Lackawanna County] Jur. 229 (Pa., 1946), the court held that graded schools, being the preferred method, could stand and that the court would not interfere when a board of education directed that instruction should be given by this method and that children should be sent from a one-teacher school to a larger, graded school.

Boards of education, operating within statutory and constitutional requirements and limitations, shall determine what grades and schools are to be operated within the system. Furthermore, school boards are permitted substantial discretion in determining and adopting courses of study that respond to local conditions.

Each LEA possesses the authority to determine instructional levels and assignment of pupils to grades and classes. At the same time, assignment and promotion and promotion of pupils has been a source of considerable litigation, with parents at odds with the arrangements established by their own local board. In affirming the board's authority for placement of pupils, the court in *Isquith v. Levitt*, 137 N.Y.2d 497 (1955), held, "A board of education is within its legal right in placing children in the kindergarten or 1st or 2nd or any other grade in accordance with its judgment based upon the mental attainment of the child." In this instance, parents had insisted that their son, being of appropriate age and having spent a portion of a year in school, be placed in the first grade. The board of education disagreed, basing its decision on the fact that the boy's attendance in kindergarten could not be considered adequate; furthermore, the board had doubts that the son's scholarship was adequate for first-grade work.

Challenges to board authority in promotion, retention, and demotion have been numerous and are not new to the education scene. One, in particular, that affirms the board's right to determine methods of promotion—including permission to "skip" a grade—is found in *Sycamore Board of Education v. State*, 88 N.E. 412 (Ohio, 1909). A child had completed the sixth grade successfully. The parents provided tutoring during the summer so that he would be prepared to enter the eighth grade at the beginning of the next school year. In the fall, when he attempted to enter the eighth grade, his admission was refused because there had been no authorization for him to "skip" the seventh grade. The parents sought a writ of mandamus, which the Ohio Supreme Court denied. In doing so, the court said, "Double promotion of a pupil from one grade to the second higher grade is discretionary with the board of education, and in the absence of evidence of permission by the board the court will not order it to be done."

The courts have been asked to rule on the use of grades as a part of the school's disciplinary policy. In *Wermuth v. Bernstein*, 1965 S.L.D. 128, the New Jersey commissioner of education held: "The use of marks and grades as deterrents or as punishment is likewise usually ineffective in producing the desired results and is educationally not defensible. Whatever system of marks and grades a school may devise will have serious inherent limitations at best, and it must not be further handicapped by attempting to serve disciplinary purposes also." That is, grades should represent a professional assessment of the pupil's academic accomplishment during a discrete period—and should not be diverted to another service.

At the same time, public school boards do have substantial powers that are in harmony with generally accepted behavioral norms for students. Boards and administrators need to control instruction in some specific curricular areas, and they are obligated to curtail student behavior that is aimed toward viciousness and hostility. Speech can be injurious, and freedom of speech is not an absolute, it is relative.

Hazelwood School District v. Kuhlmeier, **484 U.S. 260 (Mo., 1988)**

Generalization

Students who are in journalism classes, including those who are editors of student newspapers, are still enrolled in the curriculum of the school, which is under the control and direction of the local board of education.

Description

At issue was constraint by the high school principal of printed words in stories that had been written by members of the staff of the school newspaper, the *Spectrum*. Finding in an upcoming issue two stories that went beyond what could be considered "good taste" and that could certainly injure some of the students who were identifiable in the stories, he directed that the stories be deleted. This case, then, arose out of the anger of students who contended that censorship had been inappropriately applied to them, denying them freedom of speech.

The facts of the case evolved from an incident in which the principal insisted on the deletion of certain stories that had been scheduled for release in the *Spectrum*, the school newspaper. One story recounted certain personal experiences of pregnant girls in the school. The other told personal accounts of siblings whose parents were carrying through a divorce proceeding and was strongly accusative toward the father. On reviewing the paper before publication, the principal objected to the name identification of the family and objected to the pregnancy story on the basis of the immaturity of many of the regular readers of the *Spectrum*. Staff members of the paper and students in the school filed suit, alleging prior restraint in violation of the First Amendment. The federal district court ruled for the school; on appeal, the Eighth Circuit Court of Appeals ruled against the school. The United States Supreme Court reversed, ruling for the school and commenting that the "First Amendment rights of students in the public schools are not automatically coextensive with the rights of adults in other settings, and must be applied in light of the special characteristics of the school environment."

Stipulating that school control over the speech of students had to be based in legitimate concerns for education, the Court narrowed and refined its broader ruling of 20 years earlier in *Tinker*. The ruling was received with some alarm by the commercial press of the nation, but there is a very clear distinction between how and what a city newspaper may print and what is reasonable and allowable in a school paper that is a part of the curriculum of that school. In *Kuhlmeier*, the testimony of the principal revealed that when he had met with the student staff to explain his actions, he had told them that their stories were "inappropriate, personal, sensitive, and unsuitable." The episode became a classic example of the tensions that exist between First Amendment rights of students and the states' rights to structure educational programs that may include an intent to inculcate certain community values. Angered, the students on the staff of the *Spectrum* brought suit in federal court.

The Court identified several specific activities that pertain to any building principal.

The initial paragraph of the pregnancy article declared that "[a]ll names have been changed to keep the identity of these girls a secret." The principal concluded that the students' anonymity was not adequately protected, however, given the other identifying information in the article and the small number of pregnant students at the school. Indeed, a teacher at the school credibly testified that she could positively identify at least one of the girls and possibly all three. It is likely that many students at Hazelwood East would have been at least as successful in identifying the girls. Reynolds therefore could reasonably have feared that the article violated whatever pledge of anonymity had been given to the pregnant students. In addition, he could reasonably have been concerned that the article was not sufficiently sensitive to the privacy interests of the students' boyfriends and parents, who were discussed in the article but who were given no opportunity to consent to its publication or to offer a response. The article did not contain graphic accounts of sexual activity. The girls did comment in the article, however, concerning their sexual histories and their use or nonuse of birth control. It was not unreasonable for the principal to have concluded that such frank talk was inappropriate in a school-sponsored publication distributed to 14-year-old freshmen and presumably taken home to be read by students' even younger brothers and sisters.

The student who was quoted by name in the version of the divorce article seen by Principal Reynolds made comments sharply critical of her father. The principal could reasonably have concluded that an individual publicly identified as an inattentive parent— indeed, as one who chose "playing cards with the guys" over home and family—was entitled to an opportunity to defend himself as a matter of journalistic fairness. These concerns were shared by both of *Spectrum's* faculty advisers for the 1982–1983 school year, who testified that they would not have allowed the article to be printed without deletion of the student's name.

There are, then, certain things that may not be said before an immature audience. This is not a new concept in Western civilization or in American culture.

The Eighth Circuit Court had wrestled with the question of what constituted a public forum. That is, the First Amendment provides great latitude for what may be said in a public forum. In this instance, the Hazelwood School Board Policy 348.51 and the "Hazelwood East Curriculum Guide" spoke in harmony to the fact that the school paper was a laboratory experiment within the journalism classes; that is, it was a part of the school curriculum and, like all other parts of the curriculum, was under the jurisdiction of the local governing board. The circuit court based much of its holding on its particular interpretation of *Tinker*, an interpretation that the Supreme Court said "does not, of course, even accurately reflect our holding in *Tinker*." Noting, also, that in *Fraser* it had held that "a school need not tolerate student speech that is inconsistent with its basic educational mission, the justices of the Supreme Court lined up to reverse the circuit court in a 5–3 decision.

The policy of school officials toward *Spectrum* was reflected in Hazelwood School Board Policy 348.51 and the Hazelwood East Curriculum Guide. Board Policy 348.51 provided that "[s]chool sponsored publications are developed within the adopted curriculum and its educational implications in regular classroom activities." The Hazelwood East Curriculum Guide described the Journalism II course as a "Laboratory situation in which the students publish the school newspaper applying skills they have learned in Journalism I." The lessons that were to be learned from the Journalism II course, according to the Curriculum Guide, included development of journalistic skills under deadline pressure, "the legal, moral, and ethical restrictions imposed upon journalists within the school community," and "responsibility and acceptance of criticism for articles of opinion." Journalism II was taught by a faculty member during regular class hours. Students received grades and academic credit for their performance in the course.

School officials did not deviate in practice from their policy that production of *Spectrum* was to be part of the educational curriculum and a "regular classroom activit[y]." The District Court found that Robert Stergos, the journalism teacher during most of the 1982–1983 school year, "both had the authority to exercise and in fact exercised a great deal of control over *Spectrum*." (607 F. Supp., at 1453)

Finally, it is pertinent to observe that the Court spent some time analyzing the question of what constitutes a forum for public expression. It pointed out that public schools are not public streets, public parks, or the other "traditional public forums" that have been used for citizen assembly and communication in the history of the nation. With no public forum having been created, it followed that school officials "may impose reasonable restrictions on the speech of students."

The question of degrees of board control also arouse in *Bethel School District #403 v. Fraser*, 478 U.S. 675 (Wash., 1986). The First Amendment provides for the freedoms of speech, religion, press, and assembly and the right of citizens to petition the government, seeking a redress of grievances. It was freedom of speech, delivered orally, that was at issue in *Fraser*. Alleging that Matthew Fraser had acted outside the standards of appropriate speech for students, in violation of school rules and in disregard of warnings from faculty not to proceed, the LEA lost the issue at the level of the district court, lost it at the circuit court of appeals, and won before the United States Supreme Court.

Speaking before an assembly of about 600 students, many of whom were not yet 15 years of age, Matthew Fraser had delivered a speech that featured sexual innuendo. He was speaking during school hours, nominating a fellow student for a school elective office. Showing the manuscript of the speech before it was delivered, Fraser consulted with several faculty members, some of whom warned him not to deliver the speech and pointed out why it was inappropriate. Called to account to an assistant principal on the next day, Fraser admitted that some listeners might have considered his speech to be vulgar, obscene, or lewd.

Because of that episode, Fraser was penalized, losing days in school and having his name removed from the list of speakers at the impending graduation ceremonies.

The case moved quickly into the district court, and that court directed that because the student's rights to freedom of speech had been violated, the school should pay the damages and legal fees, should reinstate Fraser in school, and should allow him to proceed as a speaker at commencement.

It is quite possible that the ingeniously constructed metaphor, based in explicit allusions to sexual activity but used to describe the vigor of the political candidate being nominated, deserved admiration for its imagination and creativity. It could also have been heard as an insult to any female. However, in that auditorium setting, and in the face of the school's disruptive-conduct rule, it was at least suspect as outside the standards of behavior demanded of students in the Bethel schools. Taking note of *Tinker* and the First Amendment, the Court proceeded to reverse the Eighth Circuit of Appeals, commenting, "It is a highly appropriate function of public school education to prohibit the use of vulgar and offensive terms in public discourse." Further, the Court stipulated, "Given the school's need to be able to impose disciplinary sanctions for a wide range of unanticipated conduct disruptive of the educational process, the school disciplinary rules need not be as detailed as a criminal code."

The well-known Bethel public school rule stated:

In addition to the criminal acts defined above, the commission of, or participation in certain noncriminal activities or acts may lead to disciplinary action. Generically, these are acts which disrupt and interfere with the educational process.

Earlier, the judiciary had defined disruptive conduct in schools as follows:

Disruptive Conduct. Conduct which materially and substantially interferes with the educational process is prohibited, including the use of obscene, profane language or gestures. (755 F. 2d 1356, 1357)

With those two parts taken together to compose a standard, the Court then measured the speech that Fraser had delivered in support of a candidate for an office in student government:

I know a man who is firm—he's firm in his pants, he's firm in his shirt, his character is firm—but most . . . of all, his belief in you, the students in Bethel, is firm.

Jeff Kuhlman is a man who takes his point and pounds it in. If necessary, he'll take an issue and nail it to the wall. He doesn't attack things in spurts—he drives hard, pushing and pushing until finally—he succeeds.

Jeff is a man who will go to the very end—even the climax, for each and every one of you.

So vote for Jeff for A.S.B. vice president—he'll never come between you and the best our high school can be.

Ruling for the school district and against Fraser, the Court observed that the necessity for controlled proceedings in any comments delivered in an organization had been recognized by no less an advocate of freedom from the rules of government than Thomas Jefferson. It was Jefferson's *Manual of Parliamentary Practice* that set forward the prohibition of "impertinent" speech and that provided that "no person is to use indecent language against the proceedings of the House [of Representatives]." The Court stated, "The determination of what manner of speech in the classroom or in school assembly is inappropriate properly rests with the (local) school board." The Court added, "The role and purpose of the American public school system were well described by two historians, who stated: '[P]ublic education must prepare pupils for citizenship in the Republic.' "

Boards, in the absence of specific statutory limitations, may prescribe graduation requirements provided they are reasonable. Given the authority to prescribe reasonable graduation requirements, the board of education may deny graduation to students who for any reason fail or refuse to meet them. Once the student has completed the required courses and possesses the necessary qualifications to entitle him or her to a diploma, the board must perform a ministerial act that is mandatory and must issue the student a diploma.

Participation in graduation exercises has been the subject of litigation. In *Valentine v. Independent School District*, 183 N.W. 434 (Iowa, 1921), the court held that a student may not have his diploma withheld for refusal to wear a cap and gown at graduation exercises, but he may legally be denied the privilege of participation in the exercises of his Iowa high school. As the legitimate governing agency, boards do exert substantial control at different points of a school's operation.

CONTROL OF THE CURRICULUM

The school system has the function and the professional staff has the authority to determine the proper mode of instruction for the students. Early in the history of American education, as noted in *Trustees of School v. People*, 87 Ill. 303 (1877), the court held that although the parents may make a reasonable selection of courses, this does not give the parents the right to insist that their child be taught courses not in the curriculum of the school. In another holding, *Wulff v. Inhabitants of Wakefield*, 109 N.E. 358 (Miss., 1915), the court held that pupils may not refuse to study a subject because the parents object to the method of instruction used by the teacher if that subject is a bona fide part of the adopted curriculum.

Study of State Legal Standards for the Provision of Public Education, a study conducted by the National Institute for Education, summarized the law on public school curriculum and concluded that in all states, the local public school district must offer a curriculum that the state prescribes. Furthermore, it was found that the degree of control exercised by each LEA differs from state to state. States do set guidelines within which local school districts must operate in establishing their curriculum. Some states are able to enforce their requirements by considering the district's curriculum a requirement for accreditation. Among the sanctions that may be applied for noncompliance could be the loss of state-approved status or the loss of state aid.

Curriculum is a word of extended definitions, a professional term also used widely by anyone speaking about the content of the schools. Taken in a narrow context, curriculum pertains only to courses that are given regularly for credit; the broader context would include all life experiences that are provided by the school. Generally, the courts have accepted the judgment of local school authorities about what subject matter is appropriate to public education and what is intended as the curriculum in their schools.

With the expansion of school endeavors into areas that, formerly, had been reserved for other institutions—including the home—we have found increased legal conflict. We see an expression of this in *West Virginia Board of Education v. Barnette*, 319 U.S. 624 (W.Va., 1943), a landmark flag-salute case, when the Court said, "As government pressure toward unity becomes greater, so strife becomes more bitter as to whose unity it shall be." The Court allowed the pupils to choose whether to participate in the salute to the flag.

Local boards of education possess implied delegated powers to offer courses beyond those required by the state. Reviewing the many decisions dealing with the curriculum, we find quite liberal treatment by the courts of these powers. This treatment can be traced back to *Kalamazoo* (1874). There, the Michigan Supreme Court held that a local board of education did have the power to maintain a high school. The reverse is true, also, in that the courts have upheld the right of boards of education to drop a course or a portion of the curriculum that is not mandated by the state but that has been offered locally over a period of time. In supporting the right of the board of education to deal with curricular matters, the court, in *Jones v. Holes*, 6 A.2d 101 (Pa. 1939), recognized that it is an administrative function of boards of education and administrators to meet changing conditions and to create new courses, reassign teachers, and rearrange the curriculum.

Selection of textbooks, library books, and supplementary materials must be pursuant to statutes. Under New York statutes, a *textbook* is "a book which a pupil is required to use as a text for a semester or more in a particular class in the school he legally attends." Again, it is "a book which is selected and approved by the board of a school district and which contains a presentation of principles of a subject, or which is a literary work relevant to the study of a subject required for the use of classroom pupils" under the Michigan School Code. In the state of Georgia, all textbooks purchased with state funds must be selected from a list approved by the state board of education.

Thus with respect to selection of textbooks, states fall into two categories. There are the "text-adoption" states—for example, Alabama, California, Georgia, North Carolina, Tennessee, Texas, and Wisconsin—where the local board of education selects its textbooks from a list prepared by the state education agency. And there are the "local adoption" states—Colorado, Iowa, Massachusetts, New York, Pennsylvania, and Wyoming—where the local board of education may adopt any textbook.

There is no question about the legal right of the state to prescribe textbooks or, through statutory enactment, delegate that responsibility to local boards of education. Providing supplementary books and instructional materials has been within the discretion of local boards if these items are appropriate for the course or program being taught. Citizens cannot require a board of education to remove a book from use in the curriculum in the absence of proof that it is sectarian, "subversive," or "maliciously written," as affirmed in *Rosenburg v. Board of Education of City of New York*, 92 N.Y.S.2d 344 (1949). More recently, in a conflict in West Virginia between patrons and the board, a case that achieved national attention, the federal district court held in *Williams v. Board of Education of County of Kanawha*, 388 F.Supp. 92 (W.Va., 1975), that the use of controversial textbooks does not violate the constitutional principle of separation of church and state. Parents had objected to the books on the ground that they discourage Christian principles and good citizenship. In its decision, the court said that the First Amendment "does not guarantee that nothing about religion will be taught in the schools." Furthermore, the court noted that material in some of these controversial textbooks was "offensive to plaintiff's beliefs, choices of language, and code of conduct." Nonetheless, the court could find no cause for reversing the board of education's position.

In a related case, *Minarcini v. Strongsville City School District*, 541 F.2d 577 (Ohio, 1976), the plaintiffs challenged the board of education's right to exclude certain books from its selection of high school texts and the right of this board of education to remove from the school library those books that had been approved by a prior board. In the first instance, the court upheld the right of the board of education to refuse to approve new texts and, in the second instance, ruled that the board could not constitutionally censor or remove books that had been lawfully placed in the library by a predecessor board. This finding lacks for administrative practicality and has not found widespread acceptance by other courts.

In recent years there has been an increasing number of challenges to the selection of text and library books. Many of the literary works of importance in this century have been banned, according to an American Library Association report that appeared in the January 1975 issue of the *Phi Delta Kappan*. The books most often banned are Salinger's *Catcher in the Rye*, Steinbeck's *Grapes of Wrath*, and Vonnegut's *Slaughterhouse Five*. Among the other books that have been banned by schools are *Jonathan Livingston Seagull, Silas Marner, Moby Dick, Brave New World, 1984,* and *Fahrenheit 451*.

There is not universal agreement on text and library book matters. Each state's court system will rule on complaints in the light of that particular state's statutes. Wisconsin, in an attempt to prohibit the use of subversive textbooks in its schools, specifies in Section 118.03(2)(1972) of its statutes, "No book shall be adopted for use or be used in any public school which falsifies the facts regarding the history of our nation, or which defames our nation's founders, or misrepresents the ideals and causes for which they struggled and sacrificed, or which contains propaganda favorable to any foreign government." Continued litigation with respect to text and library books seems likely. Boards of education and school administrators should consider, develop, and adopt policies governing the selection and review of complaints in this regard.

Tests have widespread uses in schools. Those tests that are used for placement of children are the subject of considerable litigation. Of concern to the courts are the outcomes of testing. Guidelines that schools should follow when administering tests that may discriminate against some of the children in a school are found in the Fifth Circuit Court of Appeals ruling in *U.S. v. Georgia Power Co.*, 474 F.2d 906 (Ga., 1973). First, the school must demonstrate that the test has separate validation scores for each minority group on which it is to be used. This is known as *differential validity*. It differs from *content validity*—the question of whether the test measures characteristics that are found among people in a particular grouping—and *predictive validity*—the ability of scores on the test to relate highly to success in a school curriculum or on a job.

The second guideline deals with the level of confidence of the test. This should be at the 5 percent (0.05) level, meaning that the probability of obtaining the same test results through mere chance is no greater than 1 in 20. The third guideline deals with statistical significance. Thus there should be a sample of sufficient size to be statistically significant. When a test is given to a small group (sample) that may not be typical of a larger population, the results may be suspect and subject to being declared void. The fourth guideline requires that the test be administered to all testees under substantially similar circumstances as were present for those pupils who were used in standardizing the test originally.

Grouping is a mode of operation in American schools; our economy precludes the ideal of one pupil per teacher. Thus it is incumbent upon each board of education to take the necessary steps to avoid discrimination and to assure that placement is fair at the same time that it is used as a matter of economical education. If that is done and if there are provisions for a periodic review of the policy, generally the school district can withstand challenges to its testing and grouping system.

In 1967 the grouping policies and practices in the Washington, D.C., school system were challenged. The charge was that the practices unconstitutionally deprived black and other poor public schoolchildren of their rights to educational opportunity equal to that of majority and more affluent public schoolchildren. On the basis of examinations given early in the school career of each child, children were assigned to curricular tracks. There was no provision for compensatory education, and once assigned to a track, children found it difficult to move to another track. In *Hobson v. Hansen*, 269 F.Supp. 401 (D.C., 1967), the United States District Court found the concept used by the school system to be "undemocratic and discriminatory." The court thus barred the school system from using ability grouping that failed to include and implement a concept of compensatory education. On appeal, the United States Court of Appeals, D.C. Circuit, upheld the order that the track system of pupil classification be abandoned.

In *Larry P. v. Riles*, 343 F.Supp. 1306 (Cal., 1972), *aff'd* 502 F.2d 963 (1974), the Federal District Court for the Northern District of California on October 16, 1979, permanently enjoined the use of standardized intelligence tests in California for the purpose of identifying black schoolchildren for placement in classes for the educable mentally retarded (EMR). In its decision, the court noted that a clearly disproportionate number of black schoolchildren were represented in California's EMR classes. On the average, black schoolchildren made up 10 percent of the school-age population but represented 27 percent of the enrollment in EMR classes. The court's order enjoined the use of standardized I.Q. tests on black children for the purpose of determining EMR placement unless the court gives prior approval for the testing. Permission may be secured only if the defendants can demonstrate to the court's satisfaction that the test is not culturally or racially biased, that the test will be administered in a nondiscriminatory manner, and that the intended test has been determined to be reasonably accurate in its ability to diagnose mild mental retardation.

In *PASE v. Hannon*, 49 L.Wk 2087 (Ill., 1980), the decision was diametrically opposed to *Larry P. v. Riles*. Judge John Grady issued a 117-page decision in which he upheld the use of I.Q. tests, when used in conjunction with other criteria, for the placement of Illinois schoolchildren in special classes for the mentally handicapped. In acknowledging that the two children named in the suit were inappropriately placed, he said those mistakes were caused by misinterpretation of the tests, not racial bias. He attributed differences in test scores between blacks and whites to differences in socioeconomic conditions. "Plaintiffs' theory of cultural bias simply ignores the fact that black children perform differently from each other on the tests. It also fails to explain the fact that some black children perform better than most whites."

The plaintiff in *Hunter v. Board of Education of Montgomery County*, 425 A.2d 681 (Mo., 1981), sued the board of education and three teachers for "educational malpractice," claiming that the defendants failed to teach him properly. The trial court held that the maintenance of such a suit would not be permitted in the state. On appeal, the trial court's decision was affirmed, and the court said that public policy bars an action for educational malpractice. To allow such suits would require courts to sit in judgment not only of educational policies and matters entrusted by the legislature to each state department of education and to the LEAs but also of the day-to-day implementation of those policies as teachers function in their classrooms.

A recent test of board control was *Board of Education of Westside Community Schools v. Mergens*, 110 S.Ct. 3356 (Neb., 1990). That litigation had its origin in P.L. 93–377, signed into law on August 11, 1984, by President Ronald

Reagan. Bearing on facilities use and on interpretation of the term *curriculum*, the law is entitled the Equal Access Act. Westside (Omaha) High School operated under a board policy directing that all groups and clubs, recognized by the school and meeting after school hours, should have faculty sponsorship. Mergens sought recognition and permission for a Christian religious group to meet after school hours, but without faculty sponsorship. Denied, she sought an injunction against the school on the basis of violation of the Equal Access Act.

Winning at the district court, but losing at the circuit level, the board of education appealed to the Supreme Court. Justice O'Connor wrote the opinion; three justices concurred, and four others concurred in the judgment that Westside High did not have a closed forum but did have a limited open forum and that the act, applied to Westside, did not advance religion but did withstand scrutiny under the Establishment Clause.

The reasons for the decision, as voiced in the opinion, were that (1) accommodation of religion in the Equal Access Act is neutral; (2) only a closed forum is assurance that the act does not apply to any high school that receives any amount of federal support; (3) the existence of even one noninstructional group or club is evidence of an open forum or a limited open forum; and (4) allowing clubs or groups to meet on premises, after school hours but without official recognition, is denial of equal access.

This finding appears to represent a philosophical shift by the Supreme Court from, say, the strict separation pronounced in *Vitale*. It hinges on a definition of the term *curriculum* that is exceedingly narrow and substantially out of phase with the comprehensive American high school. The definition seems to say that any school that has any extracurricular program for which there is not a corresponding grade given must be open to the Equal Access Act.

STUDENT CONTROL

Partially addressed above, some other aspects of student control merit consideration. Questions over how schools can control student behavior continue to provide sources of litigation. The reasonableness of student searches on school premises is one such issue. The courts continue to use a lower standard for searches performed by school personnel than for searches by law-enforcement personnel outside the school premises. A recent case has received considerable publicity. In *Doe v. Renfrow*, 475 F.Supp. 1012 (Ind., 1979), an Indiana federal court upheld the use of dogs in a classroom as a means for detecting the presence of drugs on students and in their possessions. The plaintiff argued that her Fourth Amendment rights were violated through the use of the dogs and the search of her pockets and person. The court ruled that the use of the dogs, per se, did not constitute an unreasonable search, nor did the holding of students in their homerooms for one and one-half hours constitute a mass detention in violation of the Fourth Amendment. The court reasoned that the use of dogs was undertaken in accordance with the in loco parentis doctrine, and since the school officials had substantial evidence that the use of drugs had increased substantially before the search, there was reasonable cause to believe that school rules had been violated.

However, the judge did note that the searches undertaken that day were only for the purpose of determining violations of school rules. No criminal charges were filed, through a previous agreement with the participating police officers. The school district did mete out suspensions and expulsions from school as penalties, but no issues were raised about the appropriateness or severity of these penalties. On the other hand, had criminal charges been filed, the "court's reasoning and conclusion may well have been different . . . the school may well have had to satisfy a standard of probable cause rather than reasonable cause to believe" that drugs might be found.

With respect to the nude search of the student after the dog alert, the court ruled that the search was unreasonable under the lesser standard of reasonable cause applied in the case. To make such a search permissible, there needed to be evidence that the student, in fact, did possess contraband. The court, in relying on *Bellnier v. Lund*, 485 F.Supp. 47 (N.Y., 1977), noted that in determining reasonableness of the search, the following factors were important: the student's age, the student's history and record in school, the seriousness and prevalence of the problem to which the search is directed, and the exigency requiring an immediate warrantless search. The court could find nothing in the student's record that supported the reasonableness of this nude search. The court did, however, find that the school officials had acted in good faith and with a regard for the welfare and health of the plaintiff, and the court then held the defendant school officials to be immune from liability in the case.

Locker searches require a lesser burden of reasonable cause than do searches of a student's person or effects. Lockers belong to the school and are merely loaned to the student, and this should be made clear in all communications to students. The courts do agree, generally, that a student can claim privacy in his/her locker with respect to other students but not against school officials. In meeting the test of providing a safe place, the principal has the right, even the duty, to search lockers for contraband so that the safety of the students might be protected. This right becomes a duty when there is a suspicion that contraband may be deposited in a locker.

The case *State v. Stein*, 456 P.2d 1 (Kan., 1969), *cert. denied*, 90 U.S. 966 (Kan., 1970), dealt with a burglary. On the day after a burglary at a coin shop, two police officers appeared in the principal's office of this Kansas school and requested that the locker of a certain boy—a student at the high school—be opened. The boy consented to the opening of the locker. The principal opened the locker and found a key to a locker at the bus depot. The police officers, armed with a search warrant, searched the bus depot locker and found some of the stolen coins. As a result, the boy was found guilty of burglary. In upholding the conviction, the court held that the principal had acted properly in searching the locker and, also, was not required to give a Miranda-type warning of citizen rights to the student in doing so.

The presence of student-operated vehicles on school property may bring them under the authority of the school official. It would appear that the best course of action by a principal who suspects that articles of a dangerous nature are concealed in a car would be to notify the police. Without a search warrant, there is some doubt that the principal could search the car unless contraband was in plain sight or the principal had *probable* cause to suspect that the vehicle was being used for illegal purposes.

New Jersey v. T.L.O., 105 S.Ct. 733 (N.J., 1985), established current precedent for the use of student searches. A prominent factor bearing on expansion of the conditions of warrantless searches is the debilitating presence of drugs in American society.

The origin of this case was a teacher's report to an assistant principal that two girls were seen smoking in a restroom. Accosted, T.L.O. denied smoking but did give over her purse on request. Opening it and looking, the principal found cigarettes and rolling papers. Looking further, he found a tobacco-like substance in a plastic bag, a marijuana pipe, a debtor's ledger, and $44, most of it in dollar bills.

Both parents and police were called. T.L.O. was arrested as a minor in possession with intent to distribute. In court, her attorney moved to suppress the evidence as taken during an unreasonable search and seizure, violating the Fourth Amendment. At trial court, T.L.O. lost; at appeal, the New Jersey Supreme Court ruled the search as unreasonable. The state appealed to the United States Supreme Court, and the justices balanced the student's interests in privacy against the interest of educators to provide discipline, control, and a safe place at school.

By this 6–3 decision, the traditional restrictions imposed on searches from the Fourth Amendment were reduced. That is, (1) school officials do not need a warrant before searching a student suspected of breaking the law or the rules of the school; (2) school officials do not need probable cause to do a warrantless search; (3) school officials must act reasonably when searching without a warrant. In the view of the Supreme Court, the finding of one item in T.L.O.'s purse very reasonably led the administrator to look further. This opinion decreased the standards necessary to conduct warrantless searches of students.

Boards of education and administrators should develop and put into effect policies governing warrantless searches. Specifically, such searches should not occur unless the administrator has a *reasonable* basis for believing that illegal contraband is secreted in a locker or unless the student has freely consented in writing to such a search. If a reasonable basis for a search does not exist, then consent must be obtained from individual students for each search. Thus such a policy should provide adequate authority to the school officials to keep dangerous contraband out of the school while, at the same time, giving students a small, secure place of privacy from peers that ought to be each citizen's right.

In order that teachers may teach and an appropriate environment be provided for learning, students in school are expected to conduct themselves in a manner that will not infringe on the rights of others by creating distractions in the classroom. Educators do have considerable latitude in controlling student be-havior. A legal term that defines the relationship of educator to pupil is *in loco parentis* ("in place of the parent"). Sir William Blackstone in his *Commentaries* explained it thus: "A parent may also delegate part of his parental authority, during his life, to the tutor or schoolmaster of his child; who is then *in loco parentis*, and has such a portion of the power of the parents viz. that of restraint and correction as may be necessary to answer the purposes for which he is employed."

Since Blackstone developed that definition, there has been much modification of the concept of in loco parentis. No longer can school authorities make arbitrary decisions about pupil behavior and discipline without facing some challenges. The courts have set conditions that boards of education must meet if the boards expect that their actions, designed to control student behavior, will be upheld.

Corporal punishment in schools is the infliction of physical pain upon a student for his/her misconduct. The statutes of the particular states deal with this matter in unique ways. Some states authorize it, some states forbid it, and other states do not mention it but, by implication, authorize or allow it. New Jersey, Ne-braska, and Massachusetts are among a growing number of states that forbid it by statute. Some states forbid it by a policy of the state boards of education. In light of the federal and state statutes designed to prevent child abuse, corporal punishment is a fading method of student control.

In *Baker v. Owen*, 395 F.Supp. 294, *aff'd mem.* 423 U.S. 907 (N.C., 1975), the court held that as long as the child knows beforehand what misconduct will result in physical punishment and is told why he or she is being punished, school officials may corporally punish pupils in the absence of a state law to the contrary. In addition, the court generally set forth the requirements that are expressed in Section 32–836 of the Georgia Code, above. The court held, furthermore, that parents may not veto corporal punishment for their children.

The second case, *Ingraham v. Wright*, 430 U.S. 651, 711 (Fla., 1977), dealt with cruel and unusual punishment. In this instance, Ingraham was sent to the office to receive "licks," but he refused to assumed the "paddling position." After this, two assistant principals held him over a desk while the principal administered twenty "licks" with a wooden board. As a result, Ingraham was severely bruised, suffered a hematoma, and required compresses, laxatives, sleeping pills, pain pills, and ten days of rest and suffered discomfort for three weeks. Despite its constitutional test, corporal punishment is an ill-advised method for student control.

Dismissal from school is one other method of student control. In *Dixon v. Alabama State Board of Education*, 294 F.2d 150 (Ala., 1961), *cert. denied* 368 U.S. 930 (1961), the matter centered on the expulsion or placing on probation of students for a sit-in at a lunch counter. These students were disciplined without any notice of charges and were not granted a hearing. The rights of notice and hearing are guaranteed and protected by the due process clause of the Fourteenth Amendment. Under the provisions of this amendment, students are entitled to the names of witnesses against them, an oral or written report on the facts to which each witness testified, an opportunity to defend themselves against the charges that have been filed, and an opportunity to call witnesses on their behalf.

Dixon dealt with students in the higher education area, and it was not until the 1967 landmark case *In re Gault*, 387 U.S. 1 (Ariz., 1967), that the applicability to the elementary and secondary levels was clarified. When this case was decided, the Supreme Court held that a minor in juvenile court was entitled to the following protection under the Constitution: specific notice of the charges against him with time to prepare for a hearing; notification of the right to counsel or, if counsel cannot be afforded, the right to court-appointed counsel; privilege against self-incrimination; and right to confrontation and cross-examination of witnesses. The Supreme Court clarified the rights of children in exclusionary hearings.

Goss v. Lopez, 419 U.S. 565 (Ohio, 1975)

Generalization

Even in short-term suspensions, that is, less than 10 days, a pupil is entitled to the rudiments of due process procedure: notice of charges against the student, an opportunity for denial, a statement of the evidence that school authorities possess; and an opportunity to present the student version of the incident. All procedures should be accomplished as soon after the incident as possible.

Description

A disruption of substantial dimensions occurred in the Columbus Public Schools. Several offending students were suspended in accordance with Ohio law. Although that state mandated free public education, ages 6 to 16, other statutes empowered school principals to suspend pupils for up to 10 days in situations of misconduct. Different students seemed to get justice at different levels of sophistication.

Rudolph Sutton, in the presence of the principal, physically attacked a police officer who was attempting to remove Tyrone Washington from the auditorium. He was immediately suspended. The other four Marion-Franklin students were suspended for similar conduct. None was given a hearing to determine the operative facts underlying the suspension, but each, together with his or her parents, was offered the opportunity to attend a conference, subsequent to the effective date of the suspension, to discuss the students' future.

Two named plaintiffs, Dwight Lopez and Betty Crome, were students at the Central High School and McGuffey Junior High School, respectively. The former was suspended in connection with a disturbance in the lunchroom which involved some physical damage to school property. Lopez testified that at least 75 other students were suspended from his school on the same day. He also testified below that he was not a party to the destructive conduct but was instead an innocent bystander. Because no one from the school testified with regard to this incident, there is no evidence in the record indicating the official basis for concluding otherwise. Lopez never had a hearing.

Betty Crome was present at a demonstration at a high school other than the one she was attending. There she was arrested together with others, taken to the police station, and released without being formally charged. Before she went to school on the following day, she was notified that she had been suspended for a 10-day period. Because no one from the school testified with respect to this incident, the record does not disclose how the McGuffey Junior High School principal went about making the decision to suspend Crome, nor does it disclose on what information the decision was based. It is clear from the record that no hearing was ever held. . . .

On the basis of this evidence, the three-judge court declared that plaintiffs were denied due process of law because they were "suspended without hearing prior to suspension or within a reasonable time thereafter," and that Ohio Rev. Code . . . and regulations issued pursuant thereto were unconstitutional in permitting such suspensions. It was ordered that all references to plaintiffs' suspensions be removed from school files.

We stop short of construing the Due Process Clause to require, countrywide, that hearings in connection with short suspensions must afford the student the opportunity to secure counsel, to confront and cross-examine witnesses supporting the charge, or to call his own witnesses to verify his version of the incident. Brief disciplinary suspensions are almost countless. To impose in each such case even truncated trial-type procedures might well overwhelm administrative facilities in many places and, by diverting resources, cost more than it would save in educational effectiveness. Moreover, further formalizing the suspension process and escalating its formality and adversary nature may not only make it too costly as a regular disciplinary tool but also destroy its effectiveness as part of the teaching process.

Since suspension is normally defined as a temporary exclusion, not to exceed 10 days, from school, the Court held that the student must be given at least an informal notice of the charges against him or her and the opportunity for at least an informal hearing. (This process could occur as the teacher is escorting an obstreperous student from the room.) If the student denies the charges, the student must hear the evidence and be given an opportunity to respond to it and tell his/her side of the story.

In this instance, the Court ruled that the student does have a property right—which is protected by the Fourteenth Amendment—to an education. Thus if that right is to be removed, it can be done only through the application of procedural due process. (It should be noted, here, that there are two types of due process: *substantive*, which deals with the rights and authority of boards of education to act; and *procedural*, which refers to the process, or manner, in which due process is applied.) In school suspensions, due process can be flexible, and its flexibility is determined by the nature of the transgression and the severity of the penalty that is assessed. It stands to reason, therefore, that the more serious the misconduct and the stricter the penalty, the higher the standard of due process that must be applied.

Expulsion is a much more severe punishment than suspension and thus requires substantial due process before the actual expulsion can be carried out. Expulsion connotes exclusion from school for a period in excess of 10 days and may extend to the semester or school year. A decision with a different twist, but still dealing with expulsion, was handed down in *Wood v. Strickland*, 420 U.S. 308 (Ark., 1975). Two sophomore girls in the Mena, Arkansas, school brought suit against the board and the school district, including the superintendent, because they were expelled for spiking the punch at a school function, thus breaking a board rule forbidding the use "of any intoxicating beverage" at such affairs. Although the board of education never really established that the students either possessed or used an "intoxicating" beverage, the girls did admit to the act, and the board expelled them for three months. The Court held that such a lack of evidence, and such precipitous action by the board of education in expelling the girls, amounted to a denial of their rights to due process of law. The decision in this case addressed the degree of immunity individual board of education members enjoy in the total conduct of their official duties and also to the standard of conduct that board members must meet in carrying out their official duties. In the language of the Court, the individual board of education member, to escape personal liability for violating the constitutional rights of students or employees,

must himself be acting sincerely and with a belief that he is doing right, but *an act violating a student's constitutional rights can be no more justified by ignorance or disregard settled, indisputable law on the part of one entrusted with supervision of students' daily lives than by the presence of actual malice*. To be entitled to a special exemption from the categorical remedial language of Sec. 1983 in a case in which the action violated a student's constitutional rights, a school board member who has voluntarily undertaken the task of supervising the operation of the schools and the activities of the students, *must be held to a standard of conduct based not only on permissible intentions, but also on knowledge of the basic, unquestioned constitutional rights of his charges*. Such a standard neither imposes an unfair burden upon a person assuming a responsible public office requiring a high degree of intelligence and judgment for the proper fulfillment of its duties, nor an unwarranted burden in light of the value which civil rights have in our legal system. Any lesser standard would deny much of the promise of 1983 of the civil rights act.

Thus any individual board of education member who knows—*or should have known*, in the eyes of a federal court—that he or she is violating the constitutional rights of a student or employee may be held personally liable for such actions. This is known as the *knowledge-malice* test.

Fully developed and implemented, the following 10 steps assure adequate procedural due process. Some schemes portray more than 10, but these 10 steps are a comprehensive pattern for procedural due process. It is imperative that school officials closely follow these steps if they are to avoid losing cases because of defective procedures. Although requirements may vary from state to state and may vary according to the circumstances of a given situation, the following standards will, generally, apply and be sufficient:

1. *Notice of Charges.* A statement of the violation, that is, notice of charges, must be given to the student. This notice may be oral if there is no question or disagreement that the student was clearly involved in the misconduct. Where a higher standard of due process is required, written notice not only is preferred but is essential. Such

notice should state the specific charges against the student, the school policy or rule that was broken, and the date, time, and place of the hearing, at the student's choice. The student may waive the hearing and have an informal conference with the principal to dispose of the matter.

2. *Right to Counsel.* Although the courts are divided on whether or not the student is entitled to have counsel, it is common practice that whenever there is a hearing, the accused has the right to be represented. Some students of due process accept representation by parents to be sufficient if a lesser standard is required, that is, for a suspension rather than an expulsion. Without a ruling to the contrary, representation by counsel may be permitted at hearing.

3. *Right to a Hearing before an Impartial Tribunal.* In this instance, the hearing officer must not be involved in the situation. In larger school districts, there is usually a permanent hearing officer who has been appointed by the board of education. If the board of education is to be the hearing tribunal, care must be taken not to destroy its impartial status by briefing the board on the issues before the case is heard.

4. *Right to Avoid Self-Incrimination.* The Fifth Amendment protection against self-incrimination does not apply to school disciplinary proceedings; it applied only to criminal proceedings. But if the testimony given by a student in a school hearing is used later in a criminal proceeding, the student may then object to the use of statements made at the school hearing. The concept of double jeopardy is not applicable when school officials discipline a student for breaking a school rule; the individual may then be tried for the same offense in a court of law. In a civil suit, the jury may draw inferences from a refusal to testify.

5. *Evidence Presented against the Accused.* It should be noted that the formal rules of evidence that govern a court trial do not apply in an exclusionary hearing. This was affirmed in *Boykins v. Fairfield Board of Education*, 492 F.2d 697 (5th Cir., Ala., 1974), *cert. denied* 420 U.S. 962 (1975). However, before exclusion, students should have the opportunity to examine the evidence against them, question the hearing officer, and refute the testimony of witnesses. Only when it can be determined that the charges are supportable by substantial evidence or guilt *beyond a reasonable doubt* should one be declared guilty of the charges. That standard requires a higher degree of proof than the lesser ones of circumstantial evidence or preponderance of the evidence.

6. *Right to Cross-Examine the Witnesses.* An element of due process is the right of the accused to cross-examine the witnesses. Although there is not full agreement in this respect, when in doubt, school administrators should accord this right to any individual who is in danger of being excluded from attendance on instruction. This right implies that an administrator may no longer take as an accepted or unquestioned fact the statement of a person reporting a student for violation of a school rule or regulation—especially if the accused denies the accusation.

7. *Compulsion of Witnesses to Testify.* For example, in *Givens v. Poe*, 346 F.Supp. 202 (N.C., 1972), it was held that the right of a student to confront and cross-examine witnesses is fundamental. It is not universal that boards of education have the power of subpoena. In the few states where this power is present, witnesses are compelled to testify.

8. *Standard (Burden) of Proof on the Part of the Accuser.* In criminal cases this standard

is higher, and proof must be beyond a reasonable shadow of a doubt. This too is applicable in a hearing that may lead to the exclusion of a student from school. In civil cases a lesser standard is applied, and the proof may be by preponderance of the evidence.

9. *A Record of the Hearings.* If there is to be any appeal from the decision of the hearing officer or board, it is essential that a record be kept. Although the courts are not in agreement about whether a student is entitled, as a matter of right, to a transcript of the proceedings, it would appear that the full provision of procedural due process would require this. Thus it would seem to be appropriate to provide the student with a transcript at the student's expense.

10. *Right to Appeal.* In any hearing, full procedural due process requires that some procedure or mechanism be made available to the accused to appeal an adverse decision. In the case of a student, this may involve a series of steps terminating with the state department of education. In recent years students have chosen to go directly to the courts. Some courts have refused to hear such cases until the student has exhausted all administrative remedies. More recently, with increased frequency, students have resorted to federal rather than state courts and have argued for a reversal on the basis of a denial of due process under the Fourteenth Amendment.

Throughout the discussion of these several aspects of due process rights, two key elements—fairness and reasonableness—have been stressed. When boards of education and administrators have applied them, the courts have usually upheld the schools. When these elements have been absent, the students have often been upheld.

With the passage of Public Law 93–380, the Family Educational Rights and Privacy Act, parents and students over 18 years of age could no longer be denied access to the complete educational record of the student. Furthermore, P.L. 93–380 denied unauthorized third parties access to these records and imposed strict standards on schools for the handling of student records.

What, then, constitutes a record? Directory information, including student name, address, date and place of birth, dates of attendance, major and minor fields of study, and awards received, plus the academic record, would be there. In addition, there may be comments and descriptive evaluations of student personality, student discipline, student interests, and student attitudes.

Two categories of complaints about student records have arisen. The first deals with the access to confidential information by unauthorized third parties; the second concerns information contained in the record that is unwarranted or is false and irrelevant. Usually, the latter complaint involves charges of defamation, and the complainant may seek damage awards.

Despite increased statutory protection of student records by limiting access and by forbidding scrutiny to unauthorized third parties, school records are still open to inspection by people who "have the right to know" what is contained in the record. School professional personnel do have protection available and are excused from liability when the statements made about the pupil are reasonable and true. Nonetheless, to avoid charges of defamation, certain precautions should be taken by school personnel.

1. Be certain that all statements made about students and all evaluations of students are made by individuals whose professional status permits and may require such statements and/or evaluations.
2. Separate fact from fiction before placing a statement about a student in the record. Be objective.
3. Document the source and circumstances of each comment and evaluation.
4. Be able to demonstrate the direct connection between the statement or evaluation and the educational need and development of the student.
5. When in doubt about the need to record a particular bit of information in a student's record (other than that required to be kept), do not record that information.

Once information is recorded in a student's file, who shall decide what can be purged from that record? The principal has the ultimate responsibility for all things that occur in the school building. This includes student record keeping. Although this has been assumed to be the role of the principal in the past, currently most laws, rules, and regulations require that a professional person in each school be designated as the official custodian of the records. Purging dates may be by statute.

Outdated, irrelevant, and inaccurate data should be removed from student records. Accordingly, it is the responsibility of school officials to subject such records to continuous examination and scrutiny. Parents (and students, where legally permissible) must be given opportunities to purge the child's school record.

To purge or expunge an item from the record is to remove, strike, or erase the item completely. When the parent (or student) has required that an item be purged, and when the school officials have, with a valid reason, denied this request, and when all avenues of appeal have failed, the parent or students may place a statement of their position in the record.

Board of education policy statements on student records are one of the best guarantees of due process—both substantive and procedural—in this matter. Statutes on retention and destruction of records, records management, and requirements concerning retention/destruction vary from state to state. In several jurisdictions, these decisions are left to local school districts. Generally, the entire student record is kept for a period, usually five years, after the student's graduation. After that time the academic record, dates of attendance, and directory information—including verification of birth—are retained (often on microfilm) as permanent records.

SUMMARY

Schools exist to educate the children within the community. Thus the states have enacted statutes that grant the right and stipulate the requirement that children attend instruction. In that context, then, the administration of student personnel has a number of legal issues and implications that must be addressed. In recent years, the school administrator has been called on to serve as a student advocate. There are times when this role has placed the administrator in an adversarial relationship with the board of education. A new, delicate balance has come to be a part of school administration.

Early, in the 1925 decision of *Pierce*, the United States Supreme Court ruled that parents could comply with the compulsory-attendance law by attending private or public schools. The usual age requirement for compulsory attendance is from the child's sixth to sixteenth birthday, although this may vary in some states. An exception to the compulsory-attendance law was found in *Yoder*, wherein Amish children were not required to attend school beyond the eighth grade. The question of equivalent instruction was addressed by the Washington Supreme Court, which held that home instruction did not satisfy the compulsory attendance law. A few other cases have found to the contrary. Eligibility to attend tuition-free the schools of a public school district is extended to school-age youth who are residents of the district and to some others under statutes providing for choice.

Instruction of pupils is determined by state statutes, state boards of education, and local boards of education. Courses of study are assumed to be in the public interest, and where the state board of education has mandated certain courses, the local board of education must comply with the mandate. The curriculum includes more than the usual academic subjects; that is, organized sports are often considered to be part of the curriculum. On the question of whether a state athletic or activities association may prescribe rules that are counter to LEA policies, rules, and regulations, the prevailing opinion is that a board of education cannot delegate its powers in this respect.

Local boards have the authority to determine the grade levels to be maintained in the school district. Boards of education, operating within statutory and con-stitutional requirements and limitations, shall determine what grades and schools are to be operated within the system. Each LEA possesses the authority to determine instructional levels and assignment of pupils to grades and classes. Generally, courts have held against the use of marks and grades for disciplinary purposes. Although boards may prescribe reasonable graduation requirements, they may not deny diplomas to students who have earned them. Participation in graduation exercises is controlled by the local board of education.

The LEA has the authority, and the professional staff has the function, to determine the proper mode of instruction for the students. Defining *curriculum* in a narrow context would indicate that the term applies only to courses that are given regularly for credit; in a broader context we would include all life expe-riences that are provided by the school. Local boards of education possess implied delegated powers to offer courses beyond those required by the state. Selection of textbooks, library books, and supplementary materials must be pursuant to statutes. There is no question about the legal right of the state to prescribe textbooks or, through statutory enactment, to delegate that responsibility to local boards of education. There is not universal agreement in either statutory or case law on text and library book matters. We foresee continued litigation concerning those books that are, in the eyes of some patrons, perceived as controversial or offensive.

Tests have widespread uses in schools. Those tests that are used for placement of children are the subject of considerable litigation. Four guidelines were stated in a Fifth Circuit Court of Appeals ruling. They required separate validation scores, the level of confidence of the test, statistical significance, and the administration of the test. Grouping, through the use of tests, has been the subject of a number of court tests. In one, ability grouping was found to be "undemocratic and discriminating"; in another, the court enjoined the use of standardized I.Q. tests on black children for the purpose of EMR placement; and in still another, the court approved the use of I.Q. tests, in conjunction with other criteria, for placement of children in special classes for the mentally handicapped. Such judicial uncertainty tends to stimulate questions, and "malpractice" suits are beginning to emerge. Uniformly, courts have held in favor of the defendant boards of education.

If school officials determine that there is substantial evidence of contraband being present, a search—including the use of dogs—may be conducted. Locker searches require a lesser burden of reasonable cause than do searches of a student's person or effects. Boards should develop and put into effect policies governing warrantless searches. Searches must be reasonable.

Due process consists of two types—substantive and procedural. In a suspension (short-term exclusion) proceeding, a lesser standard is applied and consists of three requirements before suspension may be decreed: oral or written notice of the charges, an explanation of the evidence if the student denies the charges, and some kind of hearing that includes an opportunity to present the student's view of the incident. Expulsion (long-term or permanent exclusion) requires a much higher standard, and due process, in this instance, consists of the following steps: notice of charges; right to counsel; right to a hearing before an impartial tribunal; right to avoid self-incrimination; evidence presented against the accused; right to cross-examine the witnesses; compulsion of witnesses to testify; standard (burden) of proof on the part of the accuser; a record of the hearings; and right to appeal. Throughout due process, two elements—reasonableness and fairness—must be present.

Records and record management have been the subject of increased litigation since the passage of Public Law 93–380, the Family Educational Rights and Privacy Act, also called the Buckley Amendment. Complaints concern access to confidential information by unauthorized third parties and false and irrelevant information being contained in the file. Records are a part of the education process, and material placed in the records should be there to help students develop their educational potential. Outdated, irrelevant, and inaccurate data should be removed from student records. Policy statements on student records are one of the best guarantees of due process—both substantive and procedural.

7

The Law and the Handicapped

THE REHABILITATION ACT OF 1973

Title V of the Rehabilitation Act of 1973 reads, "No otherwise qualified individual in the United States . . . shall, solely by reason of his handicap, be excluded from participation in, be denied the benefits of, or be subjected to discrimination under any program or activity receiving Federal financial assistance." Section 504, when added to Title VI of the Civil Rights Act of 1964 (which outlawed discrimination based on sex), signaled a new era in protecting the rights of the handicapped.

The then Department of Health, Education, and Welfare, in promulgating guidelines for Section 504, included these words:

Handicapped persons may require different treatment in order to be afforded equal access to federally assisted programs and activities and identical treatment may, in fact, constitute discrimination. The problem of establishing general rules as to when different treatment is prohibited or required is compounded by the diversity of existing handicaps and the differing degree to which particular persons may be affected.

The placement of children under Section 504 requires the board of education to defend its action in providing an education to the handicapped by proving that it was acting to fill a valid state purpose. Such proof should be demonstrable and rational. Mainstreaming a child or placing a child in a segregated group of peers requires such a test. A school that receives federal financial assistance must ensure that no qualified handicapped individual is excluded from participating in or benefiting from any program or activity because of inaccessibility of facilities. Furthermore, along with the Education for All Handicapped Children Act (P.L. 94–142), which was enacted in 1975, the federal government requires that, to the maximum extent appropriate, handicapped children be educated with peers who are not handicapped and that only when the nature or severity of the handicap is such that education in the regular peer group cannot be achieved satisfactorily may special classes, separate schooling, or other removal of handicapped children from the regular school setting be permitted.

EDUCATION FOR ALL HANDICAPPED CHILDREN ACT (P.L. 94–142)

Under the terms of the Education for All Handicapped Children Act (EAHCA) of 1975, funds to be used for special education flow from the federal government to the states. To receive these funds, each state is required to submit its plan for educating the handicapped to the federal government for approval. Each district must establish its plans for carrying out the provisions of EAHCA (P.L. 94–142). Thus, there does remain a modicum of local control, even though this must be consistent with the state plans and be subject to federal audit. Programmatically, this federal statute shifted responsibility away from the LEA (Local Educational Agency); operational design and supervision remains with the local boards.

Parents, through the law's provisions, have the right to participate in the diagnosis, placement, education, and periodic evaluation of their children. The provisions of the EAHCA are specific and include the following rights for handicapped children:

1. The right to a free and *appropriate* public education if they are between the ages of three and twenty-one (effective September 1980)

2. The right to the same spread of programs and services, including nonacademic subjects and extracurricular activities, that are available to nonhandicapped children

3. The right to placement in the least restrictive learning environment, insofar as possible, with nonhandicapped children and, whenever possible, at the same school they would attend if they were not handicapped

4. The right to the availability of a number of alternative learning settings if attending a local public school is not possible

5. The right to have a person appointed to act as a surrogate parent, to be the child's advocate, and to participate in meetings of the program and evaluation committees if the natural parents are unavailable or if the child is a ward of the state

6. The right to participate in the writing of their own Individual Education Program (IEP) where appropriate

7. The right to placement outside the local school district in another public or private school, at public expense, if local schools do not have an adequate program

8. The right to testing for purposes of evaluation and placement that is free of racial and cultural discrimination

9. The right to an annual review of placement, based on the IEP, and at least an annual

review of that program before each school year begins and the right to review proposed changes in long-range and short-range program goals whenever this is appropriate

10. The right to remain in present placement during any administrative or judicial proceedings or the right to attend a public school if the complaint involves an application for admission to public school

11. The right to privacy and confidentiality of all personal records

The school district is required to plan its program to meet the requirements of Section 504. Should there be discrepancies in the district model, the district should proceed first with remedial action to eliminate any violations with which it has been charged. Following that, the district should undertake voluntary action to eliminate any lack of accessibility to local programs by the handicapped. Finally, to carry out its full responsibilities, the district must establish and maintain a design that provides for continuous self-evaluation. To erase discrepancy, the district might consider a model that is closely allied to the scientific method. The steps in this model are determination of the need, setting of objectives, determination of the constraints that affect the objectives, development of alternatives, testing of alternatives, testing of alternatives to determine "best fit," selection of the most appropriate alternative, implementation of the selected alternative, evaluation of the alternative, and feedback and modification, if necessary, of the alternative.

Pennsylvania Association for Retarded Children (PARC) v. Commonwealth, 334 F.Supp. 1257 (Pa., 1972)

Generalization

Children who are handicapped must be provided an educational opportunity, under the applicable statutes, that gives promise of enabling them to develop to the fullest possible extent.

Description

This case was brought as a class-action suit, seeking an order that public schools should place mentally retarded children in regular school classrooms to the greatest extent possible. It was contended that discrimination would be decreased in a mixed-student setting.

The plaintiffs in this case indicated that nowhere in the commonwealth was there a suitable commonwealth-supported local program for children of school age who were adjudged uneducable and untrainable by the public schools. The plaintiffs argued for equal protection under the law. Citing *Brown*, they questioned whether the state, having undertaken to provide public education to some children (perhaps all children), may deny it to the plaintiffs entirely.

The court, after examining evidence and declaring the state liable for whatever funds might be necessary to hire the extra personnel needed to raise the quality of education for handicapped children, pronounced a finding in which the obligations of the state to provide education for all handicapped children were ordered. Those obligations were stipulated in detail:

And now, this 5th day of May, 1972, it is ordered that the Amended Stipulation and Amended Consent Agreement are approved and adopted as fair and reasonable to all members of both the plaintiff and defendant classes.

It is further ordered that the defendants: The Commonwealth of Pennsylvania, the Secretary of the Department of Education, the State Board of Education, the Secretary of the Department of Public Welfare, the named defendant school districts and intermediate units in the commonwealth of Pennsylvania, their officers, employees, agents and successors are enjoined as follows:

(a) from applying Section 1304 of the Public School Code of 1949, 24 Purd. Stat. Sec. 1304, so as to postpone or in any way to deny any mentally retarded child access to a free public program of education and training.

(b) from applying Section 1326 or Section 1330(2) of the School Code of 1949, 24 Purd. Stat. Secs. 13–1326 and 1330(2) so as to postpone, to terminate or in any way deny to any mentally retarded child access to a free program of education and training.

(c) from applying section 1371(1) of the School Code of 1949, 24 Purd. Stat. sec. 13–1376, so as to deny tuition or tuition and maintenance to any mentally retarded person on the same terms as may be applied to other exceptional children, including brain damaged children generally. Additional requirements, specific to Pennsylvania, were harbingers of what was to be the set of requirements in other states.

Litigation over handicapped children complaints is increasing as different types of programs are being examined in light of new legislation. In *Kruse v. Campbell*, 431 F.Supp. 180 (Va., 1977), the court held that a plan that picks up 75 percent of the cost of educating a handicapped child, leaving 25 percent for the parents to pay, discriminates against poor parents.

In *In re Kirkpatrick*, 354 N.Y.S.2d 499 (1972), the decision was that a school district may be financially liable for a handicapped child's education in a private institution, even though the schools have a program that is otherwise suitable for a child with those handicaps.

In *Doe v. Laconia Supervisors Union #30*, 396 F.Supp. 1295 (N.H., 1975), the state was challenged on its plan for allocating funds for the private education of the handicapped. The statutory requirement was for the state to pay any part of the tuition cost not paid by the school district. The state board of education lacked the funds to pay the costs of all programs. Thus, the board established a priority list and funded the categories in that order. Under this system, no funds were available to fund the emotionally handicapped. A student from that group charged denial of equal protection. The court disagreed with the action of the local board and said that the state was fulfilling a valid state purpose and need not consider the financial need of every LEA when meting out the state's benefits.

An interesting case, *Dellmuth v. Muth*, 109 S.Ct. 2397 (Pa., 1989), relates the issue of governmental immunity to the placement of handicapped persons. A handicapped student with a language learning disability, in addition to emotional problems, was enrolled in a Pennsylvania public school. The father disagreed with the student's individualized education program (IEP) and requested a hearing so that he might challenge it. The hearing examiner held that the IEP was inappropriate. Both the school district and the father then appealed to the Pennsylvania secretary of education, who remanded the case to the hearing officer with instructions to revise the IEP. The hearing officer, after the revision, held that the IEP was appropriate, and the secretary affirmed this decision. The father then sued the school district and the secretary of education in a federal district court, claiming that the IEP was inappropriate, that the state's administrative proceedings violated the EAHCA because the secretary was not impartial, and that extensive delays had occurred because of the remand. The court ruled in the father's favor and held that he was entitled to reimbursement for the student's private school tuition plus attorney's fees. The court determined that the Commonwealth of Pennsylvania and the school district were jointly and severally liable under the EAHCA. The court reasoned that the EAHCA abrogated the state's Eleventh Amendment immunity-from-damage suits.

The secretary appealed to the United States Court of Appeals for the Third Circuit. This court affirmed the district court's decision, and the secretary then appealed to the United States Supreme Court, which agreed to hear the case. The Court noted that Congress does not abrogate sovereign immunity unless it specifically states so within a legislative act. The EAHCA did not specify an intent to abrogate state immunity from lawsuit. The Court reversed the court of appeals' decision and remanded for proceedings consistent with this decision.

LENGTH OF THE SCHOOL YEAR

Shall the LEA provide an education beyond the length of the normal school year for handicapped children? In *Georgia Association of Retarded Citizens v. McDaniel*, 511 F.Supp. 1236 (Ga., 1981), the court held that implicit in P.L. 94–142 and in Section 504 of the Vocational Rehabilitation Act of 1973 was the requirement that an education in excess of 180 days must be provided when the IEP committee determines extra days are necessary to meet the unique needs of the child; that the policies and practices of the local and state board effectively limited the school year to 180 days in violation of these two acts; and that IEP committees from then on were to mind the law's requirements. Ironically, the court held, furthermore, that the plaintiffs had not carried their burden of proof in showing that a year-round program or any education in excess of 180 days was necessary for these particular children. In so ruling, the court denied the requested injunction for such a program. This case turned on the fact that the IEP committee, despite the objections of the parent, had determined that an extended educational program was unnecessary in this instance. Even so, it seems clear that an entitlement for an extended school year is present in existing statutes and can be a part of any IEP.

The question of regression during periods when school is not in session—or when handicapped children are not receiving services—has given rise to several lawsuits. Because handicapped children tend to regress far more quickly when out of school than do normal children, the courts have been very liberal in granting requests for year-round schooling for these children.

After a Pennsylvania student exhibited bizarre behavior, she was placed in a treatment program at a residential school. She was diagnosed as being schizo-phrenic, and an IEP was developed for her. Her performance in the academic areas was satisfactory, but she made little progress in emotional and social areas and had serious problems readjusting after vacation periods spent at home. Authorities at the residential school asked her home school district to declare her eligible for an extended-year program so that she could remain at the resi-dential school during the summer months. The local school district declined to do this, and the parents enrolled her in the summer program anyway.

The parents contested the school district's decision. A hearing officer, claiming that her classroom performance had been satisfactory, declared her ineligible for the extended year at the residential school. The parents appealed to the Penn-sylvania secretary of education, who reversed the hearing officer, reasoning that the girl's emotional, behavioral, and social problems must also be considered. Because of the regression suffered during the summer breaks, the secretary ordered the local school district to reimburse the parents for the cost of the summer program. The school district appealed to the Commonwealth Court.

This court held that a handicapped student is entitled to an educational program in excess of 180 days per year if regression caused by an interruption in edu-cational programming, together with the student's limited recoupment capacity, renders it unlikely that the student will attain the independence from caretakers that the student would otherwise have been expected to reach in view of his/her handicapping condition. The court concluded that the student's emotional and social regression had been established, and the court then affirmed the secretary of education's determination that the school district had to reimburse the parents for the cost of the summer residential program (*Bucks County Public Schools v. Commonwealth*, 529 A.2d 1201 [Pa. 1987]).

In two somewhat similar cases, the courts ruled in favor of the students. In the first, *Alamo Heights Independent School District v. State Board of Education*, 790 F.2d 1153 (5th Cir., Tex., 1986) a mother's request for a summer program, including transportation, for a severely handicapped boy was denied. When she appealed to the Texas Education Agency, a hearing examiner ruled in her favor. The school district sought review in the United States District Court. The court found that there had been significant regression. In a further appeal to the United States Court of Appeals, this court held in favor of the district court and held, further, that the child was entitled to year-round service. Further, the court held that the request for transportation was reasonable because the mother worked full-time and the cost did not create an undue burden on the school district. In the second case, *Crawford v. Pittman*, 708 F.2d 1028 (5th Cir., Miss., 1983), the United States Court of Appeals struck down a Mississippi rule limiting the length of the school year to 180 days for all schoolchildren, saying that rigid rules such as 180-day limitations violate the EAHCA's procedural command that each child receive individual consideration and also the substantive requirement that each child receive some benefit from his education.

PROVIDING A "FREE APPROPRIATE PUBLIC EDUCATION"

Section 1401(1) requires that public schools provide all handicapped children with a *free appropriate public education*, which means "special education and related services which (A) have been provided at public expense, under public supervision and direction, and without charge, (B) meet the standards of the State educational agency, (C) include an appropriate preschool, elementary, or secondary school education in the State involved, and (D) are provided in conformity with the individualized education program required under section 1414(a)(5) of this title" (§1401[18]). The question, then, became one of defining the appropriateness of the handicapped child's education.

Board of Education v. Rowley, 458 U.S. 176 (N.Y., 1982)

Generalization

The United States Supreme Court, in establishing a standard for evaluating the appropriateness of a handicapped child's education, held that the child's program must be reasonably calculated to allow him or her to receive educational benefits.

Description

This case was brought by the parents of an eight-year-old child, deaf since birth. The parents claimed that their daughter was entitled to have a sign-language interpreter in her classroom so that she might have the same educational opportunity as her classmates. The district court held in favor of the parents (483 F.Supp. 528), and on appeal, the United States Court of Appeals, Second Circuit, affirmed the district court's decision (632 F.2d. 945). In reversing the decisions of the two lower courts, the Supreme Court held that the provisions of the EAHCA are satisfied when a school provides the handicapped child instruction with sufficient support services to permit that child to *benefit educationally* from that instruction. The court held:

1. The Act's requirement of a "free appropriate public education" is satisfied when the State provides personalized instruction with sufficient support services to permit the handicapped child to benefit educationally from that instruction. Such instruction and services must be provided at public expense, must meet the State's educational stan-

dards, must approximate grade levels used in the State's regular education, and must comport with the child's IEP, as formulated in accordance with the Act's requirements. If the child is being educated in regular classrooms, as here, the IEP should be reasonably calculated to enable the child to achieve passing marks and advance from grade to grade.

(a) This interpretation is supported by the definitions contained in the Act, as well as by other provisions imposing procedural requirements and setting forth statutory findings and priorities for States to follow in extending educational services to handicapped children. The Act's language contains no express substantive standard prescribing the level of education to be accorded handicapped children.

(b) The Act's legislative history shows that Congress sought to make public education available to handicapped children, but did not intend to impose upon the States any greater substantive educational standard than is necessary to make such access to public education meaningful. The Act's intent was more to open the door of public education to handicapped children by means of specialized educational services than to guarantee any particular substantive level of education once inside.

2. In suits brought under the Act's judicial review provisions, a court must first determine whether the State has complied with the statutory procedures, and must then determine whether the individualized program developed through such procedures is reasonably calculated to enable the child to receive educational benefits. If these requirements are met, the State has complied with the obligations imposed by Congress and the courts can require no more. . . .

3. Entrusting a child's education to state and local agencies does not leave the child without protection. As demonstrated by this case, parents and guardians will not lack ardor in seeking to ensure that handicapped children receive all of the benefits to which they are entitled by the Act.

4. The Act does not require the provision of a sign-language interpreter here. Neither of the courts below found that there had been a failure to comply with the Act's procedures, and the findings of neither court will support a conclusion that the child's educational program failed to comply with the substantive requirements of the Act.

It should be noted that five justices (Rehnquist, who delivered the opinion, Chief Justice Burger, and Justices Powell, Stevens, and O'Connor) supported the decision; one, Justice Blackmon, concurred; and three justices dissented (White, Brennan, and Marshall).

Under EAHCA, a school is not required to maximize the potential of each handicapped child; nor is it required to provide educational opportunities commensurate with those provided to nonhandicapped children. However, if a state has an education law that surpasses the EAHCA standard, that state standard is incorporated into the EAHCA, and the state is required to meet the standard in educating handicapped students in that state.

Several cases illustrate that point. In *Geis v. Board of Education of Parsippany-Troy Hills*, 774 F.2d 575 (3d Cir., N.J. 1985), the United States Court of Appeals, Third Circuit, affirmed a district court decision that held that the state of New Jersey must follow its State Board of Education's administrative code. That code required that handicapped students be provided a special education "according to how the pupil can *best* [emphasis supplied] achieve success in learning." In this instance, the state of New Jersey had chosen to exceed EAHCA standards.

In *Geis*, a 15-year-old trainable mentally retarded child with a neurological impairment brought suit against a New Jersey school district. The district had determined to change the child's placement from a residential school to his home and the local schools. A hearing officer had held in favor of the local school district in finding that the child required a specialized program with major assistance in communication skills and that such a program could be provided in the local schools. Further, the hearing officer maintained that it had not been established that the child required a 24-hour residential placement in order to learn.

A United States district court concluded that the residential program was best for this child and that to remove the child from this setting would adversely affect the child's ability to learn and develop to the maximum possible extent. Accordingly, the hearing officer's determination was overturned.

A second case involved a 17-year-old Massachusetts child with Down's syndrome. *David D. v. Dartmouth School Community*, 775 F.2d 411 (1st Cir., Mass., 1985), *cert. Denied*, 106 S.Ct. 1790 (1986). The parents were dissatisfied with their child's IEP because they felt that it didn't adequately address the child's sexual misbehavior. It was their belief that the child required a 24-hour residential program. A United States district court held that the child was entitled to a 24-hour residential placement based on Massachusetts law. Under the laws of that state, a special-education program must "assure the maximum possible development of a child with special needs." Referring to this language, the court noted that the child was entitled to the more comprehensive behavior therapy available in a residential program, especially in light of the degree of his sexual maladjustment. The school district appealed. The United States Court of Appeals, First Circuit, upheld the district court and said that where state law sets a minimum educational standard for handicapped children, those standards are incorporated by reference into the EAHCA.

Determining what exactly constitutes an "appropriate" education received no guidance from Congress when the EAHCA was enacted into law. In practice, parents and schools do not always agree on what is "appropriate" for the education of a particular handicapped child. Although *Rowley* provided a standard to which the courts might look in determining whether an education is appropriate, we do not always find that the final answer can be achieved easily. The following cases are examples of some applications of the "appropriate" test.

In *Lachman v. Illinois Board of Education*, 852 F.2d 290 (7th Cir., 1988), an Illinois school district had proposed the placement of a seven-year-old deaf student in the self-contained classroom for hearing-impaired students for at least half the school day. The parents requested placement in a regular classroom with the assistance of a full-time speech instructor, near their home. The proposed IEP called for integration into regular classrooms when possible. The parents were dissatisfied and requested a due process hearing. The hearing officer affirmed the school district's placement, and the parents filed a lawsuit in the federal district court, alleging that the district had failed to provide their son with a free appropriate public education under the EAHCA. The court applied the *Rowley* test and found that the IEP was reasonably calculated to enable their son to receive educational benefits. Thus, the court held that the district had satisfied the *Rowley* requirements and held in favor of the school district. The parents appealed.

The appeals court held the district had properly applied the *Rowley* test. The court noted that the EAHCA preference for mainstreaming must be balanced against the possibility that some students could be better educated in segregated facilities. The court noted, further, that the EAHCA granted school districts the primary responsibilities for formulating IEPs. It said that although parents have an important role to play in proposed IEPs, the dispute was primarily over the appropriate methodology, which was within the school district's primary function. The appeals court affirmed the district court's dismissal of the lawsuit.

In a Virginia case, *Bales v. Clarke*, 523 F.Supp. 1366 (Va., 1981), the court was called on to rule on the parents' claim that their child, who had suffered severe head trauma when she was injured in an automobile accident and who had become mentally impaired as a result, was denied a "free appropriate public education" as required by EAHCA. The parents argued that the local school district opted to implement its own program rather than the one that had been proposed by the parents and, thereby, was in violation of the EAHCA. In answer to the parents' suit, the United States district court found the parents' plan to be unreasonable and the school's plan appropriate, saying: "The State is not required to pay all of the expenses incurred by parents in educating a child, whether the child is handicapped or non-handicapped. . . . [P]arents [do not] have the right under the law to write a prescription for an ideal education for their child and to have the prescription filled at public expense."

What can happen when a local school district fails to implement a hearing officer's decision is found in a Maryland decision. (Such inaction may result in a failure to provide an appropriate education.) In the case *Robinson v. Pinderhughes*, 810 F.2d 1270 (4th Cir., Md., 1987), a hearing officer, in reviewing the status of an 18-year-old handicapped student in October 1984, found four procedural violations of the EAHCA by the Baltimore City Schools. The hearing officer determined that the student was a seriously emotionally disturbed adolescent who required a residential placement, and the officer ordered the Baltimore City Schools to permanently place the student in a residential setting by November 30, 1984. On December 5, 1984, the student and his mother sued the city in a United States district court because there had been no change in the student's educational program. The district court dismissed the student's claims, and he appealed to the United States Court of Appeals, Fourth Circuit.

In his argument before the court of appeals, the student claimed that he was denied a free appropriate public education when the city school district failed to implement the hearing officer's decision in a timely manner. The district court had dismissed his complaint, holding that the student failed to exhaust his administrative remedies under the EAHCA. The court of appeals disagreed, noting that the student had received a final administrative decision under the EAHCA and that the student had neither the responsibility nor the right to appeal the favorable decision of the hearing officer, since he was not the aggrieved party.

The court of appeals also concluded that since the EAHCA did not contain any provision for enforcing administrative orders by a hearing officer, the student was entitled to a claim under §1983 of the Civil Rights Act. By failing to carry out the hearing officer's decision to place the student in a residential placement, the Baltimore City Schools had, under color of state law, violated the EAHCA. Thus, the district court erred in dismissing the student's §1983 claim. The student's §1983 claim was remanded to the district court for further proceedings.

The last case in this section, *John A. by and through Valerie A. v. Gill*, 565 F.Supp. 372 (Ill., 1983), deals with a suit brought by a mother against the state superintendent of education on behalf of her severely emotionally disturbed 12-year-old child and all handicapped children in Illinois. Her son's school district recommended that his placement be in a self-contained classroom for behavior-disordered students. The mother objected and said that she had been advised by experts that a highly structured residential program would be an appropriate placement for her son. The mother appealed the school district's decision to the state superintendent, but after five months, the state superintendent had made no decision. The mother claimed that the superintendent was obligated to decide within 30 days. She then charged that the long delay and inappropriate setting had caused the deterioration of her son's condition to the extent that he had had to be placed in a mental hospital.

The mother then brought suit against the superintendent. The superintendent moved to dismiss the suit on the basis that the EAHCA creates no substantive rights for handicapped children. The United States district court disagreed and went on to say that the EAHCA is the source of a federal statutory right to a free appropriate public education in every state electing to receive federal assistance and that it is more than merely a "funding statute." The court held, further, that the passage of time caused the deprivation of a child's substantive right to an appropriate public education.

ATTORNEY'S FEES: HANDICAPPED CHILDREN'S PROTECTION ACT OF 1986

Before 1986, there was no provision in the EAHCA for attorney's fees. The United States Supreme Court, in *Smith v. Robinson*, 468 U.S. 992 (R.I., 1984), held that attorney's fees were not recoverable for special-education claims made under the EAHCA, §1983, or the Rehabilitation Act. However, Congress responded to this situation by enacting the Handicapped Children's Protection Act of 1986 (HCPA)(P.L. 99–372), which amended the EAHCA and authorized attorney fee awards to handicapped students who prevail in special-education lawsuits. Moreover the HCPA provided that in addition to the EAHCA, the Rehabilitation Act and the Civil Rights Act may also be utilized by handicapped students. The only requirement is that the handicapped student must exhaust all EAHCA procedures before seeking relief or money damages under the other federal statutes. Money damages are generally still unavailable under the EAHCA itself.

The Handicapped Children's Protection Act of 1986, for all intents and purposes, overturned the United Supreme Court decision in *Smith v. Robinson* and gave a new thrust to the EAHCA as it applied to attorney's fees. This can best be stated by citing directly from the statute:

EDUCATION OF THE HANDICAPPED ACT
§1415. Procedural Safeguards

(e) Civil action; jurisdiction; attorney's fees

(4)(A) The district courts of the United States shall have jurisdiction of actions brought under this subsection without regard to the amount in controversy.

(B) In any action or proceeding brought under this subsection, the court, in its discretion, may award reasonable attorney's fees as part of the costs to the parents or guardian of a handicapped child or youth who is the prevailing party.

(C) For the purpose of this subsection, fees awarded under this subsection shall be based on rates prevailing in the community in which the action or proceeding arose for the kind and quality of services furnished. No bonus or multiplier may be used in calculating the fees awarded under this subsection. . . .

(D) No award or attorney's fees and related costs may be made in any action or proceeding under this subsection for services performed subsequent to the time of a written offer of settlement to a parent or guardian. . . .

(E) Notwithstanding the provisions of subparagraph (D), an award of attorney's fees and related costs may be made to a parent or guardian who is the prevailing party and who was substantially justified in rejecting the settlement offer.

(F) Whenever the court finds that—

(i) the parent or guardian, during the course of the action or proceeding, unreasonably protracted the final resolution of the controversy;

(ii) the amount of the attorneys' fees otherwise authorized to be awarded unreasonably exceeds hourly rate prevailing in the community for similar services for attorneys of reasonably comparable skill, experience, and reputation; or

(iii) the time spent and legal services furnished were excessive, considering the nature of the action or proceeding, the court shall reduce, accordingly, the amount of the attorneys' fees awarded under this subsection.

(G) The provisions of subparagraph (F) shall not apply in any action or proceeding if the court finds that the State or local educational agency unreasonably protracted the final resolution of the action or proceeding or there was a violation of this section.

Attorney's fees are at issue in several cases. They are included here so that the application of this particular statute may be reviewed.

In the first case, two sets of parents of severely handicapped students sued the New York education commissioner for placement costs at an out-of-state facility for severely handicapped persons. When this case went to trial, the New York trial court found in favor of the parents and ordered the placement of the children in the out-of-state facility. This order was handed down despite the fact that the parents had failed to exhaust the administrative remedies under the EAHCA. However, pursuing these remedies was considered to be futile given the commissioner's previous refusal to implement each student's special committee recommendation. Then, the parents sought a motion for attorney's fees under the HCPA. Both sets of parents were represented by the same attorneys from the same law firm. The trial court granted the motion for attorney's fees totaling over $34,000 in the first case and $43,805.25 in the second. The commissioner then appealed, claiming that HCPA counsel fees were not available under the EAHCA and that the fees were, therefore, improperly determined.

Using the United States Supreme Court decision in *Honig v. Doe*, the appellate division ruled that the parents were permitted to seek EAHCA review by a court when the administrative process was futile or inadequate. Thus, the appellate division ruled that the parents had properly filed the matter in court. The court said, however, that the parents' attorneys had failed to submit sufficient evidence to determine their fees. There was concern that because the attorneys had represented the parents of both children, there was a possibility that they were being paid twice for the same research. The appellate division remanded the case to the trial court for a determination, directing the attorneys to submit their time sheets (*Behavior Research Institute v. Ambach*, 535 N.Y.S.2d 465 [A.D.3d Dep't, 1988]).

In *Fontenot v. Louisiana Board of Elementary and Secondary Education*, 835 F.2d 117 (5th Cir., La., 1988), an orthopedically handicapped student was involved. In March 1985, this student, who was then at the Louisiana Special Education Center (LSEC), was transferred to a hospital to be treated for respiratory problems. On his release, when he attempted to return to LSEC, he was denied admission, the LSEC claiming that it was not equipped to deal with his medical problems. The student sued the LSEC under the EAHCA. A federal district court ordered the school to admit the student, who later sued for attorney's fees. The district court denied the attorney's fees on the basis of *Smith v. Robinson*. The student appealed, but before the appeal reached the court, Congress passed the HCPA of 1986. Then, the United States Court of Appeals, Fifth Circuit, ruled that he was entitled to attorney's fees and remanded the case to the district court to determine the amount. The district court awarded attorney's fees to the student in the amount of $9,300, and the LSEC appealed. The student then requested attorney's fees to cover the costs in the appeal.

The LSEC based its defense on two arguments: first, that it had acted in good faith in denying admission to the student and, second, that he could not bring a claim in his own right. The court denied both of the arguments and declared that the LSEC could not avoid paying the attorney's fees. Further, it held that the legislative history of the EAHCA indicated that handicapped children could seek attorney's fees on their own behalf if they were old enough and were otherwise competent to bring suit. The court of appeals ruled in the student's favor and remanded the case to the district court for a determination of the amount of additional attorney's fees that he should receive for the appeal.

In another case that dealt with the award of attorney's fees under §504 of the Rehabilitation Act, a 1980 United States District Court decision held that the District of Columbia Board of Education's IEP for an autistic child was inadequate and ordered the board to place the child in a residential school in West Virginia. It also awarded attorney's fees under §504. However, in 1984, the fee awarded was vacated in response to *Smith v. Robinson*. When Congress passed the Handicapped Children's Protection Act in 1986, the parents asked the district court to reinstate the attorney's fee award.

The HCPA provided that courts may award attorney's fees to prevailing children or parents in EAHCA actions or proceedings brought after July 3, 1984, and actions or proceedings brought before July 4, 1984, which were pending on July 4, 1984. The parents argued that since their earlier attorney's fees award had been vacated on August 17, 1984, their action had still been pending on July 4, 1984 and was, therefore, actionable under HCPA. The district court agreed with the parents' interpretation. The board of education had argued that the HCPA was unconstitutional retroactive legislation, and the court rejected that argument. The court ordered that the parents were entitled to the amount of the previous fee award, which was $8,420 (*Capello v. District of Columbia Board of Education*, 669 F.Supp. 14 [D.C., 1987]).

Some cases have involved a consent decree. A group of handicapped students in Rochester, New York, brought suit against the city board of education and the state department of education in 1981 in a United States district court. They alleged that they were being denied an appropriate public education and sought relief under the EAHCA. The students and the city board of education resolved the complaint with a consent decree in August 1983. In July 1986, the students moved in United States district court to have the complaint dismissed and to be awarded attorney's fees. The judge granted the motion to dismiss but denied the request for an award of the fees, since the consent decree was relief under the EAHCA, which did not provide for the award. The students filed an appeal, but when Congress passed the HCPA and it was signed into law, the students withdrew their appeal and moved for reconsideration.

A review of the HCPA revealed a clause that provided attorney's fees for a "prevailing party." The district court ruled in favor of the students and held that they were the prevailing party, since the consent decree had resulted in significant systemwide relief to the students. However, the court pointed out that the students "prevailed" only against the city board of education because the state department of education had refused to enter into the consent decree. In making its determination, the court relied on the following language of the law: "Fee awards . . . shall be based on rates prevailing in the community . . . and the kind and quality of services furnished."

In reviewing the consent decree, the court held that it provided for monitoring the program during the 1986–87 school year and the award was for attorney's fees for the time spent monitoring the program. The court observed that the intent of Congress was that nonprofit law firms could recover attorney's fees at the same hourly rate as conventional law firms. The court awarded $204,748 to the students' three public-interest attorneys, and the city board of education alone was ordered to pay the award on behalf of the students (*J.G. v. Board of Education of Rochester City School District*, 648 F.Supp. 1452 [W.D.N.Y., 1986]). The local school district appealed this award of attorney's fees to the United States Court of Appeals, Second Circuit.

The court of appeals considered the local school district's argument that attorney's fees could not be awarded under the EAHCA because the parents in this case were not challenging a final decision of a state administrative agency relating to the evaluation or placement of a specific handicapped student. The court noted that the generalized procedural violations challenged by the parents "lend themselves well to class action treatment" and that administrative remedies need not be exhausted when they would not provide adequate relief. The court of appeals then noted that the consent judgment in this case provided substantial relief to the parents, relief that could not have been obtained through administrative appeal processes. It therefore concluded that the parents were entitled to attorney's fees (*J.G. v. Rochester City School Board of Education*, 830 F.2d 444 [N.Y., 1987]).

RELATED SERVICES

Section 1401(a)(17) of the Education of All Handicapped Children Act (EAHCA) reads as follows: "The term 'related services' means transportation and such developmental, corrective, and other supportive services (including speech pathology and audiology, psychological services, physical and occupational therapy, recreation, and medical and counseling services), except that such medical services shall be for diagnostic and evaluation purposes only, as may be *required to assist a handicapped child to benefit from special education* [emphasis supplied], and includes the early identification and assessment of handicapping conditions to children."

Irving Independent School District v. Tatro, **104 S.Ct. 3371** (**Tex., 1984**)

Generalization

Related services are those that are required to assist a handicapped child to benefit from an appropriate public education program. These are classified as "supportive services" and are defined in the description of the law, above.

Description

This case concerns an eight-year-old child, Amber, who was born with a defect known as spina bifida. As a result, the child suffered from orthopedic and speech impairments and a neurogenic bladder. She was unable to empty her bladder voluntarily and had to be catheterized every three or four hours to avoid injury to her kidneys. The remedy for this was to provide her with a procedure known as clean intermittent catheterization (CIC). This procedure is a relatively simple one and can be performed in a few minutes by a layperson with less than an hour's training. Amber's parents, babysitter, and teenage brother were all qualified to administer CIC, and Amber soon would be able to perform this procedure herself. For Amber to benefit from instruction in a daily program, the parents requested that this service be provided. The school district considered it a medical service and refused; the parents appealed, and this 1984 decision was the result of a series of actions brought to resolve the matter.

Chief Justice Burger delivered the majority opinion for the court, in which Justices White, Blackmun, Powell, Rehnquist, and O'Connor concurred; Justices Brennan, Marshall, and Stevens joined in all but part 3 of the decision and filed opinions concurring in part and dissenting in part.

In October 1979 respondents brought the present action in District Court against petitioner, the State Board of Education, and others. See §1415(e)(2). They sought an injunction ordering petitioner to provide Amber with CIC and sought damages and attorney's fees. First, respondents invoked the Education of the Handicapped Act. Because Texas received funding under that statute, petitioner was required to provide Amber with a "free appropriate public education." §§1412(1), 1414(a)(1)(CO(ii)), which is defined to include "related services." §1401(18). Respondents argued that CIC is one such "related service." Second, respondents invoked §504, which forbids an individual, by reason of a handicap, to be "excluded from the participation in, be denied the benefits of, or be subjected to discrimination under" any program receiving federal aid.

The district court denied the parents' request for a preliminary injunction and concluded that CIC was not a "related service" under the EAHCA because it did not serve a need arising from the effort to be educated. It also held that §504 of the Rehabilitation Act did not require "the setting up of governmental health care for people seeking to participate" in federally funded programs (*Tatro v. Texas*, 481 F.Supp. 1224, 1229 [N.D. Tex., 1979]).

The court of appeals reversed, in *Tatro v. Texas*, 625 F.2d 557 (CA 5 1980) (Tatro I). It held, first, that CIC was a "related service" and, second, that the refusal to provide CIC effectively excluded Amber from a federally funded educational program in violation of §504 of the Rehabilitation Act. The court of appeals remanded for the district court to develop a factual record and apply these legal principles.

The district court found CIC to be a "related service" and ordered the school district and the state board of education to modify Amber's IEP to include provision of CIC during school hours. It also awarded compensatory damages. Further, it found a violation of §504 of the Rehabilitation Act and ordered an award of attorney's fees against the school district and the state board of education.

The court of appeals affirmed in *Tatro v. Texas*, 703 F.2d 823 (CA 5, Tex., 1983)(Tatro II).

We come, again, to the U.S. Supreme Court decision which continues. . . . It would be strange indeed if Congress, in attempting to extend special services to handicapped children, were unwilling to guarantee them services of a kind that are routinely provided to the non-handicapped.

To keep in perspective the obligation to provide services that relate to both the health and educational needs of handicapped students, we note several limitations that should minimize the burden petitioner fears. First, to be entitled to related services, a child must be handicapped so as to require special education. See 20 U.S.C. S1401(1); 34 CFR §300.5(1983). In the absence of a handicap that requires special education, the need for what otherwise might qualify as a related service does not create an obligation under the Act. See 34 CFR §300.14, Comment (1)(1983).

Second, only those services necessary to aid a handicapped child to benefit from special education must be provided, regardless of how easily a school nurse or lay person could furnish them. For example, if a particular medication or treatment may appropriately be administered to a handicapped child other than during the school day, a school is not required to provide nursing services to administer it.

Third, the regulations state that school nursing services must be provided only if they can be performed by a nurse or other qualified person, not if they must be performed by a physician. See 34 CFR §300.13(a),(b)(4),(b)(10)(1983). It bears mentioning that here not even the services of a nurse are required; as is conceded, a lay person with minimal training is qualified to provide CIC.

Finally, we note that respondents are not asking petitioner to provide *equipment* that Amber needs for CIC. . . . They seek only the services of a qualified person at the school.

We conclude that provision of CIC to Amber is not subject to exclusion as a "medical service," and we affirm the Court of Appeals' holding that CIC is a "related service" under the Education of the Handicapped Act.

The U.S. Supreme Court concluded:

Respondents sought relief not only under the Education of the Handicapped Act but under §504 of the Rehabilitation Act as well. After finding petitioner liable to provide CIC under the former, the District Court proceeded to hold that petitioner was similarly liable under §504 and that respondents were therefore entitled to attorney's fees under §505 of the Rehabilitation Act, 29, U.S.C. §724a. We hold today, in *Smith v. Robinson*, 468 U.S. 992 (1984) that §504 is inapplicable when relief is available under the Education of the Handicapped Act to remedy a denial of educational services. Respondents are therefore not entitled to relief under §504, and we reverse the Court of Appeals' holding that respondents are entitled to recover attorney's fees. In all other aspects, the judgment of the Court of Appeals is affirmed.

In another case based on related services, *Bevin v. Wright*, 666 F.Supp. 71 (W.D. Pa., 1987), a profoundly mentally handicapped and legally blind child was admitted to a classroom for handicapped children in Pennsylvania. This child was admitted on the condition that her parents would pay the cost of nursing services and the related equipment that was required by the child. The child breathed through a tracheostomy tube and was fed and medicated through a gastrostomy tube. It was necessary for a nurse to be in attendance to care for this child's needs on a regular basis. The nurse administered a constant oxygen supply, administered chest physical therapy each day, suctioned mucous from the child's lungs, supervised her positioning for physical and occupational therapy, and cleared her tracheostomy tube when it became clogged by mucous. When this occurred, several times each day, the tube had to be cleared within thirty seconds to prevent injury to the child.

The child's parents and the school district agreed that the program to which she had been admitted was the most appropriate and least restrictive for her. The parents then requested that the school district assume the costs of the nursing services as "related services" under the EAHCA, and the school district refused. A hearing officer ruled in favor of the parents, but the Pennsylvania secretary of education reversed that ruling. The parents then appealed to a United States district court.

The court reviewed the provisions of the EAHCA and, in particular, those that referred to "related services." Attention was paid to the provisions for medical services. The court then addressed the parents' argument that the services that were required by the child could not be excluded as medical services because they were not provided by a physician.

The court concluded that the nursing services required by the child in this case were so extensive that placing the burden of providing them on the school district did not "appear to be consistent with the spirit" of the EAHCA and its regulations. The court then concluded, "The nursing services required are so varied, intensive and costly, and more in the nature of 'medical services' that they are not properly includable as 'related services.' "

Barnett v. Fairfax County School Board, 721 F.Supp. 755 (E.D. Va., 1989), involved a 16-year-old profoundly deaf student who was eligible for special education. Since this student had been in the first grade, he had participated in the school system's cued-speech program and had advanced through school with the aid of a cued-speech interpreter and other support services. As he progressed, he was increasingly mainstreamed into regular classes so that by the time he reached high school, he was taking academic classes with nonhandicapped students, with the assistance of a cued-speech interpreter. He also played on the high school baseball and basketball team.

The student's public school support areas included one period per day in a special resource class taught by a full-time staff teacher for the hearing impaired and several weekly speech and language therapy sessions taught by a therapist.

It should be noted that this county was one of a few in the nation that offered a cued-speech program.

In establishing its program, the school district placed its hearing-impaired programs at centrally located schools close to major arterials. Many of the 300 participating students came from across the county and from other Virginia counties. The schools that participated in the program were located close together to allow the interpreters to travel easily to the different schools.

The high school that this student attended was 5.1 miles farther from his home than the neighborhood high school he would have attended in the absence of his hearing impairment. In spite of the fact that the student was successful in his current placement and that the district was achieving success in its mainstreaming efforts, the parents felt that the program should be offered in the closer school. They requested an administrative hearing to respond to their request. The local hearing officer agreed with the parents. When the school district appealed, the state hearing officer determined that the student's present placement satisfied the requirement of a free appropriate public education in the least restrictive environment. Under his ruling, the district was not required to duplicate its cued-speech service at the neighborhood school. The parents then sued in a federal district court, and the court issued two separate opinions.

In the first opinion, the court granted summary judgment for the school district in denying the student's request for $100,000 for alleged mental and emotional distress from his inability to attend the neighborhood school. The court noted that the EAHCA allowed for tuition reimbursement but did not authorize compensatory damage awards and noted, further, that to allow such damages would create a cause of action for educational malpractice, which was not the EAHCA's intent. The court also rejected the student's §504 complaint as another impermissible educational malpractice complaint.

In the second opinion, the court considered the student's request for an order to provide cued-speech services at the neighboring high school. The court noted that the student had been provided an appropriate public education, and that he had progressed academically and had maintained a B average in regular academic classes while participating in two sports. The court held that the cued-speech program was offered at a regular public high school and constituted the least restrictive environment for handicapped students under the EAHCA. The court held, further, that the EAHCA did not create an absolute duty to place a student in a neighborhood school and that the school district was free to locate its special program at central sites and to determine the particular methods for providing services. The court held, also, that the school district had complied with §504 of the Rehabilitation Act. Given these findings, the court granted the school district's motion for summary judgment.

The provision of transportation services to handicapped children has been viewed by the courts to be part of a free appropriate public education. In *School District of Philadelphia v. Department of Education*, 547 A.2d 520 (Pa., 1988), a hearing-impaired Philadelphia student received a scholarship for biweekly hearing treatment at a therapy clinic. The student's mother requested that the school district provide transportation for the son to the clinic. The school district refused, and the mother requested a due process hearing. The local hearing officer determined that the school district was not obligated to provide transportation to the clinic. The mother appealed this decision to the Pennsylvania Secretary of Education, who determined that additional therapy would allow the student to make better use of his residual hearing. The secretary held, also, that additional therapy would assist the student in his current classroom and ensure that he continue to function independently and successfully in the future. The secretary determined that the district should provide transportation because the combination of the student's regular education and the additional therapy constituted "sufficient services reasonably calculated to give real educational benefit." The school district then appealed this decision to the Pennsylvania Commonwealth Court.

The district's argument was that it was already providing the student with an appropriate education. The court, however, in upholding the secretary's decision, determined that the combined therapies constituted services calculated to afford the student real educational benefit. Since the additional therapy program was approved by the department of education, the school district was obligated to provide free transportation. The court continued with its comments, noting that although the student was progressing satisfactorily, evidence showed that students with the same problem require additional assistance later on in their education and that providing additional therapy now would allow the student to become more independent. Thus, the court held that the district was required to provide transportation to the clinic.

TUITION REIMBURSEMENT

Parents or guardians who unilaterally change the placement of their handicapped children during the pendency of any review proceedings often seek reimbursement from their school district for tuition expenses. The United States Supreme Court ruled that parents who violate the status quo provision may nevertheless, in extenuating circumstances (e.g., inappropriate IEP, unreasonable delay in reaching a decision, discrimination, etc.), receive tuition reimbursement from the school district. However, if the proposed IEP is found to be appropriate, if the decision is reached in a timely fashion, of if there is not discrimination, the parents will not be entitled to reimbursement for expenses incurred in unilaterally changing their child's placement.

Burlington School Community v. Department of Education of Massachusetts, 105 S.Ct. 1966 (Mass., 1985)

Generalization

EAHCA §1415(e)(3): During the pendency of any proceedings conducted pursuant to this section, unless the state or local educational agency and the parents or guardian otherwise agree, the child shall remain in the then current educational placement of such child.

Description

This is a procedural safeguard to the due process provisions of the EAHCA, which relate to the development of the individualized education program (IEP), and provides a process whereby the child may challenge in administrative and court proceedings a proposed IEP with which the parents and child disagree. In this situation, the father of a handicapped child rejected the school district's proposed IEP for the 1979–80 school year, calling for the placement of the child in a certain public school. The father sought a review by the Massachusetts Department of Education's Bureau of Special Education Appeals. In the meantime, the father, at his own expense, enrolled the child in a state-approved private school for special education.

In its review, the Bureau of Special Education Appeals held that the district's proposed IEP was inappropriate and that the private school was better suited to the child's educational needs and ordered the school district (town) to pay the child's expenses at the private school for the 1979–80 school year. The school committee then appealed to the federal courts, where a United States district court held that the parents had violated the status quo provisions of the EAHCA by enrolling their child in the private school without the agreement of the public school officials. Thus, they were not entitled to reimbursement. The United States Court of Appeals, First Circuit, reversed the district court's ruling, and the school committee appealed to the United States Supreme Court. We go now to the language of the opinion:

The first question on which we granted certiori requires us to decide whether this grant of authority, including the power to order school authorities to reimburse parents for their expenditures on private special education for a proposed IEP, is proper under the Act.

We conclude that the Act authorizes such reimbursement. The statute directs the court to "grant such relief as [it] determines is appropriate." The type of relief is not further specified, except that it must be "appropriate." Absent other reference, the only possible interpretation is that the relief is to be "appropriate" in light of the purpose of the Act. As already noted this is principally to provide handicapped children with "a free appropriate public education which emphasizes special education and related services designed to meet their unique needs." The Act contemplates that such education will be provided where possible in regular public schools, with the child participating as much as possible in the same activities as non-handicapped children, but the Act also provides for placement in private schools at public expense where this is not possible. . . . In a case where a court determines that a private placement desired by the parents was proper under the Act and that an IEP calling for placement in a public school was inappropriate, it seems clear beyond cavil that "appropriate" relief would include a prospective injunction directing the school officials to develop and implement at public expense an IEP placing the child in a private school.

The Court went on to discuss the matter of time required to reach a decision:

If the administrative and judicial relief under the Act could be completed in a matter of weeks, rather than years, it would be difficult to imagine a case in which such prospective injunctive relief would not be sufficient. As this case so vividly demonstrates, however, the review process is ponderous. A final judicial decision on the merits of an IEP will in most instances come a year or more after the school term covered by that IEP has passed. In the meantime, the parents who disagree with the proposed IEP are faced with a choice; go along with the IEP to the detriment of their child if it turns out to be inappropriate or pay for what they consider to be the appropriate placement. If they choose the latter course, which conscientious parents who have adequate means and who are reasonably confident of their assessment normally would, it would be an empty victory to have a court tell them several years later that they were right but that these expenditures could not in a proper case be reimbursed by school officials. If that were the case, the child's right to a *free* appropriate public education, the parents' right to participate fully in developing a proper IEP, and all of the procedural safeguards would be less than complete. Because Congress undoubtedly did not intend this result, we are confident that by empowering the court to grant "appropriate" relief Congress meant to include retroactive reimbursement to parents as an available remedy in a proper case.

Referring to the question of the child's placement, the Court said:

We need not resolve the academic question of what Michael's "then current placement" was in the summer of 1979, when both the Town and the parents had agreed that a new school was in order. For the purposes of our decision, we assume that the Pine Glen School, proposed in the IEP, was Michael's current placement and, therefore, that the Panicos did "change" his placement after they had rejected the IEP and had set the administrative review in motion. In so doing, the Panicos contravened the conditional command of §1415(e)(3) that "the child shall remain in the current educational placement."

As an initial matter, we note that the section calls for agreement by *either* the *state or* the *local educational agency*. The BSEA's decision in favor of the Panicos and the Carroll School placement would seem to constitute agreement by the State to the change of placement. The decision was issued in January 1980, so from then on the Panicos were no longer in violation of §1415(e)(3). This conclusion, however, does not entirely resolve the instant dispute because the Panicos are also seeking reimbursement for Michael's expenses during the Fall of 1979, prior to the State's concurrence in the Carroll School placement.

Looking at this decision in its perspective, we see that the United States Supreme Court reviewed two issues:

1. Whether the act authorized the courts to order school authorities to reimburse parents for their expenditures on private special education for a child if the court determines that such placement, rather than a proposed IEP, is proper under the Act

2. Whether the act barred such reimbursement to parents who reject a proposed IEP and place a child in a private school without the consent of the school district

As one will note in the language above, the Court answered both of these issues in the affirmative. That decision is a partial guide for dispute resolution regarding IEPs.

1. Those parents who have sufficient means will use *Burlington* as a basis for unilaterally seeking appropriate private special education for their children, pending the exhaustion of administrative and judicial reviews.

2. Parents will use *Burlington* as a bargaining chip to negotiate compromises and agreements on alternative school placements.

3. Districts will expedite administrative reviews under the EAHCA. No longer will there be any advantage in a protracted review.

4. Opportunities for alternative types of special education will be enhanced.

Burlington has been applied in several cases. *Eugene B. Jr. v. Great Neck Union Free School District*, 635 F.Supp. 753 (E.D.N.Y., 1986), concerned a kindergartner. It soon became apparent that the child had difficulty learning in a normal classroom setting; he was diagnosed as neurologically impaired and placed in a nonmainstreamed special-education program, where he remained for several years.

During the 1980–81 school year, the child was placed in mainstreamed education classes, where he spent approximately 60 percent of his time in special-education classes and 40 percent with regular education students. The child's parents complained that this mainstreaming was exacerbating their son's emotional problems, and they requested (1) that the school district Committee on the Handicapped (COH) reevaluate their son's educational placement and (2) that the district provide a summer program for 1981 to compensate for the son's lack of achievement during the preceding school year. The response of the COH was to change the child's classification from neurologically impaired to emotionally disturbed, thereby leaving the child in his former educational placement by default. When the parents complained, they were told that an evaluation meeting could not be held until the fall of 1981.

During the summer of 1981, the parents had their son evaluated at the Hillsdale Center, which recommended placement at the Lowell School, a state-approved private school. In September 1981, the school district's COH met to reconsider the child's case. The parents presented the Hillside evaluations. The COH reclassified the child as neurologically impaired and, though recognizing that mainstreaming had "traumatized" him, proposed continued placement in the public school with "special support" during mainstreaming. Two days later the parents responded to this decision by placing their son in the Lowell School, where he remained from 1981 through 1984. In January 1983, a hearing officer ruled that the Lowell School placement was appropriate, and the COH agreed to fund the placement beginning with the 1983–84 school year. At this point, the parents brought suit in a United States district court to obtain reimbursement for the 1981 through 1983 school years.

The district court observed that both an impartial hearing officer and the New York state education commissioner had concluded that the school district had offered an inappropriate educational placement for the child and that the Lowell School placement was appropriate. Citing *Burlington*, the court ruled that the parents were entitled to reimbursement for the years their child was at the Lowell School. Further, the court held that any delays alleged by the parents were irrelevant because the crucial inquiry was whether the school district had proposed an appropriate educational program for the child, which it had not done. Therefore, the court ordered the Great Neck District to reimburse the parents for all tuition and related expenses at the Lowell School.

In *Board of Education of the County of Cabell v. Dienelt*, 843 F.2d 813 (4th Cir., W.V., 1988), a child had been educated in the public schools for seven years. His parents were dissatisfied with his progress and rejected the IEP proposed by his teacher. The parents had an unsatisfactory meeting with the school officials and then proceeded to obtain a loan and place the child in a private school. They then sought tuition reimbursement under the EAHCA. This was denied, and after exhausting all administrative procedures, the parents sued the school district in a federal district court. The court held for the parents, and the school district appealed to the United States Court of Appeals, Fourth Circuit.

The school district based its defense on a claim that the parents' administrative appeal was untimely—since they had waited approximately 10 months before appealing to the state educational agency. The district claimed that because the parents had received partial reimbursement from the state educational agency, they were not an "aggrieved party" for further appeal under the EAHCA. It claimed further that the trial court did not find sufficient procedural defects to support its decision that the district had failed to provide the child with a free appropriate public education. The court of appeals upheld the district court decision. In its holding, it said that retroactive imposition of a time limitation on the parents' administrative appeal was contrary to the EAHCA goals. It also found that the state agency did not compensate the parents for all tuition expenses and did not reimburse them for room, board, travel expenses, or interest on their loan. These expenses qualified the parents as "aggrieved parties." In its review of the case, the court of appeals found that the district court hearing established that the school district had failed to conduct the multidisciplinary review for the child. In addition, the district had not conducted a placement advisory committee meeting or otherwise adequately involved the parents in the preparation of the child's IEP. The court held that the parents were entitled to *full* (emphasis supplied) tuition reimbursement.

The last case in this section dealt with a mentally retarded Nebraska child who had cerebral palsy and severe behavior impairment. During the 1984–85 school year, the child's behavior gave cause for great concern. Her most severe tantrums included head banging and screaming. Her teacher believed a program with stronger behavior management and with a lower pupil-teacher ratio might be necessary. The mother was worried abut a different placement. When the child's teacher met with the mother to review the child's 1984–85 IEP, in May 1985, the mother was given a pamphlet that described her EAHCA rights. At, or near this time, a school official allegedly advised the mother of her procedural rights and told her to talk to the appropriate school official about an alternative placement for the child. The mother informed the official that she was considering a private-school placement. Sometime, during the summer or early fall of 1985, the school district learned that the child was going to be placed in a private Kansas school.

The parents filed an application for tuition reimbursement with the Nebraska Department of Education. This was denied. Then, the parents asked the department to order 24-hour private placement for the child at the Kansas school and payment for past and future costs of such care. A hearing officer, in July 1986, denied the relief, and the parents sued the school district in a United States district court. This court held for the school district, and the parents appealed to the United States Court of Appeals, Eighth Circuit. The parents argued that the school district had refused to change the child's placement on their request and had failed to give the parents proper written notice of its refusal, as required under the EAHCA. They argued, also, that the district failed to comply with the EAHCA regulations regarding reevaluations while the child was still in the school district during 1984–85. The court of appeals affirmed the district court decision. The parents unilaterally placed the child in the Kansas school and were not entitled to tuition reimbursement (*Evans v. District #17 of Douglas County, Nebraska*, 841 F.2d 824 [8th Cir., Neb., 1988]).

SUSPENSION AND EXPULSION OF HANDICAPPED STUDENTS

One of the most heavily litigated portions of law dealing with handicapped students pertains to suspension and expulsion. Going back to 1975, in *Goss v. Lopez*, 419 U.S. 595 (Ohio, 1975), the Supreme Court decided the landmark student-expulsion case in which the 10-day rule took hold nationally. In this decision, the Court held that, under the due process clause of the Fourteenth Amendment, suspension for up to 10 days required only informal notice and hearing, whereas longer exclusions required more formal procedural protections. The United States Supreme Court has clarified the issue for handicapped students.

Honig v. Doe, 108 S.Ct. 592 (Cal., 1988)

Generalization

Indefinite suspensions violate the "stay-put" provisions of the EAHCA. Suspensions for up to 10 days do not constitute a change in placement. The Court seemed to leave intact the principle that when a student's misbehavior is caused by his or her handicap, any attempt to expel the student from school will be turned aside.

Description

Honig v. Doe involved two emotionally disturbed California children who were given five-day suspensions from school for misbehavior that included destroying school property and assaulting and making sexual comments to other students. Pursuant to California state law, the suspensions were continued indefinitely during the pendency of expulsion hearings. The students sued, claiming a violation of the stay-put provisions of the EAHCA. The district court issued an injunction against expulsion for misbehavior that arises from a student's handicap, and the district appealed.

The United States Court of Appeals, Ninth Circuit, determined that indefinite suspensions constituted a prohibited "change in placement" under the EAHCA but held, further, that fixed suspensions of up to 30 days did not constitute a "change in placement." It determined, also, that a state must directly provide services to a disabled child when a local school district fails to do so. The California superintendent of public instruction filed for a review by the United States Supreme Court on the issues of whether a dangerous exception existed to the stay-put provision and whether the state had to provide services directly when a local school district failed to do so. We now quote from the language of the Court's decision:

The language of 1415(e)(3) is unequivocal. It states plainly that during the pendency of any proceedings initiated under the Act, unless the state or local educational agency and the parents or guardian of a disabled child otherwise agree, "the child *shall* remain in the then current educational placement." 1415(e)(3) [emphasis added]. Faced with the clear directive, petitioner asks us to read a "dangerous" exception into the stay-put provision on the basis of either of two essentially inconsistent assumptions: first, that Congress thought the residual authority of school officials to exclude dangerous students from the classroom too obvious to comment; or second, that Congress inadvertently failed to provide such authority and this Court must therefore remedy the oversight. Because we cannot accept either premise, we decline petitioner's invitation to rewrite the statute. . . .

Petitioner's arguments proceed, he suggests, from a simple, common sense proposition: Congress could not have intended the stay-put provision to be read literally, for such a construction leads to the clearly unintended, and untenable result that the school districts must return violent or dangerous students to school while the often lengthy EHA proceedings run their course. We think it clear, however, that Congress very much meant to strip schools of the *unilateral* authority they had traditionally employed to exclude disabled students, particularly emotionally disturbed students, from school. In so doing, Congress did not leave school administrators powerless to deal with dangerous students; it did, however, deny school officials their former right to "self-help," and directed that in the future the removal of disabled students could be accomplished only with the permission of the parents or, as a last resort, the courts.

Here, the Court proceeded to give its rationale for this decision, drawing on *Mills v. Board of Education of District of Columbia*, 348 F.Supp. 866 (D.C.,

1972), and *PARC*, 343 F.Supp. 279 (Pa., 1972), both of which involved the exclusion of hard-to-handle disabled students. The Court cited the following:

> *Mills* in particular demonstrated the extent to which schools used disciplinary measures to bar children from the classroom. There, school officials had labeled four of the seven minor plaintiffs "behavioral problems," and had excluded them from classes without providing any alternative education to them or any notice to their parents, 348 F.Supp., at 869–870. After finding that this practice was not limited to the named student, *id*, at 868–869, 875, the District Court enjoined future exclusions, suspensions, or expulsions "on grounds of discipline." *Id.*, at 880.

The Court continued with its discussion of exclusionary practices and emphasized the provision for meaningful parental participation in all aspects of a child's educational placement, and it barred schools, through the stay-put provision, from changing that placement over the parents' objection until all review proceedings were completed. Recognizing that the proceedings might prove to be long and tedious, the Court held that the act's drafters had not intended to operate inflexibly and that they had allowed for interim placements when the parents and school officials could agree on one. The Court noted, however, that any emergency exception was "conspicuously absent" from §1415(e)(3) and noted, further, that the Court was not at liberty to "engraft onto the statute an exception Congress chose not to create." The Court concluded:

> In short, then, we believe that school officials are entitled to seek injunctive relief under §1415(e)(2) in appropriate cases. In any such action, §1415(e)(3) effectively creates a presumption in favor of the child's current educational placement which school officials can overcome only by showing that maintaining the child in his or her current placement is substantially likely to result in injury either to himself or herself, or to others.

The Supreme Court held in favor of the lower court decisions, with the exception of the court of appeals holding that a suspension in excess of 10 days did not constitute a "change in placement." This was modified to hold that any suspension in excess of 10 days did constitute a "change in placement."

Many questions have been raised about the 10-day suspension rule. For example, are the 10 days only consecutive or also cumulative? In the case just cited, *Honig v. Doe*, the court addressed the exclusions of handicapped students and held that, under the EAHCA, school officials may not exclude handicapped students for more than 10 days without exhausting the due process placement procedures of the EAHCA. The only exception to this is a very narrow one— when the school officials are able to persuade the court to issue a preliminary injunction because the handicapped student is clearly dangerous.

The *Honig* court did not address the issue of consecutive or cumulative days. The court did determine that any exclusion in excess of ten days constituted a "change in placement." Three legal sources provide some possible guidance in this matter: the EAHCA, §504 of the Rehabilitation Act of 1973, or state law.

The EAHCA and its regulations do not resolve this question. In early 1973, the United States Department of Education Office of Special Education (OSE) issued a policy letter in which it stated that it had "not developed a position on when a series of shorter suspensions would cumulate to constitute a change in placement." The OSE did alert the states and school districts to a future possibility of a cumulative triggering of the placement procedures and went on to say that it had not "established a specific rule or guidance on how many nonconsecutive days of suspension constitutes a change in placement under the EAHCA."

Section 504 of the Rehabilitation Act of 1973 is more instructive. This statue and its regulations both preceded and overlapped the EAHCA but did not directly address the question of consecutive or cumulative days. In 1988, the Office of Civil Rights (OCR) issued a memorandum that provided specific guidance on how to approach nonconsecutive days (Memorandum from LeGree S. Daniels, Assistant Secretary for Civil Rights to OCR Senior Staff, ct. 28, 1988; EHLR SA–52 [Supp. 233, Jan. 25, 1989]).

This memorandum provided an interpretation of OCR's policy in §104.35(a) of §504 regulations. "A significant change in placement" was a permanent exclusion, an exclusion for an indefinite period, an exclusion of more than 10 consecutive school days, and "a series of suspensions that are each of ten days or fewer in duration [that] creates a pattern." A determination of when such a series of suspensions constitutes a significant change of placement "must," in the language of the OCR, "be made on a case-by-case basis." When this is done, the following factors must be considered: "the length of each suspension, the proximity of the suspension to one another, and the total amount of time the child is excluded from school." For students who "are handicapped solely by virtue of being alcoholics or drug addicts" with regard to offenses against school disciplinary rules as to the use and possession of drugs and alcohol, OCR provided an exception to the several variations of the 10-day limit, an exception that, in effect, limited their procedural protections to *Goss* and any applicable state law.

The third legal source to be used in looking at the 10-day suspension question is state law. It is well to research, carefully, state law on suspensions and expulsions as it applies, specifically, to the handicapped student. Two examples of very rigorous requirements are in Massachusetts, where the department of education policy requires alternative educational arrangements when suspensions of a handicapped student exceed 10 cumulative days in a school year, and in Pennsylvania, where the department of education policy requires that placement reevaluation procedures be applied when special-education students receive suspensions of more than 10 days in a school "term."

In a case that was decided after *Honig*, graduation was considered to be a "change in placement" under the EAHCA. The student was a 20-year-old emotionally disturbed boy who resided with his parents in New York state.

Beginning in 1985, the boy attended a vocational training program offered through the Board of Cooperative Educational Services (BOCES) in addition to special-education classes offered by his school district. The BOCES course in electrical mechanical systems was a ''mainstream'' course not designed primarily for handicapped students. He received passing grades in this course.

In March 1987, the school district notified the parents that the Committee on the Handicapped (COH) had determined to graduate their son at the end of the 1986–87 school year. On March 30, 1987, the parents received a letter from the BOCES stating that their son should continue in the BOCES program for another year. In light of the conflict between the two communications, the parents requested that an impartial hearing officer resolve the conflict. In the meantime, however, the son received his diploma and was not permitted to continue in the BOCES program.

After appeal to the commissioner of education, the commissioner agreed with the hearing officer that the school district had properly awarded a high school diploma to the boy. The parents appealed to the federal district court. The court granted a preliminary injunction requiring the district to reinstate the boy in the BOCES program. The district court ruled that graduation was a ''change in placement'' under the EAHCA, implicating the mandatory procedural safeguards of the act. The stay-put provision of the EAHCA required that the handicapped student ''remain in the then current education placement'' during the pendency of the proceedings. In its decision, the court noted that this was an issue of first impression in the federal courts and that a Massachusetts court had also held that graduation is a change in placement under the EAHCA (*Cronin v. Board of Education of the East Ramapo Central School District*, 689 F.Supp. 197 [S.D.N.Y., 1988]).

DISCRIMINATION

The Rehabilitation Act of 1973 prohibits discrimination against the handicapped in programs receiving federal assistance. Under the act, no otherwise qualified handicapped individual is to be excluded from employment, programs, or services to which he or she is entitled. Additionally, claims for alleged discriminations are sometimes brought under the Equal Protection Clause of the United States Constitution, which also prohibits discrimination by guaranteeing that laws will be applied equally to all citizens.

The duty not to discriminate against handicapped individuals may arise by statute and/or may be concomitant with the receipt of federal funding. When a state's asserted interest in discriminating against the handicapped is outweighed by the liberty interests of the handicapped, the state must affirmatively act to eliminate the source of the discrimination or, in other cases, must refrain from acting when doing so would promote unfair discrimination. A foremost example of the issue of illness and handicaps in employee relations emerged in the *School Board of Nassau County v. Arline* (see Chapter 5).

School officials are well advised to read and understand the holding in *Arline*. This is especially important before any action is taken concerning an employee with a contagious disease. A school board cannot fire an employee who has a contagious disease but who is "otherwise qualified" unless it can be shown that the disease is likely to be transmitted through normal, routine contacts within the school. Even so, the school must make a "reasonable accommodation," meaning that the individual is entitled to a position that poses less risk to students and employees in the school.

There is a body of law developing in the area of the acquired immune deficiency syndrome (AIDS). In reviewing a case, *Chalk v. U.S. District Court*, 840 F.2d 701 (9th Cir., Cal., 1988), which was brought before it, the U.S. Court of Appeals, Ninth Circuit, applied *Arline*. A teacher of hearing-impaired children had been transferred to an administrative position when the school district discovered that he had AIDS. The teacher brought suit against the board, claiming it had violated his rights under the Rehabilitation Act of 1973 by taking him from the classroom. A U.S. district court denied the teacher's request for a preliminary injunction, which would have allowed him to teach until the court could hold a trial and issue a ruling. The U.S. Court of Appeals, Ninth Circuit, reversed and issued the preliminary injunction.

In reaching its decision to grant the preliminary injunction, the court noted that the teacher had to demonstrate a combination of probable success at trial and a possibility of irreparable injury. Considering the Rehabilitation Act, the teacher could not be dismissed because of the handicapping condition (AIDS) if he was otherwise qualified to teach. The court then applied a test that the U.S. Supreme Court had fashioned in *Arline*. This test provided that "[a] person who poses a significant risk of communicating an infectious disease to others in the work place will not be otherwise qualified for his or her job if reasonable accommodations will not eliminate that risk." The court then went on to point out that the district court's finding was that transmission of AIDS was unlikely to occur in the classroom. The court then held that the teacher was otherwise qualified for his position because his presence in the classroom would not pose "a significant risk of communicating an infectious disease to others." The court then concluded that this finding meant that the teacher would probably succeed at trial.

Then, the court noted that although the teacher's salary had not been reduced when he was transferred to the administrative position, the transfer had removed him from a job for which he had been especially prepared and from which he derived "tremendous personal satisfaction and joy." Having determined that the previously required combination of factors existed, the court held in favor of the teacher and awarded the preliminary injunction. The teacher was returned to the classroom.

The placement of a student with AIDS was the issue in *Martinez v. School Board of Hillsboro County, Florida*, 861 F.2d 1502 (11th Cir., Fla., 1988). The United States District Court for the Middle District of Florida refused, on two different occasions, to permit an incontinent, trainable, mentally handicapped (TMH) student with AIDS to join a TMH classroom. The student's mother attempted to enroll her in the public school, and the school excluded her. The mother, after exhausting her administrative remedies, filed suit in a United States district court. The court permitted the student to join the school's TMH classroom with the proviso that she be segregated from the class in a specially constructed room with a large picture window. The mother objected and appealed to the United States Court of Appeals, Eleventh Circuit.

The court of appeals held that the two federal statutes applied when determining the appropriate placement for mentally handicapped children—the Education of All Handicapped Children Act (EAHCA) and §504 of the Rehabilitation Act of 1973. The EAHCA required schools to provide a free appropriate public education to handicapped children. Section 504 of the Rehabilitation Act held that handicapped students should not be excluded if otherwise qualified for the activity.

In determining this student's status, the court held that the student was entitled to a free appropriate education under the EAHCA. She suffered from two handicaps under §504, since she was both mentally handicapped and had AIDS. The court's finding was that the appropriate educational placement was the regular TMH classroom. Then, the district court's finding of a "remote theoretical possibility" of transmission of AIDS was insufficient to exclude her from the TMH classroom. There were other matters that the district court had failed to determine. For example, if the student was not "otherwise qualified" to attend the TMH classroom, what, if any, reasonable accommodations would qualify her? Also, the lower court would be required, on remand, to determine if segregating the student in a separate room would have a stigmatizing effect on her. The court of appeals vacated the district court's decision and returned the case for rehearing.

In *Doe v. Dalton Elementary School District #148*, 694 F.Supp. 440 (N.D. Ill., 1988), a 12-year-old student had undergone open-heart surgery as a child. As a result, he contracted the AIDS virus through blood transfusions. When the board of education of his school district learned of his affliction, it excluded him from attending the school's regular classes and its extracurricular activities. The student, then, filed an action in a federal district court, claiming that his rights were being violated.

Weighing the possibilities in this case, the court found that the student, at trial, very likely would be considered a handicapped individual. His malady impaired one or more of his major life activities. The court also determined that the student was "otherwise qualified" to attend school. Medical authorities had found no significant risk of transmission of AIDS in the classroom setting. The court held that the boy's exclusion from school had been damaging to his self-esteem and allowed that this could be partially alleviated by returning him to the normal classroom environment. The court said, also that any injury that might occur by issuing the order was insufficient to outweigh the harm to the student. In addition, there would be no disservice to the public by allowing the student to return to school, since the threat of transmitting the AIDS virus to others was minimal. The court order was in two parts: (1) the student was entitled to return to school, and (2) the school district should provide carefully drawn procedures to ensure that any potential risk of harm to the student's classmates and teachers was eliminated.

SUMMARY

The law and the handicapped is a rapidly growing body of law that has escalated since the enactment of §504 of the Rehabilitation Act of 1973 and the Education of All Handicapped Children Act (EAHCA) of 1975. These two statutes were expanded with the enactment of the Handicapped Children's Protection Act (HCPA) in 1986. Adding the debilitating force of AIDS to these statutes creates a multifaceted basis for increased litigation in behalf of the handicapped. We have come a long way from the time when the handicapped, or those who are "unable to profit from education," were excluded from school to the present day, when every child is entitled to a free appropriate public education.

Current statutes, court decisions, and federal and local board of education policies provide the guidelines under which local school districts deliver services to the handicapped. We can expect that litigation will continue as litigants seek to obtain clarification of these decisions, policies, regulations, and statutes. All people who deal with the handicapped would be well advised to follow very carefully the most recent interpretation that governs the situation facing them. Even that is no guarantee that they will avoid litigation, but it may place them in a more favorable position should they have to defend their action in court.

8

Discrimination and Equality of Opportunity

CONCEPTS OF EQUALITY

Discrimination involves choice: one thing or one person is chosen over another; one is selected while another is ignored; preference for one is accorded over another. Discrimination has come to have a socially and morally offensive connotation only recently, since adjectives have been attached indicating an unjustifiable discrimination or invidious discrimination. That is, bias and prejudice have become prominent parts in the decisions about choice. When some individuals or institutions in society act toward others in that society with bias, prejudice, malice, or hostility, an invidious discrimination is being practiced. It was at about the end of World War II that Americans became conscious of unjust discrimination and began to work at identifying groups that had been victims of unjust discrimination. Various remedies have been provided in law for those earlier unjust actions.

Equality among the citizens of a society is a concept that was stated magnificently by Thomas Jefferson when he said, "We hold these truths to be self-evident; that all [people] are created equal." That is a reasonable starting point from which to try to grasp the meaning of equality in America. *Equality* is a word that has various meanings, and different aspects of the word are embraced as the whole truth by different segments of the American citizenry. It is a slippery concept, difficult to grasp, and if it is generally accepted as a minimum political birthright, it raises a whole host of new questions for the society conferring those rights of political equality on all citizens. No one has yet seriously argued that it means economic, psychological, or physiological equality, although some of those concepts can be seen in both statutory law and case law of the present. Surely, equality cannot prevail in any society that allows discrimination toward minority groups. On recognizing and acknowledging the existence of discrimination, Americans have continued to move toward perfecting the ideal of equality, which demands conscious effort to eliminate the social and economic inequalities that have plagued minority groups.

Much of the effort expended over the past few decades to eradicate racial discrimination has involved the public schools. That focus has been enlarged beyond its initial scope to include discrimination on the basis of sex and several additional categories. Students and staff have been the objects of antidiscrimination efforts in schools as programs that recognize the values of a multicultural society have been implemented.

When equality is accepted as a base for political opportunity, it means one thing. When it is accepted as a base for economic opportunity, it means something else. When it is accepted by one segment of the population to mean one thing and by another to mean something else, conflict is probable because expectations differ. In the American system, where substantial liberties are guaranteed in law to individuals, equality cannot relate to effort or results. That is, equalized opportunity may be embraced at very different levels of effort, and rewards may be sharply unequal. An additional complication is that individual abilities are unequal—by a variety of measurements. Is it any wonder, then, that the concept of equality leads to unrealistic expectations, given the tensions, the restrictions, and the opportunities in American society? It is a concept that can be more easily stated on paper than legislated and practiced in society.

For many Americans, the disparity between expectations and socioeconomic positions is a reality contradiction, to some extent, of the whole notion of equality. But the facts of reality must include the characteristic of American free competition. The employee personnel marketplace responds to achievement; the payoff is for achievement as it is perceived to be valuable. Earnings may be spent by consumers without restriction. Some Americans earn and acquire; some save; some do not. From an economic vantage point, inequality is surely as much the rule as is equality. It is an irrevocable irony resulting from the capitalistic system blended with the very substantial political liberties that are uniquely American.

The concepts embodied in inequality gained a statutory voice immediately after the Civil War. It was the intent of Congress in the Civil Rights Act of 1871 to provide safeguards for those American black freedmen who only a few years previously had been slaves. Section 1983 of that act is the least restrictive federal statute for rectifying violations of federally protected rights. Nearly 100 years elapsed before the civil rights concept again came to the fore with comparable political emphasis. In 1964 Congress passed the Civil Rights Act. That statute, of several titles, was a culmination of the actual efforts calling for elimination of discrimination; at the same time, it was a starting point for the continuation of those efforts, providing a statutory base for litigation and further exploration of the meaning of the term *equality*. Part of that exploration has led toward the idea that for certain minority groups who can identify a time in the nation's history when they were treated with inequality—penalized or stigmatized by way of bias and prejudice—some sort of compensation should be delivered. Briefly said, there are now three federal laws that are of primary concern to school districts. Title IX deals with sex discrimination. Title VI deals with race discrimination. Section 504 deals with discrimination against the handicapped. For each of these areas, there have been refinements and successor legislation.

The essence of compensation is that injustices have been committed against groups that were vulnerable and politically powerless. Furthermore, because of powerlessness, those injustices were not halted. Because the injustices caused suffering, compensation is due the victims. If this idea may be called the "principle of compensation," a number of problems spring from the principle when it is examined. For example, in American law and culture, there is a period when an individual's guilt for injustices must be established or any claims against the accused forsaken. If one committed an act that might be considered a wrong, for how long a period would one be held accountable? On an individual basis, statutes of limitations speak to this, and a citizen may not be pursued, or held in potential guilt, longer than a specific period. However, when compensation is addressed to acts committed in the distant past, it is not addressed to an individual. It is addressed to groups, by groups.

In contemporary America, it is claimed by one group—the victims—against another group—the perpetrators. For example, American blacks may charge other Americans with human slavery and establish an expectation of compensation for the charge, which is historically verifiable but which could not involve any of the people who were actually parties to the slave-master situation. They have all died. Likewise, American Indians could charge other Americans with fraud, misrepresentation, and other similar unjust activities by which Indian territories were reduced, relocated, or lost and by which other Americans gained territory. There may be truth in such charges, although strictly they may have little to do with legality.

If articulated bluntly, the principle of compensation states: "You, or yours, took something from me, or mine, too cheaply. Now it is time to pay up." There is an attraction for elected officials in that theme, for it has provided a rationale from which to design programs to help the downtrodden of our society. Americans have a history of altruistic help to the downtrodden. The principle stipulates that the disadvantaged in society should receive help from the more fortunate, and it is the corollary of that American ethic that the strong should help the weak. The political manifestations of the principle of compensation provide for help from the stronger groups to weaker groups. Compensation is delivered on the basis of group membership, not on the basis of individual needs. Needs are assumed for all in the group, and compensation is a group entitlement. The fact that those very groups being compensated have, in their history, a record of some very intolerant, very biased acts does not bear on the issue.

Specifically, compensation has found legal expression in a number of anti-discrimination programs. Included would be legislation devoted to civil rights, equal educational and employment opportunities, salary restrictions calling for equal pay, and organizational obligations for affirmative actions with some sort of equalization as a goal. In the evolving American notion of a continually extending and expanding equality, various laws have been passed to guide citizens toward accomplishing greater equality and toward reducing discrimination that rests on bias or prejudice.

CIVIL RIGHTS LEGISLATION

More than any other single event that focused on the shortcomings in American society to provide a nondiscriminatory environment for citizens, *Brown v. Topeka Board of Education*, 347 U.S. 483 (Kan., 1954), serves as the reference point from which to consider the civil rights movement. The Topeka Board of Education, under state laws that made such an arrangement permissible, created public schools for black children only. The black children were segregated from white children, and the Supreme Court accepted the plaintiffs' claim that separate facilities were "inherently unequal," a violation of the Fourteenth Amendment. From this finding a new awareness of discrimination developed and found expression in several federal statues:

1. The Civil Rights Acts of 1957 and 1960, intended to encourage equality in voting rights and encourage school desegregation
2. The Equal Pay Act of 1963, intended to eliminate employees' pay differentials that were based solely upon sex
3. The comprehensive Civil Rights Act of 1964, attending several problem areas of citizen inequality
4. Successor statutes in the same view, devoted to topics such as voting rights, model cities, open housing, sex discrimination, and the rights of handicapped, pregnant, and aged citizens

The civil rights thrust of the twentieth century got an initial impetus from the judiciary branch, which continued its interest after *Brown*. The energy of that original thrust was picked up in a long series of executive orders as one president after another issued orders extending the comprehensiveness of civil rights. Advocacy for civil rights was strong from within and from outside of government, and Congress passed laws that had an accretionary effect, providing protection for more and more people under more and more varied social conditions. All three branches of government became active in the civil rights effort.

In a legislative expression of clear political commitment to the disadvantaged, the Civil Rights Act of 1964 (P.L. 88–252) took a comprehensive approach to the problems included in its several sections, called titles. The titles separately addressed aspects of discrimination such as voting registration, community-relations services, judicial procedures in civil rights litigation, and opportunities for equal employment. Title VII of the act, "Equal Employment Opportunity," provides definitions and accounts for state laws dealing with employment and details how complaints by minority citizens should be investigated. Two portions bear so heavily on school organization and administration that they merit extended examination.

DISCRIMINATION BECAUSE OF RACE, COLOR, RELIGION, SEX, OR NATIONAL ORIGIN

Sec. 703. (a) It shall be an unlawful employment practice for an employer—

(1) to fail or refuse to hire or to discharge any individual, or otherwise to discriminate against any individual with respect to his compensation terms, conditions, or privileges of employment, because of such individual's race, color, religion, sex, or national origin; or

(2) to limit, segregate, or classify his employees in any way which would deprive or tend to deprive any individual of employment opportunities or otherwise adversely affect his status as an employee, because of such individual's race, color, religion, sex, or national origin.

(b) It shall be unlawful employment practice for an employment agency to fail or refuse to refer for employment, or otherwise to discriminate against, any individual because of his race, color, religion, sex, or national origin, or to classify or refer for employment any individual on the basis of his race, color, religion, sex, or national origin.

(c) It shall be an unlawful employment practice for a labor organization, or joint labor-management committee controlling apprenticeship or other training or retraining, including on-the-job training programs, to discriminate against any individual because of his race, color, religion, sex, or national origin in admission to, or employment in, any program established to provide apprenticeship or other training.

The act later states, in the same title:

EQUAL EMPLOYMENT OPPORTUNITY COMMISSION

Sec. 705. (a) There is hereby created a commission to be known as the Equal Employment Opportunity Commission, which shall be composed of five members, not more than three of whom shall be members of the same political party, who shall be appointed by the President by and with the advice and consent of the Senate. One of the original members shall be appointed for a term of one year, one for a term of two years, one for a term of three years, one for a term of four years, and one for a term of five years, beginning from the date of enactment of this title, but their successors shall be appointed for terms of five years each, except that any individual chosen to fill a vacancy shall be appointed only for the unexpired term of the member whom he shall succeed. The President shall designate one member to serve as Chairman of the Commission, and one member to serve as Vice Chairman. The Chairman shall be responsible on behalf of the Commission for the administrative operations of the Commission, and shall appoint, in accordance with the civil service laws, such officers, agents, attorneys, and employees as it deems necessary to assist it in the performance of its functions and to fix their compensation in accordance with the Classification Act of 1949, as amended. The Vice Chairman shall act as Chairman in the absence or disability of the Chairman or in the event of a vacancy in that office. . . .

(g) The Commission shall have power—

(1) to cooperate with and, with their consent, utilize regional, state, local, and other agencies, both public and private, and individuals;

(2) to pay to witnesses whose depositions are taken or who are summoned before the Commission or any of its agents the same witness and mileage fees as are paid to witnesses of the courts of the United States;

(3) to furnish to persons subject to this title such technical assistance as they may request to further their compliance with this title or an order issued thereunder;

(4) upon the request of (i) any employer, whose employees or some of them, or (ii) any labor organization, whose members or some of them refuse or threaten to refuse to cooperate in effectuating the provisions of this title, to assist in such effectuation by conciliation or such other remedial action as is provided by this title;

(5) to make such technical studies as are appropriate to effectuate the purposes and policies of this title and to make the results of such studies available to the public;

(6) to refer matters to the Attorney General with recommendations for intervention in a civil action brought by an aggrieved party under section 706, or for the institution of a civil action by the Attorney General under 707, and to advise, consult, and assist the Attorney General on such matters.

The statutes have been extended by subsequent legislation to include other groups. That is, in addition to the five citizen groups identified in 1964 as worthy of special protection, the categories of age, handicap, and pregnancy have been added. In some states, and under some negotiated contracts, an even longer list of specifically protected conditions or characteristics may pertain. The translation of those stipulations into the operation of public school programs particularly concerns the area of school administration.

RACE AND EQUAL OPPORTUNITY

Initially, the litigation dealing with unequal opportunities that resulted from discrimination by one race against another was founded in that part of the Fourteenth Amendment that protected everyone, as citizens of the United States, against the unnecessary or arbitrary discrimination of officialdom in any of the states. That litigation also tended toward a simplified division of the American citizenry into black and white citizens. The entire situation is further complicated by the fact that *race*, when used as a term to identify certain groups of American citizens who are protected against present discrimination, is a political term. That is, it is a label that can be used for political purposes even though racial certainty, as determined by blood strain, is only a myth. Americans have engaged in far too much intergroup procreation for the term to have any meaning beyond identification for political purposes. For the operation of the public schools, *race* has come to mean any of those people who are not white and for whom there is either a history of discrimination in educational opportunities or a current condition that makes education a special problem for that group. Presently, the governmentally acknowledged categories of citizens, by race, are five: black, not Hispanic; white, not Hispanic; Hispanic; Asian and Pacific Islander; and American Indian and Alaskan native.

Brown v. Topeka Board of Education, 347 U.S. 483 (Kan., 1954)

Generalization

Local boards of education are obligated to provide educational opportunities of minimum-quality standards as set forward in the statutes of their state. They may not carry out those programs in facilities that are separated on the basis of pupil assignment by race.

Description

For several years preceding *Brown*, a series of cases before the Supreme Court had questioned the lack of facilities, or their inadequacy, to care for the professional needs of black students from several states that did not allow qualified black students to attend postbaccalaureate programs in state universities. Court holdings had consistently ordered the admission of blacks or the creation of equal educational opportunities, and in retrospect, those findings can be seen as indicators of what the Supreme Court might decide about elementary and secondary education. The arguments for and against in *Brown* were presented twice. First, they were heard by a Court chaired by Chief Justice Vinson. A year later, after his death, they were heard by a Court chaired by Chief Justice Earl Warren, who spoke for the Court.

These cases come to us from the states of Kansas, South Carolina, Virginia, and Delaware. They are premised on different facts and different local conditions, but a common legal question justifies their consideration together in this consolidated opinion.

In each of the cases, minors of the Negro race, through their representatives, seek the aid of the courts in obtaining admission to the public schools of their community on a non-segregated basis. In each instance, they had been denied admission to schools attended by white children under laws requiring or permitting segregation according to race. This segregation was alleged to deprive the plaintiffs of the equal protection of the laws under the Fourteenth Amendment. In each of the cases other than the Delaware case, a three-judge federal district court denied relief to the plaintiffs on the so-called ''separate but equal'' doctrine, announced by this court in *Plessy v. Ferguson*, 163 U.S. 537. Under that doctrine, equality of treatment is accorded when the races are provided substantially equal facilities, even though these facilities be separate. In the Delaware case, the Supreme Court of Delaware adhered to that doctrine, but ordered that the plaintiffs be admitted to the white schools because of their superiority to the Negro schools.

In approaching this problem, we cannot turn the clock back to 1868 when the Amendment was adopted, or even to 1896 when *Plessy v. Ferguson* was written. We must consider public education in the light of its full development and its present place in American life throughout the Nation. Only in this way can it be determined if segregation in public schools deprives these plaintiffs of the equal protection of the laws.

We come then to the question provided; Does segregation of children in public school solely on the basis of race, even though the physical facilities and other "tangible" factors may be equal, deprive the children of the minority of equal educational opportunities? We believe that it does.

We conclude that in the field of public education the doctrine of "separate but equal" has no place. Separate educational facilities are inherently unequal.

In a subsequent decision a year later, *Brown II*, the Court frankly addressed problems of implementation. At that time the Court directed that desegregation should occur "with all deliberate speed," a phrase that has continued to raise questions about how rapidly the changes should be accomplished.

After *Brown*, some school districts voluntarily set out to establish programs for the racial desegregation of their students on the premise that, in a democracy, there are educational values in population mixes; that is, students gain more accurate pictures of "real-life" communities when they are in schools with students from other cultures and races. In *Van Blerkom v. Donovan*, 207 N.E.2d 503 (N.Y., 1965), the courts refused to set aside efforts of the board of education to reduce de facto segregation. Declaring the question to be primarily educational, the court accepted the sociological and psychological rationale of the board as an adequate basis for the reassignment of student personnel based on racial identification.

Green v. New Kent County School Board, 391 U.S. 430 (Va., 1968)

Generalization

In the efforts to eliminate racially discriminatory assignments of pupils, local boards have wide latitude in what may be done. However, whatever is done must show by results or fair promise that the segregation of pupils by race will be reduced inasmuch as segregation is the manifestation of unequal opportunity.

Description

New Kent County, Virginia, was a school district in a state that had statutorily demanded that local boards establish and keep a dual system of schools, some for white students and some were for black students. In the New Kent district, there were only two attendance centers, one for blacks and one for whites.

Evidence from the many cases that occurred between *Brown* and *Green*, since they had come from one of the other 16 states with similar statutes, indicated that the facilities could seldom stand comparison in tests for whether they were, in fact, equal facilities. As viewed by the Court, they were not only inherently unequal but were literally unequal as well; the facilities with a primarily black student body were inferior.

The New Kent County Board of Education had responded to its obligation by describing and installing a freedom-of-choice plan. Citizens of the school district were both black and white, dispersed in a racial mix throughout the district but without attendance boundaries. One school received all of the district's black pupils; the other received all of the white pupils. This meant that some pupils did not go to the school nearest their own home but rode buses to a more distant school. With the installation of the freedom-of-choice plan, it became possible for children of either race to elect to attend the other school. The board did not dictate attendance boundaries for its schools and did not demand that parents living in certain areas must, by the location of their residence, be bound to one school. What the board did was offer an option that had not been previously available to patrons of that school district. However, in *Green* the Court chose to pass over evidence of effort and to ask, instead, for evidence that the effort was producing diminished discrimination against black students by segregating them in separate facilities. From the evidence, the Court deduced that the dual system persisted and that a unitary system had not been developed. Justice Brennan spoke for the Court.

New Kent County is a rural county in eastern Virginia. About one-half of its population of some 4,500 are Negroes. There is no residential segregation in the county; persons of both races reside throughout. . . . The segregated system (of schools) was initially established and maintained under the compulsion of Virginia. . . . The pattern of separate "white" and "Negro" schools in New Kent . . . established under compulsion of state laws is precisely the pattern of segregation to which *Brown I* and *Brown II* were particularly addressed. . . .

It is against this background that 13 years after *Brown II* commanded the abolition of dual systems we must measure the effectiveness of respondent school board's "freedom-of-choice" plan to achieve that end. The School Board contends that it has fully discharged its obligation by adopting a plan by which every student, regardless of race, may "freely" choose the school he will attend. The Board attempts to cast the issue in its broadest form. . . . But that argument ignores the thrust of *Brown II*. In light of the command of that case, what is involved here is the question whether the Board has achieved the "racially nondiscriminatory school system" *Brown II* held must be effectuated in order to remedy the established unconstitutional deficiencies of its segregated system.

The New Kent School Board's "freedom-of-choice" plan cannot be accepted as a sufficient step to "effectuate a transition" to a unitary system. In three years of operation not a single white child has chosen to attend (the black) school. . . . In other words, the school system remains a dual system.

In *Green* the Court took a new direction and asked the very direct question, "Does the plan work?" The Court determined that if the plan did not work, then it was invalid as an affirmative response to *Brown*.

Swann v. Charlotte-Mecklenburg Board of Education, 402 U.S. 11 (N.C., 1971)

Generalization

Boards of education should not hesitate to use a variety of techniques to overcome any vestige of a dual school system. Any obligation for local initiative cannot be set aside; if a local school district defaults in its obligations to eliminate discrimination, courts may intervene with detailed plans to accomplish the elimination.

Description

The Charlotte-Mecklenberg (North Carolina) School District was a large consolidated school. That board had proposed several plans for desegregating the schools, all of which had been rejected by a federal district court as inadequate. The Supreme Court addressed segregation imposed by state law, that is, de jure segregation. It was stated that the local board had failed to initiate adequate plans for desegregation, and the Court cited four areas that demanded attention: racial quotas as targets or balances, one-race schools, alteration of school-attendance zones, and transportation of students.

At the same time that some of the questions about the Charlotte schools were settled, other questions, perhaps larger ones, arose. Population proportions have proved troublesome. The exceedingly fine line between an attendance quota derived from population proportions in a school district or some definable community and an attendance target based on that same data has not been operationally helpful in addressing problems of racial desegregation. The same problem exists for the condition of population shifts that may occur in a school district after a court has ordered some sort of desegregation plan. In a decision that included a comment that boards in dual school systems had to carry the burden of proof to show that they were making racially nondiscriminatory pupil assignments, Chief Justice Burger also made a statement on the necessity of busing as a desegregation tool. Ironically, long used as a tool for segregation, it became the most controversial of all techniques yet applied to reduce segregation by race.

No rigid guidelines as to student transportation can be given for application to the infinite variety of problems presented in thousands of situations. Bus transportation has been an integral part of the public education system for years. . . . Desegregation plans cannot be limited to the walk-in school.

An objection to transportation of students may have validity when the time or distance of travel is so great as to either risk the health of the children or significantly impinge on the educational process. District courts must weigh the soundness of any transportation plan in light of what (has been said, above). . . . The reconciliation of competing values in a desegregation case is, of course, a difficult task with many sensitive facets, but fundamentally no more so than remedial measures courts of equity have traditionally employed.

After commenting on the general powers of district courts to carry out the sentiments and directives of the Supreme Court, and the inherent difficulties in achieving a balance that would accommodate both equity and fairness, the Court concluded with a comment on the obligations that were left to a school district after a unitary school system began operation. It was a candid recognition of the phenomenon of resegregation.

It does not follow that the communities served by such (unitary) systems will remain demographically stable, for in a growing, mobile society, few will do so. Neither school authorities nor district courts are constitutionally required to make year-by-year adjustments of the racial composition of student bodies once the affirmative duty to desegregate has been accomplished and racial discrimination through official action is eliminated from the system. This does not mean that federal courts are without power to deal with future problems; but in the absence of a showing that either the school authorities or some other agency of the State has deliberately attempted to fix or alter demographic patterns to affect the racial composition of the schools, further intervention by a district court should not be necessary.

At the time of *Brown*, 17 states demanded racially segregated school systems, that is, dual school systems. Four other states had passed permissive legislation concerning pupil assignment by race in some of the school districts. Other states had, or came to have, de facto segregation. In the latter circumstance, pupils were not assigned by race but by attendance boundaries. Given the social characteristic of like-type clustering, which is reinforced by the economic status that prevails in large-city school systems, many schools have been nearly one-race schools because the residents within that attendance area were of one race. It is a part of the cultural-economic phenomenon, seen long before the massive migrations of southern rural blacks to northern urban settings. Skin color added another factor to the affinity for clustering by like types and decreased the pervasive melting-pot phenomenon of earlier migrations.

It would be difficult to argue convincingly that racial prejudice has ceased to exist as a consequence of *Brown*. What has become apparent is that the racial desegregation of public schools, as a means to provide equal opportunity and to rid our society of discrimination, is difficult to accomplish. It may be more of a process than an end or goal. Court pronouncements are internalized by different citizens in different ways—and are rejected by some. There are several reasons for such different perceptions and expectations, which are best expressed as questions:

1. How can it be determined when a school system is desegregated? How about a single school—an attendance center—within a large school district?
2. Should proportions of the five identified races be used in making pupil assignments to overcome segregation?
3. How can a school census be developed that will include stable and accurate labels of the student body by race?
4. When a larger proportion of one race is designated as gifted, has discrimination been involved? If a similar disproportion has been identified as handicapped, has discrimination been involved?

More questions could be developed, but this short list serves to point out the difficulty in addressing problems of racial discrimination. The above questions have all been limited to the pupil population; the necessary and suitable management techniques selected to deal with employee personnel by race—hiring, placement, evaluation, and so on—pose yet another substantial organizational problem for public schools.

Over the years the difference between de facto and de jure segregation has diminished in the eyes of the Supreme Court. For example, the state constitution of Colorado specifically, and with strong wording, disallows any kind of dual school system. Yet a major case on this topic came from Colorado in 1973.

Keyes v. School District #1, Denver, 413 U.S. 921 (Colo., 1973)

Generalization

Decisions made by boards about school-building locations, attendance boundaries, and curriculum are all affirmative actions; that is, they demand board initiative. Boards cannot allow that initiative to produce schools that tend to be racially segregated and that, thereby, produce "an unequal educational opportunity in violation of the Fourteenth Amendment equal protection clause."

Description

Over the year, the Denver School District grew in population, and new groups of Americans arrived as residents. In 1970 the racial and ethnic composition of the school district included significant numbers of whites, blacks, and Hispanics. Characteristically, those groups showed up as affinity clusters in the school district, not evenly dispersed through the territory of the district. The *Keyes* case brought to the fore several new aspects about racial segregation in schools, as noticed by the judiciary:

1. It was a northern school district.
2. It was in a state with a strong statement against dual systems.
3. It included three racial groups in substantial numbers.
4. Assignment of staff by race had occurred.
5. There was no cultural-racial curriculum designed to speak to minority interests.

Speaking for the Court, Justice Brennan stated, among other things, a new definition of a dual school system:

This is not a case, however, where a statutory dual system has ever existed. Nevertheless, where plaintiffs prove that the school authorities have carried out a systematic program of segregation affecting a substantial portion of the students, schools, teachers, and facilities within the school system, it is only common sense to conclude that there exists a predicate for a finding of the existence of a dual school system. Several considerations support this conclusion. First, it is obvious that a practice of concentrating Negroes in certain schools by structuring attendance zones or designating "feeder" schools on the basis of race has the reciprocal effect of keeping other nearby schools predominantly white. Similarly, the practice of building a school—such as the Barrett Elementary School in this case—to a certain size and in a certain location, "with conscious knowledge that it would be a segregated school,"... has a substantial reciprocal effect on the racial composition of other nearby schools. So also, the use of mobile classrooms, the drafting of student transfer policies, the transportation of students....

In short, common sense dictates the conclusion that racially inspired school board actions have an impact beyond the particular schools that are the subjects of those actions. ... We emphasize that the differentiating factor between de jure segregation and so-called de facto segregation to which we referred in *Swann* is purpose or intent to segregate. Where school authorities have been found to have practiced purposeful segregation in part of a school system, they may be expected to oppose system-wide desegregation, as did the respondents in this case.

The Court specified that the local board had to assume the burden of proof, that it had to explain any of its actions or district conditions to which the plaintiffs ascribed racially discriminatory motives.

In discharging that burden, it is not enough, of course, that the school authorities rely upon some allegedly logical, racially neutral explanation for their actions. Their burden is to adduce proof sufficient to support a finding that segregative intent was not among the factors that motivated their actions.

The ruling in *Keyes* greatly broadened the responsibility of all local boards in school districts with multiracial populations. With a new dimension established as the burden of proof to be assumed by any local board, findings were delivered in the form of court orders for desegregation in school districts of northern cities that had never explicitly advocated dual systems but that could not meet the test stipulated in *Keyes* about why they did not have desegregated schools in the several forms also stated in *Keyes*.

Of all techniques that have been ordered by the courts to reduce segregation, busing pupils has been the most burdensome for school patrons. Magnet schools, clustered and paired schools, and other techniques have had, compared with busing, a ready acceptance. Costs in money and time are apparent. It is also the technique that has been most shattering to some commonly held concepts of community and the neighborhood school. The patron who sees a school building one or two blocks away at the same time that his or her child is selected to attend a school eight or ten miles away is very likely to become personally and emotionally—but negatively—involved in the problem. Intense personal involvement in addressing large social questions is not a goal of every citizen who is caught up in the court orders for busing, so that many feel trapped and make judgments about the relative adequacy of the political system that demands their involvement. At least one implication that can be noted from this or similar orders imposed, from without, on an LEA is a loss of affection for the institution, that is, the public schools, by the citizenry. Although an order is directed at an LEA, it is the private citizens residing in the affected school district who become the subjects of that court order. Many citizens have refused to participate in the large problem of racial separation and have elected to spend energy in solving their very personal part of that problem, acting to avoid the impact of the court orders—in effect, a kind of personal evasion. At least two discernible lines of reactionary avoidance have emerged since *Brown*.

In one such reaction, people merely remove themselves from the geographical territory encompassed in the court order and go to another place for their residence. Although this residence changing tends to include people of some socio-economic homogeneity, it has been called "white flight." It is the movement of whites—and others on a socioeconomic par—from school districts under a court order to desegregate their schools racially to some other area where that school district has no such obligation. Another reaction has occurred, primarily in several of those states that had dual school systems at the time of *Brown*. Private schools, or academies, were formed. Voluntary private schools burgeoned, both in numbers and in student registrations. Until 25 years after *Brown*, many of the counties in those states had more than 25 percent of the whole student body registered in private academies offering elementary and secondary curriculums. Some academies are church-related; some are not. Quality levels vary from place to place, partially a function of variable quality control from the SDEs in those several states. In the custom of American private education, these academies exercise selective admission and, as a matter of practice, register white children only. Both school settings, above, describe conditions in which court orders for racial desegregation in schools have been a prelude to resegregation.

Actually, resegregation may be a consequence of other actions that Americans are at liberty to take. There is an obvious tension between what the courts can order public institutions, such as schools, to do in regard to the education of their children and what citizens will accept as their reasonable obligation. If whites really constitute the group that the other four racial groups (the racial minorities) need to be protected from, the loss of wholehearted white support of public education is a loss that has not been frankly discussed and calculated.

For example, manifestations of this tension were at work in two major school districts in 1981. In the St. Louis Public School District, the resegregation phenomenon developed through the 1960s and 1970s until it was contended that racial desegregation was not a possibility—only black students were left in that LEA. In 1981 it was proposed that only by busing black children from the St. Louis schools into several adjacent school districts, and busing white children from those districts into the St. Louis schools, could racial desegregation occur. That plan has been variously effective, with disputes over funding and program.

In the Los Angeles Public Schools, a busing order from a state court necessitated the transportation of over 80,000 schoolchildren each day to achieve a desired racial balance. Strongly resisted by the local board and many school patrons, public school registrations dropped as children were transferred to private schools or parents moved to other public school districts. Uniquely, that order had come from a state, rather than from a federal, court. The citizens of the state passed at referendum a constitutional change that resulted in the withdrawal of the order, after conclusive judicial tests of the amendment to the state's constitution.

Private schools with selective admissions policies now register more than 10 percent of the elementary and secondary students. In *New Life Baptist Church Academy v. East Longmeadow*, 825 F.2d (Mass., 1989), the Massachusetts statute that conveyed regulatory powers to local school boards was upheld. That is, the local board had to approve as adequate the secular program of the church-sponsored school. Other states have waffled on issues of regulating private education. As a consequence of *Nebraska v. Faith Baptist*, 301 N.W.2d 572 (Neb., 1981), the Nebraska legislature created new terminology. Those who were nominally teachers in certain church-sponsored schools became instructional monitors. By that label, the question of teachers without certification was "solved," although such people could not become classroom leaders in any other setting. In *People v. DeJonge*, 445 N.W.2d 503 (Mich., 1989), the Michigan court upheld a conviction of parents, who had evaded the compulsory education law by home study, because the parents lacked the required teacher's certificate. States have handled issues of religious-sponsored education and state regulations in different ways.

The public school's portion of the problems of equal opportunity by race is substantial. Even though great progress has been made in the American polity over the past two or three decades, the expectations of many minority groups in regard to progress toward equality have not been met. Further, progress toward desegregated schools has not been endorsed by all minority groups as, in several locales, the position of separatism and identity has been advocated. There are substantial problems, then, in addressing racial equality by way of desegregated schooling.

SEX AND EQUAL OPPORTUNITY

Masculinity has prevailed in social life, in the work world, and in politics. American society has been male-dominated. The meanings of that short sentence are several, and a few examples can provide an explicit treatment of the meanings. Men have had much more locational flexibility than women. That is, when a man wanted to go to another place, he went, without any risk of a disapproving society. Men were decision makers, and in family households the "man of the house" decided where and when to spend money and, probably, how much money to spend. Not entirely irrelevant, it is fair to note that some observers have commented that conventional marriage is an institution that cannot function or endure when decisional equality exists, for with two equal partners no majority can prevail at times of disagreement, and disagreements become locked in. Men have been given preference over women in job selection when the "head of the household"—the man—got the job. Whether true or false, that condition does not stand the test of equal opportunity, with sex an allowed factor for consideration. In the past, there have been powerful American women, but they have been relatively few, so that, looking backward into the twentieth century and beyond, one sees a "man's world."

On reflection, it is clear that sex identification has played a major role in American culture, a predetermination of what citizens could or could not do. These individual roles were based on the biological identification of people as being of one or the other sex. The historical heritage includes a record of protection being afforded to females as the childbearers and especially providing relief from exertion during pregnancy. In a postindustrial society with an extensive health-care industry, and with sociology bearing heavily on the way the culture functions, pregnancy has ceased to loom as such a large health risk. Childbearing rates have decreased. New functions and new opportunities for females in society have had their origin in change patterns that are both biological and sociological.

In the administration of schools, it has become necessary for each local school district to be sure that it is in compliance with the various aspects of the federal laws dealing with civil rights. In focusing on the Educational Amendments of 1972, Title IX, "Prohibition of Sex Discrimination," it is appropriate to examine the statute itself.

TITLE IX—PROHIBITION OF SEX DISCRIMINATION

Sex Discrimination Prohibited

Sec. 901. (a) no person in the United States shall, on the basis of sex, be excluded from participation in, be denied the benefits of, or be subjected to discrimination under any education program or activity receiving Federal financial assistance, except that:

(1) in regard to admissions to educational institutions, this section shall apply only to institutions of vocational education, professional education, and graduate higher education, and to public institutions of undergraduate high education;

(2) in regard to admissions to educational institutions, this section shall not apply (a) for one year from the date of enactment of this act, nor for six years after such date in the case of an educational institution which has begun the process of changing from being an institution which admits only students of one sex to being an institution which admits students of both sexes, but only if it is carrying out a plan for such a change which is approved by the Commissioner of Education, whichever is the later;

(3) this section shall not apply to an educational institution which is controlled by a religious organization if the application of this subsection would not be consistent with the religious tenets of such organization;

(4) this section shall not apply to an educational institution whose primary purpose is the training of individuals for the military services of the United States, or the merchant marine; and

(5) in regard to admissions this section shall not apply to any public institution of

undergraduate higher education which is an institution traditionally and continually from its establishment has had a policy of admitting only students of one sex.

Nothing contained in subsection (a) of this section shall be interpreted to require any educational institution to grant preferential or disparate treatment to the members of one sex on account of an imbalance which may exist with respect to the total number or percentage of persons of that sex in any community, State, section, or other area: *Provided*, that this subsection shall not be construed to prevent the consideration in any hearing or proceeding under this title to statistical evidence tending to show that such an imbalance exists with respect to participation in, or receipt of the benefits of, any such program or activity by the members of one sex.

(c) For purposes of this title, an educational institution means any public or private preschool, elementary, or secondary school, or any institution of vocational, professional, or higher education, except that in the case of an educational institution composed of more than one school, college, or department which are administratively separate units, such term means each school, college, or department.

Statutory and case law since 1972 solidified the social views that work—in aspects such as hiring, placing, and compensating—should be equitable, without preference for one sex over the other. Those views have found expression in employing organizations' statements that they are equal opportunity employers and that they conduct affirmative-action programs, that is, programs designed to discover, recruit, and place in employment more women than ordinarily occur.

The principle of comparable worth dictates that females should be paid the same as males. That is money is paid for the performance of a function. Sex, color, size, and so on of the performer are not pertinent. In education, that principle was the baseline for the single-salary schedule. For several decades, the single-salary schedule determined through a prearranged system that dollars were to be delivered for the function, by year and academic preparation. Sex has been an excluded variable. Within the single-salary schedule, it is even possible for a female to receive a higher salary than a male performing the same function—if the female is ahead in longevity and/or academic preparation. It is ironic, then, that after making such pioneering strides in salary-for-work, the education profession does not show a high entry rate for females in the area of school administration. There are many reasons that have nothing to do with sex discrimination, but this circumstance is also related, in many cases, to the nation's cultural history.

Actually, the question of discrimination by sex is one of degree and one that may occur at any point in the professional life, from time of first hiring to retirement. In *Rodriguez v. Eastchester Union Free Schools*, 620 F.2d 362 (N.Y., 1980), the Second Circuit Court ruled that even though the teacher's transfer did not decrease her seniority or salary, the transfer did place her in a situation calling for radical professional change and constituted "interference . . . of employment adversely affecting her status within the meaning of (Title VII)." In *Dougherty County School System v. Harris*, 622 F.2d 735 (Ga., 1980), the Fifth Circuit Court stated that the secretary of Health, Education, and Welfare had exceeded statutory and regulatory authority when she acted against and charged a local school board that paid a salary supplement to industrial arts teachers but not to home economics teachers when those salary funds were not from a federal source. In *Kunda v. Muhlenburg* College, 621 F.2d 532 (Pa., 1980), a question of tenure arose. The plaintiff contended that she had not gotten the same counseling about the necessity for advanced degrees as had been provided to her male colleagues and had thereby lacked motivation to complete her studies. The circuit court agreed and accepted the ruling from the district court that she should be reinstated and given the opportunity to complete the academic work in a reasonable time. These cases indicate that substantial power has been placed in the federal government in its view of local schools. It is federal agencies that police alleged discrimination against females by school districts, but some of those cases also show that the federal police power has limits that must be honored.

Pregnancy and the administration of pregnant employees in a school have raised many questions. Some rose to court challenges. The disputes that have surrounded pregnancy have been varied, and some of them are seen in the following questions:

1. At what time may a district demand that a teacher go on maternity leave?
2. What restrictions may a district place upon return from a maternity leave?
3. What may a district do in maternity leave policies that have conservation of funds as the rationale?
4. What may a district do in maternity leave policies that have protection of instructional integrity as the rationale?
5. At what level must a district continue to pay teachers who are on maternity leave?

Not all, but several, of those disputes have been heard in the federal courts. To provide an impression of courts' views on pregnant school employees during the 1970s, three cases have been selected and are presented chronologically. They reveal the judicial background from which came P.L. 95–555, passed by the United States Congress on October 31, 1978, and identified as an amendment to the Civil Rights Act of 1964, Title VII. The cases are *Green, Buckley*, and *LaFleur*.

In *Green v. Waterford Board of Education*, 473 F.2d 629 (Conn., 1973), the Second Circuit Court ruled for the Connecticut teacher. It declared that the time picked by the board for unpaid leave, that is, four months before the expected delivery, was arbitrary. Agreeing with the board's contention that continuity of instruction was an important concern, the court noted that continuity was not dependent on a particular start date for a substitute teacher. The board had also argued that uniform maternity leaves reduced the work load for administrators, an argument that the court acknowledged might be real but was insufficient. In *Buckley v. Coyle Public Schools*, 476 F.2d 92 (Okla., 1973), the Tenth Circuit Court addressed the question, "Did board policy violate any constitutionally protected rights?'' Ruling for Buckley, the court answered ''yes,'' because although there existed no constitutional right to the job of teacher, there did exist the right to be free of unconstitutional restrictions placed on that employment. This Oklahoma board presented no compelling reasons for its arbitrary rule of termination for pregnancy. The court also reasoned that marriage and procreation are essential to the extension of humanity and should not be the objects of punishing regulations levied on women, that is, on women who became pregnant. The signal case in pregnancy and teacher leave was *LaFleur*.

Cleveland Board of Education v. LaFleur, 414 U.S. 632 (Ohio, 1974)

Generalization

Arbitrary leave dates may not be established in advance. They must be established on an individual basis and in response to the pregnant female's physical condition, as attested by a physician.

Description

LaFleur and her colleagues were married teachers who did not want to take unpaid maternity leave during the time stipulated by board policy. The policy stated that pregnant teachers had to take leave beginning five months before the ''expected date of the normal birth of the child.'' The teachers took leave in March, but under duress, for they had wanted to teach the remainder of the semester. Policy also fixed the date of return as no earlier than the beginning of the semester following the child's age of three months. Practically, the policy excluded the possibility that a teacher could deliver a child during the summer and not be forced to miss some work. The rationale for the policy was stated as being twofold: continuity of instruction and protection of the health of the mother and the child.

The United States Supreme Court addressed the question, ''Did the policy violate the due process clause of the Fourteenth Amendment and/or civil barriers to the deprivation of rights?'' Ruling for LaFleur, the Court answered that arbitrary termination dates had no ''rational relationship to the valid state interest of preserving continuity of education.'' Medical evidence, not rigidly predetermined dates, was identified as the appropriate informational source for decision making in matters of personal health; at the same time, the Court noted that pregnancy put on the employee the responsibility for substantial advance notice to the administration. With ample time for planning, personal health and classroom continuity could both be accommodated, the Court declared. Justice Stewart, speaking for the Court, said:

This Court has long recognized that freedom of personal choice in matters of marriage and family is one of the liberties protected by the Due Process Clause of the Fourteenth Amendment . . . there is a right to be free from unwarranted governmental intrusion into matters so fundamentally affecting a person as the decision whether to bear or beget a child.

By acting to penalize the pregnant teacher for deciding to bear a child, overly restrictive maternity leave regulations can constitute a heavy burden on the exercise of these protected freedoms. Because public school maternity leave rules directly affect one of the basic civil rights of man, . . . the Due Process Clause of the Fourteenth Amendment requires that such rules must not needlessly, arbitrarily, or capriciously impinge upon this vital area of a teacher's constitutional liberty. The question before us in these cases is whether the interests advanced in support of the rules of the Cleveland and Chesterfield County School Boards can justify the particular procedures they have adopted.

The school boards in these cases have offered two essentially overlapping explanations for their mandatory maternity leave rules. First, they contend that the firm cut-off dates are necessary to maintain the continuity of classroom instruction, since advance knowledge of when a pregnant teacher must leave facilitates the finding and hiring of a qualified substitute. Secondly, the school boards seek to justify their maternity rules by arguing that at least some teachers become physically incapable of adequately performing certain of their duties during the latter part of pregnancy. By keeping the pregnant teacher out of the classroom during these final months, the maternity leave rules are said to protect the health of the teacher and her unborn child, while at the same time assuring that students have a physically capable instructor in the classroom at all times.

It cannot be denied that continuity of instruction is a significant and legitimate educational goal. Regulations requiring pregnant teachers to provide early notice of their condition to school authorities undoubtedly facilitate administrative planning toward the important objective of continuity. But, as the Court of Appeals for the Second Circuit noted in *Green v. Waterford Board of Education*, 473 F.2d 629, 635:

> Where a pregnant teacher provides the Board with a date certain for commencement of leave, however, that value (continuity) is preserved; an arbitrary leave date set at the end of the fifth month is no more calculated to facilitate a planned and orderly transition between the teacher and a substitute than is a date fixed closer to confinement. Indeed, the latter . . . would afford the Board more, not less, time to procure a satisfactory long-term substitute. [Footnote omitted.]

Thus, while the advance notice provisions in the Cleveland and Chesterfield County rules are wholly rational and may well be necessary to serve the objective of continuity of instruction, the absolute requirements of termination at the end of the fourth or fifth month of pregnancy are not. Were continuity the only goal, cut-off dates much later during pregnancy would serve as well or better than the challenged rules, providing that ample advance notice requirements were retained. Indeed, continuity would seem just as well attained if the teacher herself were allowed to choose the date upon which to commence her leave, at least so long as the decision was required to be made and notice given of it well in advance of the date selected. In fact, since the fifth or sixth months of pregnancy will obviously begin at different times in the school year for different teachers, the present Cleveland and Chesterfield County rules may serve to hinder attainment of the very continuity objectives that they are purportedly designed to promote.

Under the Cleveland rule, the teacher is not eligible to return to work until the beginning of the next regular school semester following the time when her child attains the age of three months. A doctor's certificate attesting to the teacher's health is required before return; an additional physical examination may be required at the option of the school board . . . To the extent that the three months provision reflects the school board's thinking that no mother is fit to return until that point in time, it suffers from the same constitutional deficiencies that plague the irrebuttable presumption in the termination rules. The presumption, moreover, is patently unnecessary, since the requirement of a physician's certificate or medical examination fully protects the school's interests in this regard. And finally, the three month provision simply has nothing to do with continuity of instruction, since the precise point at which the child will reach the relevant age will obviously occur at a different point throughout the school year for each teacher.

Thus, we conclude that the Cleveland return rule, insofar as it embodies the three months age provision, is wholly arbitrary and irrational, and hence violates the Due Process Clause of the Fourteenth Amendment. The age limitation serves no legitimate state interest, and unnecessarily penalizes the female teacher for asserting her right to bear children.

The two cases, from Ohio and Virginia, epitomize the surge of activity during the 1960s and 1970s as employees in many occupations, but certainly including teachers, moved to test local rules and regulations against constitutional and statutory benchmarks. Those tests were initiated to secure for the employee more latitude, which included new degrees of freedom for females. *LaFleur* and *Cohen* did not release pregnant employees from the control of boards and education but did alter the management processes, linking them to facts of health. As a result of these and similar cases from many other sections of the economy, a politically persuasive influence developed, and Congress passed P.L. 95–555, entitled "Pregnancy Sex Discrimination Prohibition."

The act provided 180 days (until April 29, 1979) during which employers could bring fringe-benefit or insurance programs into conformity—or longer if a negotiated contract was in force until some later time. Substantially, the act stipulated:

The terms "because of sex" or "on the basis of sex" include, but are not limited to, because of or on the basis of pregnancy, childbirth, or related medical conditions; and women affected by pregnancy, childbirth, or related medical conditions shall be treated the same for all employment related purposes, including receipt of benefits under fringe benefit programs, as other persons not so affected but similar in their ability or inability to work, and nothing in section 703(h) of this title shall be interpreted to permit otherwise . . . nothing herein shall preclude an employer from providing abortion benefits or otherwise affect bargaining agreements in regard to abortion.

The liability of public schools has been expanded as a consequence of cases brought, recently, under the nation's civil rights legislation. Many of those alleged wrongs committed by public schools are in the area of sex discrimination. Teachers have sought relief from many of the customary personnel-management processes, such as hiring, transfer, leave, promotion, and demotion, in instances where discrimination has been perceived. Affected employees—primarily, teachers—have sought court relief in forms such as damage awards, injunctions, and court orders for appointment or reinstatement.

Title VII of the Civil Rights Act of 1974 prohibits discrimination based on color, race, national origin, religion, and sex. Title IX of the Education Amendments of 1972 prohibits sex discrimination against the beneficiaries of any educational program that is receiving federal financial assistance. These, coupled with the equal-protection clause of the Fourteenth Amendment to the Constitution, provide a formidable array of legal protection against sex-based discrimination. The Equal Employment Opportunities Commission (EEOC) is the agency charged with the administration of Title VII, and the EEOC has periodically issued statements of condition and position as well as regulations for the accomplishment of the legal mandates of Title VII.

A source of current debate is whether Title IX protections cover only those students in schools that receive some federal funding or whether those protections extend to all employees. This question was first addressed in *Romeo Community Schools v. HEW*, U.S. Dept. of Health, 438 F. Supp. 1021 (Mich., 1977), and has since been raised in several circuit courts. The original ruling was that Title IX did not apply to teachers, that they could not seek the protection of that law, and that the HEW had overstepped its own bounds in the development of unlawful regulations. Most of the circuit courts of appeal have agreed. The United States Office of Civil Rights has refused to accept the court opinion that Title IX does not cover teachers. This argument will be resolved by Supreme Court decision.

Finally, two other areas in discrimination by sex should be noted by school administrators. In 1980 the EEOC defined sexual harassment as

unwelcome sexual advances, requests for sexual favors, and other verbal or physical conducts of a sexual nature . . . when (1) submission to such conduct is made either explicitly or implicitly a term or condition of an individual's employment; (2) submission to or rejection of such conduct by an individual is used as the basis for employment decisions affecting such individual; or (3) such conduct has the purpose or effect of unreasonably interfering with the individual's work performance or creating an intimidating, hostile, or offensive working environment.

Given the predominantly female work force of the public schools, it is appropriate for each LEA to take affirmative action to prevent sexual harassment by developing a program of information before incidents and accusations occur.

Second, many of the questions about discrimination by sex have involved the restricted access to extracurricular activities in which female students have ordinarily had fewer opportunities than have their male counterparts. Charges have been brought against local school districts and state activities associations when either had rules that disqualified females from noncontact sports. In fact, some courts have ordered local schools to allow females to participate in coed football, a contact sport. See *Clinton v. Nagy*, 411 F.Supp. 1396 (Ohio 1974). In *Brenden v. Independent School District #742*, 477 F.2d 1292 (1973), the Eighth Circuit Court ruled that when a school did not provide teams for females in tennis, skiing, and running, qualified females could compete with males, and a rule to the contrary was unenforceable. Qualified females may not be deprived of opportunities to participate, and such a provision may exist as equivalency in girls' teams or in invitations into coed activities. In either case, the initiative is the responsibility of the local education agency. In *O'Connor v. School District #23*, 101 S.Ct. 72 (Ill., 1980), Justice Stevens pointed up a very pertinent problem in this whole area when he said, "Without a gender based classification in competitive contact sports, there would be a substantial risk that boys would dominate the girls' programs and deny them an equal opportunity to compete in inter-scholastic sports." That is, sports opportunities, classified by gender, increase the opportunities for participation for girls.

In *Yellow Springs Schools v. Ohio High School Athletic Association*, 443 F.Supp. 753 (Ohio, 1978), the question involved participation of girls on a high-school basketball team for boys, a violation of the state association rule. Citing such accomplished female athletes as Babe Didrickson, the court decided that the exclusionary rule deprived girls of liberty without due process. Accordingly, the rule was set aside, and schoolgirls had to be given the opportunity to compete with boys for positions on teams in interscholastic contact sports. Many observers would describe as a more substantive aspect of this whole issue of gender bias a New York case that addressed eligibility for scholastic scholarships. In *Sharif v. New York State Education Department*, 709 F.Supp. 345 (N.Y., 1989), the court viewed evidence that showed that for more than 15 consecutive years, the test scores of males had exceeded the scores of females. Further, it noted that only two states, one of which was New York, awarded scholarships exclusively on the results of that particular test. Consequently, the state department of education was ordered to consider other aspects of academic accomplishment and to award scholarships accordingly.

AGE AND DISCRIMINATION

The Age Discrimination in Employment Act, enacted by Congress in 1967, provided special protection for people aged 40–70 in the American work force. In *EEOC v. Atlantic Community School District*, 879 F.2d 434 (Iowa, 1989), the Eighth Circuit Court considered a hiring procedure in which a 23-year-old applicant with two years of experience was hired in preference to a 40-year-old applicant with ten years of experience. Finding no evidence that the LEA board used age as a criterion, the court agreed that the board could choose on the basis of a reduced salary obligation to the person with lesser experience.

Although there was some criticism of the LEA's hiring policies by district court jury members after the verdict in *Lowe v. Commack Union Free Schools*, 886 F.2d 1364 (N.Y., 1989) had been delivered, those comments could not be construed in any way except as American citizens expressing individually held opinions. The LEA had hired from the applicant pool of 13 people, and in that group, eight were 40 years of age. The plaintiffs were both 52 years old. Stipulating that if evidence could be found that age had been used as a criterion for hiring, the finding would be for the plaintiffs, the Second Circuit Court could find no such criterion. The court did take note of hiring irregularities in that LEA for other years, but found none in the particular time frame under consideration. The age of the 52-year-old plaintiffs was not found to be the reason they were not hired, and even if hiring criteria were, in the eyes of the court, unwise, that alone could not constitute illegality.

HANDICAPS AND EQUAL OPPORTUNITY

The statutes are replete with definitions and lists of qualifications. P.L. 94–142 identified handicapped children as those who are hard of hearing, speech impaired, visually impaired, mentally retarded, emotionally disturbed, orthopedically impaired, or suffering from some specific learning disabilities. Section 504 defined a handicapped person as anyone having a physical or medical impairment that creates a substantive limit on one or more major life activities, which include walking, seeing, hearing, breathing, learning, working, and self-care. Section 504 includes all of the handicaps in P.L. 94–142 and is even more extensive, including people addicted to the use of drugs or alcohol. Both laws are aimed against the warehousing of children. Together, the laws mandate that local schools must provide a free appropriate education to anyone who has a qualifying handicap and who falls within the age range for public education as set forward in the laws of the individual states.

The prime social areas for litigation in the wide realm of discrimination were for race in the 1950s, 1960s, 1970s; for sex in the 1970s; for the handicapped, apparently, in the 1980s and 1990s. Office of Education rulings and policy letters on the interpretations of P.L. 94–142 numbered into the hundreds by the 1980s—a good indication of the high-quality level of litigation likely to materialize in the decade.

In a conceptual expansion of this civil rights legislation for the handicapped, Congress passed the Americans with Disabilities Act in July 1990. With this act now of such magnitude in the whole education enterprise, the relationships and obligations of schools are given a full treatment in chapter 7.

SUMMARY

As America has consciously moved toward an increasingly egalitarian position, the public schools have become the primary agency for the accomplishment of those goals. People of rational viewpoints differ about whether it is appropriate that this performance burden be given to and accepted by the public schools of the nation. Some people contend that too broad a mission has been put on the schools, given their history, personnel, funding, and so on. However, it is true that in the latter half of the twentieth century, public schools have extended their programs very substantially, trying to provide adequate—equal—educational opportunities to a student population that is much more diverse than was the population in those same schools during the first half of the century.

Requests for educational programs differing from the norm, from community cultural patterns, and from a century of tradition have been mandated by statutory and case law. The nation's executive branch has been very active in this whole endeavor too, for the executive orders of the presidents of the 1960s and 1970s often set the pattern for the legislation that followed. This was true, for example, of the developing concept of equality of educational and employment opportunity and its research and enforcement branches.

Now, the nation has codified in statutes from the legislative branch, opinions from the judiciary, and regulations from administrative agencies a vast array of statements about how people can—and cannot—be treated. Primarily, all of this activity in law has been designed to provide protections for groups of citizens who can be identified as having been extended a lesser opportunity than was offered to other citizens and whose relative position in society reflects that lack of opportunity. The protected groups include members of racial minorities, females, the handicapped, the aged, those of national origin other than native-born American, and those with unusual political and religious views. These are delicate balances to provide fairness in a multicultural society.

The public schools (LEAs) are obligated to accommodate all of these protected groups. That protection must be available to pupils as well as employees. It calls for ingenuity and care in personnel search and hiring, and it may necessitate, for many of the nation's more than 15,000 LEAs, an identification of new or different characteristics when attempts are made to select the highest quality from among several applicants. Some affirmative-action plans have necessitated such revisions in which the realities of the labor market play a much decreased role in recruitment and hiring.

In many ways, the public school is American society in microcosm. The American social condition is characterized by an increased tension that has matched the movement of that society through the twentieth century. For school administration, the condition demands an awareness that is visible and a performance that is balanced. School administrations must know of the real pressures from diverse agencies such as the Leadership Conference on Civil Rights, the American Civil Liberties Union, and the Office of Civil Rights. Representing a much wider spectrum of advocacy and enforcement agencies, the sentiments of those agencies have been in the forefront in securing new rights for new groups by way of legal demands for new performances in each LEA.

All of this action is indicative of a free, inventive, and lively society. It confronts every LEA with a very basic problem, that is, where to get the money to fund the new programs. It is a condition of tension, and some groups in the clientele of public schools want to move at a much more rapid pace of change than do others. Schools are left to cope with many ambiguous areas. It is surely fair to speculate that the tension will continue and that clashes will continue to arise in the courts of the nation as people seek the service of the judiciary to resolve perceptions of inequalities in public schools.

9

Injury and Negligence

Injuries range in severity from an inconsequential level to one so serious as to cause death. They may be the result of negligent actions or may be the result of purely accidental circumstances. The damages that come from some injuries are very apparent; others are less so. For example, when a student falls on the playground and breaks a bone, the injury is obvious or will become so. Eventually, the medical costs of that injury can be totaled. The pain and suffering from the injury may have been quite real but cannot be set forward as an actual, unquestioned total number of dollars. The injury may have caused a loss of services from the student to the parents, but that too is a type of claim from which it is very difficult to develop a reliable total cost. Therefore, the least disputable costs of physical injuries are the medical costs consequent to the injury; yet other costs may be claimed in a suit and may be awarded, depending on the facts of an individual case.

In other words, the consequences of an injury may be complex and pervasive, and it is those characteristics that lead to litigation, for if an injury has been caused by negligence, a damage award may follow. There is a duty of care imposed on public school districts, demanding that the responsibility for the safety of the students and employees be accepted and fulfilled. School boards can fulfill a part of that responsibility through regulations for the control and operation of the school. Ordinarily, injuries that are the result of purely accidental situations are not actionable for damages.

Action seeking damages for injuries coming from attendance in public schools do not have a long history because such schools were protected from suit under the common-law concept of sovereign immunity. Literally, that concept meant that the king could do no wrong, that whatever a king did, as the head of government, was right. Altered slightly to fit the American government patterns, the concept was expressed as governmental immunity, meaning that the people controlled the government process and had never acted explicitly to make their governmental agencies liable for the negligent acts of their employees even though those acts might have contributed to accident and/or injury. This all began to change with the pronouncement in *Molitar v. Kaneland Community School*, 18 Ill.2d 11 (Ill., 1959). Speaking for the Illinois Supreme Court, Justice Klingbiel noted that the sovereign-immunity concept was first extended to a political subdivision in England in 1788 (*Russell v. Men of Devon*). A century later that concept of immunity was reversed in England but continued to prevail in America, leaving American citizens with no protection from governmental units' unjust and negligent acts that could lead to injury. The Illinois court refused to accept the arguments supporting school-district immunity as out of phase with the times, since they excluded school districts from their appropriate civil responsibility, and reversed the lower court, ruling for Thomas Molitar, who had been injured in a school bus accident.

The arguments for governmental immunity are several:

1. Legislatures, as representatives of the people, can set aside governmental immunity by statute, if desired.
2. The treasuries of political subdivisions should not be spent to satisfy a claim, for the taxes were not collected for that purpose. Neither should public properties be sold to satisfy a claim.
3. Public quasi-corporations, such as school districts, are not perfectly comparable to private corporations.
4. Allowance of damage claims creates budgetary unpredictability.
5. Public endeavors should not be endangered by individuals claiming damages for injury at a cost to the public treasury.

The list could be extended, but the circumstance has been that in state after state, the legislatures of the 1960s took their cue from *Molitar* and acted to set aside governmental immunity. Such actions made school districts and other political subdivisions liable for the negligence of their employees. Injury, negligence, and damages go together. Injury in a setting of obvious attention to care for the welfare and safety of schoolchildren is not likely to produce awards for damages, even in those states that statutorily set aside governmental immunity.

Governmental immunity is not a constant, either in its elimination or maintenance. In *Jones v. State Highway Commission*, 557 S.W.2d 225 (Mo., 1977), the Missouri Supreme Court set aside governmental immunity for the political subdivisions and the agencies of the state. At the same time the court, acknowledging the legislative function, specified that the state legislature could reinstate the immunity by specific statute if it chose to do so, and it did. (In this case, the Missouri Supreme Court followed the pattern of the Wisconsin Supreme Court when, in 1962, it ruled similarly but gave the legislature a period to prepare for the financial ramifications of the loss of immunity.) There is not a perfect understanding, either, of who fits within the shield of governmental immunity. In *Webb v. Hennessy*, 257 S.E.2d 315 (Ga., 1978), the Georgia court of appeals ruled that immunity from suit provided to the governing boards of Georgia school districts did not necessarily include the employees of the board and found a school principal negligent of performing certain basic duties. Employees and board members are well advised to carry liability insurance covering errors and omissions. The cost of premiums for board members may be charged against the district treasury.

One consequence of enveloping school districts in the group of social organizations subject to suit for injury has been a new budget cost. Schools have purchased insurance to protect the district treasury from a disastrous claim and to protect the trustees of the governing board from claims against them as individuals. Such an insurance program is nearly universal among school districts in states that have set aside governmental immunity. Likewise, many local schools and/or local education associations have secured liability insurance for the administrators and teachers. As a "cost of doing business," liability insurance has become a recent addition—but a very necessary one—to LEA budgets. The history of liability insurance costs to school districts through the 1980s revealed a sharply progressive premium cost, even for districts with very good loss records and with an increased deductible.

The purchase of insurance for injuries has in no way diminished the ethics of the obligation to care for children compelled by law to attend schools. Schools owe to the students and to the parents of those students the exercise of reasonable care in accepting the children as students. If the students are injured by wrongful acts of the professional adults in whose care they have been placed, penalties may be imposed by law on individuals or the whole organization. A tort is a wrong committed against the person, reputation, or property of another. It has three elements: (1) the generally understood duty; (2) a breach of that duty; and (3) the extent of damage consequent of that breach. Students who are injured and who seek restitution through an award for damages generally base that claim on some point of negligence, that is, a failure to exercise the necessary and prudent degree of care. From the concept, a civil action may be brought against a board of education, administrators, teachers, or whatever party or parties are alleged to have caused or contributed to the injury. School districts are not necessarily exempt from liability resulting from the negligence or tortious action of employees as they perform their duties. Neither are they automatically liable for such injuries. Liability can be deduced only from the facts of a given situation, but a judgment may include punitive damages as well as actual damages to the injured party.

LIABILITY OF TEACHERS AND ADMINISTRATORS

Each teacher is the instructional leader for the assigned students and stands as the professional representative of the board's responsibility to provide safe instruction to every child. If a student is injured while under the supervision of the teacher, it is natural to follow with questions to determine who was responsible for the injury. In the classroom, the teacher stands in place of the parent, a position of special responsibility that articulates with the position of professional responsibility. The teacher must always act in such a way as to prevent, or minimize, injury to the student. Teachers not only instruct but also supervise, plan, intervene, reward, punish, and engage in other actions necessary to fulfill a position of trust. Their scope of employment is broad, necessitating thoughtful consideration of what should be done—or not done—to provide protection for the students, especially against bodily injury. To the degree that teachers cannot produce evidence of such a high level of job performance, they increase the likelihood that, as one consequence of injury to a student, civil suits for the recovery damages will be successful.

To say that students do get injured in school is no detraction from the preponderant evidence that schools are safe places. Yet some students are injured; some even die from the injuries. Others are injured in school-related incidents. In *Tinkham v. Kole*, 110 N.W.2d 258 (Iowa, 1961), Marius Kole disciplined a student by striking him about the face and ears, and as a result the student suffered a punctured eardrum. This was an avoidable injury. Considering the student's misconduct, the Iowa Supreme Court stated that a teacher's right to use physical punishment is limited, was excessive in this case, and was the direct cause of the injury to the student Michael Tinkham. In *Wire v. Williams*, 133 N.W.2d 840 (Minn., 1965), suit was brought against an elementary physical education teacher. While Diane Wire, a second grader, was jumping rope, one end was held by Patricia Williams, the teacher. The rope, which had a wooden handle, was jerked from her hand and struck the student in her upper front teeth. This was an unavoidable injury. The court found that the teacher was using proven equipment as part of a well-planned curriculum and attributed the injury to an unavoidable accident. In *Cook v. Crain*, 288 N.W.2d 609 (Mich., 1980), suit was brought by the parents of an injured child against both a teacher and a principal. The injury occurred at recess on a day when the teacher was not present and a substitute teacher was in charge. The court found that the absent teacher had no liability; likewise, the substitute teacher and the school district were exonerated. However, the court found that the principal had broad supervisory powers that she exercised in such small degree that she did not minimize potential injury to pupils in her building and that such an omission was neglectful performance of her duty. In *Lake County School Board v. Talmadge*, 381 So.2d 698 (Fla., 1980), a teacher was judged negligent on an act of commission. There, the teacher physically placed a student on a trampoline over the objections of that student and then forced the student to perform. The student complied and fell, injuring himself. Negligence may be by commission or omission.

Teachers should be advised by administrators not to leave a classroom unattended. The adult presence of a teacher, as instructional leader, is part of any school's safety program. In *Segermann v. Jones*, 259 A.2d 794 (Md., 1969), a

Maryland teacher left her fourth-grade class for about five minutes. Before leaving, the teacher instructed the class to do physical exercises, and the class had started the exercises, with recorded music to give rhythm. During her absence, and while the class was exercising, one pupil was hit by another in such a way that two of her front teeth were badly chipped. When the case was appealed to the Maryland Supreme Court, strict tests for negligence were applied, and the teacher was exonerated because the accident might have occurred in the teacher's presence and the teacher had very carefully prepared the class for the exercise. Despite this finding, teachers are ill-advised to leave the classroom unattended, except for emergencies.

A small number of states have provided a statutory protection under which teachers and administrators are protected and indemnified from judgments rendered in school-connected injuries. Such statutes are referred to as save harmless laws. The prevailing condition, however, is that as adult professionals, certificated school district employees are responsible for the consequences of their acts and must answer for injury to students.

Lutterman v. Studer et al., 217 N.W.2d 756 (Minn. SC., 1974)

Generalization

When injury to one student results from the action of another student, the actions of the injured student and the actions of the teacher in charge must also be considered before any action for fixing negligence and awarding damages can be made.

Description

John Lutterman was a student in Independent School District #456. He was injured by a baseball bat, released by another student during a supervised batting practice, and through his father brought suit for damages against Wayne Studer, the boy who released the bat; Douglas Ringnell, the coach; the Gopher Athletic Supply Company, seller of the bat; the Hillerich and Bradsby Company, manufacturers of the bat; and the public school district. The defendant listing was inclusive. Lutterman was a student in the school but not a member of the group designated to practice batting on the day of the accident. He had, however, come into the school gymnasium to watch the practice, which had been moved inside because of inclement weather.

The students participating in a simulated batting practice were lined up in five columns, the columns consisting of five students, extending in a north-south direction. All participants wore baseball helmets. Studer was in the front row of either the first or second column numbered from the west. The distance between Ringnell and Studer was approximately 20 feet. Ringnell would simulate pitching a ball, and as he announced its location over an imaginary homeplate, the students would swing their bats in the area where the ball would cross homeplate. Plaintiff, a nonparticipant, stood at a distance of

30 or 40 feet watching the drill. During the drill the bat slipped out of Studer's hand and struck plaintiff on the left side of his head.

Plaintiff was standing in front of a batting machine when the track coach entered the gymnasium and spoke with one of the baseball players. This player went to the weight room leaving by the door at the northwest corner of the gym. Plaintiff watched this player leave the gym, turning his head from the batting drill for approximately 1 minute. He was struck as he was turning back to watch the batting practice again.

(1) Plaintiff contends on this appeal that Studer was negligent as a matter of law and that the negligence of Ringnell, as a matter of law, was direct cause of the injury. We find no support in the circumstances of the case for plaintiff's position that Studer was negligent as a matter of law.

(2) Plaintiff contends more strenuously, however, that Ringnell's negligence was, as a matter of law, the proximate cause of the injury. The applicable legal principles, which are not disputed by either side, are captured in the following statement from *Pluwak v. Lindberg*, 268 Minn. 524, 528, 130 N.W.2d 134 (1964):

... (4, 5) Let it be assumed only for the purpose of this consideration that the jury would have been justified under the evidence finding that plaintiff had permission to be in the gymnasium during the practice. Plaintiff was knowledgeable of dangers connected with baseball. Additionally, he failed to keep a proper lookout during the drill. Admittedly, he was aware that his fellow students were swinging 25 to 30 bats in his direction. He was aware of the possibility of flying bats. The evidence sustains the jury's finding of his negligence. It may be that the jury's finding that his negligence was not a direct cause of the injury to him is more difficult to follow. This court's statement is in *Seivert v. Bass*, 288 Minn. 547, 466, 181.

... The facts present a combination of circumstances without which the accident would not have occurred. Had the coach been more careful in surveying the area and the boy more alert to the danger in which he placed himself, the accident would not have occurred. Neither the failures of the coach nor the acts of the boy standing alone were sufficient to lodge legal liability. This combination of the acts of both very probably was the basis for the jury's verdict. The facts did not establish a situation where, as a matter of law, the court could determine the issue of causation. The answers to the interrogatories by the jury can be reconciled and are consistent with the evidence.

Affirmed.

Lutterman points up two important aspects of litigation seeking damage awards. First, when the plaintiff decides to launch the suit, and if the defendants are not clearly identifiable and isolated, there may be an inclusive list of defendants, lest a decision be made that negligence caused the injury but the negligent party not among the named defendants. Originally, there were five defendants named in *Lutterman*. Second, contributory negligence is one defense against a charge of negligence. People who suffer injuries have some responsibility for their own welfare, and if they expose themselves needlessly to danger, they must be willing to accept some of the consequences. In this case, young Lutterman was experienced in batting practice and positioned himself in a dangerous place on his own choice, taking some risk himself.

Rixmann v. Somerset Public Schools et al., **266 N.W.2d 326**
(Wis. SC, 1978)

Generalization

When teachers are confronted with emergency situations created by students, they must act. When that action is reasonable, even though it may be ineffective, that teacher cannot be held liable for negligence.

Description

This action for damages came from an incident in a laboratory experiment being conducted in a high-school science class. Harold Ammerman was the teacher and one of the defendants. Other defendants were the school district, insurance company, and two students who shared the laboratory station with Ronald Rixmann.

Ammerman had demonstrated the experiment the previous day. The experiment involved heating a beaker of water and beaker of alcohol on an electric plate and using these liquids to remove starch from a leaf. Because alcohol is flammable, the students were instructed to have no open flames near the experiment.

The class was divided into two groups for the purpose of conducting the experiment. Ronald, the defendants-respondents, Thomas LeMire and Robert Kieckhoefer, and three other students were in one group. During the course of the experiment, Kieckhoefer used a plastic spoon to pour a small puddle of the heated alcohol onto the table for the purpose of lighting it with a match. LeMire then set fire to the puddle with a match furnished by Ronald. Eventually, the spoon itself caught fire. Kieckhoefer, in an attempt to extinguish the burning spoon, waved it in the air. He then proceeded to place the spoon in the beaker of water, but in so doing ignited the fumes from the beaker of heated alcohol.

Ammerman, who was at that time with the other group of students, saw the beaker on fire and attempted to extinguish it by placing a notebook over its mouth. The alcohol beaker tipped over, spilling the flaming liquid onto Ronald. He was severely burned.

On an amended complaint, this action was maintained against the school district, the district's liability insurer, LeMire, Kieckhoefer, Ammerman and his liability insurer. The case was tried to a jury and during the course of the trial the plaintiffs proffered a document under which Ronald's father's health insurer, Guardian Life Insurance Co., purported to assign to him any interest it might have by reason of payments made for medical expenses arising out of this incident. The trial court, however, ruled that Guardian Life had no interest to assign to the father, and that his recovery for medical expenses would be limited to that amount which had not been covered by the insurance.

The jury returned a verdict finding only the school district and Ammerman causally negligent, and apportioned 40% of the causal negligence to the school district and 60% to Ammerman. The jury awarded the plaintiff $656.33 for past medical expenses (the amount set by the trial court to reflect the unpaid portion of those expenses); $8,400 for future medical expenses, and $25,000 for past and $30,000 for future pain, suffering and disability.

(3) It may be true, as the trial court stated, that these students "weren't the brightest." But all three of the students were bright enough to know that alcohol was flammable and

that they were not supposed to have open flames near it. On the basis of these admitted and undisputed facts, we conclude that the students, by collaborating to set fire to the puddle of alcohol on the table, did not conform their conduct to that which would be expected of a similarly situated child of the same age and with the same capacity discretion, knowledge and experience in creating the initial fire. The evidence does not reasonably admit an alternate conclusion. Thus, the trial court erred in not holding these students, Ronald included, negligent as a matter of law.

The plaintiffs also contend that the trial court erred in not finding as a matter of law the students' negligence a cause of Ronald's injuries. The concept of causation as it pertains to negligence cases in this state has been described as follows:

In this state negligence is causal if it is a substantial factor in producing the injuries or death complained of. The cause of an accident is not determined by its most immediate factor. The doctrine of proximate cause in the strict sense of that term has been abandoned for the substantial-factor concept of causation to properly express "cause" or "legal cause." Consequently, there may be several substantial factors contributing to the same result. The contribution of these factors under our comparative negligence doctrine are all considered and determined in terms of percentages of total cause. It follows that, in resolving questions as to causation in the case before us, we will apply what this court has termed " . . . the substantial-factor concept of causation, under which there may be several substantial factors contributing to the same result. . . . " *Sampson v. Laskin*, 66 Wis.2d 318, 32s–26, 224, N.W.2d 594, 597 (1975).

(4) The defendants, LeMire and Kieckhoefer, contend that the acts of the teacher, Ammerman, constituted a superseding cause of Ronald's injuries.

After exploring the legal concepts of "superseding cause" and "intervening force" and their relationship to negligence and liability, the Wisconsin court made its pronouncement.

It does not shock the conscience of this court to hold the defendant students liable for their negligence; indeed, it would be shocking if the court were to relieve them of liability.

Therefore, on the basis of this record, we hold that the negligence of the students— Kieckhoefer, LeMire, as well as Ronald himself—was a substantial factor in bringing about Ronald's injuries. These three, to various degrees, joined forces to create an open flame in the proximity of a heated beaker of alcohol. Once this condition was created, none of the boys alerted Ammerman to the danger, nor did Ronald take even the most elementary steps to remove himself from the scene. Rather, Kieckhoefer increased the danger by setting fire to the spoon and then to the beaker of alcohol. Though Ammerman's negligence intervened at this juncture, it did not supersede the boy's negligence in bringing about Ronald's injuries.

Because liability must be reapportioned in light of our conclusions above, we reverse and remand this case for a new trial on this as well as the damage issue. In view of the above, we do not reach the remaining issues concerning the constitutionality of sec. 89s43 Stat. 859.43.

Judgement reversed and remanded for further proceedings not inconsistent with this opinion.

There is a difference between proprietary and educational functions, and public schools do both. In *Meyerhoffer v. East Hanover Schools*, 280 F.Supp. 81 (Pa.,

1968), Rae Ann Meyerhoffer was struck by a school bus. Cursorily acknowledging some of the unique aspects of this case in which damages in the amount
of $10,000 were asked, Judge Folmer ruled that the case against the school
district should be dismissed; however, he left in place the case against Lloyd
Umberger, driver of the bus. That provided the opportunity for the Meyerhoffers
to pursue their case.

There is some risk attached to attending school, just as there is a risk attached
to participation in society in any way. Yet by the use of police powers, every
state compels the attendance of children for some time. Teachers and administrators are responsible for the instructional programs that will encourage educational growth but also must act to protect the students from harm. Lack of
such thoughtful, affirmative action in the face of injuries may leave any school
employee open to charges for negligence. This is true for physical injuries, where
damage is most obvious. It is also true of psychological, reputational, and
emotional injuries, to the extent that they become known and that their occurrence
may be presented before a court in a reasonable and persuasive way.

LIABILITY OF SCHOOL DISTRICTS

As the political subdivision charged in each state to carry out, at the local
level, the state responsibility for education, each district is also responsible to
provide a safe, clean, supervised environment for that education. Boards of
education may not allow their physical facilities to fall into disrepair and endanger
the well-being of the students (or of the teachers, for that matter). Parents must
have confidence that the local board will keep a safe place, and that is as true
for the routines of the school's operation as for the facilities where the child
must go, under the compulsory-education statutes of each state. Like a legislature
and its statutes, like a governmental agency and its guidelines, courts will not
accept a plea that because of lack of funds, a local board operated a dangerous
school. For example, it may be demanded that dangerous asbestos be removed
and the levels of radon reduced. Each local board must find the necessary funds.
Practically, the necessary funding situation is much more complex when consideration is given to the fact that funds come from various sources, often with
maximum dollar limits and with yearly vacillation in amounts and sources. All
of the complexities of securing adequate funds for the operation of each local
school district and doing so without evidence of neglect are part and parcel of
the obligation of the governing board of each of the nation's nearly 15,000 public
school districts.

With substantial case law and statutory law to indicate the liability of each
board for its potentially injurious acts, it is now common practice for local boards
to carry liability insurance—on the board itself, to protect the district's treasury,
and on individual members of the board, to protect their personal wealth from
adverse judgments. Inevitably, schoolchildren will get injured; parents or guardians may seek damages through litigation; liability insurance should be in force

to cover such claims as may be awarded. Although consideration of circumstances in which such protection would be most needed would lead toward protection from physical injury, other kinds of liability protection should be sought too. In *Wood v. Strickland*, 420 U.S. 308 (Ark., 1975), suit was brought against some members of the local board of education and two administrators by two suspended students, Peggy Strickland and Virginia Crain. The girls contended that by their suspension for a relatively small matter, some board members acted inappropriately and denied them basic constitutional rights. The Supreme Court discussed standards of conduct and degrees of governmental immunity and stated, "In the specific context of school discipline, we hold that a school board member is not immune from liability for damages under 1983 if he knew or reasonably should have known that the action he took within his sphere of official responsibility would violate the constitutional rights of the students affected, or if he took the action with malicious intention to cause a deprivation of constitutional rights or injury to the student."

In *Wong v. Waterloo School District*, 232 N.W.2d 865 (Iowa SC, 1975), Peter Wong was enrolled in a summer swimming class held at a public school and supervised by school employees. Evidence presented in court included the plans for the instruction, statements on the abilities of the instructors, and the condition of the pool and led to a decision that the local district was not liable, for it had engaged in reasonable and careful planning. This was so even though Wong's parents sought damages on his death by drowning during the last session of the swimming class. In *Stevens v. St. Clair Schools*, 115 N.W.2d 69 (Mich. SC, 1962), action was brought, declaring that injuries sustained to the plaintiff while playing on a school playground occurred because the playground was unsafe. Lacking proof of any breach of duty, the Michigan court ruled that the declarations against a school district (even though it carried liability insurance) were insufficient to entitle the plaintiff to prosecute, given the defense of governmental immunity. In *Brahatcek v. Millard Schools*, 202 Neb. 86 (1979), David Brahatcek was injured and died as a result of being struck in the head by a golf club during a physical education class. In the class were 57 students, supervised by one teacher and one student teacher. The Nebraska Supreme Court, citing failure to follow existing procedures and a lack of adequate supervision, granted a total damage award of $53,370.06 as an indication of the school district's liability for the malperformance of its employees.

Keiffer v. Southern Pacific Transportation and Corrigan-Camden Schools, 486 F.Supp. 798 (Tex., 1980)

Generalization

States may statutorily set aside the common-law doctrine of governmental immunity. When that occurs, political entities are liable for any of the activities and the limits generally specified in law.

Description

The Texas legislature had passed the Texas Tort Claims Act. James Keiffer represented the parents and children who brought a suit for damages against Southern Pacific after a collision between a school bus and a train. The railroad filed a third-party claim, bringing in the school district on the grounds that it was the owner of the vehicle that was operated by one of its employees. The school district asked to be released from the suit, but that request was denied by the court.

Traditionally, a political entity such as a local school district is immune from liability in tort so long as it acts in its governmental, rather than proprietary, capacity. This is the rule adopted by Texas, and, without more, it blankets the School District with a cloak of immunity 844, 846 (Tex. 1978) ("an independent school district is an agency of the state and, while exercising governmental functions, is not answerable for its negligence in a suit sounding in tort.")

Texas, however, has chosen to partially shed this immunity and has done so by enacting the Texas Tort Claims Act. Under the Act, a school district is liable for money damages for personal injuries or death when proximately caused by the negligence or wrongful act or omission of any officer or employee acting within the scope of his employment or office arising from the operation or use of a motor vehicle . . . under circumstances where such officer or employee would be personally liable to the claimant in accordance with the law of this state. . . . Liability hereunder shall be limited to $100,000 per person and $300,000 for any single occurrence for bodily injury or death.

At the outset, it is clear that the Texas Tort Claims Act may be used by a third party plaintiff to implead a third-party defendant for a claim of contribution or indemnity ("the right of indemnity is available under the [Texas Tort Claims] Act even though [the third-party plaintiff] suffered no personal injuries"). Accordingly, any argument of the School District that the third-party claim for contribution under the Act fails to state a claim upon which relief can be granted is without merit.

In *Mount Pleasant Schools v. Estate of Linburg*, 766 S.W.2d 208 (Tex., 1989), the school district prevailed against a suit for damages on two premises: (1) the standard of care in the operation of school buses was sufficiently high; and more important, (2) the school district had protection under the concept of sovereign immunity. In a minority of states, selected government entities are still entitled to protection under sovereign immunity. The standard of care also played an important part in *Benitz v. N.Y.C. Board*, 543 N.Y.S.2d 29 (1989). An injured football player, with a jury-supplied damage award of $878,300, lost on appeal because the court recognized that his participation in football had been voluntary. His injury was described as a "luckless accident."

Larson v. Independent School District #314, 289 N.W.2d 112 (Minn. SC, 1979)

Generalization

School districts hire professionals to carry out the mission of the school. When injury occurs through their negligence, the local district may not be held responsible to indemnify any judgment for damages made against them.

Description

Steven Larson was injured in a physical education class at a time when one teacher had just left and another teacher, Lundquist, had been hired to take his place. It was determined by a jury that the new teacher and the principal, Peterson, were negligent, and an award, plus other costs, was made in the amount of $1,013,639.75 to Steven. Substantial expert testimony about the teaching of physical education and the adequacy and intent of Minnesota's curriculum guides was taken.

Because of Lundquist's inexperience, the jury could reasonably have believed that Peterson should have exercised closer supervision over planning and administering the physical education curriculum by specifically instructing Lundquist to refer to Curriculum Bulletin No. 11, by instructing an experienced physical education instructor like Embretson to closely plan the curriculum and submit a detailed report, or by requiring detailed written plans from Lundquist. It could also have believed that Peterson should have more closely supervised the transition between Embretson and Lundquist by formulating definite goals and requiring detailed reports. The jury's finding that Peterson was negligent is supported by the evidence.

The crux of plaintiff's position is that Curriculum Bulletin No. 11 established mandatory activities and courses of study which could not be departed from in a physical education curriculum. At the time of the accident, Minn. Reg. Edu. 162(b) provided:

"(b) Secondary school course. There shall be taught in every Secondary school the prescribed course of study prepared and published by the commissioner of education in accordance with M.S. 121.11, Subd. 7 and M.S. 126.02, which is Curriculum Bulletin No. 11, 'A Guide for Instruction in Physical Education, Secondary School, Grades 7–12, Boys and Girls,' . . . " Plaintiffs contend this regulation demonstrates that Curriculum Bulletin No. 11 established mandatory affirmative duties for physical education instruction. We disagree.

Lundquist and Peterson also argued that any liability on their part for Steven's accident is precluded by the common-law doctrine of discretionary immunity. Under the doctrine of discretionary immunity, state officials and employees are not absolutely immune from suit but ordinarily may be held liable only in the performance of ministerial rather than discretionary duties. As we observed in *Susla v. State*, 247 N.W.2d 907, 912 (1976), "It is settled law in Minnesota that a public official charged by law with duties which call for the exercise of his judgment or discretion is not personally liable to an individual for damages unless he is guilty of a willful or malicious wrong."

Discretionary immunity must be narrowly construed in light of the fact that it is an exception to the general rule of liability. Because of the special protection that the law affords school children, *Spanel v. Mounds View School District #621* 118 N.W.2d 795 (Minn., 1962), failure by Peterson, in this case, to adequately supervise the planning and administering by Lundquist of the physical education curriculum cannot be considered decision-making that the doctrine of discretionary immunity is designed to protect. We therefore hold that Peterson's liability is not precluded by the doctrine of discretionary immunity.

Peterson also argues that his liability should be less than the amount determined by the trial court. He argues, and we reject, that (1) his liability is limited to the insurance coverage prescribed by Minn. St. 1971, 466.04, and (2) that he is entitled to indemnity from the school district.

Peterson is not entitled to indemnity from the school district. His attempt to obtain indemnity is barred by governmental immunity conveyed to the school district under 466.12 subd. 2. The limited waiver of immunity provided in 466. subd. 3a, was the result of the legislature's desire that persons injured by the negligence of a school district's employee have recourse to the school district's insurance coverage. Peterson does not come within the class to whom waiver of the school district's governmental immunity has been granted. His quest for indemnity is therefore barred by c. 466. Furthermore, Peterson was found personally negligent, and he may not seek indemnity from his employer, whose only liability to plaintiffs in this case is vicarious.

Affirmed.

Larson is a good illustration of the manner in which school district treasuries are protected in states that have set aside governmental immunity. In instances of large dollar awards, both the plaintiff and the defendant may seek to shift the responsibility for payment. Unless Peterson, personally, had an unusually large liability insurance policy, all of his assets could have been liquidated and, still, the award for damages not be paid in full. So he would have sought the financial protection, by way of employee indemnification, of the school district's liability insurance under state statutes. Likewise, the plaintiff would have sought incorporation of the school district into the liable group as a much larger source of money from which to satisfy the damage award. However, when negligence is strictly attributable to the poor performance of employees, the school district may be exonerated, as it was.

Boards of education are not responsible for actions of employees who are in violation of board policy. In *Walker v. St. Louis Board*, 776 S.W.2d 474 (Mo., 1989), a sixth-grade child died while on a field trip. The teachers sought protection from damage awards under a board regulation that stated that the board would defend and hold harmless its employees up to a maximum amount of $1,000,000. Examining the descriptions of the accident, it was revealed that the teachers had violated board policy, so the board declined to protect the involved teachers. Claiming breach of contract and seeking board support for judgments and other money costs, the teachers lost.

SUMMARY

Largely as a matter of convenience, this discussion of injury and negligence has focused on injuries to schoolchildren. Injuries can occur to others including employees and patrons, who might subsequently have an interest in attempting to prove negligence as a basis for an award of damages. The focus has also been on physical injury. Adults may suffer injuries, physical or reputational. Many other kinds of injuries may have their origin in schools or school-related activities, but the vast preponderance of injuries are physical and involve children.

School boards must pass strict tests of responsible action when called on to explain injuries that occur to children in their schools. Boards, and their professional employees, stand in loco parentis. Although that concept is not applied as literally as it was in the first half of the twentieth century, it still pertains in many cases. The obligation of a local school board to provide a safe place can hardly be overemphasized. It is a legal understanding with strong and widely spread roots in the ethics of American culture: adults are responsible for the care and protection of children.

Employees of school districts must accept their professional responsibilities without reservations. They cannot expect their own school to indemnify them for their own inattention to the job. Just as school board members are obligated to fulfill their official duties in good faith, without malice, and with appropriate attention to the overall operation of the school district, teachers and administrators are similarly obligated. In addition, it is the professionals who are entrusted with the supervision of students on a daily basis, and a high standard of performance will be demanded from them by any court.

10

Religion and Schooling

BELIEFS AND AMERICAN SOCIETY

People with a religious faith subscribe to some more or less orderly theological system. It includes the relationship between people and the Divinity, that is, God. Theism is the belief in a god or gods and, representing conditions that are prevalent in the recorded history of contemporary cultures, is the opposite of the deism denial of the American Humanist Association, for example. Theism includes a belief in that higher being, the Divinity; states the kind and amount of influence exerted by the Divinity on the lives of humans, and denies the necessity for the Divinity to engage in unequivocal self-revelation. Religious faith is detached from commonly accepted and logical systems of proof. That is, if God exists and the believer has faith in that existence, there is no need for proof. Religious faith has emotional overtones, since each believer accepts and embraces all of the incidental items that mark one religion as different from another. No believer wants to have his/her religion assailed, and ordinarily, believers would like to have other citizens join them, sharing their beliefs. In many aspects of American society, religious faith holds an exalted position.

For most religious denominations or sects, new members are actively sought by existing members. Each member tends to think that his/her own religion includes the most important and the best beliefs. Other religions are viewed as less satisfactory and less accurate presentations from the basic scriptures or holy books. For example, Christians base their beliefs on the old and the new testaments of the Holy Bible, and there is sectarian dispute over when parts are identified as important or unimportant.

Attempting to define *religious* legalistically and, by inference, the characteristics of people who have religious faith, is not a very promising intellectual exercise. Theology is the proper source from which to define *religious beliefs*, and theologians are the people most competent to develop those definitions if the terms are to be both comprehensive and accurate. Yet the churches, as units of organized religious believers, have had such a pervasive influence on elementary and secondary education in America that it would plainly be a mistake not to provide a systematic, if primary, description of the church-state-school relationships in a book devoted to school law. Therefore, this brief but systematic description is included as a necessary reference point from which to approach some of the church-state arguments.

Churches are units in which believers meet to share aspects of their faith with other believers. For each church there are two audiences: the groups attending and those who might be persuaded to join. Some of the church's efforts are directed toward this second group. Much of the controversy that has been so extensively litigated in the church-state arena has its origin in two approaches to the question "How can the tenets of this religious faith be extended so that others may accept it?" The First Amendment provides assurance that citizens may believe selectively and be protected, but it also assures that government cannot be used coercively to build membership. These are restrictions that are especially pertinent to public schools.

Relationships between a public school district—a tax-collecting agency—and the private sectarian schools within the district are variable. Philosophical viewpoints vary. Some public school boards, viewing the public-service of the sectarian schools, deliver all support services that can legally be given to the children attending private, fee-charging, sectarian schools. Other boards, viewing the sectarian characteristic and denominational influence, refuse to deliver any services other than those that have been demanded of the local educational agency by the legislature.

Although sectarian schools represent one answer to the question of how to perpetuate a particular faith, another approach to education is to create a religiously neutral educational setting. Public schools are commonly seen in this light. No single church can dominate the public schools, and no single set of religious beliefs can be extolled over any other sect. Likewise, unbelievers receive governmental protection. There is an aspect of fair play at work. To preserve the freedom of choice in religious beliefs, the secular public school does not have a curriculum that includes the religious tenets of any church, for to do so would unduly influence the children in each school. Schoolchildren could be proselytized by teachers-believers who would have nearly unrestricted access through compulsory attendance.

Theoretically, the secular school has been sanitized of religious beliefs. Practically, the problem is not that neat and clean. Many religious beliefs are pervasive in social behavior and are evident in art and music. Most organized religions include ethical and moral systems, and since schoolchildren form their own values in the secular school, the separation of those value systems from any and all religions is not easy, if it is even possible. Moreover, the moral and ethical values of some churches are unique and recognizable as based in the religious tenets of one certain church. This, coupled with the fact that many parents want their children to be exposed to, to learn, and to accept religiously based moral systems, may penetrate the protective shroud of secularism from several directions.

Another approach to the question has problems of its own. In this other approach, a candidly biased religious setting is also the place where the child is educated. Churches sponsor private elementary and secondary schools, also called sectarian or parochial schools. The legality of such schools has been questioned, and it was settled in *Pierce v. Society of Sisters*, 268 U.S. 510 (Or., 1925). In *Pierce* the Supreme Court established several principles. First, it was decided that states could not use the police power to compel students into public schools exclusively. Other principles of school law included the right of parents to enter into decision making about where their child would attend school; the power of the state to regulate private schools, as an assurance of a minimum acceptable curriculum; and the right of private groups, including churches, to own property, hire personnel, and establish schools that might include both secular and sectarian components in the education.

Private schools, sponsored by churches, may exist. In many states the SDE is responsible for regulating quality in private as well as public schools, providing an assurance to all parents that schools in the state meet some standards of minimum quality. Religion can be studied as a part of the curriculum or as a pervasive influence spread through the entire endeavor of the school or both. Commonly, it is both. The church that has been most aggressive in establishing elementary and secondary schools is the Roman Catholic church. Although some other churches, such as the Lutheran, Baptist, and Seventh-Day Adventist, have also established elementary and secondary schools, no group is close to the Catholics in this endeavor. In 1990, over 80 percent of the children who attended church-sponsored nonpublic schools were in Roman Catholic schools.

To the extent that the church-sponsored school openly teaches specific religious beliefs and an accompanying system of morality, the desires of parents to see their offspring grow and mature in that church are satisfied. Not everything in this plan is satisfying, however. Although public nonsectarian schools are tax-supported, the private sectarian schools may not receive tax funds, lest they be in violation of the First Amendment clause that forbids government support for the establishment of a religion. Patrons of those schools pay the taxes levied by the public school district where they reside and also pay tuition or fees to the private school they have selected. Fees, even if paid directly or through contributions to their church, are still educational costs over and above local taxes paid to support public schools.

Each school type, the secular public or the sectarian private, leaves parents less than entirely satisfied. From time to time, parents of children in public schools have attempted to incorporate into that curriculum various religious aspects, including Bible reading and prayer. On the other side of that dissatisfaction question, parents of children in sectarian private schools have attempted to get tax money for the support of their schools. Viewed in the short term, the American system that calls for separation of church and state does not fit the desires of either parent group. It does provide for a distribution of dissatisfaction that meets certain tests of fair play, however, and that is no small accomplishment for any political system.

In the United States Constitution, the First Amendment states, in part, "Congress shall make no law respecting an establishment of religion, or prohibiting the free exercise thereof." The clause contains two prohibitions: Congress shall not establish a religion, and Congress shall not forbid citizens to exercise freedom of choice in religion and worship. The first is called the establishment clause; the second is called the free-exercise clause. The prohibitions were made applicable to each state through the Fourteenth Amendment. State constitutions have followed the federal lead, and their terminology has been at least as strong in describing the church-state separation that must be maintained. The Nebraska Constitution, representative of a few with unusually strong wording, states that "neither the State Legislature . . . or other public corporation shall ever make any appropriations from any public fund" to any church-related enterprise.

NONPUBLIC SECTARIAN EDUCATION

A historical examination of sectarian schools reveals that the large-city school districts, as they were forming in the latter part of the nineteenth century, also became the locales in which large numbers of Catholic-sponsored elementary and secondary schools first flourished. On the rationale that the church should be a dominant force in the education of the young, and because a Protestant-influenced nonsectarianism was perceived by many Catholics to exist in public schools, the movement spread. Even very small parishes started schools. Many failed, but many prevailed. Parents were proud of their schools, and in the pattern of extensive parental involvement in schools, many other religious denominations have entered the schooling arena. If those latter efforts are not as apparent, it may be because of the comparatively large number of Catholic schools in the United States. A church with a large membership, families that have been atypically large, and, originally, a strong teaching group in religious orders produced a very visible "system" of church-dominated elementary and secondary schools.

The efforts of other churches have been more recent. Christian schools and academies, especially, have flourished since the early 1970s. Groups that might be generically described as Fundamentalist Christians have moved toward supporting their own schools and have also fostered systematized, centrally directed home tutorials. Questions of state control over those schools, and of exceptionality from compulsory-attendance laws for children in home tutorials, are imperfectly resolved.

Questions of educational obligation have arisen. Must sectarian schools fulfill all obligations that are put on public schools? Answers to this question have varied from state to state, but in *State of Ohio v. Whisner*, 351 N.E.2d 750 (Ohio, 1976), that court stipulated a differential test for public and private schools. The state could require of (church-sponsored) private schools only those programs and procedures necessary to assure that students would get an education leading to economic self-sufficiency and performance as socially responsible citizens on reaching adulthood—a lesser demand than that imposed on the state's public schools. Some states have demanded that church-sponsored schools be comparable to public schools.

The term *church* has been defined here only by implication. The situation of church-sponsored schools has been viewed from the larger perspective. Specific and local questions have been omitted. The consideration has been specific only in that Christian churches have been the sponsoring churches. Other religious beliefs have secured the support of members toward the establishment of their schools too. Jewish and Islamic schools and several schools of Asiatic religions were among the many church-sponsored elementary and secondary schools on the American educational scene by 1980. Churches are groups of believers who accept a set of tenets in common. Those groups, large or small, may set out to establish sectarian private schools for the education of their children.

Those schools are a different kind of educational setting from the home tutorial, in which a parent has chosen to teach his or her child at home. Both are private, and even though that choice for the home tutorial may have been motivated in part by religious beliefs, a home tutorial is not a school in the sense that it is a nonsocial, separatist situation. Instruction in isolation from other children is, in many ways, the opposite from a school. Presently, states do not provide for any kind of financial relief for the home tutorial, although many who are advocates for educational vouchers may envision such applications. Nonpublic sectarian education is schooling that is church-sponsored, fee-supported, and selective in admissions. Conceptually, it is separatist.

The principle that education could meet the demands of the state and still be strongly sectarian was enunciated in *Pierce* in 1925. As stated earlier, the United States Supreme Court struck the Oregon statute that demanded that all students in the compulsory-education age range had to attend public schools and established the constitutionality of attendance at academically equivalent private schools, sectarian or nonsectarian. Viewed in retrospect, a rather systematic sequence of cases slowly followed. The "child-benefit theory" was discussed in *Cochran v. Louisiana State Board of Education*, 281 U.S. 370 (1930), as the high court allowed public school districts to furnish textbooks to pupils in nonpublic schools. *Everson v. Board of Education of Ewing Township District*, 330 U.S. I (1947), followed, and no conflict was found in the New Jersey statute that directed local school districts to pay the school transportation costs incurred by parents, even when those children were attending sectarian schools. That is, transportation was described as a service lacking in any aspects of religiosity.

In both cases, there was a judicial differentiation between aid to children and aid to the schools they attended. An aid, or a benefit to a schoolchild, was not seen as aid to a sectarian school—which would have been unconstitutional.

The following selected cases are representative of current judicial thinking and are also in a direct logical line from the precedents set by those earlier Supreme Court decisions, above.

American United, Inc., as Protestants and Other Americans United for the Separation of Church and State, et al. v. School District #622, Ramsey County, 179 N.W.2d 146 (Minn. SC, 1970)

Generalization

Local boards of education can pay the transportation costs for children in sectarian schools, if the legislature has empowered them to do so and if the state constitution does not forbid it.

Description

A census revealed that in School District #622, there were 13,600 school-children of elementary and secondary age and that of that total, 2,000 were enrolled in sectarian schools during the 1969–70 school year. At a midsummer meeting of the local board, it was voted to pay the costs for transporting these children who lived in the district and who attended sectarian schools in the district. The resolution was a benefit to about 1,200 children, all of whom attended schools that conformed to minimum standards promulgated by the Minnesota Department of Education. The cost was $70,200, with nearly half of that to come from state aid.

The court noted that any support that came to private education by way of public payment for pupil transportation was incidental. Citing *Everson v. Board of Education of Ewing Township*, the state court showed that the question of violation of the United States Constitution was settled, and the court followed with the conclusion that there was no prohibition in the state constitution. With an enabling state statute, it was appropriate to use public funds to pay for the transportation costs of all schoolchildren. Transportation was construed as a kind of general welfare, similar to other services such as streets, sewers, sidewalks, and fire and police protection. Transportation is secular. Such services are available to all citizens without reference to any religious inclination or lack of it.

Religious sects may hold schools that are academically equivalent. They are free from interference in conducting such schools, even when they are heavy with doctrinal teaching. Lacking evidence to the extent that would have proved beyond a reasonable doubt that the Minnesota statute was unconstitutional, the validity of the law was upheld.

The question of using tax funds to reimburse certain educational costs incurred by parents who choose to enroll their children in private schools in not entirely settled. In regard to payment for transportation costs, most states allow recovery of those costs or mandate that local districts provide transportation without regard to whether the student goes to a private or public school. However, the question of providing textbooks for all students is not so clear. The constitutional question was resolved in *Cochran*, above, and reiterated in *Board of Education v. Allen*, 392 U.S. 236 (N.Y., 1968), when the United States Supreme Court, by a 6-to-3 vote, held true to the "child-benefit theory" and ruled that New York schoolchildren could borrow, on request to their local public school district, suitable secular textbooks for their grade and subject. The question in the case was whether the statute conflicted with the First and Fourteenth amendments, and the ruling was that it did not. When state constitutions contain sections forbidding such action, as in Nebraska, this cannot be done, even though there is no federal conflict. In *Gaffney v. State Department of Education*, 220 N.W.2d 550 (Neb. SC, 1974), the court declared such help to be a benefit.

Two instructive cases came before the Supreme Court in the 1970s. The question of support was addressed: "What can be purchased or funded from public school tax funds to enhance the education of schoolchildren in private schools?" This question is complicated because state constitutions differ.

Committee for Public Education & Religious Liberty et al. v. Nyquist, Commissioner of Education of New York et al., 413 U.S. 756 (USSC, N.Y., 1976)

Generalization

Under the United States Constitution, aid that may be extended by a state legislature to families with children in nonpublic schools is sharply restricted in both the specific items and the procedure for such aid.

Description

New York's Education and Tax Laws were signed by the governor in May 1972 and established three financial-aid programs for nonpublic schools and parents of children in those schools. The first section provided aid for the maintenance and repair of nonpublic schools that served a high concentration of low-income families. Thirty dollars per pupil was set aside for buildings constructed within the last 25 years, and $40 per pupil was set aside for those buildings over 25 years in age. Section 2 established tuition reimbursement for parents of nonpublic schoolchildren. The rate was $50 for each elementary child and $100 for each secondary child. The reimbursement could not exceed 50 percent of the total tuition cost. Other sections established income-tax relief for parents of children in nonpublic schools. Incomes from $5,000 to $25,000 were made eligible for tax credits on the state income tax return. The amount that could be claimed was established in graduated amounts and linked to ability to pay tuition costs. A schedule for calculating amounts was included in Section 5 of the statute. The legislation was challenged by the plaintiffs as a violation of the establishment clause of the First Amendment. In the state of New York, about 700,000 to 800,000 students, or about 20 percent of the entire elementary and secondary student population, attended nonpublic schools.

After examining the statute, the Supreme Court ruled that Section I was direct payment to a sectarian institution. Ample precedent disallowed such action. Monetary reimbursement to parents may represent a kind of enhanced freedom of choice, but that money obviously found its way as direct support to the sectarian institutions. Other sections encouraged the excessive entanglement between church and state.

Most Supreme Court cases raising establishment-clause questions have involved the relationship between religion and education. Among these religion-education precedents, two general categories of cases may be identified: those dealing with religious activities within the public schools and those involving public aid in varying forms to sectarian educational institutions. Although the New York legislation places this case in the latter category, its resolution requires consideration not only of the several aid-to-sectarian-education cases but also of other educational precedents and several important noneducation cases. The now well-defined, three-part test that has emerged from our decisions is a product of considerations derived from the full sweep of the establishment-clause cases.

To pass scrutiny under the establishment clause, legislation must do three things. It must clearly reflect a secular legislative purpose. It must neither advance nor inhibit religion. It must avoid excessive entanglement with religion. This three-pronged test has been used in later arguments. Justice Powell wrote the opinion of the Court, stating that although *Everson* and *Allen* did aid parents of nonpublic schoolchildren, they did not directly aid the school because the school could have avoided the transportation and textbook costs by placing the burden directly on the parents' shoulders. In contrast, he pointed out that any assistance such as tuition, reimbursements, or tax credits does eventually find its way back as financial support to nonpublic schools.

In the 6-to-3 decision, Chief Justice Burger dissented, along with Justices Rehnquist and White. As support for his position, Burger pointed out that there was no restriction of federal monies provided for education under the G.I. Bill of Rights. He maintained that if the money is well spent on quality education, it doesn't matter which schools receive it. In his view, parochial schools serve a public purpose. Justice White pointed out that if the nonpublic schools closed, the public schools would receive an overwhelming cost burden. He also pointed out that parents desiring a secular and religious education for their children might find it unaffordable, placing them under an undue strain of conscience and violating their freedom of choice.

Meek v. Pittenger, Secretary of Education, 421 U.S. 349 (USSC, Pa., 1975)

Generalization

When a legislature passes an omnibus bill with many kinds of aid to children attending nonpublic schools and to the instructional effort of such schools as well, each part of that bill will be scrutinized for constitutionality.

Description

"The commonwealth of Pennsylvania was authorized to provide directly to all children enrolled in nonpublic elementary and secondary schools meeting Pennsylvania's compulsory-attendance requirements 'auxiliary services' (Act 194) and loans of textbooks (Act 195)," with those textbooks being made available by purchase through publicly collected taxes. "The auxiliary services include counseling, testing, psychological services, speech and hearing therapy, and related services for exceptional, remedial, or educationally disadvantaged students." In that same act was a provision for the loan from public to nonpublic for materials and equipment to be used directly in the instructional endeavor. The plaintiff questioned the constitutionality of both acts; the instructional materials included periodicals, photographs, maps, charts, recordings, and films. The equipment itself included things such as projectors, recorders, and a variety of laboratory paraphernalia.

The justices examined all parts of each act. The justices did not agree on which parts were constitutional and which were not. That is, some justices were in the majority on some aspects and in the minority on others. Nonetheless, their decision was so organized that it provided very good guidance about what services, materials, and equipment may be purchased by public funds and provided to nonpublic schoolchildren.

First, Act 194 violated the establishment clause because the auxiliary services were provided at predominantly church-related schools. The district court erred in holding that such services were permissible because they are only secular, neutral, and nonideological. Excessive entanglement would be required for Pennsylvania's department of education to be assured that the public school professional staff members providing those services would not advance the religious mission of the church-related schools in which they might be assigned.

Second, the direct loan of instructional materials and equipment to nonpublic schools authorized in Act 195 had the unconstitutional primary effect of establishing a religion, because 75 percent of the nonpublic schools in Pennsylvania that qualified for aid were church-related or religiously affiliated. With aid that was neither indirect nor incidental, it was clear that religious establishment would be enhanced by that aid.

Third, Part III of Act 195—the textbook-loan provision—was limited to text-books acceptable for use in the public schools and was constitutional. It merely made "available to all children the benefits of a general program to lend books free of charge" and yielded a financial benefit that was not to the schools but rather was to the children and their parents.

Finally, Act 194 and all but the textbook-loan provisions of Act 195 violated the establishment clause of the First Amendment as made applicable to the states by the Fourteenth Amendment.

In *Wolman v. Walter*, 433 U.S. 229 (Ohio, 1977), the Supreme Court examined another omnibus bill, this time passed by the Ohio legislature. Noting the great preponderance of Catholic sponsorship among private schools in Ohio, Justice Blackmun wrote a badly split decision for the Court. In general, the decision was harmonious with *Meek* and stipulated that the provisions for textbooks loaned from public agencies to children attending any school—public or private—were constitutional and that diagnostic and therapeutic services to certain handicapped children enrolled in private schools could be supplied by public agencies. However, in *Mueller v. Allen*, 483 U.S. 388 (Minn., 1983), the Court upheld a Minnesota statute that allowed tax deductions for tuition, textbooks, and transportation to parents of schoolchildren whether they attended public or private schools—which would seem to contradict *Public Funds for Public Schools of New Jersey v. Brendan T. Byrne, Governor*, 590 F.2d 514 (USCA 3rd, N.J., 1979). In that case, the appeals court struck a New Jersey statute that provided state income-tax relief grants as a way to meet the costs of tuition and fees, assisting parents with children in nonpublic schools. Questions of tax equity, when matched with religious fervor, are difficult to answer.

This contention over funding is one of the recurring themes in a troublesome area. Early on in the nation's development, Thomas Jefferson admonished that there should be a "wall of separation between church and state." The court called up the three standards, enunciated during the 1960s by the Supreme Court, for dealing with cases that may violate the establishment clause and reiterated them. To satisfy the Constitution, a challenged law

1. must have a secular legislative intent;

2. must have, as its principal or primary effect, neither the advancement nor inhibition of religion; and

3. must avoid excessive entanglement between government and religion.

Court decisions have indicated a line of allowable support. Specifically, that is support to the citizens involved in nonpublic education, parents, and their children. At the same time, those decisions have indicated that support aimed directly at nonpublic institutions is not allowable.

Every institution is financially dependent. Said another way, when an institution's money source is halted, the institution halts too. There is a direct relationship between money flowing to an institution and its establishment and continuation.

One signal case involving disputes over funds was *Aguilar v. Felton*, 105 S.Ct. 3232 (USSC, N.Y., 1985), which answered questions about resources supplied by public school districts to private (sectarian) schools. The New York City schools used funds received under Title I of the ESEA of 1965 to pay the salaries of teachers hired by the public school district but assigned to teach in qualifying sectarian schools. Justice Brennan spoke for the Court and stated that this arrangement (and the arrangement in another, similar case from Grand Rapids, Mich.) violated the First Amendment establishment clause. The fact that the children being served qualified as low-income, educationally deprived children did not remedy an unconstitutional practice. As in *Nyquist* (above), and for substantially the same reasons, the dissenters were Burger, Rehnquist, and White. The consequence of this case is that Title I–supported instruction must occur at a "religiously neutral" site.

In a text on school law, it is pertinent to identify some organizations that have as their mission the thwarting of legislative attempts to divert public tax funds to the support of nonpublic education. One is the Public Funds for Public Schools of New Jersey, above. Others are the Committee for Public Education of New York and the Americans United for the Separation of Church and State. There are many others. Still, other organizations, such as the American Civil Liberties Union, approach such questions of religious freedom from a broader viewpoint. When all such organizations are considered, there emerges a formidable citizen force that frequently engages in litigation to test studies enacted by legislatures in response to political pressures for new considerations to children enrolled in private schools. The phenomenon provides an excellent example of the power balance that exists in the American system as the judiciary is used by some citizens who find the legislative branch oppressive—without regard to whoever might prevail in court decisions. The American system provides the opportunity for challenge on both sides of the several church-state questions and does not foreordain the winner. It is a picture of the fair play that is central within a political system of checks and balances.

CURRICULUM DISPUTES

Even though curriculum constriction is under the purview of the states, curriculum disputes involving some aspects of religions provide an ongoing story in litigation. In *Ring et al. v. Grand Forks Public Schools*, 483 F.Supp. 272 N.D., 1980), the district court declared unconstitutional a North Dakota statute stating that every public school board "shall cause a placard containing the Ten Commandments of the Christian religion to be displayed in a conspicuous place in every school room, classroom, or other place where classes convene for instruction." The court ordered the placards removed, as being in violation of the establishment clause. That legislative effort is a good reminder of the constant desire of some people to integrate into publicly supported education some basic religious tenets as among the foremost part of a program of study.

Similar desires have been evidenced in legislative activity within the federal Congress. Although some members of Congress have spoken out against religion in public schools, declaring that the public schools cannot—by both definition and function—train children either in piety or morality, others disagree. In 1980 both senators and representatives were actively pursuing means by which federal court jurisdiction in school-prayer cases could be ended. Typically, proposed federal statutes and committee resolutions describe a need for public schools to set aside a short period for silent prayer, meditation, or contemplation.

The question is not new. Its difficulty is extended by the fact that religion, as practiced in the United States, lacks commonality. What is a religious exercise for one has nothing of religiosity for another. In *West Virginia Board of Education v. Barnette*, 319 U.S. 624 (W.Va., 1943), the Supreme Court protected the religious integrity of students who saw, in the flag salute, a violation of the biblical admonition that believers should not bow down to a graven image. Those affected schoolchildren were excused from the state requirement that all students should stand and salute the flag in a daily routine.

Zorach v. Clauson, 343 U.S. 306 (USSC, N.Y., 1952)

Generalization

If schoolchildren are released from school classes to go to another location for religious instruction, there does not seem to be a conflict with either religious clause of the First Amendment.

Description

New York City has a program that permits its public schools to release students during the school day so that they may leave the school buildings and school grounds and go to religious centers for religious instruction or devotional exercises. Students are released on the written request of their parents. Those not released stay in the classrooms. The churches make weekly reports to the schools, sending a list of children who have been released from public school but who have not reported for religious instruction.

This "released-time" program involved neither religious instruction in public school classrooms nor the expenditure of public funds. All costs, including the application blanks, were paid by the religious organizations.

Zorach and Gluck were taxpayers and residents in the New York City Public School District, and they attacked this released-time program as violating the provisions of the First Amendment, which, as embodied in the Fourteenth Amendment, prohibits the states from establishing religion or prohibiting its exercise.

The Court viewed this as a narrow question: whether the New York schools prohibited the free exercise of religion or created a system "respecting the establishment of religion," as depicted in the First Amendment. The Court paid scant attention to factors such as the degree to which the state's compulsory-attendance laws influenced children to attend religious classes or the role of the teachers who received parental excuses for each child. Although three justices—Black, Frankfurter, and Jackson—dissented, the majority stated, "We cannot read into the Bill of Rights such a hostility toward religion."

Several reasons were set forward to support the decision. First, no one was forced to attend the religious instruction, and no religious instruction was brought into the public schools. Second, the religious program required no expenditures from public funds. Third, school authorities were neutral in regard to the program, and no attempt was made by the staff to persuade or coerce students to participate in the religious instruction. Fourth, the First Amendment reflected the philosophy that church and state should be separated; however, it did not say that in every and all respects there must be a separation of church and state. Finally, the Court declared that the history of the First Amendment did not reveal that religion and the state shall be aliens to each other—hostile, suspicious, and unfriendly.

The establishment-of-religion clause of the First Amendment means at least this: Neither state nor federal government can set up a church; pass laws that aid one religion, aid all religions, or prefer one religion over another; force or influence a person to go to or to remain away from church against his or her will or force a person to profess a belief or disbelief in any religion; punish a person for entertaining or professing religious beliefs or disbeliefs or for church attendance or nonattendance; levy a tax to support any religious organizations or groups and vice versa; finance religious groups, undertake religious instruction, blend secular and sectarian education, or use secular institutions to force some religion on any person.

Preceding Zorach was *McCollum v. Board of Education*, 333 U.S. 203 (Ill., 1948). In that case, Vashti McCollum, a resident of the school district, was successful in her efforts to end religious instruction that was delivered on public school premises by ordained clergymen of various denominations. Although attendance was voluntary, as it was in *Zorach*, the place of attendance was the critical factor, and the Champagne, Illinois, board of education was ordered to halt its on-premises religious instructional program.

In *Holt v. Thompson*, 225 N.W.2d 678 (Wis., 1975), the Wisconsin Supreme Court ruled on the Released Time for Religious Instruction Act. In that law, the Wisconsin legislature stipulated the procedures for pupil flow, accounting on attendance rolls, and the number of instructional minutes per week (60–180) that could be allotted to religion. The statute provided that such instruction was at the discretion of each local school board and, on testing, was declared in harmony with the state constitution.

Several cases have arisen concerning prayer and Bible reading in public school classrooms. In *State v. Sheve*, 91 N.S. 946 (Neb., 1902), the Nebraska

Supreme Court ordered that daily readings from teacher-selected Bible verses should halt, since they were forbidden by the state constitution. Occurring early in the twentieth century, that case was not very influential, even in the schools of the state where it was pronounced. More recently, similar cases have found their way into federal courts. *School District of Abington Township v. Schempp* and *Murray v. Curlett*, 374 U.S. 203, came before the Supreme Court in 1963. In one, the Court ruled against the schools in which students' readings of various versions of the Holy Bible were piped through school loud-speaker systems. In the other, the Court ruled against teacher-led prayers in the Baltimore public schools.

Engle v. Vitale, 370 U.S. 421 (USSC, N.Y., 1962)

Generalization

Local or state boards of education may not write prayers to be said by all schoolchildren each day. In fact, the writing of prayers by boards of education is an inappropriate function.

Description

The New York State regents recommended a daily procedure that included this prayer: "Almighty God, we acknowledge our dependence upon Thee, and we beg Thy blessings upon us, our parents, our teachers, and our Country." Not surprisingly, this came to be known as the *Regent's Prayer* case.

The Union Free School District #9, New Hyde Park, initiated the prayer, to be said aloud by all students. The parents of 10 pupils brought this action, "insisting the use of this official prayer in the public schools was contrary to the beliefs, religions, or religious practices of both themselves and their children." They challenged the constitutionality of the state enabling law and the local school regulation ordering the recitation of this particular prayer and alleged that the practice violated the establishment clause of the First Amendment. The Court reviewed history and especially those times when people found the church in ascendancy over the political state. This led to a declaration on the importance of religious liberty and on the fact that this value was what led James Madison to write the First Amendment as he did. That is, only when there is protection against the political ascendancy of religion can there be freedom of religion. The Court also pointed out that although some might see hostility toward religion in a decision that set aside the Regent's Prayer, the decision was really one of friendliness toward all religions but preference for none. Prayer, then, to any deity cannot be a part of the instructional routine of a public school, for it would amount to the state's establishing a religion.

Two other cases, from among several, demonstrate still other aspects of the church-state conflict as it arises in public schools. When there is honest dispute among citizens on some unsettled point in the spectrum of human knowledge, can a public school follow a theological interpretation of that problem? When national holidays and religious holidays coincide, must public schools ignore the religious aspects of those days, even when they are deeply ingrained in the nation's culture?

Epperson v. State of Arkansas, 393 U.S. 97 (USSC, Ark., 1968)

Generalization

A legislature cannot dictate an exclusive treatment of a questionable and controversial subject for the public schools, when that treatment adheres to some religious belief and excludes all other considerations on the subject.

Description

Susan Epperson was a teacher with a master's degree, employed by the Little Rock Public Schools to teach biology in 1964–65. Arkansas law made it unlawful for any public schoolteachers "to teach the theory or doctrine that mankind ascended or descended from a lower order of animals." The statute had been passed in 1925 and seemed to have been, and apparently was, one product of an upsurge of religious fervor at that time. It was derived from Tennessee's "monkey law," a law that gained some fame in the celebrated *Scopes* case of 1927.

After one successful year, in the fall of 1965, Susan Epperson was assigned to teach from a new text. That new text contained a chapter adapting much of the essence of Darwin's theory of the origin of species. Her dilemma was either to skip that chapter or to teach it and face possible criminal prosecution and dismissal. (The record indicated that Epperson was also interested in bringing the Arkansas statute into a constitutional test, to the end that it would be set aside.)

The Arkansas Supreme Court sustained the statute as an exercise of the state legislature to control the schools and specify the curriculum. The United States Supreme Court recognized that the Arkansas law demanded a curriculum that was attuned to a literal interpretation of the Book of Genesis as the adequate and exclusive explanation for the presence of life. Noting that the First Amendment "does not tolerate laws that cast a pall of orthodoxy over the classroom," the Court specifically observed that Arkansas had "sought to prevent its teachers from discussing the theory of evolution." Speaking for the Court, Justice Fortas stated:

Judicial interposition in the operation of the public school system of the nation raises problems requiring care and restraint. Our courts, however, have not failed to apply the First Amendment's mandate in our educational system where essential to safeguard the fundamental values of freedom of speech and inquiry, and of belief. By and large, public education in our nation is committed to the control of state and local authorities. Courts do not and cannot intervene in the resolution of conflicts which arise in the daily operation of school systems and which do not directly and sharply implicate basic constitutional values. . . .

In the present case, there can be no doubt that Arkansas has sought to prevent its teachers from discussing the theory of evolution because it is contrary to the belief of some that the Book of Genesis must be the exclusive source of doctrine as to the origin of man. No suggestion has been made that Arkansas' law may be justified by considerations of state policy other than the religious views of some of its citizens. It is clear that fundamentalist sectarian conviction was and is the law's reason for existence. Its antecedent, Tennessee's "monkey law," candidly stated its purpose: to make it unlawful "to teach any theory that denies the story of the Divine Creation of man as taught in the Bible, and to teach instead that man has descended from a lower order of animals" . . . there is no doubt that the motivation for the laws was the same: to suppress the teaching of a theory which, it was thought, "denied" the divine creation of man.

Arkansas' law cannot be defended as an act of religious neutrality. Arkansas did not seek to excise from the curriculum of its schools and universities all discussion of the origin of man. The law's effort was confined to an attempt to blot out a particular theory because of its supposed conflict with the Biblical account, literally read. Plainly, the law is contrary to the mandate of the First, and in violation of the Fourteenth Amendment to the Constitution.

The decision was that the Arkansas' statute was not one of religious neutrality, and the state supreme court decision was reversed. This finding was reaffirmed in *Edwards v. Aguillard*, 107 S.Ct. 2573 (1987), as the Supreme Court set aside the Louisiana act entitled "Balanced Treatment for Creation-Science and Evolution-Science in Public School Instruction."

Florey et al. v. Sioux Falls Schools, 619 F.2d 1311 (USCA 8th S.D., 1980)

Generalization

Some aspects of our culture, such as music and painting, are so permeated with religious themes that to avoid scrupulously every such composition or work of art would be to present an art curriculum with terrible voids; however, schools cannot teach such subjects in a way that gives aid to any religion.

Description

In a pattern not too different from previous years, two kindergarten classes in the Sioux Falls public schools prepared a program for parents during the Christmas season of 1977. It contained substantial religious content. After receiving complaints, the superintendent of schools called for the establishment of a citizen's committee to study the church-state issue as related to school functions. A recommendation from the committee became board policy in 1978 as a guide to Christmas-season programs. Plaintiffs alleged that the new policy still violated the establishment clause of the First Amendment.

The policy was a substantive change from previous guidelines. If the policy had been in place in 1977, the two kindergarten programs that had originally caused the complaint could not have been done. The new policy stated that schools could observe holidays having both religious and secular importance, such as Christmas; that schools could present holiday programs containing religious art, literature, and music; that such materials had to be displayed in a prudent and objective way; and that religious symbols having deep cultural significance could be displayed as part of such programs if pertinent.

The district court ruled that the new board policy was not in violation of the establishment clause. The circuit court of appeals upheld that ruling. The board's policies did not result in any relationship between the schools and any religious authority; hence there could be no excessive entanglement. The policies represented a substantial change from the previous posture of the local school board. From the evidence describing the 1978 presentations, the courts found no aid to religion or to any religious institution.

The school district made a substantial change in both policy and practice between 1977 and 1978. Justice Jackson's comment from *McCollum* was quoted by the district court, and it is pertinent here:

Music without sacred music, architecture minus the cathedral, or painting without scriptural themes would be eccentric and incomplete, even from a secular point of view. . . . The fact is that, for good or for ill, nearly everything in our culture worth transmitting, everything which gives meaning to life, is saturated with religious influences, derived from paganism, Judaism, Christianity—both Catholic and Protestant—and other faiths accepted by a large part of the world's people. Ironically, it is this condition which provides both impetus and barrier in questions of invocations and benedictions at high school graduations. When raised to litigation, recent decisions in such states as Oregon, California and Michigan are unified on the impermissibility of any prayer that is not exceedingly innocuous. See *Bennett v. Livermore Schools* 238 Cal. Rptr. 819 (1987) or *Graham v. Central (IA) Schools*, 608 F. Supp. 531 (1985).

Without constitutional violation and lacking any historical basis for hostility, the efforts of the local school district were allowed to stand by the courts.

FINANCE AND ORGANIZATION

Can a church own property? Can a church own property and have it exempted from local property taxation? Can a local school district rent space for instructional purposes? Can such a rental include space owned by a church? Can students enrolled in a church-sponsored nonpublic school attend any classes in public schools, if they live in that school district? When does excessive entanglement occur?

The questions that arise on sober reflection over how to keep church and state separated are both many and complicated. In part, this is true because the questions are part of a never-ending parade of questions—new ones and refinements of old ones that are constantly arising. No sooner is one question settled by a court decision than another one arises, because many Americans are not satisfied with the conditions that no public funds be given to private education and no religious activities be allowed in public education. Given the American characteristics of aggressiveness and inventiveness, new proposals will doubtless continue to flow as citizens seek ways to accomplish, constitutionally, the goals they deem to be important.

The professionals in educational administration have seen all of this activity. Many administrators have played active roles in some of the controversies. Yet there is very little evidence of any long-range planning on some of the basic questions of the church-state controversy. With compulsory-education laws in every state, the public schools are the organizations that must receive all who are qualified to attend. This differentiating characteristic between public and private schools merits thoughtful organizational planning from school administrators before some court decision is made that private schools—sectarian or not—perform such a pervasive public service that they are entitled to support from public tax funds. In fact, at least three critical areas in the realm of money and organization deserve such extended professional attention. The following questions should be asked if, in any fashion that may be invented, more tax money is to flow to students in private schools or to the schools themselves.

1. Who should control the curriculum and hire the faculty in the private schools?
2. Who should own the physical plant and the instructional equipment in the private schools?
3. Who should set standards and control admission and assignment of students in private schools?

If school administrators do not give attention to these matters, and to a very few other similarly basic questions, court decisions on the larger question of money support may very likely have an adverse effect on education, generally, if in no other way than by the sundering of community support for the whole concept of elementary and secondary education for all.

Walz v. Tax Commission of New York City, 397 U.S. 664 (USSC, N.Y., 1970)

Generalization

Property owned by a church and used for religious or educational purposes can be exempted from property taxation by state constitution or statute, for such a practice is not in violation of the United States Constitution.

Description

The appellant property owner unsuccessfully sought an injunction to prevent the New York State Tax Commission from granting property-tax exemptions to buildings used for religious worship. The state constitution and statutes provided for tax exemptions for property used for religious, educational, or charitable purposes. It was argued that tax exemption as applied to religious bodies violated the provisions prohibiting the establishment of religion under the First and Fourteenth amendments. The First Amendment to the Constitution provides in part that "Congress shall make no laws respecting an establishment of religion, or prohibiting the free exercise thereof," and the Fourteenth Amendment made that provision binding on all of the states. In essence, the contention was that since all taxes were public funds, and since the Constitution prohibited the use of public funds for religious purposes, the state was indirectly requiring Walz to make contributions to religious bodies.

To understand the First Amendment, a person must understand the times in which it was written and the historical antecedents that caused Madison and Jefferson to dwell on it. The establishment of religion at that time connoted the active involvement of the sovereign in religious activity, as was the case in England. There, the Church of England was established, sponsored, and financed by the Crown. Exemptions from property tax for the church under provisions of the United States Constitution and its First Amendment does not, and cannot, mean establishing, sponsoring, or financing the church by the state out of public funds. It is an act of benevolent neutrality that enhances the Constitution by granting the church the freedom of existence and exercise without interference. Also, it frees the government from certain obligations and commitments to the church.

The constitutional purpose of the property-tax exemption is neither sponsorship nor hostility but respect for the peaceful coexistence of church and state and a recognition of the religious nature of the American people. Government derives its main support from tax money. Receiving tax from the church puts the issue the other way around—the church supporting the state—and tends to tie the two together, rather than separating them. Property-tax exemption by the state for the church's property is no more or less an aid, in principle, than is the federally granted exemption of contributions to churches from income taxes.

The church, through its program of health, education, and other social welfare services to a large population of the community, relieves the government of such burdens that would have consumed a reasonable proportion of the nation's tax money. Tax exemption, equated with subsidy and used this way, has not promoted religion, rather, it has promoted secular and social services by the churches for the community. Churches not only provide for religious experiences but also carry on many secular services. Absolute separation or noninvolvement between church and state, which is pursued in this case, does not exist and cannot exist. The ruling was for continuation of the exemption. This ruling was a reaffirmation of a longtime American societal practice.

SUMMARY

In candor, it is a very narrow line that separates constitutional support given to children attending private schools and unconstitutional support given to the school itself. If parents find relief from the costs of books and transportation, for example, they are surely in better financial shape to face the tuition for and donations to the private school. Yet the line is discernible, and the fact that it is a narrow line does not make it any less acceptable legally or socially. The Equal Access Act and *Westside Community Schools v. Mergens*, are treated in chapter 6, above.

From court tests of state and federal statutes, it is now clear that if not precluded by state constitutions, several kinds of support from public funds to children attending nonpublic, church-sponsored elementary and secondary schools are constitutional: bus transportation (or transportation costs), secular textbook loans, health services, psychological services, reimbursements on a per-pupil-cost basis for the administration of state-mandated standardized tests, tests for speech and hearing defects, and remedial help for the handicapped. Assistance from public funds, aimed specifically at the children who will benefit from that assistance, has been the guiding rule since about 1930.

Some kinds of support from public funds have been consistently ruled un-constitutional: salary supplements to parochial teachers, direct money grants to nonpublic schools, and tax credits or exemptions to parents of parochial school students.

The question of prayer and meditation, as religious expression in public schools, is not so clear. The religious beliefs of schoolchildren deserve extended protection and yet not to the extent that children should be exempted from obligations for vaccination—unless statutes provide exemption for people holding religious tenets against medical practices such as vaccination. Can children pause in the school day for silent meditation but not for silent prayer? Even a cursory examination of *Karcher v. May*, 108 S.Ct. 388 (N.J., 1987), shows that they may not have that "minute of silence." Children can be released from public schools to go to another location for instruction in a religious denomination. In some states, shared-time enrollment or dual enrollment can be carefully structured and meet tests of constitutionality. But that is determined by state, for what proved to be acceptable in Nebraska was unacceptable in Michigan. With so many unsettled questions about the church-state relationship in education, this will continue to be a frequently litigated area.

11

Collective Bargaining

The decade of the 1960s witnessed substantial growth in collective bargaining in public education. Emerging from a time when initial efforts by teachers to organize and bargain collectively met with public criticism, more than 90 percent of today's teachers in the United States are covered by a contract that is the result of collective bargaining. Semantic terms—*collective negotiations, collective bargaining,* and others—are used in several states. For our purposes, we refer to *collective bargaining* as the process through which the parties (the board of education and the employee organization) reach an agreement.

At last count—and this number has been changing—over 40 states provide for some form of collective bargaining by school employees. Six of them approved teacher collective bargaining in the 1960s; the remaining states granted statutory approval in the 1970s and 1980s.

Because of the very nature of the employment relationship, there are substantial differences between the rights of employees in the public sector and the rights of employees in the private sector. One issue that has not yet been resolved satisfactorily is the right of public employees to strike.

Federal legislation has had an impact on organized labor in all states. In 1935, the Wagner Act (which established the National Labor Relations Board [NLRB]) provided employees the right to organize and bargain. Furthermore, this act granted the employees the right to strike and picket. The constitutionality of the act was upheld in *National Labor Relations Board v. Jones and Laughlin Steel Corp.*, 81 L.Ed. 893 (1937). This act specifically excluded workers in public employment, but it established a political tone in labor relations.

Believing that there should be a better balance between labor and management, Congress enacted the Taft-Hartley Act of 1947. Section 14b of this act, known as the "right-to-work" provision, set the stage for states to adopt legislation that grants employees the right to work whether or not they join a labor union.

With that very brief acknowledgment of federal statutes that changed the government's position toward bargaining, let us examine a landmark case that deals with the issue of the sovereignty of the board of education and with the issue of strikes by public employees.

Norwalk Teachers' Association v. Board of Education, 83 A.2d 482 (Conn. SC, 1951)

Generalization

In the American system of government, sovereignty is inherent in the people. The people can delegate this sovereignty to a government that they create and operate by law. People employed by such a government are agents who are to carry out the government's task. The status of these employees is different from that of employees in the private sector; that is, the former serve the public welfare. The profit motive of free enterprise is absent. To say that those in the public employ, without statutory authority to do so, have the right to strike is the equivalent of saying that they can deny the authority of government and contravene the public welfare.

Description

In April 1946 there was a dispute between the parties over salary rates. After protracted negotiations, 230 of the approximately 300 members of the teachers' association rejected the individual contracts tendered to them and refused to return to their teaching duties. The governor and the state board of education entered the negotiations, and finally a settlement was reached. This was carried forward through the school year of 1950–51. Doubt and uncertainty arose concerning the rights and duties of the respective parties, the interpretation of the contract, and the construction of the state statutes relating to schools, education, and boards of education. The parties joined in an action to seek judicial determination of their respective rights, privileges, duties, and immunities. Questions were raised about the right to strike, the right to organize as a labor union, the right to demand recognition and collective bargaining, and the question of whether collective bargaining between the plaintiff and the defendant was permissible.

The court first held that teachers did not have the right to strike. Questions (a) and (b) related to the right of the plaintiff to organize itself as a labor union and to demand recognition and collective bargaining. The right to organize is *sometimes* [emphasis supplied] accorded by statute or ordinance. . . . The right to organize has also been forbidden by statute or regulation. In Connecticut the statutes are silent on the subject. Union organization in industry is now the rule rather than the exception. In the absence of prohibitory statute or regulation, no good reason appears why public employees should not organize as a labor union. . . . It is the second part of the question (a) that causes difficulty. The question reads: "Is it permitted to the plaintiff under our laws to organize itself as a labor union for the purpose of demanding and receiving recognition and collective bargaining?" The question is phrased in a very peremptory form. The common method of enforcing recognition and collective bargaining is the strike. It appears that this method has already been used by the plaintiff and the threat of its use again is one of the reasons for the present suit. As has been said, the strike is not a permissible method of enforcing the plaintiff's demands. The answer to questions (a) and (b) is a qualified "yes." There is no objection to the organization of the plaintiff as a labor union, but if its organization is for the purpose of "demanding" recognition and collective bargaining, the demands must be kept within legal bounds. What we have said does not mean that the plaintiff has the right to organize for all the purposes for which employees in private enterprise may unite, as those are defined in Sec. 7391 of the General Statutes. Nor does it mean that, having organized, it is necessarily protected against unfair labor practices as specified in Sec. 7392 or that it shall be the exclusive bargaining agent for all employees of the unit, as provided in Sec. 7393. It means nothing more than that the plaintiff may organize and bargain collectively for the pay and working conditions which it may be in the power of the board of education to grant.

Questions (a) and (b) in effect ask whether collective bargaining between the plaintiff and the defendant is permissible. The statutes and private acts give broad powers to the defendant with reference to educational matters and school management in Norwalk. If it chooses to negotiate with the plaintiff with regard to the employment, salaries, grievance procedure and working conditions of its members, there is no statute, public or private, which forbids such negotiations. It is matter of common knowledge that this is the method pursued in most school systems large enough to support a teachers' association in some form. It would seem to make no difference theoretically whether the negotiations are with a committee of the whole association or with individuals or small related groups, so long as any agreement made with the committee is confined to members of the association. If the strike threat is absent and the defendant prefers to handle the matter through negotiation with the plaintiff, no reason exists why it should not do so. *The claim of the defendant that this would be an illegal delegation of authority is without merit.* The authority is and remains in the board. This statement is not to be construed as approval of the existing contracts attached to the complaint. Their validity is not an issue.

As in the case of questions (a) and (b), (c) and (d) are in too general a form to permit a categorical answer. The qualified "yes" which we give to them should not be construed as authority to negotiate a contract which involves the surrender of the board's legal discretion, is contrary to law or is otherwise ultra vires. For example, an agreement by the board to hire only union members would clearly be an illegal discrimination. . . . Any salary schedule must be subject to the powers of the board of estimate and education. "The salaries of all persons appointed by the board of education . . . shall be fixed by said board, but the aggregate amount of such salaries . . . shall not exceed the amount determined by the board of estimate and taxation."

This case, for many years, set guidelines on the right of the board of education to negotiate with teachers. The following precedents were established by the decision in this instance:

1. Without a statute or regulation to the contrary, public employees may organize as a labor union.

2. The board of education may recognize the union as the bargaining agent for the teachers and, having done so, may bargain collectively for pay and employment conditions that may be within the power of the board to grant.

3. Even though the board of education has recognized the union and agreed to bargain collectively with it, the board may not abrogate its right to have the last word in the bargaining process.

4. Public employees may not strike, individually or collectively, to enforce their demands.

5. On reaching an impasse, the parties may agree, legally and voluntarily, to arbitration of specific issues with the proviso that the board may not surrender its power to have the last word; these same provisions apply to fact finding and mediation.

6. The board—throughout the collective bargaining process—may not delegate its statutory and/or constitutional powers to other parties.

ELEMENTS OF COLLECTIVE BARGAINING

There is no constitutional right to bargain, nor is there a prohibition; each state legislature establishes that right through its enactments. These statutes will vary from state to state even as the application of the statutory provisions will vary from school district to school district within the state. However, although a court decision is based on an interpretation of the language of a particular state's collective bargaining act and the language of a specific school district's contract, this may or may not be controlling in another jurisdiction.

In states that have enacted collective bargaining statutes, formal bargaining is the generally accepted practice. These statutes call for the formal pattern but not necessarily the full content of federal labor laws. The major topics that are included in these statutes include the bargaining unit and representation, processes for resolving disputes, rights and security of the bargaining representation, handling of unfair labor practices, and the creation of state boards and agencies to administer the statutes. Minus the exceptions noted above, these collective bargaining statutes prohibit strikes by public employees.

DESIGNATION OF THE BARGAINING UNIT AND THE BARGAINING REPRESENTATIVE

The first step in the process is the designation of the bargaining unit. There is no clear-cut universal definition of such a unit; the guidelines to determine the "appropriate bargaining unit" vary and are subject to the provisions of particular state statutes. Generally, the following criteria are controlling:

1. There should be as few bargaining units as possible to represent the membership.

2. The units should include members who have a "community of interest" in the same collective bargaining procedure (Wis. Stat. Ann., Sec. 14.70 [4] [d] 2).

Having employees with conflicting interests and duties in the same bargaining unit would be counterproductive and would, thereby, tend to defeat the purpose of the collective bargaining process—the fair representation for all employees in the unit.

Although most states do provide wide latitude in determining the appropriate bargaining unit, certain state statutes place restrictions on bargaining unit composition. For example, Connecticut, Delaware, and Hawaii require separation of certificated employees according to their certification classes or administrative duties (Conn. Gen. Stat. Ann., Sec. 10–1536; Del. Code Ann., Tit. 14, Sec. 4001 [5]; Haw. Rev'd Stat. 89–6 [a] [5–8]), and the Minnesota statute requires that all teachers be placed in the same unit (Minn. Stat. Ann., Sec. 17963, Subd. 17). One of the more difficult problems to be resolved in determining the composition of the bargaining unit is the placement of supervisors and administrative personnel. Section 207(1) of the New York State Civil Service Laws leaves the inclusion of such personnel in a teachers' unit to the discretion of the Public Employees Relations Board (PERB). New Jersey and Pennsylvania statutes place supervisors in units that are limited to supervisors, and Rhode Island and Wisconsin prohibit any representation of supervisors by any labor organization (R.I. Gen. Laws, Sec. 28–9.3–2; Wis. Stat. Ann., Sec.III.81 [12]).

Where the statutes are unclear and/or where the particular circumstances of a school district create some doubt about the proper placement of employees, expert legal counsel should be sought before bargaining units are designated for specific groups of employees.

After the bargaining unit is established, the bargaining representative is selected in accordance with the provisions of the statute(s) of the state within which the unit is located. For the most part, states have authorized the organization that receives the majority vote of the unit members to act as the exclusive bargaining agent for all unit members—including those who have elected not to join the union or association. There is very little provision for proportional representation. It should be noted that in any election to determine the bargaining representative, the ballot not only should contain the names of competing organizations but also should contain a provision whereby the members of the bargaining unit may elect not to be represented by any bargaining agent.

The matter of recognition of bargaining units continues to be litigated, and several interesting decisions were handed down in the past decade. Two cases, in particular, dealt with the role of employees as related to management and supervision. In *Lawrence Township Educational Association v. Indiana Educational Employment Relations Board*, 536 N.E.2d 563 (Ind., 1989), the court of appeals in Indiana reversed and remanded a lower court finding that an athletic director, a head football coach, and a head basketball coach were supervisors and thereby were excluded from the bargaining unit of school employees. The question to be answered dealt with the employees whom they supervised. If the staff were noncertificated, then these employees did not fulfill the definition of school employees as specified in the labor relations act, and the director and the coaches in question would not be, in the technical sense, supervisors. The remand called for an examination of the certification status of the supervised staff members.

In the second case, *Chicago Principals Association v. Educational Labor Relations Board*, 543 N.E.2d 166 (Ill., 1989), a voluntary group of principals in Chicago sought recognition as a representative labor organization, contending that they were not supervisory employees because board policy limited their supervisory roles. The court found otherwise and held that the principals were not educational employees and could not be recognized as a collective bargaining unit.

Whether substitute teachers may be represented by a bargaining agent is another question that has been litigated. In *DeLafleur v. Independent School District #11*, 727 P.2d 1352 (Okla., 1986), the school board refused recognition of the Owasso Education Association (OWEA) as the bargaining agent for the teachers after a majority of the school district's teachers had signed authorization cards. The board claimed that a secret ballot election was the only acceptable method by which the teachers could designate a bargaining agent but refused the OWEA's request for such an election. The basis for this decision was the passage of legislation requiring such a referendum. However, the legislation did not invalidate prior selections based on the authorization-card method. Therefore, the court ordered the school board to either grant or withhold recognition of the OWEA on the basis of the authorization cards.

A Louisiana case demonstrated the limitations placed on the powers of the board of education. After a 40-day strike, the St. John the Baptist Parish School Board and the teachers union entered into an agreement that provided that the board would call a referendum election to decide whether or not to recognize the union. To be placed on the ballot, the request had to be made to the Louisiana secretary of state, who refused the board's request. The Louisiana Supreme Court held that the local board possessed only the powers that had been expressly granted to it by statute and that no Louisiana statute presently enabled a school board to call a referendum on its own initiative (*St. John the Baptist Parish Association of Educators v. Brown*, 465 So.2d 674 (La., 1985).

An area of much concern is—and has been—that of fair share fees. Two main cases, and their related actions, are worthy of consideration at this time. The United States Supreme Court, in *Abood v. Detroit Board*, 431 U.S. 209 (1977), found that the granting of exclusive bargaining rights to a certified union or association, by statute, was constitutional. In this case a group of teachers was challenging the validity of an agency-shop clause in a collective bargaining agreement between the Detroit Board of Education and the Detroit Federation of Teachers. Under the agency-shop provision, the Michigan statute required that teachers who did not become a union member within 60 days of their employment had to pay the union an amount equal to the regular dues or face discharge. The nonunion teachers cited their opposition to collective bargaining and their disapproval of a number of the union's political activities (for example, support of political candidates) that were unrelated to the collective bargaining process. They then asked the Court to declare the agency-shop clause unconstitutional and argued that their constitutional right to freedom of association, under the First and Fourteenth amendments, had been violated. The Court ruled that the agency-shop clause was constitutional and noted that a previous labor relations decision in the private sector had held that such arrangements were viable in that bargaining activities benefited all employees and that, therefore, all employees should help defray the union's expenses in negotiations. Citing a union-shop arrangement, the Court reasoned that agency-shop arrangements were valid for public employees in that a "union shop arrangement has been thought to distribute fairly the cost of these activities among those who benefit, and it counteracts the incentive that employees might otherwise have to become 'free riders'—to refuse to contribute to the union while obtaining benefits of union representation that necessarily accrue to all employees."

In *Abood*, the Supreme Court ruled that requiring a public employee to pay dues to support a union's political activities was in violation of the First Amendment. However, the Court did not define "political activities" and noted, instead, that there would be "difficult problems in drawing lines between collective bargaining activities, for which contributions may be compelled, and ideological activities unrelated to collective bargaining, for which compulsion is prohibited." A successor case arose in Chicago.

Chicago Teachers Union v. Hudson, 475 U.S. 292 (1986)

Generalization

When a school board and a teachers union enter into an agency-shop agreement that permits union dues to be deducted from the paychecks of nonunion members, the union must provide for a reasonably prompt decision by an impartial decision maker as to the use of the deductions—whether they are being used for political or ideological activities not germane to the union's duties as the collective bargaining unit. This prohibition is designed to prevent any infringement of nonmember teachers' constitutional free-speech rights in being forced to fund political or other ideological causes with which they might disagree.

Description

The Chicago Teachers Union had been the exclusive collective bargaining representative of the Chicago Board of Education's educational employees since 1967. Approximately 95 percent of the employees were members of the union. Until 1982, the members' dues financed the entire cost of the union's collective bargaining and contract administration, and nonmembers received the benefits of the union's representation without making any contributions to its cost. In an attempt to solve this "free rider" problem, the union and the board entered into an agreement requiring the board to deduct "proportionate share payments" from nonmembers' paychecks. The union determined that the "proportionate share" assessed on nonmembers was 95 percent of union dues, computed on the basis of the union's financial records. The union also established a procedure for considering nonmembers' objections to the deductions. After the deduction was made, a nonmember could object by writing the union president, and the objection would then undergo a three-stage procedure: (1) the union's executive committee would consider the objection and notify the objector within 30 days of its decision; (2) if the objector disagreed with that decision and appealed within another 30 days, the union's executive board would consider the objection; and (3) if the objector continued to protest after the executive board's decision, the union's president would select an arbitrator. If an objection was sustained at any stage, the remedy would be a reduction in future deductions and a rebate for the objector. Objecting nonmembers of the union brought suit in federal district court, challenging the union procedure on the grounds that it violated their First Amendment rights to freedom of expression and association and their Fourteenth Amendment due process rights and also permitted the use of their proportionate share for impermissible purposes. The district court rejected the challenges and upheld the procedure. The court of appeals reversed, holding that the procedure was constitutionally inadequate. The court rejected the union's defense that its subsequent adoption of an arrangement whereby it voluntarily placed all of the objectors' agency fees in escrow cured any constitutional defects.

In its holding, the Supreme Court said:

Under an agency-shop agreement, procedural safeguards are necessary to prevent compulsory subsidization of ideological activity by nonunion employees who object thereto while at the same time not restricting the union's ability to require any employee to contribute to the cost of collective bargaining activities. The fact that nonunion employees' rights are protected by the First Amendment requires that the procedure be carefully tailored to minimize an agency shop's infringement on those rights. And the nonunion employee must have a fair opportunity to identify the impact on those rights and to assert a meritorious First Amendment claim.

Here, the original union procedure contained three constitutional defects. First, it failed to minimize the risk that nonunion employees' contributions might be temporarily used for impermissible purposes. Second, it failed to provide nonmembers with adequate information about the basis for the proportionate share from which the advance deduction of dues was calculated. And third, it failed to provide for a reasonably prompt decision by an impartial decisionmaker. The nonunion employee, whose First Amendment rights are affected by the agency shop itself and who bears the burden of objecting, is entitled to have his objection addressed in an expeditious, fair, and objective manner.

The union's subsequent adoption of an escrow arrangement did not cure all of these defects. Two still remain—failure to provide an adequate explanation for the advance reduction of dues and to provide for a reasonably prompt decision by an impartial decisionmaker.

In *Hudson v. Chicago Teachers Union, Local #1*, 922 F.2d 1306 (7th Cir., Ill., 1991), the U.S. Court of Appeals, Seventh Circuit, held that the teachers union's fair share notice to nonunion employees was constitutionally adequate, regardless of any alleged errors in its calculation of fair share fee, when the notice gave nonunion members enough information to challenge the basis for the fee.

Hudson prompted other cases. An Ohio case, *Ping v. National Education Association*, 870 F.2d 1369 (7th Cir., Ohio, 1989), involved an examination of the financial disclosure requirements expected under *Hudson*. A group of non-union teachers charged that the state association had not met its obligation to provide financial data regarding the use of fair share fees charged to nonunion members. The court disagreed with the plaintiffs, citing the *Hudson* financial provisions that did not require or expect the unions to provide an exhaustive and detailed list of all their expenditures.

In *Ake v. National Education Association, South Bend*, 531 N.E. 1178 (Ind. Ct. App., 1988), *Hudson* was cited when the union held that since the payroll deduction for fair share fees in Indiana was "voluntary," the *Hudson* provisions regarding rebate practices did not apply. The court, in examining the record, determined that although payroll deduction was not mandatory, payment of the fee was required. Therefore, the court ruled that the facts were similar to *Hudson*, and the union was instructed to discontinue the rebate practice.

RIGHTS AND OBLIGATIONS OF EXCLUSIVE BARGAINING REPRESENTATIVES

Several recent cases deal with the rights and obligations of the bargaining agent. Once granted exclusivity, the union does acquire certain rights—and obligations—in standing as the recognized representative of the educational employees in the district.

A case in New York points out the union's obligation to represent a member of the bargaining unit. A full-time mathematics teacher was granted leave for a school year to pursue graduate studies in computer science, which was to be her assignment during the next school year. The teacher requested an extension of her leave so that she could complete her master's degree; the district refused to grant it, and she resigned. The teachers union refused to represent her in prosecuting the grievance against the board of education. She filed suit against the union, arguing that the union had breached its duty of fair representation. When the New York State Supreme Court, Appellate Division, dismissed her lawsuit, the teacher appealed to the New York Court of Appeals. The court held that a wrongful discharge did not sever a union's duty of fair representation when the discharge breached the collective bargaining agreement. Since her grievance arose while she was a member of the bargaining unit, her status was like that of an employee who was actually fired in violation of a collective bargaining agreement. The court overturned the previous dismissal of the lawsuit (*Baker v. Board of Education*, 520 N.Y.S.2d 538 [Ct. App. 1987]).

Nanette Hunter was a school psychologist employed by the Cherry Hill School District in Michigan from August 1976 through February 1985. During that time, she was not a member of the Cherry Hill Education Association (CHEA), the bargaining unit in the school district. She was, however, listed on the CHEA seniority list.

On February 1, 1985, Cherry Hill became part of the Wayne-Westland School District through annexation. At that time, it was agreed that CHEA bargaining unit members would be incorporated into the Wayne-Westland Education Association (WWEA) and given seniority as if they had been employed originally by the Wayne-Westland District. The new collective bargaining agreement specifically included school psychologists in the group that was being represented. Despite that provision, Hunter's seniority credit was set to begin on February 1, 1985, the date of the annexation.

When Hunter inquired about her seniority, the WWEA president responded that Hunter was not receiving retroactive seniority because she had not been a member of the CHEA bargaining unit, had not paid union dues, and was not a CHEA member.

Hunter, then, sought recognition of her seniority rights and appealed to the Michigan Employment Relations Commission. The commission held that the school district and the WWEA had violated the Public Employment Relations Act by entering into a contract that discriminated against Hunter due to her former nonunion status and that the WWEA had breached its duty of fair representation. The WWEA was ordered to grant Hunter seniority on the same basis as that of other former Cherry Hill employees.

The Michigan Court of Appeals agreed, stating, "Because the WWEA held itself out as exclusive bargaining agent for Hunter in the new Wayne-Westland School District, it cannot now argue that it didn't owe her a duty of fair representation" (*Hunter v. Wayne-Westland School District*, 436 N.W.2d 483 [Mich., 1989]).

An element of union security, related to *Abood* and *Hudson*, is the requirement for identifying membership or nonmembership. Precise identification is by way of three terms:

1. *Closed shop* is an arrangement whereby the management employs, and retains in employment, only those persons who are members in good standing of a specified labor union. This is the most extreme of all the "union-security" arrangements.

2. *Union shop* is an arrangement under which an employer may hire a nonmember of a union with the understanding that the new employee shall join the union within a specified period; failure to do so will result in the termination of the new employee's employment.

3. *Agency-shop* employees are not required to join the union but must pay, as a condition

of their employment, an "agency" fee for being represented by the bargaining agent; failure to pay the fee will result in the employee's discharge.

The employee organization that acts as the exclusive bargaining agent also has the legal duty to represent all teachers in that bargaining unit. Such "duty of fair representation" requires that there be no discrimination against any of its members in negotiating and administering collective bargaining agreements. Furthermore, this duty requires that the union represent the interest of all members of the bargaining unit in the negotiation process—even those who are not union members. Although this requires the union to be "honest and fair," it does not deny the union the use of its discretion in deciding its negotiating strategy with the board of education or in handling grievances. Unless it can be shown that the union has acted in "bad faith," the union can take positions with which some members disagree, or it can decide to settle a grievance that may not be to a unit member's satisfaction. It is, after all, a unit, represented in some central "steering" committee that is not obligated to the individual inclinations of all teachers in the unit—members or not.

Several cases have dealt with the question of seniority. We shall discuss one here. In 1962, a teacher in the Lynn School District (Massachusetts) became pregnant. At that time, pregnant teachers were required to take maternity leave four months before the expected data of delivery and could not return earlier than seven months after the birth. Any teacher who failed to return within two years from maternity leave was treated as having resigned.

This teacher was granted a maternity leave for the 1962–63 school year. She did not return to full-time teaching until 1977. In 1981, she filed a discrimination charge, with the Massachusetts Commission Against Discrimination, against the school system and the Lynn Teachers Union for failing to credit her for service before her forced resignation.

The union argued that the bargaining agreement required that teachers' seniority be computed according to the number of "consecutive years of experience" in the system. After the commission found that the union had discriminated against the teacher on the basis of her sex, the union appealed. The Massachusetts Supreme Court upheld the commission's ruling, stating that the seniority system placed a unique burden on female employees. The teacher was credited with fewer years of employment solely because she had become pregnant during her employment and had been forced to resign. (*Lynn Teachers Union, Local 1037 v. Massachusetts Commission Against Discrimination*, 549 N.E.2d 97 [Mass., 1990]).

Another case deserving attention is *Schafer v. Board of Public Education*, 903 F.2d 243 (3rd Cir., 1990). This case deals with child-rearing leave for male employees.

Gerald Schafer was employed as a teacher in the Pittsburgh School System. He applied for an emergency leave of absence in September 1981 for the purpose of child rearing. He was granted a three-month emergency leave but was denied an extension for the remainder of the year. In his letter requesting the extension for the remainder of the year, Schafer indicated that this was necessary so that he could care for his son and that, if the leave were refused, he would have to resign.

In June 1982, Schafer requested that the board reconsider the denial of his leave so that he could return to work in September 1982. The request was denied. He then filed a charge of discrimination against the board with the Equal Employment Opportunity Commission. The complaint was later amended to include both the board and the Pittsburgh Federation of Teachers. In December 1986, the Department of Justice initiated a lawsuit against the board, the federation, and a number of other unions with which the board had collective bargaining agreements with similar provisions relating to child-rearing leave.

The contract language in dispute was in Article 31 of the collective bargaining agreement and included the following provision: "Leaves without Board pay for personal reasons relating to childbearing or childrearing . . . shall be available to female teachers and other female personnel. Such leave shall not exceed one (1) year in length from the date of their inception, but may be of shorter duration as requested by the female applicant."

On March 13, 1987, the Department of Justice and the board entered into a consent agreement, and a decree was issued granting the board's male employees child-rearing leave on the same basis as that granted to female employees. The consent decree was prospective in nature and, therefore, did not offer any benefit to Schafer, who had resigned.

In its decision, the United States Court of Appeals, Third Circuit, held:

> Because we find as a matter of law that the Board violated Schafer's rights under Title VII, we will reverse the district court's grant of summary judgment to the Board and the Federation. We also conclude that the district court properly decided that there is a factual question of whether it was reasonable for Schafer to resign; thus, we will affirm the district court's denial of Schafer's motion for summary judgment but remand for a determination of whether Schafer was constructively discharged. However, we will reverse the district court's denial of the Federation's motion to dismiss, because we find that the Federation is not an indispensable party, the statute of limitations has run against it, and there is no equitable tolling in this instance.

The factual inquiry in the matter of child rearing in each case is determining when the child rearing by the father and/or the mother begins and terminates. Careful wording of the policy on child rearing is essential if major legal battles are to be avoided in the future.

THE BARGAINING TABLE

Usually, the physical setting for collective bargaining sessions includes a table at which the parties are seated and across which they conduct their bargaining session. There is a figurative sense to the table, also. In collective bargaining, the parties are assumed to come to the table as equal partners with equal powers. Labor legislation requires that the parties bargain in good faith. The parties meet at reasonable times to present and receive proposals and counterproposals. The parties are to try honestly to reach agreement on the issues. There is nothing in the law that requires either party to agree to any demand. Good-faith bargaining requires the practice of the art of compromise and includes a need for invention and substitution.

The United States Supreme Court has interpreted the requirements of "good-faith bargaining" in a number of cases drawn from the private sector, and these same standards have been cited, frequently, as the standards that shall be applied in public-sector collective bargaining. An illustration of that is found in *San Juan Teachers v. San Juan Schools*, 118 Cal. 662 (Cal., 1975), in which the California Court of Appeals, relying on the holding in a case decided under the Labor Management Relations Act, outlined the school board's obligations with regard to good-faith bargaining:

> The statutory duty to bargain collectively . . . imposes upon the parties the obligation to meet . . . and confer in good faith with respect to wages, hours, and other terms and conditions of employment with a view to the final negotiation and execution of an agreement. The statute states specifically that this obligation "does not compel either party to agree to a proposal or require the making of a concession." Thus the adamant insistence on a bargaining position is not necessarily a refusal to bargain in good faith. "If the insistence is genuinely and sincerely held, if it is not mere window dressing, it may be maintained forever though it produces a stalemate." . . . The determination as to whether negotiations which have ended in a stalemate were held in the spirit demanded by the statute is a question of fact which can only be answered by a consideration of all the "subtle and elusive factors" that, viewed as a whole, create a true picture of whether or not a negotiator has entered into discussion with a fair mind and a sincere purpose to find a basis of agreement.

The principle at stake declares, in effect, that there is to be something for something (quid pro quo), wherein those who present demands should be willing to give something in return. These items are known as *trade-offs*.

At a point in time when the bargainers have decided that they have made all the concessions they can and have not reached agreement on all issue, they have reached an impasse. There are three major methods of breaking an impasse. Each provides for intervention by a third party who must be neutral and impartial.

The first method is *mediation*. This process calls for a mediator who will attempt, through an advisory process, to bring the parties back to the bargaining table. The mediator will usually meet with the parties separately to determine if there might be some movement toward a resolution of the conflict. Typically, the mediator moves back and forth between the separated parties, carrying ideas and seeking new views on the disagreement.

The second method is *fact finding*. Each side will present its factual information to the fact finder. Some states use a team of fact finders. After reviewing this information, the fact finder will verify the facts and then will recommend a solution based solely on the facts that have been presented to the impasse. That recommendation or those recommendations flow back to the board and the teachers. If the recommendations are accepted by both parties, settlement occurs, and the impasse is broken.

The third method is *arbitration*. There are two forms of arbitration—advisory and binding. In *advisory arbitration*, the arbitrator attempts to advise the parties on what the arbitrator considers to be an equitable solution—based on the arbitrator's analysis of the impasse, the positions of the parties, and the evidence that has been gathered. Note that this arbitrator's report is advisory and will not be binding on either party. The hoped-for effect of advisory arbitration will be that once this solution has been made public, pressure will be brought to bear on the parties, and they will agree on a settlement. The second form—*binding arbitration*—requires that the parties abide by the decision of the arbitrator; it is binding on both parties. This form of arbitration may raise some questions of constitutionality when a duly constituted public body is required to surrender duties and responsibilities specifically charged to the board of education by the constitution, statutes, and/or decisions of the high state court. At the same time, in some states, binding arbitration is the statutorily mandated last effort when an impasse has not been resolved by any other method.

The parties must agree on the procedures they will follow in the bargaining process. One question that needs to be addressed at the outset of the bargaining process is the procedures to be used in handling news releases. In some instances this is determined by statute, as in the California Government Code, Section 3547a, which reads: "All initial proposals of exclusive representatives and of public school employers which relate to matters within the scope of representation, shall be presented at a public meeting of the public school employer and thereafter shall be public records." There is no set pattern for the conduct of the bargaining sessions or for determining the composition of the bargaining team. News releases that come as surprises to the other party detract from the desired level of trust and tend to increase the difficulty level of bargaining. The bargaining process usually begins when either party drafts a contract proposal or a set of demands. As a rule, this process is initiated by the union and presented to the employing board of education.

SCOPE OF BARGAINING

The states have enacted statutes that determine what can be included in the bargaining process. These laws vary widely. Some laws are very broad and permit school boards and teachers unions to bargain "in respect to rates of pay, wages, hours of employment, or other conditions of employment, and shall be so recognized by the public employer" (State of Michigan, Gen. Sch. Laws, Sec. 423.211). Other state laws are more restrictive and specific, as provided in Tennessee Code Annotated, Section 49–5510 (Cum. Supp. 1979):

The board of education and the recognized professional employees' organization shall negotiate in good faith the following conditions of employment:

a. Salaries or wages
b. Grievance procedures
c. Insurance
d. Fringe benefits, but not to include pensions or retirement programs of the Tennessee consolidated retirement system
e. Working conditions
f. Leave
g. Student discipline procedures
h. Payroll deductions

Nothing shall prohibit the parties from agreeing to discuss other terms and conditions of employment in service, but it shall not be bad faith as set forth in this chapter to refuse to negotiate on any other terms and conditions. Either party may file a complaint in a court of record of any demands to meet on other terms and conditions and have an order of the court requiring the other party to continue to meet in good faith on the required items of this section only.

The collective bargaining process between boards of education and teachers unions may occur under one of several conditions. One such condition is mandatory bargaining, which requires a board of education to negotiate with the representative teachers union. The second condition is prohibitive bargaining, which may forbid bargaining completely or, if not completely, may restrict bargaining to certain specified subjects and prohibit the inclusion of others. When the statutes are silent on bargaining, the board of education is not required to enter into any collective bargaining agreement. The third condition is permissive bargaining. If the board of education agrees to permissive bargaining, it shall bargain on those items until an agreement is reached and shall be bound by the agreement that is reached. In those states where the board of education agrees to meet and confer, usually the board is not bound to bargain to the extent that it shall reach an agreement—although an impasse appealed into the state court system may produce a decision that is, in effect, an agreement through binding arbitration.

Defining the subjects for bargaining has created many difficulties. General language in a statute has precipitated court cases seeking a determination of obligations. Some courts limit mandatory subjects of bargaining to those that are directly or significantly related to wages, hours, and other conditions of employment; other courts are more flexible and limit mandatory subjects of bargaining to matters materially related to wages, hours, and other conditions of employment. In the latter instance, the courts apply a test or balance to determine if the impact of the bargaining subject outweighs its probable effect on the school system's basic policy and to determine the relationship and possible impact of the bargaining subject(s) on wages, hours, and other conditions of employment.

We turn now to several recent cases that deal with the scope of bargaining—on both mandatory and prohibited topics. The scope of bargaining was central in a case before the District of Columbia Circuit Court. This case involved changes in the working conditions of teachers at Department of Defense overseas schools. The plaintiffs charged that the department had instituted new regulations that added a class period to the school day and mandated that teachers give up planning periods and lunch periods as necessary to cover the classes of absent teachers. The union filed a grievance, and the department refused to bargain. Then, the union filed unfair labor practice charges, holding that the new regulations had a significant effect on the working conditions of the teachers and were, therefore, a mandatory subject of bargaining. The Federal Labor Relations Authority responded that the changes were an exercise of management rights and were not bargainable. The union appealed, and the circuit court disagreed with the authority's decision. The court conducted an extensive examination of the legislative history and intent of the Federal Labor Relations Act and determined that the proposed changes altered working conditions significantly enough to be a subject of bargaining under the act's provisions (*Overseas Education Association v. Federal Labor Relations Authority*, 876 F.2d 960 [D.C., 1989]).

In *Decatur Board of Education District #61 v. Illinois Education Labor Relations Board*, 536 N.E.2d 743 (Ill., 1989), classroom size was held to be a mandatory topic. The court held that class size has a direct effect on the conditions of employment of teachers. Therefore, it was necessary to apply a balancing test between the interests of the teachers and the interest of the district in maintaining unencumbered control over managerial policy. The court found that the balance was in favor of the teachers and held that class size was a mandatory topic of bargaining.

In a case dealing with teacher evaluations, a teachers union proposed new guidelines to govern such evaluations. The Connecticut Teacher Evaluation Act provides that teacher evaluations shall "be based upon minimum performance criteria established by the state board of education and such additional performance criteria as the local or regional board of education may, by mutual agreement, establish." During their negotiations for a collective bargaining agreement, the school board refused to bargain over several of the guidelines that had been proposed, and the teachers union sought a determination that the Connecticut Teacher Evaluation Act mandated bargaining on teacher evaluation guidelines. The Connecticut Supreme Court concluded that the phrase "by mutual agreement" made teacher evaluation guidelines a permissible, rather than mandatory, subject of negotiation. A school board or a teachers union could therefore refuse to negotiate about the subject of teacher evaluations (*Wethersfield Board of Education v. Connecticut State Board of Labor Relations*, 519 A.2d 41 [Conn., 1986]).

In *Jersey City Education Association v. Board of Education*, 527 A.2d 84 (N.J., 1987), the Jersey City school board and the local teachers union were at odds over the district's affirmative action plan. The plan stated, with respect to filling administrative and supervisory positions: "All vacancies and positions shall be filled without regard to race, age, creed, color, religion, nationality, sex or marital status." This was included in the collective bargaining agreement. Later, the board implemented an affirmative-action plan that gave hiring and other preferences to blacks and Hispanics. The teachers union sued on the ground that this plan was contrary to the collective bargaining agreement. The New Jersey Superior Court, Appellate Division, upheld the board's affirmative-action plan, ruling that the implementation of such a plan was a managerial prerogative of the school board. It observed that the teachers union had been on notice that the board had an affirmative-action plan, since the board referred to itself as "an Equal Opportunity and Affirmative Action Employer." The court held, further, that the board's affirmative-action plan was acceptable under both New Jersey law and the Equal Protection Clause of the United States Constitution. The plan was a legitimate effort on the part of the board to further its educational goals through the attainment of a racially integrated work force.

A New York district challenged a Public Employment Relations Board order banning smoking in school buildings, and the court held that the district's policy prohibiting smoking in district buildings was a condition of employment and therefore a subject of collective bargaining. Addressing the issue of smoking on school buses, the court held that the prohibition against smoking was not subject to mandatory negotiation because the state commissioner of education had issued a regulation banning smoking on buses and, thus, bargaining on the topic was thereby precluded by the same regulation (*Rush-Henrietta Central School District v. Newman*, 542 N.Y.S.2d [1989]).

In yet another New York case, a district imposed regulations that mandated financial disclosure and background investigations of nontenured employees as a condition of their continued employment. The union argued that such disclosure and investigations should be mandatory topics of collective bargaining. The arbitrator held for the union, and the district appealed. The court then disagreed, holding that the strong public interest in detecting and deterring corruption was a paramount consideration in the district's policy and that the district could hardly be required to collectively bargain over anticorruption measures with the employees whose honesty and integrity were at issue (*Board of Education City School District v. State Public Employment Relations Board*, 542 N.Y.S.2d 53 [1989]).

GRIEVANCES

A grievance dispute is one in which the school district and the bargaining agent disagree on the meaning or performance of a collectively bargained contract. The grievance must be filed with respect to a provision of the contract, for it is the administration of the contract that is being questioned.

Labor statutes, as a general rule, provide a technique of dispute resolution within some form of arbitration. A number of state laws mandate arbitration of

grievances over the meaning and performance of outstanding collectively bargained agreements. When the item in dispute is genuinely negotiable, the board
of education must, generally, enter into arbitration with the teachers union if the
collective bargaining agreement calls for arbitration of such disputes.

When arbitration does take place under these conditions, a number of states
have held that arbitration awards are presumptively valid, absent a challenge
that shows them to be illegal. Courts will not uphold arbitration awards that are
prohibited by the statutes or principles of judge-made law, that is, the rule against
a board of education's delegation of discretionary duties that are vested exclusively in the board.

A nontenured teacher complained to her principal about a negative evaluation
that he had given her. Eventually, her complaints led to a nonrenewal of her
contract, and she sued in federal court. Previously, she had grieved over the
negative evaluation, and the district had refused to arbitrate the grievance because
a district policy declared that a teacher's dissatisfaction with a principal's evaluation was not a grievable subject. The court ruled that the First Amendment
offered no protection for her essentially personal, employment-related situation
(*Day v. Smith Park Independent School District*, 768 F.2d 696 [5th Cir., Tex.,
1985]).

On the subject of what is bargainable and what is not, an Oklahoma case
provides some direction. Mary Dixon, a school teacher in the Craig County
School District, was reprimanded by the superintendent, and a copy of the
reprimand was placed in her personnel file. The district and the Professional
Educators Association of Ketchum (PEAK) had a binding grievance-arbitration
provision in the collective bargaining agreement. This called for binding arbitration in the last step of a four-stage teacher grievance procedure.

Having exhausted the first three stages unsatisfactorily, Dixon requested arbitration. The board refused to participate unless the arbitrator's decision would
be advisory only. Dixon and PEAK sued to compel the school board to submit
to binding arbitration. The trial court held that the board must comply with the
arbitration provision, and the district appealed.

The Oklahoma Supreme Court stated that a school board's managerial prerogative could not be bargained away. To subject disciplinary decisions to binding
arbitration would seriously interfere with a school board's ability to maintain
adequate standards and discipline among its teachers. Management decisions
would be made by nonelected arbitrators rather than principals and superintendents who are supervised by an elected school board. Therefore, the authority
to discipline a teacher is nondelegable and nonbargainable. The trial court erred
in requiring the board to comply with the binding arbitration provision (*Raines
v. Independent School District #6, Craig County*, 796 P.2d 303 [Okla., 1990]).

STRIKES

The ultimate weapon that may be used by employees to obtain concessions
from an employer is the strike. This is permissible in the private-employment

sector but is denied, generally, to teachers and other public employees. Eight states permit a limited right to strike. On granting teachers unions the right to strike legally if mediation efforts fail, Minnesota experienced more teacher strikes in the fall of 1981 than in the previous nine years combined. Twenty-one strikes occurred, and the majority of the public school districts were working without contracts.

Not all concerted refusals to work are unlawful. Courts may be asked to determine what constitutes an unlawful strike. The mass refusal of teachers to sign new individual contracts for the coming school year has been held to be a lawful means of expressing collective demands. Mass teacher resignations, if submitted without conditions and in proper form to terminate the teachers' employment, have also been held to be legal, since the individuals who presented them are no longer employed and are no longer involved in collective bargaining. However, those resignations that are submitted to become effective only if a bargaining representative fails to achieve a satisfactory settlement have been considered to be an illegal strike, as determined in *Board of Education v. Shanker*, 283 N.Y.S.2d 548, *aff'd.* 386 N.Y.S.2d 543 (1967).

Forms of work interruption—slowdowns, "work-to-rule," mass "sickouts," cancellation of all extracurricular volunteer assignments—if used as a weapon in the collective bargaining process, may be considered to be a form of strike pressure. The Pennsylvania Statutes Annotated, Title 45, Section 215.1, shows a broad definition of a strike:

Strike means concerted action in failing to report for duty, the willful absence from one's position, the stoppage of work, slowdown, or the abstinence in whole or in part from the full, faithful and proper performance of the duties or employment for the purpose of inducing, influencing, or coercing a change in the conditions or compensation for the rights, privileges, or obligations of employment.

There are limitations on the statutory right to strike. When negotiations have reached an impasse in states permitting strikes, the requirement that the parties exhaust statutory settlement remedies—that is, third-party intervention such as mediation or fact finding—usually must be satisfied before a strike may occur. Statutes that permit strikes provide, also, for the termination of the strike by court injunction when it has been determined that the strike poses a clear and present "danger or threat to the health, safety, or welfare of the public," as found in the Oregon Revised Statutes, Section 243.725(6). The courts must determine the kinds and degrees of dangers to public health, safety, and welfare. In *State v. Delaware Education Association*, 326 A.2d 868 (Del., 1974), mere inconvenience would not satisfy the requirement for injunctive relief. In some states, for example, Pennsylvania, the courts cannot grant an injunction if no actual strike is in progress, but in other states, for example, New Jersey, the threat of a strike is sufficient grounds for the issuance of an injunction. Then too, if the court feels that the public interest is best served by promoting good-faith bargaining and third-party intervention procedures and is of greater importance than the temporary interruption of public education, it may refuse to enjoin even a harmful strike.

Teachers, or labor unions, that willfully disobey a court injunction may be held in contempt of court. Punishment for contempt may be in the form of fines assessed against individuals and/or the union or imprisonment of individuals or both. Some statutes require specific sanctions. An illustration is Article 14 in the New York Civil Service Law, the Public Employees' Fair Employment Law, commonly referred to as the Taylor Law.

That law provides two types of penalties against employee organizations that participate in a strike: If an employee organization violates a court injunction against striking, the organization may be fined for criminal contempt (Sec. 751 of the Judiciary Law), and if there has been a strike, the Public Employee Relations Board (PERB)—or in some instances, a court—may suspend the striking employee organization's right of dues check-off, after a hearing, to determine the extent of the organization's responsibility for the strike. In each case, the amount of the fine and the period of suspension of the right of check-off depend in part on whether the public employer committed acts of extreme provocation so as to diminish the organization's responsibility for the strike. Any employee who participates in a strike or a slowdown will lose two days' pay—one day's pay for the pay not earned and one day's pay as a penalty—for each day of such participation. In addition, the attorney general has ruled that an employee placed on probation because of a Taylor Law violation is to be treated, for layoff purposes, like any other probationer—and probationers must be laid off *before* *tenured* employees.

What remedies are available to a board of education for unlawful work stoppage? The most stringent is discharge for cause. Cause may be breach of contract, unauthorized absence, insubordination, or a statutory penalty. Such a dismissal occurred in *Hortonville Joint School District #1 v. Hortonville Joint School District #1 Education Association*, 426 U.S. 481 (1976). The teachers went on strike in March 1974. The superintendent of schools sent two letters requesting the teachers to return to their classrooms. A few did. The board determined to hold hearings and set dates to do so. At the first hearing most of the teachers appeared with their counsel and indicated that they did not wish individual hearings but preferred to be treated as a group.

The teachers admitted that they were on strike but argued that the board was not sufficiently impartial to hear their case and that the due process clause of the Fourteenth Amendment required an independent, impartial decision maker. The board rejected this argument and voted to terminate the employment of the striking teachers and fill the positions with replacements. The Wisconsin Supreme Court ruled in favor of the teachers. The board appealed to the United States Supreme Court, which reversed the lower court and said, in part:

First, the Board is the body with overall responsibility for the governance of the school districts. . . . Second, the state legislature has given to the Board the power to employ and dismiss teachers, as a part of the balance it has struck in the area of municipal labor relations . . . and the Court concluded: we hold that the Due Process Clause of the Fourteenth Amendment did not guarantee respondents that the decision to terminate their employment would be made or reviewed by a body other than the School Board.

In a case from New Jersey, a strike by teachers in 1984 resulted in payment to the school board of $70,000. The union challenged the amount and appealed. The court found that the $10,000-per-day payment had been determined arbitrarily and was not supported by evidence to show that the actual losses to the board were equal to that amount. The appellate division reversed the lower court decision and remanded the case for further proceedings to determine the actual cost (*East Brunswick Board of Education v. East Brunswick Education Association*, A.2d 55 [N.J., 1989]).

A labor dispute in a Michigan school district resulted in a work stoppage for a number of days. As a result, the board of education adopted an amended school calendar for a shortened school year with an attendant reduction in teachers' salaries. Twelve teachers and their bargaining unit sued for lost wages, claiming that the reduction in salary was a deprivation of a protected property interest as stated in their employment contract. The United States Court of Appeals, Sixth Circuit, concluded that there were not restrictions on the right of a board to adopt an amended school calendar with an attendant reduction in teachers' salaries due to teacher participation in an illegal strike (*Ash v. Board of Education*, 699 F.2d 822 [6th Cir., 1983]).

SUMMARY

Collective bargaining is the process through which the board of education and the employee organization reach an agreement. This process has undergone substantial growth during the past three decades, with a major case in 1951 to set the pace. *Norwalk Teachers' Association v. Board of Education*, 83 A.2d 482 (Conn., 1951), included guidelines that have become standard for schools:

1. Without a statute or regulation to the contrary, public employees may organize as a labor union.

2. The board of education may recognize the union as the bargaining agent for the teachers and, having done so, may bargain collectively for pay and employment conditions that may be within the powers of the board to grant.

3. Even though the board of education has recognized the union and agreed to bargain collectively with it, the board may not abrogate its right to have the last word in the bargaining process.

4. Public employees may not strike, individually or collectively, to enforce their demands.

5. On reaching an impasse, the parties may agree, legally and voluntarily, to arbitration of specific issues with the proviso that the board may not surrender its power to have the last word; therefore, these same provisions apply to fact finding and mediation.

6. The board—throughout the collective bargaining process—may not delegate its statutory and/or constitutional powers to other parties.

Now, 20 states, led by the early actions of Alaska, Hawaii, Minnesota, Montana, Oregon, Pennsylvania, Vermont, and Wisconsin, have provided a limited right to strike to teachers.

The first step in the bargaining process is the designation of the bargaining unit. Once this unit has been established, the bargaining representative is selected, in accordance with the state's statutory provisions. When the union has been granted exclusivity, it does acquire certain rights, such as access to faculty mailboxes and, in those states that permit it, agency-shop provisions. Another element of the bargaining process is the bargaining table, where, figuratively, the parties are assumed to come as equal partners with equal powers. Coming to the table requires that the parties bargain in good faith, which furthermore requires that the parties meet at reasonable times to present and receive proposals and counterproposals. There is nothing in the law that requires either party to agree to any demand, although, for practical purposes, the development of a contract does involve compromises and agreement.

Failure to reach agreement creates an impasse. There are three methods for resolving an impasse. Mediation involves an attempt by a mediator, through an advisory process, to bring the parties back to the bargaining table. In *fact finding*, a fact finder attempts to verify the facts presented by both parties and then recommends a solution to the impasse. *Arbitration*, whether advisory or binding, involves a third party or a third-party panel that will recommend (advisory) a resolution to the impasse or that will decide (binding) a resolution that shall then be binding on both parties.

The scope of bargaining may occur under one of several conditions. One is *mandatory bargaining*, which requires a board of education to negotiate with the union on issues that are considered to be mandatory. Another is *prohibitive bargaining*, which forbids bargaining on items that are reserved exclusively to the board of education. In the third condition, *permissive bargaining*, once the board of education has agreed to bargain on certain items, bargaining shall proceed on those items until an agreement is reached. State statutes frequently define those items that are mandatory, prohibited, or permissive subjects for bargaining. Usually, the terms *wages*, *hours*, and *conditions of employment* are found in the statutes. Among these items may be found subjects such as class size, welfare items or financial benefits, reduction in force, work load, school calendar and length of school day, and academic freedom.

A *grievance dispute* is one in which the school district and the bargaining agent disagree about the meaning or performance of a collectively bargained contract. Usually, grievances are resolved through arbitration, when and if the collection bargaining agreement calls for this procedure.

In the private sector, the strike is the ultimate weapon that may be used by an employee to obtain concessions from his/her employer. However, except for the eight states in which there is a statutorily granted, limited right to strike, the use of the strike is an illegal activity that may result in severe penalties, including dismissal, fines, and/or imprisonment. The right of a board of education to dismiss striking employees, even though the board must, ultimately act on the collectively bargained agreement, was upheld in *Hortonville*.

Collective bargaining in the public sector requires a thorough understanding of the statutes of the particular state in which the school district is located. Above all, those who represent the parties should recognize their obligations, under the statutes, and should conduct themselves in such a manner as to arrive at an agreement that will permit the school district to discharge its primary function—the education of boys and girls.

12

Finance

Public schools are creatures of state and local governments. Of the 50 states, 49 provide education funds from state and local sources. The proportions of state and local funds vary. The fiftieth state—Hawaii—operates a state school system funded completely at the state level. The basic support for most public schools comes from tax dollars. The major producer of these dollars at the local level is the *ad valorem property tax*, that is, a tax levied against some proportion of the actual value of the property in the district. Some jurisdictions provide for other sources of taxation including, but not limited to, the local income tax, a utilities tax, and—the tax used most frequently as a property-tax alternative—the sales tax. The use of the property tax has received much attention, has been labeled an oppressive and regressive tax, and has led to a number of court cases when citizens have sought relief from it.

The general argument advanced by the opponents of the present finance system is that reliance on local property-tax revenues has caused wide discrepancies in the funding of educational programs, not only when one state is compared with another but also when one public school system is compared with another in the same state. Additionally, some critics fault it as an inequitable tax on those who pay it. The property tax—the main support for public schools—is a controversial tax.

Since many of the court challenges to public school financing programs attack the constitutionality of such programs—usually under the equal-protection provision of the Fourteenth Amendment of the United States Constitution—the constitutional aspects of public school district finances merit attention.

CONSTITUTIONAL FREEDOM AND THE FEDERAL ROLE
IN EDUCATIONAL FINANCE

The Tenth Amendment of the United States reads, "The powers not delegated to the United States by the Constitution, nor prohibited by it to the States, are reserved to the States respectively, or to the people." There is no reference to education in the Constitution, and education is, thereby, reserved to the states. The 1945 Georgia State Constitution reads, "The provision of an adequate education for the citizens shall be a primary obligation of the State of Georgia, the expense of which shall be provided for by taxation." That constitutional statement typifies what is said in the other 49 states.

Even though the federal government is not charged with the direct financing of education, federal funds are made available through various congressional enactments. The basis for such funding is generally derived from the general welfare clause found both in the Preamble of the Constitution—"We the People of the United States, in order to form a more perfect Union . . . promote the General Welfare . . . do ordain and establish this Constitution for the United States of America"—and in Section 8—"The Congress shall have the power to lay and collect Taxes, Duties, Imposts, and Excises, to pay the debts and provide for the common Defense and general Welfare of the United States." In *United States v. Butler*, 297 U.S. 1 (1938), the Court addressed the question of the meaning of Section 8 (Article I). In a 6-to-3 decision, the Court declared that this clause did not refer merely to other enumerated powers of Congress but actually conferred a new and separate power. With that clarifying case, Congress secured the power to tax and to appropriate, "limited only by the requirement that it shall be exercised to provide for the general welfare of the United States." Comparatively, that could be described as a broad construction of the Constitution, and inasmuch as public education can be rationally described as within the rubric of general welfare, this provided a case-law basis for federal participation in local educational costs.

One other basis that is frequently cited as a justification for federal support of education is the child-benefit theory. This concept, enunciated in both statutory and case law, is based on the argument that the aid benefits the child directly even though there may be indirect and incidental aid to the school, public or nonpublic, that the pupil attends.

In 1785 the Congress of the Confederation authorized grants of public lands for maintenance of the public schools. This was followed, in 1787, by the Northwest Ordinance, under which federal land was granted for education—the sixteenth section of each township being reserved for schools. Additional land was reserved for a university. Thus began the complex pattern of federal support for education. This pattern established the concept of categorical aid, whereby funds are appropriated for specific purposes and are restricted to those purposes alone. The following is a selected list of federal legislation that supports educational activities and that can be taken as exemplary–not inclusive—of the federal involvement in education:

1862   First Morrill Act—Authorized public land grants to the states for the establishment and maintenance of agricultural and mechanical colleges.

1890   Second Morrill Act—Provided money grants for support of instruction in the agricultural and mechanical colleges.

1917   Smith-Hughes Act—Provided for grants to states for support of vocational education.

1935   Agricultural Adjustment Act (P.L. 74–320)—Commodities purchased under this authorization began to be used in school lunch programs in 1936.

1943   School Lunch Indemnity Plan (P.L. 78–129)—Provided funds for local school lunch food purchases.

1946   National School Lunch Act (P.L. 79–396)—Provided assistance through grants-in-aid and other means to states to assist in providing adequate foods and facilities for the establishment, maintenance, operation, and expansion of nonprofit school lunch programs.

1950   Financial Assistance for Local Educational Agencies Affected by Federal Activities (P.L. 81–815)—Provided assistance for construction and (P.L. 81–874) provided assistance for operation of schools in federally affected areas (''Impact Aid'').

1954   School Milk Program Act (P.L. 83–690)—Provided funds for purchase of milk for school lunch programs.

1958   National Defense Education Act (P.L. 88–210)—Increased federal support of vocational schools, vocational work-study programs, and research, training, and demonstrations, in vocational education. Funds could be used on a 50–50 basis for constructing and equipping vocational school facilities.

1964   Civil Rights Act of 1964 (P.L. 88–352)—Authorized the commissioner to (1) arrange through grants or contracts with institutions of higher education for the operation of short-term or regular-session institutes for special training to improve quality of elementary and secondary instructional staff in dealing effectively with special-education problems occasioned by desegregation; (2) make grants to school boards to pay, in whole or in part, the cost of providing in-service training for dealing with problems incident to desegregation; and (3) provide school boards technical assistance in desegregation and required nondiscrimination in federally assisted programs.

1965   Elementary and Secondary Education Act (P.L. 89–10)—Provided large-scale direct federal aid to elementary and secondary schools. The act specifically prohibited federal control of education. It authorized aid to children attending parochial schools but placed control of the expenditures with the public school agencies. The act authorized grants for the following uses: elementary and secondary school programs for children of low-income families; school library resources, textbooks, and other instructional materials for schoolchildren; supplementary education centers and services; strengthening of state education agencies; and educational research and research training.

1972   Emergency School Aid Act—Designed to meet the special needs incident to the elimination of minority-group segregation and discrimination among students and faculty in elementary and secondary schools; to encourage the voluntary reduction, elimination, or prevention of minority-group isolation in such schools; and to aid schoolchildren in overcoming the educational disadvantages of group isolation.

1975   The Education of All Handicapped Children Act (P.L. 94–142)—Intended that a free and appropriate education and related services be provided to all handicapped children.

1982   Education and Consolidation and Improvement Act (P.L. 97–35)—This act left programs such as Vocational Education, Education of the Handicapped, National School Lunch, Higher Education, and Impact Aid intact. The Elementary and Secondary Education Act was repealed, and most of its elements became part of this legislation. Though the block consolidated a number of programs, some, such as Title I (now Chapter I) and ESEA Title VII (Bilingual Education), survived. In essence, the impact of the block grant on the categorical aspects of federal aid to education was negligible.

TAXES AND TAXING AUTHORITY

Even though there is this evidence of the federal incursion into educational finance, school districts remain in fact, state instrumentalities that have been created by legislative enactments to carry out the constitutional mandates for providing educational opportunities for the children in that state. Having been charged with these mandates, school districts must develop financial plans for implementing them. These plans, too, commonly find their basis and boundaries in state statutes.

Students of educational finance recognize that the school budget is the financial statement of the educational program for the school district. Once the expenditure side of the budget has been determined, the revenues to support these expenditures must be put in place. School systems derive the major portion of their revenues from tax funds. These taxes may be in the form of direct receipts from local property taxes or state appropriations and collections having various forms of taxation as the money sources.

Taxing authority for school districts is a special power that must be specifically conferred by the legislature. Not all districts have the same power. This was clearly stated in the decision in *Pirrone v. City of Boston*, 305 N.E.2d 96 (Mass., 1973), when the court held that school districts are not agencies with broad powers but are limited to powers that are expressly or by implication conferred on them by the legislature. The court held, furthermore, that the legislature could classify districts and delegate varied financial powers to them dependent on their classification. However, such a legislative enactment does not preclude constitutional tax limitations. In *Hurd v. City of Buffalo*, 311 N.E.2d 504 (N.Y., 1974), a constitutional tax limitation applicable to certain school districts in the state of New York was at issue and was allowed to stand.

Basically, in considering the power to tax and raise funds, there are two types of boards of education. The first is the fiscally independent board of education. These boards are granted legal authority by the state legislature to set the ad valorem tax rate on real property (not personal and intangible property)—within constitutional and legislative limits—to levy and collect (or cause to be collected) taxes for the support and maintenance of the local schools, and to approve the expenditure of the funds collected. All must be in accord with the district's budget. The vast majority of the nearly 16,000 public school boards of education in the United States fall into the fiscally independent category. The second type is the fiscally dependent board of education. In this arrangement, the board of education commonly prepares and adopts a budget showing the anticipated expenditures and projecting the revenue needs. Then a different political subdivision has the responsibility for apportioning the school taxes. One example is the Virginia Code, Section 22–126.1, which provides that the local municipal governmental agency shall be the tax-levying authority. The code provides, furthermore, that local boards of education must go to their local governmental body for appropriations and budget approval. Another example is the board of education of the city of New York, which must receive approval of its budget and appropriation of funds from the board of estimate. The actual funds necessary to support the school's operating budget may come through different legal and organizational arrangements, varying from state to state.

In a number of states, statutes require that tax levies be annually approved by the electorate. This is true in the Central, Union Free, and Common School districts in New York State but does not apply to city school districts, 57 of which are limited by constitutional restrictions in the amount of money that can be raised by taxation, or to the five largest city school districts (Buffalo, New York, Rochester, Syracuse, and Yonkers), which are dependent on other municipal bodies for their funding.

In the state of Georgia, county school boards of education approve their budgets and then rely, generally, on the county tax commissioner for collection. Twenty-six "independent" school districts (cities that are separate from the county school system) must rely on the cities in which they are located for the funds to operate the schools. The county school districts—with a few exceptions—have a 20-mill limitation on tax rates on real property for school operating funds.

Voter resistance to increases in property taxes for school purposes has been experienced in California—with the passage of "Proposition 13"—and in Massachusetts—with the passage of "Proposition 2-½." Other states, for example, Michigan and Ohio, have experienced financial setbacks when voters have rejected increased millage referendums with the result that some school districts have had to close their doors until funds became available. Others have continued, but with programs that were drastically reduced.

There have been exceptions to the taxpayer approval of spending plans. In a 1989 decision of the New Jersey commissioner of education relating to the Depford Township Board of Education, the commissioner reinstated the budget that had been rejected by the voters and modified by the township council. The state appellate court reversed this decision, and the board appealed to the New Jersey Supreme Court, which ruled that statements of reasons must be provided for all line-item reductions to assure that budget cuts are specific and conscientious. The court held that, in this case, the commissioner had proposed too drastic a remedy for the municipality's failure to submit a statement of reasons by simply restoring the original budget and, then, proceeded to modify the lower court's decision and remanded the matter to the commissioner for a meritorious review of the budget.

Frequently, procedural defects emerge in the levying of taxes. When these irregularities occur and become the focal point of a suit, the courts are faced with alternatives that may declare the irregularly levied tax invalid and, thereby, cripple the schools; or they may find the tax to be valid and thus work a hardship on the taxpayer. Usually, the court will carefully weigh the harm to the taxpayer, and when the taxpayer has not been deprived of a substantial right, the levy will be considered to be valid.

This generalization does not hold when the taxpayer has been deprived of his/ her voice in determining whether the tax should be levied. As a rule, when there is a special referendum being held at a time and date that varies from the general election date and that has been set by the governing body (the board of education), it is the obligation of the board of education to give proper notice of the date, time, place, and purpose of the special referendum. A defect in this procedure will, in most cases, render the referendum invalid. That is, boards may not use obscurity as a technique to "sneak by" a tax increase.

Determining the amount of tax to be levied raises some interesting questions. One deals with surplus funds. Generally, a board of education cannot use its taxing power to establish a surplus fund. There are, however, exceptions to this. Section 2021.21 of the New York State Education Law provides that the anticipated balance (surplus) of the budget of a school district is limited to the amount necessary to meet expenses during the first 120 days of the fiscal year following the fiscal year in which such tax is collected. Any balance in excess of this amount must be used to reduce the new tax levy. Most states apply even more rigorous and demanding regulations on local boards.

In *C.R.T. Corp. v. Board of Equalization*, 110 N.W.2d 194 (Neb., 1961), the Nebraska Supreme Court specifically recognized the authority to levy a tax rate that would produce a relatively small surplus should the total tax levy be collected. In this instance, the court upheld a levy that was designed to produce for all purposes a surplus amount of approximately $800,000, in a total budget of $13 million. The court allowed that there were uncertainties of fluctuations in operating expenses as well as in anticipated revenues and thus that adequate estimates of the sums required to balance the budget needed to be made. In some years, actual tax collections may be only 85–90 percent of the levied amount. Some flexibility is needed.

In *Missouri v. Jenkins*, 110 S.Ct. 1651 (Mo., 1990), the district court for the Western District of Missouri imposed a property tax increase for the Kansas

City, Missouri, School District (KCMSD) so that the district would be able to pay its share of the costs of court-ordered desegregation. Missouri state statutes limited the property tax levy any school could impose, and therefore the district court concluded that state law prohibited the KCMSD from securing the revenue it needed. The State of Missouri brought suit, arguing that the district court had exceeded its authority in ordering such an increase.

The Supreme Court concluded that the district court acted within its authority. The Court reasoned that a federal court may set aside a state statute when there is reason based in the Constitution for doing so. In this case, the Constitution required that the KCMSD desegregate its district to provide equal education for students from racial minorities. That fact, based in the Constitution, and the supremacy clause of the United States Constitution are sufficient to override the state statute limiting the tax levy of any given school district. To rule otherwise, the Court concluded, would allow states to place obstructions in the way of residents' constitutional rights and in effect would allow the states to avoid fulfilling federal mandates.

INDEBTEDNESS AND FISCAL RESPONSIBILITY

Without statutory authorization to the contrary, school districts are expected to operate with balanced budgets. Thus, "pay as you go" is the basic premise under which these political subdivisions function. There are times when a short-fall in funds limits a district's cash flow, and the district is forced to resort to borrowing. For example, unexpectedly low tax collections may leave a school district's treasury depleted just at the time of the monthly payroll. Finance laws of the states prescribe the types and terms of borrowing that may be undertaken by political subdivisions—school districts included. Loans are subject to many varied legal controls depending on the term, purpose, and form. When the power to borrow money is granted for a specific purpose, the funds borrowed must be applied to that purpose and to no other.

There are several types of borrowing. The first is the short-term loan. As a general rule, such loans are to provide the cash flow necessary to meet current obligations, for example, payroll and bills payable on a monthly basis. The statutes commonly require that such loans must mature and be repaid in the same fiscal year out of revenues that are due or collectible in that year. An example of this requirement can be seen in the Pennsylvania Statutes Annotated, Title 53, Section 6780–201. When there is more than one lending institution within the school district, a wise policy is to seek quotations (bids) from all interested lenders and then accept the one that provides the best arrangement for the school district. Other procedural conditions (advertising the nature, purpose, and amount of the loan; clearance of bond forms and terms; and prior voter approval) are not usually required for short-term loans.

The second form of borrowing is concerned with long-term debt. Such bor-rowing becomes necessary when there are insufficient funds to finance long-term

school construction and other capital improvements. State constitutions and statutes set forth the provisions that regulate both the substance of the loans and the
form and procedure of the contracts covering them. One of the primary controls
is found in the establishing of debt ceilings, through the enactment of debt-
limitation laws. An old case, *McBean v. Fresno*, 44 P. 358 (Cal., 1896), early
provided the rationale for such laws:

> The framers had in mind the great and ever-growing evil to which the municipalities
> of the state were subjected by the creation of a debt in one year, which debt was not,
> and was not expected to be paid out of the revenue of that year, but was carried on into
> the next year increasing like a rolling snowball as it went until the weight of it became
> almost unbearable upon the taxpayers. It was to prevent this abuse that the constitutional
> provision was enacted.

At issue in borrowing is the calculation of "net" debt. A common definition
of *net debt* is the debt that remains after deducting from the total of all outstanding
debts the district assets that are available for the payment of existing debts.
Generally, the holding is that the assets need not actually be applied to the
payment of the indebtedness, but only that they be available.

Borrowed money, which is funded through revenue bonds rather than through
general-obligation bonds, is not considered a debt. Holders of revenue bonds
depend for their payment on income produced by the enterprise that has been
financed by the bonds. Although this form of financing is not, generally, available
to school districts, it is available to states and often through this means may be
the source of funds the state uses to finance certain types of educational ventures.
One example of revenue bonds being used directly by school districts is in those
states where this is permissible and where the district has embarked on a self-
liquidating project, such as an athletic stadium. In this instance, the holders of
the loan are paid solely from revenues generated as a result of the construction
of the stadium and the admission tickets sold. Such debt is not considered for
funding-limitation purposes.

Another means of avoiding a debt ceiling is through using another government
entity (for example, a school building authority) to finance and construct a
building for long-term lease to a school district. This overlying debt is used by
fiscally hard-pressed school districts in those states where the constitution and
statutes permit such a procedure.

Exemption from debt-ceiling limits may be achieved through a public referendum whereby the public authorizes the board of education to contract a debt
exceeding the debt limit for the construction of a new building or the recon-
struction of an existing building or for such other capital expenditure as is
statutorily permitted. When the voters approve such a financing scheme, the
courts are reluctant to overturn their decision.

Fiscal stability is the responsibility of the central administration and the board
of education. The annual budget is the board's fiscal statement of the school

district's educational program. The budget includes a statement of the anticipated expenditures and the revenues that are to support these expenditures. Detailed budget provisions and procedures vary from state to state. They may include, but are not necessarily limited to, requirements such as format of the budget, itemization within the budget, publication of the budget, public hearings on the budget, adoption of the budget, and issuance of the tax-warrant or tax-levy order to provide the tax-revenue portion of the budget.

Courts tend to respect the right of a board of education to use its discretion about those public purposes for which school funds may be expended, but they will not permit expenditures for improper purposes. At times, arguments arise over the transfer of funds from one category to another within the budget. Particular attention should be paid to the individual state's constitution and statutes. In general, courts hold to the rule that a fund that has been raised by taxation for a specific purpose cannot be diverted to another. An illustration of this would be money raised to pay the principal and interest on bonded indebtedness. Funds in that category, raised specifically by taxation for that purpose, may not be transferred to another section of the budget. From South Dakota's highest court came *Stone v. School Board of Beresford Independent School District #68*, 206 N.W.2d 69 (S.D., 1973), which upheld the transfer of funds from the general fund to the capital outlay fund. The court reasoned that there was no evidence that the transferred funds had been raised by local tax levies and added that the amount of the transfer was actually less than the amount derived from sources other than local taxes.

An outgrowth of fiscal constraints on school districts has been the consideration of student fees with which to fund certain services and activities. These fees have been the subject of numerous legal tests. Just what fees may be charged, and under what circumstances, depend on the specific wording of the statutes.

There are diverse opinions in the courts about which activities are to be included in free public education. For purposes of our discussion, we shall deal with three major classifications: instruction (including tuition, matriculation, and registration fees), materials (textbooks, other books, and instructional supplies), and special activity and service fees.

Under the classification of instruction, a federal court in Georgia ruled that an Atlanta school board policy requiring aliens who held certain types of visa classifications to pay tuition to attend the public schools violated the equal protection clause of the Fourteenth Amendment of the United States Constitution. The court also imposed personal liability on each of the board members because the plaintiff's attorney had put them on notice, before the suit, with a personal letter stating that the policy was impermissible. The court held that the board members were liable for damages but ordered a jury trial to determine the exact amount of damages to be imposed (*Pena v. Board of Education of City of Atlanta*, 620 F.Supp. 293 [Ga .,1985]).

In *Washington v. Salisbury*, 306 S.E.2d 600 (S.C., 1983), the Supreme Court of South Carolina held that the imposition of a tuition charge for summer school attendance was constitutional. The court said that since the summer session was operated in addition to the mandatory 185-day school term and received no direct state support, summer school was not part of the free public school system required by the state constitution, and thus there was no duty to make it available free of charge. In this case we see the distinction between what was required—the 185 days of the regular session—and what was not required—summer session.

There is a division of opinion about furnishing free instructional materials. Here, it is important to consult the statutes of the particular state. As an example, the states of Idaho, Michigan, and Montana require that a legal test be applied to textbooks and school supplies to determine if these items fall under the provision of a free public education.

The test is to determine if these materials are essential to the public school activity or are reasonably related to the general educational goals of the school. If they are found to be essential or related, no charge may be made for them. Conversely, if they are used in areas that are considered to be nonessential, a charge may be made for them.

The issue then becomes a definition of what is essential and what is nonessential—or what falls in the area of the extracurricular. Here, courts in two of the three states above differ. The Idaho court ruled that fees could be charged; the Montana court ruled against charging fees for extracurricular materials. Recently, state courts have predominantly held that reasonable fees, which are tied to actual costs, may be charged for textbooks and supplies. Michigan is one state, as an example, in which the courts have been very critical of such charges, however.

The charging of special-activity fees falls into the same category as charging for instructional materials. The question that must be considered is, Are the fees consistent with the state constitutional requirement of a free public education? If so, have they been authorized statutorily? In general, the courts have held that charging activity fees is impermissible where the activity is required of the student; the courts have been less stringent in applying this to voluntarily selected activities, but it is a variable condition from state to state. Notice for instance, the case from California in which the parents of high-school students brought suit against a local school board of education claiming that the imposition of fees on students for participation in extracurricular activities violated the free school and equal protection guarantees of the California Constitution. After the adoption of Proposition 13 and its attendant loss of revenues, the district imposed fees for participation in dramatic productions, musical performances, and athletic competition. The parents based their argument on the California Constitution, which requires the legislature to "provide for a system of common schools by which a free school shall be kept up and supported in each district." The school district argued that it provided for needy students with a fee-waiver policy and, thus, satisfied the requirements of the free school guarantee. The California Supreme Court rejected that argument and said that no financial burden may be imposed on the right to an education. It also held that the programs in this case were educational in character, and it held, further, that once a community had decided that a particular educational program was important enough to be offered by its public schools, a student's participation in that program cannot be made dependent on his or her family's financial situation (*Hartzell v. Connell*, 201 Cal. Rptr. 601 [1984]).

During the past several years, the topic of transportation has been litigated often. In *Kadrmas v. Dickinson Public Schools*, 108 S.Ct. 2495 (N.D., 1988), the North Dakota statutes provided that when sparsely populated districts did not reorganize, they could charge students a portion of their costs for transportation. Claiming violation of the equal protection clause and the state constitution, the parents appealed this case to the United States Supreme Court, having lost in all the lower courts. The Supreme Court held that transportation was not a fundamental right, that the state statute did bear a reasonable relationship to the state's legitimate objective of encouraging local school districts to provide bus service, and that the state did not impose a fee directly. There was no discrimination against any class, and the statute did not interfere with any constitutional rights. Holding the reverse, because transportation was considered to be a fundamental right under the California Constitution, a California appellate court struck down a California statute that authorized school districts to assess transportation fees for nonindigent students (*Salazar v. Honig*, 246 Cal. Rptr. 837 [1988]).

There is a need to address fiscal responsibility in dealing with expenditure controls, particularly in the area of contracts. A contract is an agreement or promise that is legally enforceable. In addition, the following requirements pertain to contracts: the parties are sufficiently competent to enter into a contract; the parties have the legal capacity to enter into a contract; there are proper offers that are properly accepted with a sufficient consideration (an agreed-upon exchange between the parties) to be enforceable; and there is nothing illegal about the contract. All of these requirements must be present in a valid personnel-services contract between an employing board and all employees.

It should be remembered that boards of education must enter into a contract in an open, public meeting of the board, which is properly constituted and prepared to act on the business before it. In that way, every contract becomes a matter of public record. In cases where a board of education never formally approved the contract, or attempted to do so in a manner unauthorized by statute, or attempted to authorize an agreement beyond its powers, or failed in some other manner (for example, reducing an oral agreement to writing) to carry out its statutorily required duties, the resulting agreements have been declared null and void and are unenforceable. Such restrictions create a protection of the public funds administered by each local board of education.

An area of great concern in contracts is that of bid laws. Most states have enacted statutes that govern public competitive bidding by outside independent contractors who want to do business with school districts. Although the need for such statutes may seem to be obvious, such legislation seeks to prevent fraud, collusion, favoritism, and improvidence in contract administration in the public sector. Furthermore, it is the intent of these statutes to ensure that public schools and agencies receive the best products and services at the lowest available price from a responsible bidder. Bid specifications usually place in the hands of the board of education the responsibility for using its discretion in determining what bid is actually lowest in net cost, who is a qualified or responsible bidder, the equivalency of items submitted as alternates to those that were specified, and whether it is prudent to "standardize" selection of goods and services because of special needs, services, or materials that are unique and justify a negotiated, nonbid procurement, regardless of the contract amount.

From time to time, there are attempts to use unlawful devices to eliminate bidding and,thereby, circumvent the bidding statutes. The courts have tended to accept broad board discretion about how much and when work may be ordered by contract. However, an obvious attempt to avoid the bid statutes by splitting a continuous service into small successive contracts is an unlawful practice. This board discretion is permitted, also, when dealing with alternatives. In this instance, the board of education must determine which alternative best meets its need and then must award the contract to the lowest responsible bidder within the same alternative package.

In developing bid proposals, and to ensure fair and open competition, boards of education should pay particular attention to the advertisements for bids. These should provide sufficient facts to enable bidders to submit intelligent bids. All facts should be disclosed fully to avoid giving any bidder an unfair advantage from undisclosed facts. The board of education's requirements should be stated in full and complete terms to avoid disqualifying bidders for not complying with intended, but unstated, requirements. The goods and services specifications, from which vendors and/or contractors prepare their bids, must furnish the same information to all prospective bidders as the basic minimum fairness. Normally, the development of specifications and advertisements is a task assigned to central-office administrators.

Once a board of education formally accepts a low bid and awards a contract for the work or material, it cannot seek other bids for the same work or material. However, before the award of a contract, the board of education has the right to reject any and all bids—provided that such right exists by statute, charter law, or terms of the invitation to bid. Courts have upheld low-bid rejections for a bidder's failure to attach a bid security in the form of a bid bond or certified check, failure to comply with the requirements of the invitation to bid, and failure to sign the bid form. The courts are not in agreement about whether a bidder has a right to a hearing before being disqualified. In at least one instance, a court has found that a denial of a hearing on bidder responsibility could amount to arbitrary abuse of administrative discretion. The point of the bidding process is to assure, through open competition, that public school funds are spent in a prudent fashion.

USES OF SCHOOL BUILDINGS AND GROUNDS

A difficult concept for most citizens to comprehend is the legal nature of school buildings. Most people feel that since primarily local funds were used to construct and equip school buildings,the buildings belong to the local community. As one manifestation of the concept, requests come from various local groups seeking to use the school buildings for purposes that are often unrelated to education. The fact remains that, generally, school property is state property, and its use rests completely with the legislature except where there may be constitutional restrictions.

Although the use of school buildings rests with the legislature, restrictive legislation is lacking, and the local board of education is given the discretion for the management and control of school buildings. In some instances, there are occasional requirements (for example, the use of schools as polling places for official elections) that must be met. Likewise, it is generally held that school buildings may not be used for some purposes—secret society activities or religious services. It is a legally justifiable action to permit the use of school buildings for school-connected activities to which parents, friends, and the general public are invited, even where admission fees are charged. However, the general rule is that school buildings may not be used for commercial enterprises when there is a monetary gain for private individuals or entities.

One of the most far-reaching concepts of school building use for nonschool purposes can be found in the California Civic Center Act. This act requires boards of education to permit community use of school property free of charge for meetings to discuss subjects that, in the judgment of the group, "appertain to the educational, political, economic, artistic, and moral interests of the citizens."

Boards of education do have the authority, unless specifically prohibited by state statute or constitution, to deny access to the school buildings to outside persons or groups. However, if a board chooses to do this, all persons or groups similarly situated must be denied access. Fairness must prevail. In denying the use of the building, a board of education may use constitutionally protected rights as the basis for its denial. A case in point will be found in *East Meadow Community Concerts Association v. Board of Education*, 219 N.E.2d 172 (N.Y., 1966), in which the New York Court of Appeals applied the rule that, although school authorities could close the door to all outside organizations, if they closed the door to any, they had to treat alike all organizations in the same category. Furthermore, although a board could deny use of the building if proof was presented of a clear and present danger that public disorder and possible damage to the building would result, the board could not bar an organization simply because the board, or even a part of the public, might be hostile to the opinions or the program of the organization, provided the same was not unlawful per se. In this instance, the board of education sought to bar one of a series of concerts because it was to feature as a performing artist a "highly controversial figure." The performer had sung a concert in Moscow, and some of the songs he sang were critical of American policy in Vietnam. The court held that the board of education's reason for cancelling the concert was unconstitutional because it rested on the unpopularity of the singer's views rather than on the unlawfulness of the concert. The court, in its opinion, stated, "The expression of controversial and unpopular views, it is hardly necessary to observe, is precisely what is protected by both the federal and state constitutions."

There may be some question about the use of school property on a temporary basis for religious services. This use is an exception, accepted by many courts, to the majority view that buildings cannot be used for sectarian purposes. Frequently, this use occurs when a house of worship has been destroyed by flood, fire, tornado, or some other disaster and a meeting space is needed for the congregation. Certainly, such a use could not occur when the school itself was in regular session.

When faced with a surplus of classrooms due to declining enrollments, boards must decide the best use of the property that is no longer needed for school purposes. Disposition of this property, either by lease or sale, falls within the powers delegated to boards of education by statute. When leasing property, the board of education is required to limit the lessee to lawful uses. Furthermore, the board is required to receive, in return for the lease, a fair return on the property. Leasing at a nominal fee (for example, $1), even to a nonprofit organization, is an unlawful gift of public funds unless such an arrangement is authorized by statute.

Such fiscal management requires prudent action on the part of the board of education. A fair return in the form of rental fees for buildings no longer needed for school purposes is an example of good management. Before property is sold, a long-range study must be made to determine if, in the foreseeable future, such property will be needed once again for school purposes. If so, the cost of replacement must be weighed against the immediate monetary gain from selling—rather than renting or leasing—the property.

PUBLIC FUNDS FOR NONPUBLIC EDUCATION

Three basic principles under the establishment clause are involved when reviewing legislative enactments with respect to public funds for private schools and determining the constitutionality of the statutes: Does the enactment have a secular purpose? Does the principal or primary effect of the enactment neither inhibit nor advance religion? Does the enactment foster an excessive entanglement with religion? The use of these three principles can be illustrated by two cases—Levitt I and Levitt II—from New York State. In the first, *Levitt v. Committee for Public Education and Religious Liberty*, 413 U.S. 472 (N.Y., 1973), the United States Supreme Court struck down a 1970 New York State statue that provided public funds to reimburse both church-sponsored and secular nonpublic schools for performing various services mandated by the state. The Court reasoned that the statute violated the establishment clause of the First Amendment. In 1974 the New York State Legislature attempted to remedy the defect of the 1970 legislation by enacting a new statute directing the commissioner of education to apportion and pay to nonpublic schools the actual cost they incurred in complying with certain state-mandated requirements. The difference in the two statutes was that in the 1974 version, the state did not plan to reimburse nonpublic schools for preparation, administration, or grading of teacher-prepared tests, and this statute provided a means whereby payment of state funds could be audited to ensure that only the costs incurred were reimbursed from state funds. A federal district court, in *Committee for Public Education and Religious Liberty v. Levitt*, 414 F.Supp. 1174 (N.Y., 1976), invalidated this statute. On appeal to the United States Supreme Court, the Court vacated the district court's judgment and remanded the case for reconsideration. The district court, under the precedent of *Woman*, ruled that the statute did not violate the establishment clause, and the district court decision was again appealed to the United States Supreme Court. In *Committee for Public Education and Religious Liberty v. Regan*, 100 S.Ct. 840 (N.Y., 1980), the Supreme Court (in a 5-to-4 decision) held that the New York State statute did not violate the provisions of the First and Fourteenth amendments. In arriving at its decision, the majority noted:

This is not to say that this case, any more than past cases, will furnish a litmus paper test to distinguish permissible from impermissible aid to religiously oriented schools. But Establishment Clause cases are not easy, they stir deep feelings; and we are divided among ourselves, perhaps reflecting the different views on this subject of the people of this country. What is certain is that our decisions have tended to avoid categorical imperatives and absolutist approaches at either end of the range of possible outcomes. This course sacrifices clarity and predictability for flexibility, but this promises to be the case until the continuing interaction between the courts and the States—the former charged with interpreting and upholding the Constitution and the latter seeking to provide education for their youth—produces single, more encompassing construction of the Establishment Clause.

The provision of transportation to pupils who attend nonpublic schools continues to be a matter of litigation. Some states have provided the service under the child-benefit theory; others have considered the service to be unconstitutional on the theory that it actually benefits the schools in which sectarian doctrines are taught.

In *Everson* the Supreme Court held that a New Jersey statute permitting boards of education to arrange, at public expense, for the transportation of children to school was constitutional. The Court considered that the furnishing of transportation of all pupils was in the category of a public service for all and, as such, was a general program to help parents get their children, regardless of their religion, safely and expeditiously to and from their schools. In Iowa, a 1987 law provides for the reimbursement of costs that parents incur transporting their children to nonpublic schools. The law applies to transportation provided after July 1, 1986, and will reimburse a parent for up to three elementary students and one high-school student. The 1988 Montana Laws, Ch. No. 320, grant school districts the discretion to charge nonpublic schoolchildren for transportation on district school buses.

APPORTIONMENT OF STATE SCHOOL FUNDS AND CHALLENGES

Beginning in the late 1960s and intensifying during the 1970s and the 1980s, litigation appeared attacking public school finance systems. Centered on the systems that were based, primarily. on property-tax revenues, the attacks took a position that children were discriminated against when their education was dependent on the wealth or poverty of their neighbors in the school district in which they, "by accident of birth" and residence, were to be educated.

Two series of cases have been brought to the courts. The first began with what is known as the *McInnis*-type cases in 1968. *McInnis v. Shapiro*, 293 F.Supp. 327 (Ill., 1968), was a class-action suit brought in behalf of parents and public school students in four Cook County school districts in Illinois. The plaintiffs sought relief through a permanent injunction forbidding further distribution of tax funds in accordance with the existing state statutes.

After hearing the case, the United States District Court ruled against the plaintiffs. In its declaration, the court cited the following points: the Fourteenth Amendment did not require that public school expenditures be made solely on the basis of "educational need" "educational expenses" were not the "exclusive yardstick" for measuring the quality of a child's educational opportunity; and there were no "judicially manageable standards" by which a federal court could determine if and when the equal protection clause is satisfied or violated. The court further expanded its opinion in stating, "The General Assembly's delegation of authority to school districts appears designed to allow individual localities to determine their own tax burden according to the importance which they place upon public schools."

In 1971 there was a complete turn of events in California, and a second series of cases began. In *Serrano v. Priest (I)*, 561 Cal.3d 584 (1971), the California Supreme Court held that the California school-aid formula violated the equal protection clauses of the constitutions of the United States and California. In its finding, the court agreed with parents living in Los Angeles County and stated that there were inequities of educational opportunity in some districts occasioned by the state's funding plan, inequities to taxpayers in less-favored districts as a result of the heavy reliance on the property tax for schools, and discrimination between and among districts because the system unfairly made the quality of a child's education a function of the wealth of his/her district. In its holding, the court said:

By our holding today, we further the cherished idea of American education that in a democratic society free public schools shall make available to all children equally the abundant gifts of learning. This was the credo of Horace Mann, which has been the heritage and the inspiration of this country. "I believe," he wrote, "in the existence of a great, immortal, immutable principle natural law, or natural ethics—a principle antecedent to all human institutions, and incapable of being abrogated by any ordinance of man—which proved the *absolute right* to an education of every human being that comes into the world, and which, of course, proves the correlative duty of every government to see that the means of an education are provided for all.

The California Supreme Court remanded the case back for trial, saying:

The richer district is favored when it can provide the same educational quality for its children with less tax effort. Furthermore, as a statistical matter, the poorer districts are financially unable to raise their taxes high enough to match the education offering of wealthier districts.

The California Supreme Court, in *Serrano v. Priest (II)*, 18 Cal.3d 725 (1977), reaffirmed its stand in *Serrano (I)* and proceeded to list the remedies that were available to the legislature in order to cure the malaise of the public school finance program in California. Included in the list were the following proposals: full state funding, to be supported by a statewide property tax; consolidation of districts, with boundary realignments to equalize assessed valuations of real property among school districts; retention of present school district boundaries but removal of commercial and industrial property from local tax-warrant rolls for school purposes; school district power equalization; and implementation of a voucher system. Subsequent *Serrano* cases are discussed below.

The *Serrano* concept spawned a case that was heard by the United States Supreme Court. It is presented here in detail because of its importance in establishing public education as a basic responsibility of the state.

San Antonio Independent School District v. Rodriguez, 411 U.S.1 (Tex., 1973)

Generalization

Public education is not a "fundamental interest" under the equal protection clause of the United States Constitution. If one school district is wealthier than another and a state-aid formula takes that into account, the state is not structuring a constitutionally suspect classification.

Description

This suit attacking the Texas system of financing public education was initiated by Mexican-American parents whose children attended the elementary and secondary schools in the Edgewood Independent School District, an urban school district in San Antonio, Texas. They brought a class action on behalf of school-children throughout the state what were members of minority groups or who were poor and resided in school districts having a low property-tax base. Named as defendants were the state board of education, the commissioner of education, the state attorney general, and the Bexar County (San Antonio) board of trustees. The complaint was filed in the summer of 1968. In December 1971 the panel rendered its judgment in a per curiam opinion holding the Texas school finance system unconstitutional under the equal protection clause of the Fourteenth Amendment. The state appealed the decision to the United States Supreme Court. The Court agreed to hear the case because of the far-reaching constitutional questions that were involved. Justice Powell delivered the opinion of the Court:

The first Texas State Constitution, promulgated upon Texas' entry into the Union in 1845, provided for the establishment of a system of free schools. Early in its history, Texas adopted a dual approach to the financing of its schools, relying on mutual partic-ipation by the local school districts and the state. . . .

Until recent times, Texas was a predominantly rural State and its population and property wealth were spread relatively evenly across the State. Sizable differences in the value of assessable property between local school districts became increasingly evident as the State became more industrialized and as rural-to-urban population shifts became more pronounced. The location of commercial and industrial property began to play a significant role in determining the amount of tax resources available to each school district. These growing disparities in population and taxable property between districts were responsible in part for increasingly notable differences in levels of local expenditure for education. . . .

In support of their charge that the system discriminates against the "poor," appellees have made no effort to demonstrate that it operates to the peculiar disadvantage of any class fairly definable or indigent, or as composed of persons whose incomes are beneath any designated poverty level. Indeed, there is reason to believe that the poorest families are not necessarily clustered in the poorest property districts. . . .

Neither appellees nor the District Court addressed the fact that. . . . lack of personal resources has not occasioned an absolute deprivation of the desired benefit. The argument here is not that the children in districts having relatively low assessable property values are receiving no public education; rather, it is that they are receiving a poorer education. . . . Apart from the unsettled and disputed question whether the quality of education may be determined by the amount of money expended for it, a sufficient answer . . . [is] that, at least where wealth is involved, the Equal Protection Clause does not require absolute equality or precisely equal advantages. Nor, indeed, in view of the infinite variables affecting the educational process, can any system assure equal quality of education except in the most relative sense.

For these two reasons—the absence of any evidence that the financing system discrim-inates against any definable category of "poor" people or that it results in the absolute deprivation of education—the disadvantaged class is not susceptible of identification in traditional terms. . . .

It is clear that the appellees' suit asks this Court to extend its most exacting scrutiny to review a system that allegedly discriminates against a large, diverse, and amorphous class, unified only by the common factor of residence in districts that happen to have less taxable wealth than other districts. The system of alleged discrimination and the class it defines have none of the traditional indicia of suspectness. . . .

We thus conclude that the Texas system does not operate to the peculiar disadvantage of any suspect class.

But appellees have not relied solely in this contention. They also assert that the State's system impermissibly interferes with the exercise of a "fundamental" right and that accordingly the prior decisions of this Court require the application of the strict standard of judicial review. It is this question—whether education is a fundamental right, in the sense that it is among the rights and liberties protected by the Constitution–which has so consumed the attention of the courts and commentators in recent years.

. . . the key to discovering whether education is "fundamental" is not to be found in comparisons of the relative societal significance of education as opposed to subsistence or housing. . . . Rather, the answer lies in assessing whether there is a right to education explicitly or implicitly guaranteed by the Constitution. . . .

Education, of course, is not among the rights afforded explicit protection under our Federal Constitution. Nor do we find any basis for saying it is implicitly so protected . . . it is appellees' contention, however, that education is distinguishable from other services and benefits provided by the State because it bears a peculiarly close relationship to other rights and liberties accorded protection under the Constitution. Specifically, they insist that education is itself a fundamental personal right because it is essential to the effective exercise of First Amendment freedoms and to intelligent utilization of the right to vote.

. . . this is not a case in which the challenged state action must be subjected to the searching judicial scrutiny reserved for laws that create suspect classifications or impinge upon constitutionally protected rights. . . .

. . . the judiciary is well advised to refrain from imposing on the States inflexible constitutional restraints that could circumscribe or handicap the continued research and experimentation so vital to finding even partial solutions to educational problems and to keeping abreast of ever-changing solutions.

Appellees do not question the propriety of Texas' dedication to local control of education. To the contrary, they attack the school-financing system precisely because, in their view, it does not provide the same level of local control and fiscal flexibility in all districts. Appellees suggest that local control could be preserved and promoted under other financing systems that resulted in more equality in educational expenditures. While it is no doubt true that reliance on local property taxation for school revenues provides less freedom of choice with respect to expenditures for some districts than for others, the existence of "some inequality" in the manner in which the State's rationale is achieved is not alone a sufficient basis for striking down the entire system. . . . It may not be condemned simply because it imperfectly effectuates the State's goals. . . . Nor must the financing system fail because, as appellees suggest, other methods of satisfying the State's interest, which occasion "less drastic" disparities in expenditures, might be conceived. Only where state action impinges on the exercise of fundamental constitutional rights or liberties must it be found to have chosen the least restrictive alternative.

The complexity of these problems is demonstrated by the lack of consensus with respect to whether it may be said with any assurance that the poor, the racial minorities, or the children in overburdened core-city school districts would be benefited by abrogation of traditional modes of financing education.

We hardly need add that this Court's action today is not to be viewed as placing its judicial imprimatur on the status quo. The need is apparent for reform in tax systems which may well have relied too long and too heavily on the local property tax. And, certainly innovative thinking as to public education, its methods, and its funding is necessary to assure both a higher level of quality and greater uniformity of opportunity. These matters merit the continued attention of the scholars who already have contributed much by their challenges. But the ultimate solutions must come from the lawmakers and from the democratic pressures of those who elect them

Reversed.

Having brought to an end the attitude that education was a fundamental interest protected by the United States Constitution, the United States Supreme Court returned arguments regarding state financing of public school education to the state courts for determination. Since then, decisions reflecting both the *McInnis*-type and the *Serrano*-type cases have been made.

In the first of three *McInnis*-type decisions, *Fair School Finance Council of Oklahoma v. State*, 746 P.2d 1135 (Okla., 1987), the court stated that neither the state nor the federal constitution requires equal expenditures per child and that a rational basis existed for the present school finance system. The second case, *Britt v. North Carolina State Board of Education*, 357 S.E.2d 432 (N.C., 1987), centered around a claim by a group of students that the funding system denied them their right to an equal educational opportunity. The North Carolina Court of Appeals held that the constitution's command that "equal opportunities shall be provided for all students" meant only that racial discrimination in the public schools was outlawed. The disparities in school district funding were held to be permissible. The third case came from Wisconsin in *Kukor v. Grover*, 436 N.W.2d 568 (Wis., 1989). The plaintiffs in this case challenged the equal protections of the state's constitution. The supreme court stated that the state constitution's uniformity provision was intended only to assure that those resources distributed equally were applied in such a manner as to assure that the "character" of instruction was as uniform as practicable. "Character" related to such things as minimum standards for teacher certification, minimum number of school days, and standard school curriculum. The court held, also, that the finance system did not violate the equal protection provisions of the state constitution, since disparities in per-pupil expenditures were rationally based on the preservation of local control over education.

We turn, now, to four *Serrano*-type decisions. The Montana Constitution provided that equality of educational opportunity was guaranteed to each state citizen. The constitution also guaranteed that the state would fund and distribute the state's share of costs of the basic elementary and secondary school system in an equitable manner. The state's contention was that this provision was aspirational, only. A district court found that the funding scheme was unconstitutional, and the state appealed to the supreme court of Montana. The supreme court held that the mandate was clear and that the "equality of educational opportunity" was guaranteed to each person of the state and was not merely a "goal." The supreme court upheld the district court's ruling (*Helena Elementary*

School District v. State, 769 P.2d 684 [Mont., 1989]). In *Edgewood Independent School District v. Kirby*, 777 S.W.2d 391 (Tex., 1989), a group of Texas school districts, parents, and students asked a district court to declare the state's financial system unconstitutional. The group claimed that the system violated both their equal protection rights and the Texas constitution's guarantee of an efficient school system. The court of appeals ruled that the state financing system was unconstitutional, but the Texas Court of Appeals reversed. The plaintiffs appealed to the supreme court of Texas. The court held that the matter of efficiency was not a political question. It said that although the legislature has the primary responsibility to decide how to achieve an efficient system, courts may decide if that constitutional mandate has been met. Thus, the court held that the state financing system was unconstitutional. New Jersey's constitution requires that every child receive a free education that is "thorough and efficient." Although many factors contribute to making an education "thorough and efficient," the court had earlier defined this as preparing the student to become "a citizen . . . a competitor in the labor market." Despite other arguments, the court found that money was a factor in determining the quality of education. Under the state constitution, disparity in funding was permissible only if the poorer districts could achieve that certain minimum level of education. Applying this test, the court determined that the students would be unable to compete and that the education in the poorer districts did not meet the "thorough and efficient" standard. The court then ordered the legislature to create a new system of funding, within guidelines, to ensure that each child received an education that was "thorough and efficient" (*Abbott by Abbott v. Burke*, 575 A.2d 359 [N.J., 1990]).

Rose v. Council for Better Education, 790 S.W.2d 186 (Ky., 1989)

Generalization

The plaintiffs charged that the state had failed to meet its constitutional mandate to provide an efficient system of common schools. The allegations were that the entire system was so inadequate, inequitable, and unequal as to be inefficient under the Kentucky Constitution and the Fourteenth Amendment.

Description

The Kentucky Supreme Court concurred with the plaintiffs and cited *Brown* as its "polestar," stating:

The overall effect of appellants' evidence is a virtual concession that Kentucky's system of common schools is underfunded and inadequate; is fraught with inequalities and inequities throughout the 177 local school districts; is ranked nationally in the lower 20–25 percent in virtually every category that is used to evaluate educational performance; and is not uniform among the districts in educational opportunities.

In its ruling, the court held that a child's education should result in seven essential capacities: (1) sufficient oral and written communication skills to enable the student to function in a complex and rapidly changing civilization; (2) sufficient knowledge of economic, social, and political systems to enable the student to make informed choices; (3) sufficient understanding of governmental processes to enable the student to understand the issues that affect his/her community, state, and nation; (4) sufficient self-knowledge and knowledge of his/her mental and physical well-being; (5) sufficient grounding in the arts to enable the student to appreciate his/her cultural and historical heritage; (6) sufficient training or preparation for advanced training in either academic or vocational fields to enable the student to choose and pursue life work intelligently; and (7) sufficient levels of academic or vocational skills to enable the student to compete favorably with counterparts in surrounding states in academics or in the job market.

The court then went on to define an "efficient" system of common schools and listed the following essential and minimal characteristics:

1. The establishment, maintenance, and funding of common schools in Kentucky is the sole responsibility of the General Assembly.
2. Common schools shall be free to all.
3. Common schools shall be available to all Kentucky children.
4. Common schools shall be substantially uniform throughout the state.
5. Common schools shall provide equal educational opportunities to all Kentucky children, regardless of place of residence or economic circumstances.
6. Common schools shall be monitored by the General Assembly to assure that they are operated with no waste, no duplication, no mismanagement, and no political influence.
7. The premise for the existence of common schools is that all children in Kentucky have a constitutional right to an adequate education.
8. The General Assembly shall provide funding that is sufficient to provide each child in Kentucky an adequate education.
9. An adequate education is one that has as its goal the development of the seven capacities recited previously.

In its summary/conclusion, the court said:

We have decided this case solely on the basis of our Constitution, Section 183. We find it unnecessary to inject any issues raised under the United States Bill of Rights in this matter. We decline to issue any injunctions, restraining orders, writs of prohibition or writs of mandamus.

We have decided one legal issue—and one legal issue only—viz, that the General Assembly of the Commonwealth has failed to establish an efficient system of common schools throughout the Commonwealth.

Lest there be any doubt, the result of our decision is that Kentucky's *entire system* of common schools is unconstitutional. There is no allegation that only part of the common school system is invalid, and find no such circumstance. . . . This decision applies to the statutes creating, implementing and financing the *system* and to all regulations, etc., pertaining thereto. . . .

While individual statutes are not herein addressed specifically or considered and declared to be facially unconstitutional, the statutory system as a whole and the interrelationship of the parts therein are hereby declared to be in violation of Section 183 of the Kentucky Constitution. . . .

Since we have, by this decision, declared the system of common schools in Kentucky to be unconstitutional, Section 1983 places an absolute duty on the General Assembly to re-create, re-establish a new system of common schools in the Commonwealth. . . . The system, as we have said, must be efficient, and the criteria we have set are binding of the General Assembly as it develops Kentucky's new system of common schools. . . .

As we have previously emphasized, the *sole responsibility* for providing the system of common schools lies with the General Assembly. . . .

The General Assembly must provide adequate funding for the system. How they do this is their decision. . . .

Because of the enormity of the task before the General Assembly to recreate a new statutory system of common schools in the Commonwealth, and because we realize that the educational process must continue, we withhold the finality of this decision until 90 days after the adjournment of the General Assembly, *sine die*, at its regular session in 1990.

The past two decades are surely indicators of continued challenges to state public school financing systems. Whereas courts have scrutinized the systems carefully, they have never demanded that equal dollars must be spent on every child. Nonetheless, it should be expected that states will be called on to make changes in their existing systems of public school finance, and some of those changes will be by way of court decisions.

SUMMARY

Public schools are creatures of state and local governments. Even though the federal government is not charged with the direct financing of education, federal funds in comparatively small amounts are made available through various congressional enactments.

School districts, as instrumentalities of the state, must develop financial plans for carrying out state constitutional mandates for educating the citizens of the state. These districts derive the major portions of their revenues from tax funds. Taxing authority to provide these funds is a special power that must be conferred by the legislature to the LEA (Local Education Authority). Such authority is possessed in different degrees, dependent on the classification of the school district. Fiscally independent boards of education have the authority to set the ad valorem tax rate on real property, to levy and collect—or cause to be collected—taxes for the support and maintenance of the schools, and to approve the expenditure of the funds collected. Fiscally dependent boards of education depend on another political subdivision for the funds with which to operate the school system.

Taxpayers who complain about illegal taxation would do well to act before the tax is collected. The usual process is to seek to have the collection of the tax enjoined.

School districts are expected to operate within balanced budgets. There are times when funds are needed for capital projects or for situations due to a shortfall in cash flow. Under these conditions, in accordance with state statutes and constitutional limitations, districts are permitted to borrow funds. Short-term debt is debt that will be liquidated during the current tax period, and long-term debt is, usually, in the form of bonds. These are general obligation bonds, which differ from revenue bonds in that revenue bonds are redeemed from revenues derived from source of revenue for which the bonds were issued, whereas general obligation bonds are a debt obligation to be paid from tax and other revenue sources.

Although boards of education have discretion to use their school funds for public purposes, they must be sure that the use is proper. The same must be said for sources of funds. One source area that raises questions is student fees. In general, if the course is required for graduation, if the course is related to the school's educational goal, or if the course has been approved by the state board of education, fees for entry into the course are inappropriate. It should be pointed out, however, that the courts have not been definitive with respect to fees that may be charged to students.

Boards of education are permitted to enter into contracts. A contract is an agreement that is legally enforceable. In addition, the following requirements pertain to contracts: the parties are sufficiently competent to enter into a contract; the parties have the legal capacity to enter into a contract; there are proper offers that are properly accepted with a sufficient consideration; and there is nothing illegal about the contract.

Bidding laws permit boards of education some latitude in acquiring the services and materials they seek. However, boards must be meticulous in their application of the laws.

School buildings are, generally, state property, and their use rests completely with the legislature. Broad powers have been conferred on local boards of education in permitting the use of school buildings. It is commonly accepted that school buildings may be used for educational purposes. It is when a request comes from an individual or a group wanting to use the building for other than educational purposes that questions arise. If a board of education chooses to deny the use of the building to an individual or group, it must treat all other similar individuals and groups in like manner.

The courts have been asked to rule on the use of public funds for private schools. In reviewing such use under the establishment clause, the courts have addressed three basic principles: Does the enactment have a secular purpose? Does the principal or primary effect of the enactment neither inhibit nor advance religion? Does the enactment foster an excessive entanglement with religion?

Usually, money provided to private school pupils flows under the child-benefit theory. The many variations make this an unsettled issue.

Beginning in the late 1960s, intensifying in the 1970s, and continuing in the 1980s, litigation has appeared attacking public school finance systems. Basically, two types of cases have appeared: the *McInnis*-type, which have been largely unsuccessful in attacking the constitutionality of the state finance systems; and the *Serrano*-type, which have been successful in attacking the constitutionality of the systems. These cases have been based on state constitutions. In *Rodriguez*, heard by the United States Supreme Court, the Court held that public education was not a ''fundamental interest'' under the equal protection clause of the United States Constitution and that the financing system did not discriminate against a suspect class of citizens. Litigation about equity for taxpayers and equality of opportunity continues to fuel this dispute.

Public school systems in our nation will continue to face financial crises. Changes in state finance systems, tax policies, taxing structures, and school-system organization, budgeting, and administration are inevitable in the decade ahead.

Glossary

Assault: A threat to strike or harm another.

Attractive nuisance: A condition that is dangerous to young children because it is so enticing; it is dangerous because inexperienced (young) children cannot distinguish that latter characteristic from the attraction.

Bail bond: A pledge of value taken when a defendant is released from custody, conditioned for the timely appearance of that defendant.

Bona fide: Honestly; without deceit.

Breach of contract: Failure by either party to perform a part or the whole of a contract, without any legal basis for such failure.

Capacity: The ability to function as a majority citizen; to make contracts and possess property.

Case law: The body of law created from judicial decisions.

Caucus: A meeting of the leaders of a group to decide about the acceptability of conditions or persons.

Certificate: An official document intended as an indicator of performance, or of an event; an indication of authority or qualification.

Certiorari: An action to remove a case from a lower to a higher court, commonly a request directed to the United States Supreme Court.

Citation: A system of source identification in law books incorporating technical abbreviations; a reference to authority to support an argument.

Civil action: An action brought to redress a wrong or to recover some civil right.

Closed shop: In labor relations, a condition dictating union membership as preceding employment.

Codification: The systematic arrangement of the laws of the state or of the United States, with appropriate headings, index, and so on.

Collective bargaining: A process in which employees meet as a group and make demands and proposals about working conditions to their employer; negotiations.

Common law: That part of law that has come down through the culture, deriving its force from social consensus of what constitutes fair play.

Compensatory damages: A measure of actual loss when damages have been suffered by a party; not punitive damages.

Concurring opinion: A statement by a judge, indicating general agreement with the opinion of the court, but including the (different) reasons leading to that shared opinion.

Constitution: The supreme law of the land; the documents that include the basic legal principles of each state and of the United States.

Contempt: An intentional disobedience of public authority; commonly, disregard for the orders of a court.

Contract: An agreement based upon value, mutually acceptable to the parties to the agreement; the proof of that agreement; a document revealing commitment and considerations.

Contract action: A court action brought as a necessity to enforce the terms of a contract.

Contributory negligence: The proximate cause of an injury, in which both litigants share.

Court of record: A court that keeps a permanent record of its proceedings, and that commonly has its findings cited as precedent for subsequent actions.

Criminal action: The legal proceeding by which parties charged with crimes are brought to trial.

Damage: An injury that occurs to a person, reputation, or property that may have been caused by a wrongful act, negligence, or accident.

De facto: In fact.

De jure: In law.

Decision: The conclusion of a court, arrived at by its own reasoning, the court's judgment.

Declaratory relief: A judgment that declares certain rights of parties but does not order anything to be done.

Decree: A court order made to settle questions of equity.

Defamation: Words that are written or spoken about another that may be harmful and for which an action for damages would lie.

Defendant: The person against whom a suit is brought or against whom an indictment has been brought.

Demurrer: A plea by one party that the existence of a body of facts is not a basis to continue the action.

Dictum: A statement by a judge of a legal principle, not essential to the case at point and not forming a part of controlling precedents.

Discrimination: In school law, the inappropriate conferral of privileges upon one class of citizens, when there is lacking a reasonable basis for that distinction.

Dissenting opinion: An opinion by one (some) judge, disagreeing with the majority of the justices of the court, as an eight-to-one decision or a five-to-four decision.

Due process: The rules and systematic protection of individual rights when questions of access and property arise.

Eminent domain: The power of some governmental units, such as public school districts, to take private property for private use, with just compensation.

Enjoin: To require a person, by virtue of court order, to perform or to cease and desist from some act; to command positively.

Equity: A system of law providing a remedy where there is no complete and adequate remedy already at hand.

Estoppel: Prevention at law of a person from affirming or denying certain facts because of previous behavior or statements by that person.

Ex officio: By virtue of office.

Ex parte: An action that is not an adverse proceeding against another.

Ex post facto: After the fact; coming after an occurrence.

Ex relatione: In behalf of or upon the relation of information.

Fait accompli: An accomplished fact; already done.

Felony: An offense that is more significant than a misdemeanor.

Finding: The conclusion of a court after consideration of the facts of a case.

Forfeiture: A penalty imposed, calling for the loss of rights or property as punishment for an illegal act or negligence.

Fraud: The use of deceitful or unfair means to gain personal advantage to another's loss.

Fringe benefits: Supplements to wages or salary received by employees at some cost to employers.

Governmental immunity: Sovereign immunity; in common law, the circumstance in which the consequences of governmental functions are not actionable, even in the face of damages.

Grievance: A complaint or expressed dissatisfaction by an employee in connection with his job, pay or other aspects of his employment.

Gross negligence: A low standard of care; less thought than even inattentive persons give to the management of their own property.

Habeas corpus: A court command to one person who is holding another to bring that person before the court.

Hearsay evidence: Testimony by a witness relating what has been told him by another, not what is personally known of firsthand.

In loco parentis: In place of the parent; carrying out conventional duties of parents in the society.

In re: Concerning; in the matter of; commonly used to identify proceedings where there are no adversarial parties.

Indictment: A written accusation against one or more persons of crime.

Information: An accusation against a person, alleging violation of some law.

Infringement: An invasion of an individual's rights.

Injunction: A prohibitive command from a court forbidding a person or group to do, or to continue doing, some act that is injurious to the plaintiff; a restraint.

Ipse dixit: An assertion deriving to authority from an individual.

Ipso facto: By the fact itself; the consequences of an act.

Judgment: The decision of a court; also the reasons set forward by a judge to reveal the rationale of that decision.

Jurisdiction: The power of a court to decide on a matter; the geographical area over which a court has power, as the area of one of the circuit courts of appeal.

Laches: The lapse of time that is sufficient to cause a person to lose the rights to a legal remedy for redress.

Laws: Rules of human conduct to which persons are obliged to conform; statutes enacted by a legislature comprise the statutory law.

Liability: Responsibility under law.

Libel: Defamation in a written communication.

Liquidated damages: Damages in an exact amount, as the amount due from one party to another for breach of contract.

Litigation: A dispute carried into court for settlement.

Majority opinion: The statement or reasons accepted by the majority of the judges sitting to hear an argument, when a decision is less than unanimous.

Mala prohibita: Acts prohibited by law that may not run counter to generally understood standards of the culture.

Malfeasance: The commission of an act that is unlawful.

Malice: Ill will; intentionally and by design doing an unlawful act.

Mandamus: An order from a court compelling a public officer or a public body to do the thing specified in that writ.

Mediation: An attempt by an unbiased third party to assist labor negotiations toward settlement; to advise and stimulate action toward agreement.

Ministerial: The obligation of a subordinate who is bound to follow instruction; the opposite of discretionary.

Misdemeanor: Any indictable offense that is less than a felony.

Misfeasance: A wrongful act that may include the inappropriate performance of a lawful act.

Moral turpitude: An action that is base or depraved; out of harmony with the customary rules of behavior in the culture.

Municipal corporation: A voluntary political body organized for the purpose of administering local affairs; a city or village. Less precisely, any political subdivision less than a county.

Negligence: Lack of reasonable care.

Nolens volens: When done with or without consent.

Nonfeasance: Nonperformance or omission of a required duty.

Nuisance: An offensive or noxious use of property; a condition that may injure or inconvenience others; obstructing the proper use of the property.

Oath: A promise; a solemn affirmation undertaken with a sense of responsibility.

Ordinance: A rule or regulation, generally applied to the laws passed by a municipality.

Pecuniary: Having to do with money.

Per se: By itself, alone.

Perjury: A false statement made while under oath, as in a court proceeding.

Petition: An application or a prayer to the court, asking redress for some wrong.

Petitioner: The person presenting a petition; similar to the plaintiff in other kinds of cases.

Picketing: Patrol duty, typically near the place of employment, by members of the employee organization to publicize a labor relations dispute.

Plaintiff: The person who initiates a complaint by filing a complaint.

Plenary: Complete power, as the grant of power from the federal government to the states under the Tenth Amendment.

Police power: The power of the states to enact statutes for the comfort, health, and general welfare of the citizens.

Precedents: Previous court decisions that are followed by courts that, later, receive cases of parallel disputes; a system of coordinating judicial authority.

Prima facie: A first examination; evidence so strong that it will prevail unless disproved.

Quantum meruit: A contract dispute involving an amount of compensation or quality level of performance.

Quasi: Almost as if it were.

Quasi-municipal corporation: A political subdivision that functions to assist in the accomplishment of the state's obligation, for example, a public school district.

Quorum: In an organization, the minimum number necessary to constitute a lawful meeting when business can be transacted.

Ratification: The act of confirming an obligation; closing an option, as in ratification of a tendered contract.

Reasonable doubt: The circumstance of qualified conviction after comparing and considering all that can be presented in a given case.

Referee: Generally, a disinterested party to whom disagreements are referred for settlement.

Referendum: A proposition extended to voters for their acceptance or rejection; that voting procedure itself.

Remand: To send a case back to an inferior court where it was first heard, with orders to take some specific, further proceedings.

Respondent: In certain kind of cases, the defendant; the one who makes an answer.

Restrain: A court order prohibiting some action or occurrence; an injunction.

Right: A claim; a power that one party possesses against another.

Seniority: A designation of employment status useful in determining promotion, layoff, vacation, and so on.

Slander: A communication delivered by speaking that is maliciously defaming of another party's reputation or business.

Stare decisis: The adherence to precedents as a means to develop the legal principles necessary for the settlement of litigation; to cite cases already decided.

Status quo: The existing circumstance; to leave unchanged.

Statute: The law enacted by a legislature, which may be the U.S. Congress or the legislature of any state; statutes may be substantive, that is, dealing with material problems; or procedural, that is, enabling government agencies or parties to do certain things.

Strike: A temporary work stoppage by employees to express a grievance, enforce a demand, or resolve a dispute with management.

Subpoena: A legal procedure whereby a party can be commanded to appear in court and testify.

Sue: To bring a civil action in a court.

Suit: The civil action, pitting plaintiff against defendant.

Supra: A word used as an indicator in scholarly books, referring the reader to a previous part of the book.

Tacit: Understood; implied by a lack of denial or disapproval.

Tenure: Generally, a description of an employment condition indicating the expectation of continuation in position; in public employment, a demand that dismissal must be for just cause and with due process.

Tort: In civil law, a wrong committed against the person, reputation, or property of another.

Trespass: An unauthorized entry into or upon the property of another; interference with property use.

Trial: The examination of a cause before a court. The court may consist of a judge or judges, may be with or without a jury.

Ultra vires: An action, especially in contract, that exceeds the legal power of an organization.

Umpire: In labor relations, the person who decides a question in dispute.

Unfair labor practice: Action by an employer or employee group that violates labor legislation, such as a refusal to bargain in good faith.

Union shop: A provision in a contract requiring all employees to become members of the union within a short period after initial hiring. Opposite of "right-to-work" shops.

Unlawful: Contrary to the law.

Valid: Effective; with binding force.

Venue: The neighborhood; the place where an act occurred, where a trial may be held, and from where a jury is drawn.

Vested right: A right that is so obviously and specifically the possession of a party that it cannot be revoked, removed, or impaired.

Violation: An act that is contrary to another's right, which may be carried out with violence.

Void: Null; ineffective and lacking legal force, as in a contract that is defective.

Waive: To renounce or voluntarily set aside a right.

Warrant: A writ or summons; an authority.

Wilful (or Willful): To act intentionally and deliberately.

Witness: A person who sees some act performed, committed, or perpetrated.

Writ: The judicial instrument that enforces obedience to the orders of a court and its sentences.

Writ of error: In the appeals procedure, the order of a superior to an inferior court, calling for its records, which will be examined for alleged errors.

Wrong: An act infringing upon a right.

Table of Cases

Index

About the Authors

ROBERT C. O'REILLY is Professor Emeritus of Educational Administration at the University of Nebraska at Omaha. He is the senior author of *Librarians And Labor Relations; Employment Under Union Contracts* (Greenwood, 1981); (with Edward T. Green) *School Law For The Practitioner* (Greenwood, 1983); and *Understanding Collective Bargaining In Public Education*. He has also contributed numerous articles to professional journals and served as a member of the National Commission for Excellence in Educational Administration. In 1985 he was President of the National Council for Professors of Educational Administration. He is a professor in management and administration at Walden University.

EDWARD T. GREEN is Professor Emeritus at Georgia Southern University, where he served as Professor of Educational Leadership. A long-time superintendent of schools in New York State, he served on national committees devoted to finance, facilities and collective bargaining. Besides co-authoring *School Law For The Practitioner*, he has presented numerous papers to the National Council of Professors of Educational Administration.